THE MILITARY HERITAGE OF
BRITAIN & IRELAND

THE MILITARY HERITAGE OF
BRITAIN &
IRELAND

Martin Marix Evans

Preface by Richard Holmes

André Deutsch

Acknowledgements

Throughout Britain and Ireland there are tens, perhaps hundreds, of people who have contributed directly or indirectly to this book. Some are to be found in the Further Reading section as authors, many more have patiently dealt with my written or telephoned requests for information. I am particularly grateful to the following individuals for their help and encouragement: fellow members of the Battlefields Trust Clive Hollick, Peter Marren, Chris Scott, Alan Turton and C F Wesencraft; also Matthew Alexander, David Burridge, Brian Dix, Jim Earle, Doreen Grove, Pat McCarthy, Jean-Paul Marix Evans, Andrew Saunders, Brian Swynnerton and Richard Watson. I am indebted to Richard Holmes for his Preface. My thanks to Gillian Marix Evans are no mere sop to guarantee my continued enjoyment of her care, but a true recognition of her part in this work.

Martin Marix Evans

First published in Great Britain by André Deutsch Ltd, 76 Dean Street, London W1V 5HA

André Deutsch is a VCI plc company

Copyright © Martin Marix Evans 1998

The right of Martin Marix Evans to be identified as author of this work has been asserted by him in accordance with the Copyright, Designs and Patents Act 1988

A catalogue record for this title is available from the British Library

ISBN 0 233 99150 6

Book design by Adrian Hodgkins Design, Oxford

Typesetting by White Horse Graphics, Charlbury

Illustrations: Half title – cartoon of the Duke of Wellington. (By permission of Aspley House, The Wellington Museum, London.)
Frontispiece – Newhaven Redoubt; 19th and 20th century defences. (Photograph by the author.)
Area maps prepared by White Horse Graphics and Adrian Hodgkins Design and based on RH publications/Maps in Minutes material.
Battle plans prepared by White Horse Graphics and Adrian Hodgkins Design and based on author's sketches.

Printed by Butler and Tanner, Frome and London.

Contents

Preface

by Professor Richard Holmes

The threads of Britain's military past are stitched deep into her landscape. There are ancient earthworks, Norman castles, battlefields of dozens of conflicts from the Roman invasion to the age of horse and musket, defences against barbarian, gallic or teutonic invasion, the airfields of two world wars and even – now, let us hope, very much part of history – sinister relics of the Cold War. There are museums, from the great treasure-houses in cities like London and Edinburgh (and, with the recent move of the Royal Armouries, in Leeds too), to tiny collections, perhaps open only by prior arrangement, celebrating long-disbanded regiments. And then there are memorials, from huge, officially-inspired tributes, to the smaller, sometimes unutterably poignant, private or local testaments to the men and women whose sacrifice is our history.

A lifetime's interest in military history has often taken me across this landscape on journeys into the past, whether working on the English Civil War, more years ago than I care to remember, with my mentor the late Brigadier Peter Young, or, most recently, preparing the BBC series *War Walks*. Even now, when, frankly, I have been at it so long that I might expect familiarity to have bred boredom, the experience of reaching back to touch the past never fails to move me. There are haunted acres where history changed direction: the ruins of Battle Abbey, crowning the ridge where King Harold and his housecarls fell in 1066, hefting sword and axe to the end; the field of Naseby, with the shadows of a summer evening darkening the ridge and furrow of a cultivation system already old when the battle was fought in 1645; Drummossie Moor in Culloden, where the clansmen came howling across the heather to meet the Duke of Cumberland's musketry in 1646.

Relatively few of these battlefields are as well-commemorated as they ought to be. All too often there is a memorial in the wrong place, a persistently misleading local tradition, or a few artefacts on the wall of the local pub. And in any event time has not always dealt kindly with battlefields, and concrete, brick and asphalt has scarred many. Occasionally there is good reason, for it is not always possible to be sure exactly where an early battle took place. For example, the location of Bosworth, scene of Richard III's defeat by Henry Tudor in 1485, is hotly disputed, and on the balance of probabilities the excellent Battlefield Trail is in the wrong place.

But even relative certainty is little help against urban sprawl or the road-builder. The scene of the Duke of York's victory at St Albans in 1455 is submerged beneath the streets, and a motorway link clips noisily across the southern edge of Naseby. Happily, English Heritage, working closely with the Battlefields Trust has compiled a register of key sites, but even this valuable process offers no guarantee of safety. In short, constant public vigilance, informed by local knowledge, is crucial to the survival of many of these sites.

For this reason (and many others too) I welcome Martin Marix Evans's work. Other authors have addressed the battlefields of Britain: Alfred Burne, David Smurthwaite and Glen Lyndon Dodds are amongst those who deserve honourable mention. But this is the first serious attempt at a comprehensive survey of all the United Kingdom and Ireland's military sites – battlefields, buildings, airfields and museums alike. It is both academically respectable, on the one hand, and user-friendly, on the other. Its simple and logical layout makes information easy to find, and the inclusion of telephone numbers and opening times (where appropriate) reduces the chance of wasted journeys. Whether I am wondering about the site of the battle of Stirling Bridge (didn't I read somewhere that its foundations had been discovered?) or worrying about the opening times of the Green Howards' splendid regimental museum in Richmond, this will be the book I turn to first. It deserves to become part of the working library of anyone with an interest, serious or fleeting, in the military past it charts so admirably.

Richard Holmes
The Security Studies Institute,
Royal College of Military Science,
Cranfield University

Introduction

The landscapes of the British Isles are peppered with the traces of a military past dating back to pre-history. Hill tops are crowned with Iron Age forts and radar towers. Major strategic routes have been the scenes of battles many times in a thousand years. Castles, forts and bunkers have protected the shore for centuries – Pevensey Castle is furnished with machine-gun nests.

It is rarely any great distance to a site of military interest wherever you may find yourself in the United Kingdom or Ireland. The gaps that appear in this work are most likely to be gaps in my knowledge, or places where the traces of history are invisible. It is the purpose of this guide to provide a basis for the investigation of the military history of these islands, history as it can be seen in the countryside, towns and museums. It is too much to hope that the information can be complete. It has been gathered from personal observation and discovery to some extent, but to a much greater extent from the works of others, specialists in various fields, and from the leaflets, guides and catalogues published by the custodians of our heritage and by tourist authorities.

It is also my hope that an increased awareness of our military heritage will discourage vandals, amateur or official, acting in ignorance or wilful neglect, from destroying the evidence of the past.

The Structure of the Book

The work has been divided into what seem to me to be logical areas. Political boundaries have been ignored as they are, in the perspective of this book, temporary. In any case, as a writer with English, Scottish, Welsh, Irish, French and American ancestry, I cannot find a side to take in any argument. The Scotland section thus has a southern boundary well short of the official one and the Borders section straddles that line. The arrangement has been governed by considerations of the historical events combined with the practicalities of tourism.

Within each section things to see and places to visit are arranged in relation to a number of towns or cities which appear to be conveniently positioned, and the location described in a way that is intended to be clear to readers using an ordinary road atlas for reference. Once pinpointed, the target can be reached by whatever route suits the travellers, depending on where they are starting from and how they intend to travel. The battle plans are also offered assuming that the reader has a good road atlas or even an Ordnance Survey map to which to refer. Those encouraged to want greater detail will find it in the list of books for further reading and may also be interested in one of the specialist societies listed at the end of the book.

Details of precise location are based on the best information readily obtainable, and when no decent data could be located the next best has been used so as to permit inclusion of the attraction. Some spirit of exploration may be needed. Telephone numbers have been included wherever possible to assist the search and to find out about practical details – wheelchair access, for example. Opening times have been given in as brief a form as possible and the fairly obvious exceptions, such as 'closed on 25 December', are omitted. Once again, imprecise data has not led to exclusion of a worthwhile place and usually a telephone number has been found to allow those on a tight schedule to make enquiries of their own.

Finding what you want

There are two ways into the book. First, the area in which you find yourself can be examined by going to the opening pages of the relevant section where an area map shows the key location towns and symbols indicate that attractions of a given type – a fortification, a battlefield or battle base, a museum, a cemetery or, a vague category, some other thing – are to be found around it. The relevant text can then be consulted.

Second, people, places and things have been indexed. Thus a particular battle, regimental museum, castle, fort, or cemetery can be looked up in the index. Within the limitations of the space available, certain historical characters and other items are also indexed.

Nothing, of course, prevents people just reading at random.

Things that are missing

There are bound to be a lot. Sometimes this will be the result of a mistake or oversight on my part, and I apologise in advance to those whom I may disappoint. Sometimes it is because the information is not available at the time of writing. For example, an important survey into the relics of World War II, The Defence of Britain, is currently still being carried out and will enrich a future edition. Advice on these missing entries is welcome and if comments can be made in a form similar to the arrangement of the entries it would be very helpful.

Certain battles are described with the help of plans, but those sites to my knowledge supplied with visitor centres or information boards have no plans, nor do the battles for which troop movements are unknown. The plans have been made with reference to the books noted in the select bibliography.

Things that are wrong

I hope there will not be too many. I have relied on published information a great deal, but it is frequently conflicting. Few battles that took place hundreds of years ago can be located with precision and opinions differ. Sometimes I have been able to use a knowledge of the ground to resolve such conflicts, sometimes the opinion of a particular scholar has persuaded me to present the account given here. Once again, opinions and suggestions, supported by evidence, will be welcome.

Martin Marix Evans

LONDON

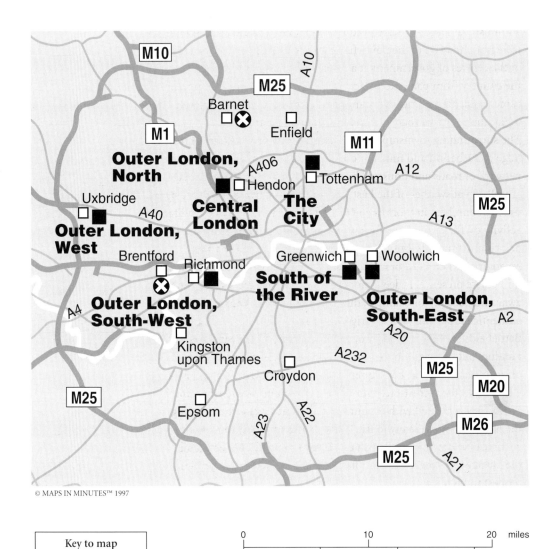

Key to map

❌ Battlefield

■ Museum

0   10   20 miles

0   10   20   30 km

Details of things to see in Central
London, The City and South of the
River sections omitted from this map

At the lowest point on the River Thames at which they could erect a bridge, the Romans created a walled town where the City now stands. Their walls can still be seen and new construction frequently turns up relics of their time. From this centre their roads ran across the land and the combination of overland mobility and the excellent port provided by the river gave London its unmatched position as an administrative and strategic headquarters. The conditions of city life were not attractive to the powerful and thus Westminster grew as one of the centres of government at a time when the ruler moved about the country from palace to palace. With military and political power came trade, nourishing an expanding metropolis from which, even today, the principal road, rail and air routes emanate.

The surrounding townships and villages steadily became part of this huge conurbation and much of our history now lies under the network of roads and houses. The advent of total war did its damage as well. Great swathes of the East End and the City were laid waste by German bombers in World War II. It follows that the traces of military activity on the ground are few and monuments and museums are the principal attractions, but the richness of the collections and the ingenuity of their curators compensates for the rarity of history as an immediate presence. Indeed, modern presentations carry the visitor away and back to, for example, the two major World Wars with an authenticity that can be truly frightening.

Battlefields are to be found, two, unsurprisingly, on the outskirts of London, but one right in the centre. The biggest battle of all took place in the air, and its consequences on the ground, the Blitz, can be glimpsed in the recreations a number of museums provide. London is generously sprinkled with monuments and statues commemorating the military, far too many to list. Those few mentioned here are of particular importance to British and Commonwealth history, while the invaluable alliances of the 20th century also receive recognition, modest though it is.

CENTRAL LONDON

Tourist information: British Travel Centre, 1 Regent Street. Victoria Station Forecourt. Tel (premium rate): 0893 123456. Visitorcall Military Museum tel (premium rate): 0893 123482.

The Cenotaph

Whitehall, in the centre of the street. Underground stations: Westminster or Charing Cross.

The national War Memorial commemorates British and Commonwealth dead of World Wars I and II as well as subsequent wars such as the Korean and Falkland Islands wars. It was designed by Sir Edwin Lutyens and is built of Portland stone. It was unveiled by George V on Armistice day, 11 November, in 1920 and is the centre of national mourning every year when the Remembrance Day ceremony takes place here and members of the Royal Family lead the laying of wreaths. Memorials, in the form of their statues, to Field Marshal the Viscount Slim, Field Marshal the Viscount Alanbrooke and Field Marshal the Viscount Montgomery of Alamein stand in Whitehall on Raleigh Green, outside the Ministry of Defence.

The Cabinet War Rooms

Clive Steps, King Charles Street. Tel: (0171) 930 6961. Open daily 9.30am to 6pm (10am from October to March).

A complex of underground rooms beneath Whitehall was the control centre of the British war effort in World War II. Here Winston Churchill and his Chiefs of Staff took the decisions that shaped the nation's survival. The 21 rooms include the Cabinet Room, the Map Room, Churchill's bedroom and the Transatlantic Telephone Room from which Churchill spoke directly to Franklin D. Roosevelt, President of the USA, in the White House.

Westminster Abbey

Parliament Square. Underground station: Westminster.

The tombs of many Kings and Queens are here, but perhaps the most moving memorial is that to the Unknown Warrior, near the West Door. The burial of the body of an anonymous soldier of World War I took place on 11 November 1920 in the presence of George V and other members of the Royal Family and the stone is inscribed 'They buried him among Kings'. Between this memorial and the door is a green marble stone in the floor dedicated to the memory of Winston Churchill. His statue stands nearby in Parliament Square. Also near the West Door is a plaque in memory of Franklin D. Roosevelt, President of the United States during World War II.

The Guards Museum

Wellington Barracks, Birdcage Walk. Tel: (0171) 414 3271. Open daily except Fridays and ceremonial occasions, 10am to 4pm.

The museum records the service of the five regiments of Foot Guards over three centuries, including their special relationship with the Sovereign and the City of London. The campaigns covered include Tangiers 1680, the Boer War, World Wars I and II and the Falklands.

Apsley House

Hyde Park Corner. Tel: (0171) 499 5676. Open Tuesday to Sunday and Bank Holidays 11am to 5pm. Underground station: Hyde Park Corner.

Number One, London is the concise address popularly given to the former residence of the Duke of Wellington. The 19th-century town house has been restored to the glory it displayed as Wellington's private palace after his acquisition in 1817 of the building created by Robert Adam between 1771 and 1778. The victorious general was rewarded by magnificent gifts from all over Europe including paintings, sculpture, furniture and porcelain to pay tribute to his success in the Peninsular War and the Battle of Waterloo. The house is a branch of the Victoria and Albert Museum.

Although not a military museum, there is much here of interest to the military enthusiast. The history of aviation as displayed in Flight and the Flight Lab not only offers an interactive introduction to the principles of flight, but includes the World War I bomber, a Vickers Vimy, in which Alcock and Brown made the first transatlantic crossing. Other aircraft include a Fokker E111, an S.E.5a, a Spitfire, a Hurricane and a Messerschmitt Me 163B. Exploration of Space provides an insight into rocketry and satellites as well as the challenge of living in space, and both a V1 flying bomb and a V2 rocket can be seen. A German Enigma machine and radar equipment are also on display.

The Science Museum

Exhibition Road, South Kensington. Tel: (0171) 938 8008/8080/8000. Open daily 10am to 6pm. Underground station: South Kensington.

The purpose of the Institute is to preserve all aspects of Polish heritage, and this includes militaria. The Krasinski collection of 17th-century armour is here, as is a comprehensive section on General Wladyslaw Sikorski, head of the exiled Polish government in World War II, amongst other items of military interest.

The Polish Institute and Sikorski Museum

20 Princes Gate, off N end of Exhibition Road. Tel: (0171) 589 9249. Open afternoons.

The history of the British Army from the raising of the Yeoman of the Guard in 1485 to the present day is the subject of the museum, including the Gulf War and service in the former Yugoslavia and Northern Ireland. The collections of the Women's Royal Army Corps and the Middlesex Regiment are here, and the Indian Army up to independence in 1947 is covered, as are Colonial armies. The Victorian Soldier Gallery tells the story of the British soldier from the Battle of Waterloo to the outbreak of World War I. The Reading Room, with over 35,000 volumes as well as documents and photographs, is open from Tuesday to Saturday.

National Army Museum

Royal Hospital Road, Chelsea. Tel: (0171) 730 0717. Open daily 10am to 5.30pm. Underground station: Sloane Square.

Charles II founded the Royal Hospital in 1682 as a retreat for army veterans who had become unfit either from wounds or after 20 years' service. It was inspired by Louis XIV's Hôtel des Invalides in Paris which had been established eight years earlier. The buildings were designed by Sir Christopher Wren and further buildings were added on East and West roads by Sir John Soane in the early 19th century. Royal Hospital Road was built across the grounds in 1846 and the original entrance was from the other side of Burton's Court north of that road. By the time the hospital opened it was too small to accommodate all the old soldiers, so some were granted pensions to live outside, Out-Pensioners, and about 400, as now, the In-Pensioners, lived in the building itself. The entrance hall of the Secretary's office in East Road is dedicated to the memory of the Duke of Wellington and displays, amongst other objects, two French eagles or regimental standards and a huge painting of the Battle of Waterloo by George Jones. The adjacent museum has a variety of exhibits related to the museum including a collection of over 2,100 medals of former Chelsea pensioners. The Chapel, the Great Hall and the Museum are open to visitors.

The Royal Hospital, Chelsea

Royal Hospital Road, Chelsea. Tel: (0171) 730 0161. Open Monday to Saturday 10am to 12 noon and 2pm to 4pm, Sunday 2pm to 4pm (museum April to September).

Grosvenor Square

Statues to two great Americans of World War II, President Franklin D. Roosevelt and General Dwight D. Eisenhower.

THE CITY

Tourist information: Liverpool Street Underground Station. Tel (premium line): 0839 123456.

St Paul's Cathedral

Underground station: St Paul's.

The cathedral has numerous memorials to individuals and military units, too many to list in their entirety. Of particular general interest are the tombs of Admiral the Viscount Nelson and the Duke of Wellington. Wellington is surrounded by memorials to men of a later war, World War II: Field Marshals Alexander, Slim, Montgomery, Alanbrooke, Wavell, Gort, Auchinleck, Dill, Wilson and Ironside. Two admirals of the same war are remembered in the Crypt, Sir Dudley Pound and Viscount Cunningham. Behind the High Altar is the American Memorial Chapel, a tribute to the 28,000 Americans based in Britain who lost their lives in World War II. It contains a 500-page roll of honour and stained-glass windows on the theme of the soldiers' sacrifice.

The Battle of Ludgate Hill, 1066

Ludgate Hill, between St Paul's Churchyard and Old Bailey. Underground station: St Paul's.

Fire Fighters' Memorial

Near St Paul's Cathedral.

In memory of the firemen and women who fought the blazes started by the Blitz on London in World War II.

After the defeat of Harold near Hastings on 14 October, William the Conqueror marched on London, but was repulsed when he attempted to cross the river by the bridge from Southwark. He then circled west to cross at Wallingford and accepted the surrender of Edgar the Aetheling at Berkhamstead, before making a fresh approach on the city. The valley along which Farringdon Road and New Bridge Street now run is the course of the River Fleet, now covered over, and the wall of the Roman town ran up it from the Thames, turned east roughly along Blackfriars Lane and then north to Lud Gate and along the east side of Old Bailey to New Gate. Within the walls a population of some 25,000 viewed William with disfavour. The Normans prepared themselves for a siege, but the opening of Lud Gate by collaborators gave them entrance to the city where a fierce battle ensued, probably in the area in front of today's St Paul's. William prevailed, slaying numerous Saxons whose graves have been discovered near the confluence of the Fleet with the Thames.

Museum of the Order of St John

St John's Gate, St John's Lane, Clerkenwell. Tel: (0171) 253 6644. Open Monday to Friday 10am to 5pm, Saturday 10am to 4pm. Underground stations: Farringdon and Barbican.

The Order of St John, whose primary mission was to care for pilgrims and the sick, developed as the military Knights Hospitaller during the Crusades. The Priory in Clerkenwell, the headquarters of the Order in England, was founded in about 1140, but the buildings were largely destroyed in the Peasants' Revolt of 1381. The Priory was dissolved by Henry VIII's Act of Dissolution in 1540, some 36 years after the construction of the new southern gate which now stands surprisingly facing a busy street in an area much damaged by bombing in World War II and uninspiringly rebuilt. It had various uses thereafter, including the publishing and printing of Edward Cave's *Gentleman's Magazine* in the 18th century, a periodical to which Dr Johnson contributed. In 1874 it was acquired by The Most Venerable Order of the Hospital of St John of Jerusalem, the founders of St John Ambulance in 1877. The museum contains the most comprehensive collection of items relating to the Order of St John outside Malta and the St John Ambulance Museum traces the history of the Association, including memorabilia of World War II POWs. The 12th-century crypt of the Grand Priory Church survives, though the church itself was bombed out in the Blitz, and may be visited as part of a guided tour at 11am and 2.30pm on Tuesdays, Fridays and Saturdays.

The Museum of London stands at the western end of the street that runs alongside the old Roman wall. It is not principally a military museum but offers an exciting understanding of life in the city from earliest times, a useful adjunct to the appreciation of the martial life of the town. The remains of the wall can be seen by walking east along the high walk from the museum.

The Museum of London
150 London Wall. Tel: (0171) 600 3699. Open Tuesday to Saturday 10am to 6pm, Sunday 12 noon to 6pm.

The Honourable Artillery Company is the oldest regiment in the British Army, and the senior Territorial regiment, having its origin in letters patent issued by Henry VIII. The official escort to the Lord Mayor of London is the HAC's Company of Pikemen and Musketeers and there is also a ceremonial Light Cavalry Troop. The museum contains items dating back to the Civil War and includes uniforms, weapons, equipment and decorations.

Museum of the Honourable Artillery Company
Armoury House, City Road. Tel: (0171) 606 4644. Open by appointment only. Underground stations: Moorgate, Old Street.

The memorial commemorates the men of the Merchant Navy and Fishing Fleets who gave their lives in World Wars I and II. The monument to those lost in World War I was designed by Sir Edwin Lutyens and was unveiled by Queen Mary in 1928. Within the corridor the names of 11,919 men with no grave but the sea are inscribed on bronze panels, listed by ship with only the Master or Skipper designated by rank. The losses of World War II are recorded in a sunken garden designed by Sir Edward Maufe, with sculptures by Charles Wheeler. From the UK Merchant Navy and Fishing Fleets there are 23,414 names, from the UK Merchant Navy (of Australia) 62, the UK Merchant Navy (of New Zealand) 72, UK Merchant Navy (of South Africa) 182, the Australian Merchant Navy 47, and from the UK Lighthouse and Pilotage Services 16 Pilots and 64 men of the Lighthouse and Steam Vessel Service – there are 23,857 names in all.

The Tower Hill Memorial
Trinity Square, Tower Hill. Underground station: Tower Hill. Commonwealth War Graves Commission.

Having secured London, William the Conqueror set about strengthening the city against both internal and external threat. He selected a site in the south-eastern angle of the Roman wall (part of which can be seen on the approach from the Underground station) which dominated the waterway. The river could also be used for transport and supply in time of internal strife. Here Bishop Gandulf of Rochester built him a tower-keep of stone, the White Tower, in the style of a motte and bailey castle. The essential difference from the motte and bailey defences that scattered the Norman kingdom was that the White Tower was also a palace, with all the facilities that would usually be spread out over a large area here arranged in vertical form. What is more, it was a statement of supremacy, decorated without to impress.

The concentric defences to be seen today were started by Richard I and the building continued under Henry III to be completed by Edward I. The work on the curtain wall with interval towers was extended to provide additional buildings for the accommodation of his court and followers by Henry III, with chapels, halls and lodgings, as at Windsor. Edward I started the outer ring of defence,

The Tower of London
Tower Hill. Tel: (0171) 600 3699. Open March to October Monday to Saturday 9am to 6pm, Sunday 10am to 5pm. November to February closes 5pm every day. Underground station: Tower Hill.

Winston Churchill's Britain at War Theme Museum

64/66 Tooley Street. Tel: (0171) 403 3171. Underground station: London Bridge.

A vision of World War II from the civilian's point of view. Special effects and original artifacts re-create the experience of war for the ordinary citizen.

completed by Edward III, which included a water-gate, St Thomas's Tower, popularly known as the Traitor's Gate. Up to the time of Henry VIII the Tower continued as a royal residence. The castle was modified for defence against internal strife in the late 17th century when, after the Restoration, the gun-towers at the north-eastern and north-western corners of the outer wall, Brass Mount and Legge's Mount, were built to carry artillery.

The Royal Armouries

The White Tower. Open March to October Sunday and Monday 10am to 6pm, Tuesday to Saturday 9am to 6pm. Closes 5pm November to February.

The bulk of the collection having been relocated in Leeds, the new displays here tell the story of the building and development of the White Tower and of the Royal Armoury itself, and of the Board of Ordnance which was responsible for the development of new weapons from 1660 to 1855. The personal armours of Tudor and Stuart royalty as well as weapons of Henry VIII's arsenal at the Tower are here.

The Royal Fusiliers Museum

Tel: (0171) 480 6082. Open 10am to 5pm. Closes 4pm November to February.

Deals with the history of the Royal Regiment of Fusiliers and its predecessor, the Royal Fusiliers, from 1685 to today. In addition to weapons, uniforms and equipment, there are dioramas of the battles of Alma, Mons and Cassino.

SOUTH OF THE RIVER

Tourist information: Unit 4, Lower Level, Cotton's Centre, Middle Yard, Southwark.

HMS *Belfast*

Morgan's Lane, Tooley Street. Tel: (0171) 407 6434. Open March to October 10am to 6pm. Closes 5pm November to February. Underground stations: Tower Hill and London Bridge. Ferry from Tower Pier.

Moored across the river from the Tower of London, HMS *Belfast* is the last of the big gun armoured warships of World War II. This cruiser was launched in 1938 and took part in the notable actions of North Cape in 1943 and the D-Day landings in Normandy in 1944. She also served in the Korean War. All seven decks are open to visitors and give the chance to see inside the triple 6-inch gun turrets and to operate her light anti-aircraft guns.

Imperial War Museum

Lambeth Road. Tel: (0171) 416 5321. Open 10am to 6pm. Underground station: Lambeth North.

The museum is devoted to all aspects of war involving Britain and the Common-wealth since 1914, and thus covers World Wars I and II in considerable depth. There are thousands of imaginatively displayed exhibits including complete aircraft, guns, a London bus converted for carrying troops and a U-boat. Special features add to the understanding. The Trench Experience is a chilling evocation of World War I and the Blitz Experience, with sound and smells, a dramatic vision of World War II. The Holocaust Exhibition, showing the actu-ality of the Nazi persecution of the Jews is, at the time of writing, under dev-elopment. Operation Jericho is a simulation of a bombing raid over Germany and there are interactive videos to portray other aspects of war. The archives of photographs, films, maps and documents are open to visitors by appointment.

The museum concerned with the life and work of Florence Nightingale naturally has material relating to the Crimean War in which she did her pioneering work in nursing.

Florence Nightingale Museum

2 Lambeth Palace Road. Tel: (0171) 620 0374. Underground stations: Lambeth North and Waterloo.

OUTER LONDON, NORTH

The World War I airfield at Hendon is now flanked by the rush of traffic on the M1 motorway. The RAF Museum deals with the history of that service, of the Royal Flying Corps and aviation in general. There are over 65 aircraft from the Bleriot XI, the Sopwith Camel, the Spitfire and the Hurricane to the Lightning as well as countless exhibits including photographs, documents, guns, bombs and uniforms. The Battle of Britain Hall has British, German and Italian aircraft of World War II and a display entitled the Battle of Britain Experience. The Bomber Command Hall shows, amongst other aircraft, a Vulcan, a Wellington and a Lancaster.

Royal Air Force Museum

Grahame Park Way, Hendon. Tel: 0181 200 1763. Open 10am to 6pm. Underground station: Colindale. Rail station: Mill Hill Broadway.

Richard Neville, Earl of Warwick, the Kingmaker, switched his loyalty to the Lancastrians and restored Henry VI to the throne in 1470 forcing Edward IV to flee to Burgundy on 2 October. Edward was back the next spring with a force supported by Charles the Bold and bottled up Warwick at Coventry before regaining London on 12 April. Warwick had brought the Lancastrian army south but Edward had quickly consolidated and was at Barnet to push back the Lancastrian advance guard at Barnet on the night of 13 April. The Yorkists camped that night astride the Great North Road north of the junction with St Albans Road with Edward in the centre, Lord Hastings to the west on St Albans Road and Richard of Gloucester far to the east on Hadley Wood Road. The Lancastrians were on the north of Hadley Green on a line through the golf clubhouse on the west and north of Dury Road and the church to the east, with the Duke of Somerset in the centre, the Earl of Oxford on the west and Warwick himself on the east.

Early in the morning, about 4am, Edward's troops advanced through the mist. The Yorkist line was overlapped on the west by Oxford but outflanked Warwick in the east. Thus, when they met, Oxford was able to push Hastings's men back through Barnet, but there the victors dispersed, either to loot the village or chase the fleeing Yorkists. On the other flank Warwick was hard pressed by Gloucester, but was holding on as the centre locked together in battle. Oxford managed to get his troops together again and they returned to the battlefield but, as they were coming from the south, their Lancastrian fellows assumed they had changed sides and fired upon them as freely as they did on the Yorkists. At this moment Edward threw his reserves into the fight and the Lancastrians broke. Warwick never reached his horse in the rear of his position, he was caught and killed. That evening Queen Margaret landed at Weymouth to reinforce the Lancastrian cause. Lacking Warwick, she was to see it destroyed at Tewkesbury three weeks later.

The Battle of Barnet, 14 April 1471

Monken Hadley, N of Barnet on A1000, from junction 24, M25. Underground station: High Barnet.

Middlesex Regimental Museum

Bruce Castle, Lordship Lane. Tel: (0181) 808 9772. Rail station: Bruce Grove.

Covers the history of the Middlesex Regiment from 1755 to 1966.

OUTER LONDON, SOUTH-EAST

Tourist information: 46 Greenwich Church Street, Greenwich. Tel: (0181) 858 6376.

Museum of Artillery

The Rotunda, Repository Road, Woolwich. Tel: (0181) 854 2242, ext. 3127. Open April to September Monday to Friday 12 noon to 5pm, weekends 1pm to 5pm. Closes 4pm October to March. Rail station: Woolwich Arsenal.

The tent-shaped building in which the museum is housed was designed by John Nash in the early 19th century. Here the history of artillery is displayed from iron guns of the 15th century to the missiles of today. Weapons to be seen include the Peninsular and Crimean War 6-pounder, the World War I 13-pounder, and the World War II 25-pounder. There are anti-tank guns, machine guns, anti-aircraft guns and part of the Iraqi supergun.

The military nature of the area dates from before the time of Henry VIII when the dockyard was flourishing; it closed in 1869. Neighbouring Woolwich Warren was acquired by the Crown in 1671 to be used as an ordnance storage depot and developed into a munitions factory. Later still the Royal Ordnance Factory was established here, to remain operational until 1967. Numerous fine buildings were erected by noted architects, James Wyatt and Sir John Vanbrugh among them. At the time of writing the future of this magnificent piece of our architectural heritage is uncertain, though a number of buildings are listed.

National Maritime Museum

Romney Road, Greenwich. Tel: (0181) 312 6565 (24 hour), (0181) 858 4422 (switchboard). Open daily 10am to 5pm. Rail station: Greenwich or Maze Hill. Pleasure boat from Westminster, Charing Cross or Tower Pier. Foot tunnel under river from Island Gardens.

The collection of the museum is vast and it is as well to plan your route to take in exactly what you want to see. The coverage is from the prehistoric to the present day. There are special exhibitions in addition to the permanent displays such as (at the time of writing) the Nelson exhibit featuring his battles with Dutch, Spanish and French fleets and illustrated paintings, artefacts, tableaux and audio descriptions. The English Civil War makes use of the portraits in the Queen's House and the 20th Century Seapower Gallery is full of background information on Jutland and more recent actions, drawing on archive film and using new-technology displays. The museum is not limited to military subjects; Captain Cook, navigation and cargo handling, for example, can be studied. By appointment with the Librarian the extensive collection of naval records, books, ships plans and manuscripts can be used. The index is computerised. Those interested in astronomy and navigation should take the opportunity to visit the Old Royal Observatory in Greenwich Park.

Royal Artillery Regimental Museum

Red Lion Lane, off Shooter's Hill, SE18. Tel: (0181) 854 2242, ext. 5628. Open Monday to Friday 12.30pm to 4.30pm. Bus 161 or 122 from Woolwich Arsenal.

OUTER LONDON, SOUTH-WEST

Tourist information: Old Town Hall, Whittaker Avenue, Richmond. Tel: (0181) 940 9125.

The Museum of Richmond is here and has a small display of militaria. Richmond Park was the home to numerous military activities in World Wars I and II, but almost nothing survives in the park itself.

The Public Record Office

Mortlake Road, Kew. Tel: (0181) 876 3444. Open Monday to Saturday

The Public Record Office has an extensive collection of material on the history of British and Commonwealth forces over seven centuries. As the national archives of the United Kingdom, the PRO holds many of the most important records of the British Army, Royal Navy, Royal Marines and Royal Air Force.

They include many personal documents and photographs of the men and women who served in the forces. Items of particular interest are to be seen in the museum, such as charts drawn up by Captain Cook, sketch maps made by Lawrence of Arabia and World War II posters. Special exhibitions are mounted from time to time.

9.30am to 5pm, 7pm Tuesday and Thursday. Rail and underground station: Kew Gardens. Rail only: Kew Bridge.

The main road from the west to London, before the Great West Road and then the M4 were built, was the Bath Road, London Road and Brentford High Street. Julius Caesar crossed the Thames here and it was the site of a battle in 1016 during the confused times at the end of Ethelred's reign, when Edmund Ironside and Cnut were contenders for the crown. On 23 October 1642 King Charles I had gained an advantage if not a real victory over the Earl of Essex's Parliamentary army at Edgehill. The Royalists made their leisurely way towards London, in spite of the urgings of Prince Rupert to make haste. The Londoners prepared themselves to resist, raising a force of 6,000 men. Charles reached Reading on 4 November but Essex got to London four days later and added the London Trained Bands to his force. On 11 November both armies were closing on Brentford.

The Battle of Brentford, 12 November 1642

High Street (A315), Brentford and Syon Park. Rail station: Brentford Central.

As Rupert, in the vanguard of the Royalists, approached along London Road on 12 November, only two regiments of Essex's army were ready to meet him, Lord Brooke's Purplecoats and Denzil Hollis's Redcoats, drawn up astride Brentford High Street west of Ealing Road. Rupert hit them hard, his cavalry and the few infantry with them scattering the Parliamentarians and driving many of them down the narrow streets such as Back Lane, Dock Road and Ferry Lane into the river. John Hampden's Greencoats came up but could not turn the tide and the Royalists took the little town, but made no further attempt to advance, turning instead to drinking the place dry.

The next day Essex tried to supply the remnants of his front line with ammunition and gunpowder, only to have the river-borne munitions destroyed by Royalist artillery deployed in Syon Park. At Turnham Green, however, the main Parliamentary army numbered some 24,000 men and blocked the way to London. Charles, with only 12,000, could not contemplate attack. He turned away, having lost his best opportunity to take the city.

OUTER LONDON, WEST

On 15 September 1940 Winston Churchill visited this operations room at a crucial phase of the Battle of Britain, an event immortalised in the well-known film of that name. The former operations room, which was responsible for the air defence of London and south-east England, is shown as on that day.

No. 11 (Fighter) Group Operations Room

RAF Uxbridge, S from A40 at first junction E of M40, by B466 Park Road and 200 yards on left in Hillingdon Road. Underground station: Uxbridge. Open by prior arrangement only with the curator, tel: (01895) 237144, ext. 6400 (answerphone).

Buried 60 feet underground and reached by a 76-step stairway, the plotting room displays the positions of both friendly and hostile forces and the illuminated tote board the readiness state and deployment of the individual fighter squadrons. The plotting room is overlooked by glass-fronted control rooms which house a display of World War II artefacts and memorabilia.

SOUTHERN ENGLAND

The country from Kent to Hampshire has been curiously untroubled by civil conflict; the principal military interest has been keeping people out of Britain. The Roman invaders probably met little resistance here as the British ruler Cogidubnus soon allied himself with the incomers. The Normans fared well but since then no invasion has taken place, though the Spanish Armada came close, Napoleon completed extensive preparations and Hitler's Luftwaffe fought, and lost, the preparatory battle.

The landscape limited what could be gained or lost in warfare before the machine age. The barrier of the North Downs swings westwards from the cliffs of Dover to pass immediately to the south of London and curl south on the Hampshire border before running east once more as the South Downs, terminating in Beachy Head. To the

Key to map

- ✖ Battlefield
- ▲ Castle/Fort
- ✚ Cemetery
- ■ Museum
- ● Other

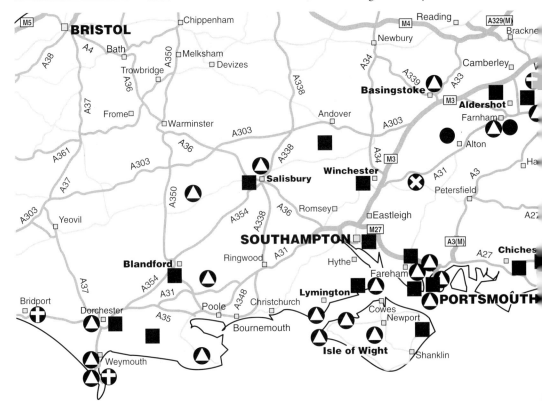

west of this feature a broad valley thrusts north from the coast until the Hampshire Downs bar the way. The major routes to the seat of power, London, thus lie along the Thames in the north and the line from the generous harbours of Portsmouth and Southampton through Winchester, and then by upland paths over chalk hills – comparatively well drained and mud-free – to the capital. The main concern in the region has been with the continent of Europe rather than with domestic conflict; the islanders leaving to attack enemies across the channel or resisting their arrival in England.

The castles built by the Normans were intended to enforce the domination of the new rulers over their unwilling subjects and the only notable civil war battle, Lewes, took place in the south-east when Henry III, attempting to get round the flank of the rebel barons to recruit support in the West Country, was caught en route. In the Civil War of the 1640s the competition was along the route north through Winchester, the south-east being held for Parliament.

The region consequently has a strong maritime heritage, both in the presence of the Royal Navy and in coastal fortifications, and in the 20th century has acquired the modern manifestation of the same challenge, the evidence of aerial warfare.

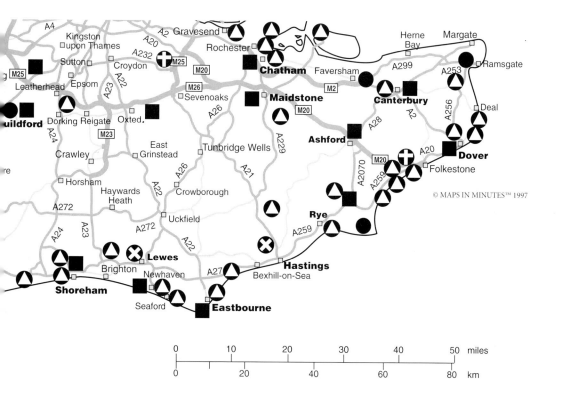

ALDERSHOT

Tourist information: Aldershot Military Museum. Tel: (01252) 320968.

In April 1854 the government approached Guildford Corporation with an offer of £100,000 to establish a camp for 20,000 soldiers on the Hog's Back. It was declined. The money was then offered to the village of Aldershot, which accepted. The growth around the army base since then has led to a complex of camps and exercise areas that can confuse the visitor, so a local road map is worth having.

Aldershot Military Museum
Queens Avenue, Aldershot. Tel: (01252) 314598.

Housed in the barrack blocks of the 1890s, the museum records the daily life of the soldiers (many of them Irish) and civilians and the story of the mechanisation of the British Army. Canadian army units of World War II are honoured here. It is open daily.

Airborne Forces Museum
Browning Barracks, Allisons Road, Aldershot. Tel: (01252) 349619.

The Parachute Regiment was formed in the early days of World War II and is now an elite unit of the Army. The museum reveals the history of airborne warfare and includes, amongst others, coverage of the D-Day landings, Arnhem and the Falklands War. It is open daily.

Army Physical Training Corps Museum
Fox Lines, Queens Avenue, Aldershot. Tel (01252) 347168.

Physical fitness, both for effectiveness in battle and for recreational, sporting purposes, was recognised as needing proper organisation in 1860. The work of the Corps and the Army's sporting achievements are portrayed. It is open Monday to Friday.

RANC Museum and the RAMC Museum
Keogh Barracks, Ash Vale, Aldershot. Tel: Nursing (01252) 340294, Medical (01252) 340212.

The story of the doctors and nurses of the British Army is told in the Royal Army Nursing Corps and the Royal Army Medical Corps museums. The experience of the Crimean War in the 1850s and the fame of Florence Nightingale led to the establishment of military medicine and nursing which is recounted up to the Falklands War. The museums are open Monday to Friday.

Brookwood Military Cemetery
Commonwealth War Graves Commission. 4 miles NE of Aldershot on the A324 Purbright and Woking road. Open daily.

This, the largest Commonwealth war cemetery in the UK, contains 1,601 World War I and 3,474 World War II graves and commemorates 3,471 men and women who have no known grave. In addition to the British, soldiers from Australia, Canada, India, New Zealand, South Africa and the West Indies lie here. There are also plots devoted to the graves of Belgian, Dutch, French, Italian, German, Polish and Serbian troops. The Canadian Records building and the American Military Cemetery of World War I are on this site.

Royal Logistics Corps Museum
Princess Royal Barracks, Deepcut. W of Brookwood by B3012. Tel: (01252) 340871.

Without logistical support, an army can achieve nothing at all. The vital roles of the Royal Corps of Transport, Royal Army Ordnance, Royal Pioneer Corps, Catering Corps and the Postal and Courier Services are revealed here. It is open Monday to Friday.

The disaster of Dieppe, where the Canadians suffered so severely on 19 August 1942, led to renewed research into the problems of overcoming coastal defences. A wall was therefore built on Hankley Common by Royal Canadian Engineers and various devices tested in order to breach it. One of the earliest devices was a wooden frame containing 1,000 pounds of explosive which was trundled into place by a Churchill Mk II tank which retired trailing 100 foot of cable used to detonate it. This was called Onion. The eventual result was the Petard demolition mortar which fired a huge charge from a converted Sherman or Valentine tank which, when fitted to a Churchill, became the first Armoured Vehicle Royal Engineers or AVRE. The Anti-Tank Experimental Unit at Hankley Common was absorbed into 79 Armoured Division under Major General P C S Hobart, the unit responsible for various special tanks, amphibious, mine-busting flails and flame-throwing, known as Hobart's Funnies. It is reported that the wall still stands, with public footpaths passing through breaches made by the prototypes of the weapons used in the D-Day landings.

The Surrey Sea Wall
Hankley Common, near Tilford, 4 miles S by minor roads.

The original castle was built by Henry of Blois, Bishop of Winchester, in about 1138 as a stone tower, but in the style of the wooden tower on a motte. The earth was piled up around stone foundations, a stone platform capping the motte and overhanging the foundations, and the tower rising above. It proved to be unstable, so later the motte itself was encased in stone. The gatehouse, in brick, was added by Bishop Waynflete in the 15th century. The castle was stormed and taken by Sir William Waller for Parliament in 1642.

Farnham Castle
Farnham, 3 miles SW by A324, N of town centre on A287. English Heritage. Tel: (01252) 713393. Open daily April to September.

ASHFORD

Tourist information: 18 The Churchyard. Tel: (01233) 629165.

The history of British Military Intelligence from the times of Elizabeth I to the present day. Amongst countless documents, maps and photographs are special exhibits on the Crimean War, the Boer War and World Wars I and II.

Intelligence Corps Museum
Templer Barracks, Ashford. Tel: (01233) 657208. Open Tuesdays and Thursdays.

There are six aircraft on display, including a rare Fieseler 103R-IV flying bomb prototype, a de Havilland Vampire T11 and a Super-Sabre F-100F twin-seater. There are also items from crash sites, photographs and other memorabilia.

Lashenden Air Warfare Museum
Headcorn, 15 miles W of Ashford by A28, A262 and A274. Tel: (01622) 890226, 890236. Open April to October, Sundays and Bank Holidays only.

BASINGSTOKE

Tourist information: Willis Museum, Old Town Hall, Market Place. Tel: (01256) 817618.

The early Norman castle had been extensively modified before it saw real action in the Civil War. A Royalist stronghold, it was the southernmost of the strategically important north/south line through Donnington Castle, Oxford and Banbury. The ruins include the extensive earthworks that repulsed Sir William Waller in

Basing House
Redbridge Lane, Basing, 2 miles NE by minor road. Open April to September, Wednesday to Sunday and Bank Holidays.

1643 and were eventually overcome in October 1645, when the house was destroyed and the defenders slaughtered.

Second World War Aircraft Preservation Society
Lasham Airfield, Near Alton. 8 miles SE by A339. Tel: (01344) 774157.

Nine aircraft are to be seen, including two Meteors, a Hawker Hunter, a Sea Hawk and a Starfighter F-104G. There are some indoor displays. Open on Sundays and Bank Holidays.

BLANDFORD FORUM

Tourist information: Marsh and Ham Car Park, West Street. Tel: (01258) 454770.

The Royal Signals Museum
Blandford Camp, E of Blandford Forum. Tel: (01258) 482248.

The story of military communications is told from primitive beginnings in the Crimean War through World Wars I and II to the satellite systems of today. Historic vehicles and equipment. Open Monday to Friday, and weekends June to September.

Badbury Rings
Kingston Lacey Estate. 8 miles SE of Blandford Forum by B3082. National Trust.

The Iron Age fort dominates the landscape and is the meeting-place of a web of Roman roads. Dorset is well supplied with hill-top forts. Hod Hill and Turnworth Down are NW of Blandford and the National Trust also cares for Pilsdon Pen, Lambert's Castle and Coney's Castle in the west of the county north of Lyme Regis.

Corfe Castle
On Wareham to Swanage road, A351, 15 miles S of Blandford. National Trust. Tel: (01929) 481294. Open daily.

Built on a promontory by the Normans, the stone keep dates from 1105 and the stone bailey was constructed soon after. The lie of the land encouraged a departure from the motte and bailey layout and subsequent development by King John added the western bailey and great hall. Today the ruins bear witness to the power of artillery; the castle was taken and slighted, that is, made weak and of no importance, by Parliamentary forces in 1646.

The Tank Museum
Bovington Camp. 10 miles S of Blandford. From junction of A35 and A31 at Bere Regis, S by minor road. Or from A352 W from Wareham. Tel: (01929) 405096. Open daily.

There are over 300 AFVs (Armoured Fighting Vehicles), tanks, armoured cars, etc., in this wonderful museum dating from 1915 onwards and brought together from 26 countries including Britain. There are regular driving days when the vehicles can be seen on the move. The attractions include a video theatre and a tank simulator, as well as a Lawrence of Arabia exhibit. Lawrence's cottage, Clouds Hill (National Trust), is one mile north.

The Keep Military Museum
Bridport Road (B3150), Dorchester, 16 miles SW of Blandford Forum by A354 and A35. Tel: (01305) 264066. Open daily except Christmas and New Year.

The Devonshire and Dorset Regiment was formed in 1858 from the Devonshire Regiment and the Dorset Regiment, each of which has a long history. From the raising of a force to resist Monmouth's Rebellion in 1685 to the present day men of these regiments have seen service in India (there is a diorama of the Battle of Plassey, 1757), the Napoleonic Wars, Australia, South Africa and in World Wars I and II as well as overseas theatres since 1945. There are also Nazi relics from Hitler's Chancellory.

This must be the finest Iron Age hill fort in Britain. The earthworks are vast and incorporate a series of ramparts and overlapping entrances. The fort was taken by the Romans in 43AD.

Maiden Castle
Dorchester, 2 miles SW by A354 and minor road N of bypass. English Heritage. Open site.

There are ten Commonwealth War Graves Commission graves of World War I, including one Australian, and thirteen of World War II. Other graves of both wars are in the main cemetery.

Bridport Cemetery
E of Bridport in Bothenhampton.

One of the forts built in the 1860s, Nothe is now a museum with displays on three levels showing the history of coastal defence. It is open daily in summer, Sunday afternoons in winter.

Nothe Fort Museum of Coastal Defence
Barrack Road, Weymouth, 7 miles S of Dorchester by A354. Tel: (01305) 787243.

The defences of Portland Harbour to be seen date back, probably, to the 15th century. Rufus or Bow and Arrow Castle is on the east side of the Isle of Portland. It is a blockhouse with five circular gunports in its walls and the remains of a machiolated parapet. More recent is the castle built by Henry VIII, Sandsfoot Castle, which is known to have been operational in 1541. The octagonal gun room has been almost entirely eroded by the sea, but the residential block survives. The defences were of importance in the Civil War and a landward defensive bastioned earthwork may be seen.

Portland Coastal Defences
Isle of Portland, Weymouth.

Portland Castle
N shore, Isle of Portland. English Heritage. Tel: (01305) 820539.
This is a well-preserved example of a Henrican fort and is built of Portland stone. It is semicircular in plan with a single-storey gun room for five guns and with an upper tier of guns as well. A two-storey barrack building stands to the rear. Open March to October 10am to 6pm.

There are 154 Commonwealth graves here, of which 59 are British dead of World War I. There is one Canadian of World War II with one New Zealand and 78 British. Fifteen further graves are of unidentified men.

Portland Royal Naval Cemetery
On the N slope of Portland, overlooking the harbour. 6 miles S of Weymouth.

CANTERBURY

Tourist information: 34 St Margaret's Street. Tel: (01227) 766567.

The towers of the gatehouse, built in 1380 to protect the town from cross-Channel raiders in the Hundred Years War, are the earliest fortifications in England designed for guns. The keyhole gunports give overlapping fields of fire. The museum contains arms and armour from the Civil War, Boer War and World War II.

West Gate and the City Walls
West Gate Museum, St Peter's Street, Canterbury. Tel: (01227) 452747. Open Monday to Saturday.

The regiment was raised in the time of Elizabeth I and its history of world-wide service is traced up to 1961. There is a section on the East Kent Volunteers and Militia. It is open Monday to Saturday except Good Friday and Christmas week.

The Buffs Regimental Museum
18 High Street. Tel: (01227) 452747.

Chart Gunpowder Mills

Westbrook Walk, Faversham. 7 miles W of Canterbury by A2. Tel: (01795) 534542.

Particularly during the Civil War, control of the gunpowder supply was of fundamental strategic importance and the ready availability of powder to the Navy was crucial in wars at sea. The manufacture of explosives has always been a dangerous business and the delicate process is explained here. Open April to October, weekend afternoons only.

Richborough Castle

11 miles E of Canterbury by A257, 2 miles N of Sandwich, N off the A257. English Heritage.

The Roman fort defended the port of Rutupiae, the principal port of entry to Roman Britain. It was here that the invaders made their landing in 43AD, and here that the Romano-British attempted to stem the next invasion by Germanic peoples. In addition to the walls, the foundations of a triumphal arch survive. Open daily April to October.

Manston Memorial

RAF Manston, W of Ramsgate. Tel: (01843) 823351.

RAF Manston was a key fighter station in World War II. A Spitfire XVI and a Hurricane II are on display as well as other exhibits in the Manston Memorial Building. Open daily.

Deal Castle

Deal, 16 miles E, SW of town centre. English Heritage. Tel: (01304) 372762. Open April to October daily, November to March Wednesday to Sunday.

In 1538 the Catholic nations of France and Spain threatened Henry VIII's England with invasion and this castle was the largest to be constructed to protect the naval anchorage of the Downs. A central tower has six small bastions, *lunettes*, around its base, from which handguns can cover the courtyard. Outside, six large bastions with 53 gunports overlook the dry moat.

Walmer Castle

2 miles S of Deal Castle. English Heritage. Tel: (01304) 364288. Open April to October as Deal.

Now the residence of the Lord Warden of the Cinque Ports, HRH The Queen Mother, the castle was built to protect the Downs. The layout is similar to, but simpler than, Deal Castle, with a central tower and four bastions. The Duke of Wellington died here and a room is devoted to his memorabilia.

CHATHAM

Chatham Historic Dockyard

Tel: (01634) 812551. Open daily April to October, Wednesday, Saturday and Sunday in February, March and November.

The vast dockyard in which HMS *Victory* was built now has some 30 buildings devoted to the display of shipbuilding from Tudor to recent times, particularly warships of the Royal Navy in the days of sail and wooden hulls. The yard dates from about 1570 when a mast pond, storehouses and a forge comprised the premises. Of special interest is the Ropery, where the 20 miles of rigging that a man o'war required was made; it is still in operation today. The sail and colour loft still produces flags and sails on a commercial basis. The Wooden Walls gallery describes the building of a wooden warship from the point of view of an apprentice and another of the exhibits is a collection of historic lifeboats. There is so much to see here that at least half a day should be allowed for a visit.

The Chatham Naval Memorial

King's Bastion Road. From A231 by Mansion Row and Sally Port Gardens or on foot from the Town Hall gardens. Open daily.

One of three memorials (see Plymouth and Portsmouth) to sailors of the Royal Navy lost at sea in World War I (8,515 names) and World War II (10,112 names). The centrepiece is a stone tower crowned with a copper globe. The register is kept in Brompton Garrison Church, Maxwell Road, off Mansion Row.

Leaving the Romans aside, William the Conqueror brought the first military engineer to Britain, and the museum traces the development since roads, fortifications, railways, canals, as well as dealing with unexploded bombs. An example of the first remote-controlled missile, the Brennan Torpedo is here, as is Wellington's map of the battle of Waterloo. The Engineers were at Rorke's Drift in the Boer War, dug amazing tunnels in World War I and contributed the Mulberry Harbour and the bridges vital to the invasion of Normandy in World War II.

Royal Engineers Museum

Brompton Barracks, Gillingham. Tel: (01634) 406397. From centre of Chatham take the Gillingham (A231) road and turn left on Prince Arthur Road (B2004).

During the Seven Years' War (1756–1763), in fear of a French invasion which was actually attempted in 1759, but was beaten off at sea, the inland defences of Chatham Dockyard were enhanced with continuous bastions from St Mary's Creek in the north to this fine example of 18th-century fortification in the south. It was completed in 1820. A reconstructed World War II operations room is to be seen. The 3.7-inch anti-aircraft gun is a memorial to 166 (City of Rochester) Battery.

Fort Amherst

Barrier Road, off Dock Road, Chatham. Tel: (01634) 847747. Open daily.

One of the ring of forts (Borstal, Bridgewoods, Horsted and Luton) built in the 1870s and 1880s. They are polygonal, low in profile and blend into the landscape.

Fort Luton

Privately owned; open in summer. To SE of Chatham.

After the destruction of the fort at the mouth of the Medway by the Dutch in 1667, Sir Bernard de Gomme, who was responsible for Tilbury Fort, designed the new shoreline bastions here, extended to enclose Blue Town nearly 100 years later. The fort itself, built in the 1860s, is not easy to visit, but the line of spanner-like supports for the launching rails of the Brennan Torpedo (see R.E. Museum, Chatham) can still be seen.

Garrison Point Fort

Sheerness, 12 miles NE, by A249 from M2, exit 5.

The 12th-century tower keep was built for Henry I by William of Corbeil, Archbishop of Canterbury, within the ringwork of an earlier castle. The massive walls were strengthened by an internal cross-wall which, when it was besieged by King John in 1215, allowed resistance to continue even when part of the external wall had been undermined. The cross-wall also contained the well from which water could be drawn as high as the third floor. By this time the castle had become a residence as well, and the fireplaces and garderobes (toilets) can be seen. Another development from the motte and bailey layout was the construction of a forebuilding to guard the entrance to the keep itself. It had to be entered on the first floor from a stair that turned from the west face of the keep to the north-west corner, still leaving a pit and drawbridge to be overcome.

Rochester Castle

Rochester, 2 miles W by A289. English Heritage. Tel: (01634) 402276. Open daily April to September 10am to 6pm, October to March 10am to 4pm.

An Elizabethan attempt to provide protection for the fleet at Chatham on the opposite bank. Built in the 1560s, it ignores the innovations for efficient use of artillery to be seen at Deal, for example, using an angled bastion that restricts the field of fire. It proved useless against the Dutch in 1667.

Upnor Castle

NE of Rochester on shore of Medway off A228. English Heritage. Tel: (01634) 827980. Open April to September 10am to 6pm.

New Tavern Fort

Fort Gardens, Milton Place, Gravesend. Open weekends in summer.

Built in 1778 to complement Tilbury Fort on the north bank of the river, and modified in 1868. A 6-inch battery was installed this century, and various other guns are to be seen. A passenger ferry from West Street to Tilbury permits access to its big brother. Gravesend Blockhouse was built by Henry VIII.

Gravesend Blockhouse

Opposite Clarendon Royal Hotel.

CHICHESTER

Tourist information: 29a South Street. Tel: (01243) 775888.

Royal Corps of Military Police Museum

Rousillon Barracks, Broyle Road. Tel: (01243) 534225.

The history of the Military Police dates back to Tudor times. Videos and a diorama enhance the account of the fight against crime and the other duties that fall to the Corps. Special exhibits on World War II, National Service and life in a modern garrison town can be seen. Open daily, except Monday, April to September; Tuesday to Friday October to March, but closed January.

Tangmere Military Aviation Museum

Tangmere Airfield. 3 miles E of Chichester by A27. Tel: (01243) 775223. Open daily February to November.

This was a fighter base from World War I until 1970. The history of aerial warfare, especially in World Wars I and II, forms the core of the museum. Six historic RAF aircraft are to be seen, including a Gloucester Meteor F4 and a Hawker Hunter F3.

DOVER

Tourist information: Townwall Street. Tel: (01304) 205108.

Dover Castle

Off Castle Hill Road, the A258 to Deal. English Heritage. Tel: (01304) 201628. Open daily March to October 9.30am to 6pm, November to March 10am to 4pm.

A mighty fortress now stands where an Iron Age earthwork was converted to a castle by the Normans and extended and enhanced by successive generations to the present day, providing a history of fortification in itself. The most radical alterations took place in the 18th century and during the Napoleonic Wars when artillery became dominant. The vulnerable medieval curtain wall was lowered and earth bastions for heavy guns, each independently defensible and connected by underground passages, were built together with vaults for ammunition.

In World War II the underground tunnels were developed to provide a command centre and hospital and the provision for gunnery modernised. For example, there is a spigot mortar mounting on Horseshoe Bastion. Dover Castle has the longest recorded history of any major fortress in Britain.

The Princess of Wales's Royal Regiment and the Queen's Regimental Museum
Dover Castle.
The Queen's is one of two regiments entitled to the battle honour *Tangier 1662–1680*, and is thus one of the founding regiments of the British Regular Army. Together with 11 other regiments, including the Buffs, the East Surrey and the Middlesex, they have been amalgamated into the Princess of Wales's. The scope of the museum is therefore very wide, including the French and Indian War in America, the taking of Quebec, the American War of Independence, the Napoleonic Wars, the Peninsular War, service in India, China and against the Maoris, the Boer War, World Wars I and II.

Extensive fortifications begun in 1803, now a Young Offender Institution, but viewable from footpaths outside. Includes the Drop Redoubt (English Heritage) to the north-east and the Grand Shaft (Dover Council), a remarkable three-part stair from the former barracks to the town. A guide book from Dover Museum.

The Western Heights
From York Street, going inland, left up Durham Hill and left into North Military Road. Tel: (01304) 241806.

The whole range of Dover's history is portrayed in the high-tech displays of the Historium, including Roman, Anglo-Saxon, Napoleonic and World War II events of war. Two hours should be allowed for the visit.

White Cliffs Experience and Dover Museum
Market Square. Tel: (01304) 214566

This 19th-century defence work still has two 16-inch Rifled Muzzle-Loaders (RMLs) in place. History from Dover Museum.

Admiralty Pier Fort
Dover Harbour Board.

One of the few surviving sound mirrors (see also entries under Rye) remains at Abbott's Cliff.

Sound Mirror
Capel-le-Ferne, 4 miles W. Approach by B2101, track to coast next Royal Oak pub.

Shore defence tower built in the 1800s. The entrance was on the first floor where there were living quarters for 24 men and one officer. The gun platform above carried a 24-pounder gun mounted on a pivoting carriage to give all-round fire.

Martello Tower No 3
Folkestone, 6 miles W by A20. Open summer.

A forward fighter station in the Battle of Britain in World War II, Hawkinge has replica aircraft of the time, including Spitfires, Hurricanes and Messerschmitts as well as military vehicles. The story of Britain's desperate days of 1940 is told in the displays. Open daily April to October.

Kent Battle of Britain Museum
Hawkinge, 2 miles N of Folkestone by A260. Tel: (01303) 893140.

The Commonwealth War Graves Commission cemetery contains 490 graves of World War I and 81 of World War II.

Shorncliffe Military Cemetery
Shorncliffe Military Barracks, 2 miles W of Folkestone, S of A20.

EASTBOURNE

Tourist information: 3 Cornfield Road. Tel: (01323) 411400.

The 11-gun redoubt was towards the western end of a line of fortifications, a series of Martello towers that included another redoubt at Dymchurch and Newhaven Fort, all built between 1804 and 1812 to meet the threat of invasion by Napoleon. It remained part of the coastal defence system until 1945. Housed within is the museum. A Martello tower, the Wish Tower, stands further west on Royal Parade.

Eastbourne Redoubt
Royal Parade, eastern end. Tel: (01323) 410300. Open Easter–November. Entrance to the fortress is free, to the museum at a charge.

The Sussex Combined Services Museum
The Royal Sussex Regiment's service since 1701 includes the American Revolution and the Napoleonic Wars while the Queen's Royal Irish Hussars collection has memorabilia of the Charge of the Light Brigade at Balaclava as well as of Korea and Bosnia. The British Model Soldier Society's collection is also here, comprising more than 1,500 figures of soldiers from Roman times to the Gulf War.

Pevensey Castle

3 miles NE of Eastbourne by A259. English Heritage. Tel: (01323) 762604. Open April to October 10am to 6pm, November to March Wednesday to Sunday 10am to 4pm.

When William the Conqueror landed at Pevensey he used the old Roman fort of Anderida as a base. The place was refortified and Robert de Mortain built a permanent castle in the south-western corner of the fort. It continued as part of the coastal defensive system, being refurbished, for example, against the threat of the Spanish Armada, 1588. Camouflaged pillboxes attest to its World War II role.

GUILDFORD

Tourist information: 14 Tunsgate. Tel: (01483) 444333.

The Henley Grove Centre

Now a Surrey CC school camp. Visit by appointment only with the Warden. Tel: (01483) 562636.

In the 1890s the defence of London was provided for by the construction of Mobilisation Centres and forts on a line from Guildford through Box Hill, Westerham, Farningham and the site of the modern Blackwall Tunnel. Henley Fort is a good example, with casemates for 15-pounder breech-loading guns, magazines and storehouses. The Volunteer forces, precursors of the Second World War Home Guard, were to assemble at these centres in time of national crisis.

Semaphore Tower

Chatley Heath. Tel: (01932) 862762. SE of M25 junction 10, immediately left from the A3 roundabout, to car park in Old Lane.

Sending urgent messages from London to Portsmouth before the age of the electric telegraph was achieved by using a chain of towers to pass signals by semaphore. The Surrey CC have preserved this example, complete with its apparatus. From the car park it is a 15-minute walk following signs. Open in summer, weekends and Bank Holiday Mondays, afternoons only.

Brooklands Museum

Brooklands Road, Weybridge, 10 miles N by A3, A245 and B374. Tel: (01932) 857381. Open daily except Monday.

Brooklands is best known as the motor racing track which was operational from 1907 to 1939, and the museum shows vehicles associated with that period. It also shows some 40 aircraft in whole or in part, including a Wellington bomber rescued from Loch Ness in 1985 and restored here.

The Queen's Royal Surrey Regiment Museum

Clandon Park, Guildford. Tel: (01483) 223419. Just N of the A246 Guildford to Leatherhead road on A247.

The Queen's Royal Regiment, formerly the Tangier Regiment, and the East Surrey Regiment are remembered here under the name of the unit formed by their amalgamation in 1959. Only the Blues and Royals share with the Queen's the battle honour *Tangier 1662–1680*. The story thus goes back to the foundation of the Regular Army. Open April to October, Tuesday, Wednesday and Thursday, Sunday and Bank Holidays, afternoon only.

Box Hill Fort

Box Hill, between Dorking and Leatherhead, off A24. National Trust Country Park.

The Mobilisation Centres that formed the London Defence Positions of the 1860s included Henley Grove near Guildford and this fortification at the beauty spot of Box Hill. They had dual purposes both as storehouses for equipment should the Volunteers have to be mobilised and as redoubts should an invading force get this far inland. The rise of the Blue Water School, the proponents of the theory that the Navy would prevent an invasion even starting, led to the abandonment of the London Defence Positions by the end of the century.

The Chilworth mills, established by the East India Company in 1626, once stood alongside the River Tillingbourne on land now owned by Guildford Borough Council. From the southern end of the Blacksmith Lane crossing of the river a public footpath runs east past West Lodge to Lockner Road, passing the relics of the gunpowder works, engine beds, a tramway and a swing bridge. The guide book (from the Guildford Museum, Castle Arch) by Glenys Crocker is fascinating.

The control of these mills was a vital contribution to the success of Parliament in the Civil War. Water power was replaced by steam in the 1860s and the works were extended in 1914–18. They closed in 1920.

The river was part of the line of the World War II GHQ Stopline of pillboxes and roadblocks organised to resist German invasion. On reaching Lockner Road traces may be seen on walking south-east, while walking the other way, towards Chilworth Manor, reveals a pillbox on the right on a footpath.

Chilworth Gunpowder Mills
N of the A248 Shalford to Albury road by Blacksmith Lane.

GHQ Stopline
The Seahorse, Shalford, S of Guildford by A281.

Roadblocks, concrete blocks slotted to hold girders or rails, were part of the GHQ Stopline system. The relic on the pavement next to the pub here is marked with a plaque.

HASTINGS

Tourist information: 4 Robertson Terrace. Tel: (01424) 718888.

William, Duke of Normandy, landed at Pevensey on 28 September, only three days after Harold had defeated the Vikings at Stamford Bridge near York. Harold hurried south, getting to London on about 6 October and leaving to block William's route inland on 11 October. The Anglo-Saxons occupied Caldbec Hill, key to both the Maidstone and Lewes routes, on 13 October. A marshy valley separated them from the Normans on Telham Hill to the south and across it ran a narrow ridge. Harold drew up his forces on the forward slope, probably on a line through the place where the Abbey's High Altar stands today.

Soon after 8.30 the next morning, descending from the hill on a narrow front, the Normans fanned out as they neared the long line of English shields. It was to take the whole day to break the dam that faced them. At one point the Breton forces on William's left were thrown back, but the over-eager pursuers were cut off and slain. It became a long, attritional fight, the Norman horsemen slowly wearing down Harold's axemen at fearful cost and redoubling their efforts as dusk approached lest the defenders slip away in the gloom. Arrows shot high in the air eroded the Anglo-Saxon force until a small knot stood around Harold's standard, finally to be overrun. Harold, despite the arrow-in-the-eye legend, fell to the sword.

The Battle of Hastings, 14 October 1066
Battle, NW of Hastings on A2100. English Heritage Visitor Centre. Tel: (01424) 773792. Open daily March to October 10am to 6pm, November to March 10am to 4pm.

Battle Museum of Local History
Memorial Hall, opposite Abbey Green. Open April to September 10.30am to 4.30pm.

Includes a print of the Bayeux Tapestry.

To secure the area from French invasion during the 14th century, Richard II granted Sir Edward Dalyngrigge leave to build a castle at the highest point navigable on the River Rother which reaches the sea at Rye. In flat country no natural defensive position existed, so the moat was vital, and vast. Both a fortress and a residence with private apartments for the lord, the castle illustrates the transition from the stark military structures of earlier times.

Bodiam Castle
Bodiam, E of the B2244, Hawkhurst to Hastings road. National Trust. Tel: (01580) 830436. Open mid-February to October daily, November to mid-January Tuesday to Sunday.

ISLE OF WIGHT

Tourist information: The Car Park, South Street, Newport. Tel: (01983) 525450.

Carisbrooke Castle

S of Newport. English Heritage. Tel: (01983) 522107. Open daily.

Aylmer Military Collection and Isle of Wight Home Guard Museum

Nunwell House, Brading. 7 miles E of Newport. Tel: (01983) 407240. Open July to September Sunday to Thursday.

Private museum exhibiting military memorabilia of the family and a section on the Home Guard in World War II.

The first fortification here was built by the Romans and adapted by the Saxons in the 8th century. Improvements were made continuously for hundreds of years, making this a prime example of the evolution of the English castle. The Norman fitzOsberns raised the banks on the line of the old walls and later built a motte surmounted by a stone shell keep, completed by the 1130s. Domestic buildings were added until, between 1270 and 1293, Isabella de Forz built a chapel and private apartments, adding to the hall, and laid out a garden to transform the castle from a fort and residence to a private palace. It became a royal castle on her death, bought by Edward I. The gatehouse was rebuilt in the 1380s and gunports with sighting slits above can be seen on the upper parts of the towers.

The fear of the Spanish Armada in 1588 led to refortification and that fear persisted so that, between 1597 and 1601, the Italian engineer Frederigo Genebelli was employed in building the last of the classic Italian-style bastions in England. Carisbrooke was a prison to Charles I before his execution and his story forms part of the exhibition to be seen here. Donkeys are another – they replaced prisoners on the treadmill to draw water from the well and perform the same service today.

Yarmouth Castle

Yarmouth, 12 miles W of Newport by A3054. English Heritage. Tel: (01983) 760678. Open daily April to October.

This was the final fort in Henry VIII's coastal defence system, built in 1547 to protect the passage up the Solent from the Needles. Originally it was square, with the sea on two sides and a ditch on the other two, with an angle bastion of the Italian type covering them. The *orillons*, the flattened barbs of the arrow-head shape, were too short to provide adequate covering fire to the ditches, and there were two tiers of gunports in the walls with a parapet above. This unsatisfactory arrangement was modified in the 1560s by lowering the structure and in-filling to make a huge gun platform. The orillon bastion remains; the earliest example surviving in Britain.

The Needles Old Battery

SW of Totland by B3322. National Trust. Tel: (01983) 754772. Open April to October Sunday to Thursday and daily in July and August. May be closed in bad weather; telephone to check.

The 1860s were marked by the greatest programme of coastal fortification since the 17th century. The battery built to dominate the approaches to the Solent was notable for its use of searchlights. Between 1889 and 1892 trials were made of searchlights in caves made at the foot of the cliffs, and in 1898 an emplacement for a light was made at the western tip of the battery with a tunnel going back into the battery itself. Electrical controls allowed the detonation of mines placed offshore under an encroaching enemy. Armament included QFs (quick-firing guns) and RMLs (rifled muzzle-loaders). Two RMLs are to be seen here.

LEWES

Tourist information: Lewes House, 32 School Hill. Tel: (01273) 483448.

One of William the Conqueror's companions, William de Warenne, built the fine Norman keep on the western motte to secure the seaport and river crossing as well as to keep the native Saxon populace in order. There are, unusually, two mottes. Brack Mount, the earlier by 30 years, stands behind the Lewes Arms to the north-east and between them an ancient bowling green occupies the centre of the bailey. Towers in the north-west and south-west walls of the keep were added in the 13th century and the imposing barbican in the 14th century. From the towers the field of the battle of 1264 can be seen to the north-west.

Lewes Castle
In the town.

In 1258, to raise money, Henry III was obliged to accede to demands for reform and accept, by the Provisions of Oxford, the involvement of his barons in the government of the realm. Henry persuaded the Pope to nullify his oath six years later, but a return to autocratic rule was resisted by a group of barons led by Simon de Montfort, Earl of Leicester. In April 1264 Simon gathered his forces at St Albans while Henry, moving south and west, was at Lewes in May with some 10,000 men, with Simon approaching from London at the head of a force of about 5,000.

On the morning of 14 May Simon took up positions on Offham Hill, possibly on the line of the footpath, from which height the land falls away both to the west and, to the east, towards the town of Lewes, and facing a spur along which another footpath now runs down towards the modern prison.

The Battle of Lewes, 14 May 1264
Offham Hill, NW of town, 2 miles by footpaths from Offham or from near H.M. Prison.

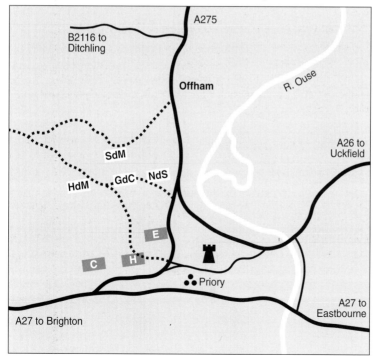

Human bones
Relics of the slain have been found in the chalk-pits on the road to Offham and, in 1810 when the turnpike road, now Brighton Road, was being made, three pits with some 500 bodies in each were found, suggesting that the final slaughter took place near the modern prison.

Anne of Cleves House

Southover High Street, Lewes.

French prisoners of the Napoleonic Wars were held in Lewes prison and made models of ships out of bones to pass the time. Some examples are here.

The king's son, Edward, had spent the night at the castle while Henry and the Earl of Cornwall were at the Priory. Edward rushed his men into action against Nicholas de Segrave's untried troops on de Montfort's left, breaking the formation and chasing them down the steep slope to the north. Henry and Cornwall were thus obliged to move swiftly to the attack, but on the left Cornwall's troops had a steep climb to face Henry de Montfort's force on Simon's right and were driven back. In the centre, on the spur, Henry III was on level terms, and terrain, against Gilbert de Clare's men but Simon's reserves, now Cornwall was out of the way, took him on the left flank and drove him back into the town before Edward could return to save the day. Defeated, Henry had to allow the barons their voice in government – the first seed of parliamentary rule in Britain.

Newhaven Fort

Fort Road. Tel: (01273) 517622. S from Lewes by the A26. Follow signs from the ring road, A259. Open April to September daily.

When the port of Lewes silted up in the 16th century the river was diverted and Newhaven created. The landing of 20 Frenchmen in 1585 led to the first defence measures – a single cannon that took 20 years to get installed. The coming of the railway made Newhaven an important harbour and this, one of the later forts constructed in the 1860s, was less a counter-invasion measure than a protection for the growing port. It was intended for 42 guns and 300 men and was finished in 1870. It is more substantial than other forts of the time and was the first in which concrete was used as a revetment for ditches. Displays include gun emplacements, a World War II Royal Observer Corps observation post, and part of a V1 flying bomb. The preparations for the Dieppe Raid in which so many Canadian troops died were made here and that event, together with the D-Day landings, is featured. The work of the RAF Marine Craft Service in air-sea rescue is also documented.

Canadian Memorial

Approaching Newhaven Fort, next to the river.

HMS *Forward*

Newhaven Local and Maritime Museum, Avis Road. Follow signs. Tel: (01273) 512123. Open April to October weekends and Bank Holidays.

HMS *Forward* was a secret underground radio and telecommunications base built under Heighton Hill in 1941. Observations of movements in the English Channel in World War II made by other coastal installations were reported every 20 minutes to maintain a detailed plot of the situation, both in the air and on the water, between Dungeness and Selsey Bill. The base was thus heavily involved in the affair of the *Scharnhorst*, *Gniesenau* and *Prinz Eugen*'s audacious dash for German waters in 1942, the Dieppe Raid in the same year and the D-Day operations of 1944. The Canadian Corps Coastal Artillery had their headquarters here. A model of the installation is on display at this museum.

Seaford Martello Tower

Marine Drive, on the seashore. It is the Museum of Local History, open Sundays and Bank Holidays all year, closed lunchtime, and on Wednesday and Saturday afternoons in summer.

Of special interest because of the gun mounted on the gun platform, so that it offers something of its operational appearance. Nearby is Bishopstone Railway Station (immediately S of A259, W of Seaford; follow signs). Incorporated in the tower of the building erected in about 1937 are loop-holes for World War II bren guns – a sort of latter-day Martello tower in the style of a 1930s cinema, now woefully shabby.

LYMINGTON

Tourist information: St Barb Museum and Visitor Centre, Main Car Park.
Tel: (01590) 672422.

Of Henry VIII's coastal defence castles, this is unusual in having a 12-sided central tower and an internally angular outer ring. In the Napoleonic Wars it had two six-gun batteries added outside (1795) and the tower was modified in 1803 to carry six 24-pounders on traversing carriages on top; a massive version of a Martello tower. In the 1860s huge casemated batteries were added with iron shields to answer the improvements in naval gunnery. There are 37 casemates on the western side and 24 on the east, replacing the earthworks of the previous decade. The gun positions were open to the rear when in action to allow fumes to disperse and closed with wooden walls and doors to serve as barracks in peacetime. There are two exhibitions open here and two 38-ton guns.

Hurst Castle
Pebble Spit, by ferry from Keyhaven, 3 miles S of Lymington. Ferry – tel: (01590) 642500 (June/Sept 9am/2pm) or (01425) 610784 (recorded info). English Heritage. Open daily April to October.

Ships were built here for the Royal Navy between 1745 and 1822. The museum explains the history of the ships, shipyard and the way of life of the workers.

Buckler's Hard Maritime Museum
Buckler's Hard, 7 miles E of Lymington by B3054 and minor road. Tel: (01590) 616203/612345.

MAIDSTONE

Tourist information: The Gatehouse, Old Palace Gardens, Mill Street. Tel: (01622) 673581.

The merging of regiments over the years has given this regiment a large portfolio of ancestors. The part of the museum devoted to military matters contains memorabilia of the 50th and 97th Regiments of Foot, the West Kent Militia, the 20th London and the Kent Cyclists Battalions. Weapons, medals, uniforms, pictures and other items are on display.

Queen's Own Royal West Kent Regimental Museum
Maidstone Museum and Art Gallery, St Faith's Street. Tel: (01622) 754497. Open daily.

There were relatively few through routes from the south coast over the heavily wooden Weald. This 12th-century keep protected the road from Rye. It is in the care of English Heritage and can be visited at any reasonable time

Sutton Valence Castle
5 miles SE of Maidstone.

General James Wolfe lived here as a child and four rooms are devoted to memorabilia of his family, life and career. The Battle of Quebec, Canada, 1759, is the subject of a special exhibition and includes material on his rival general at the Heights of Abraham, the Marquis de Montcalm.

Quebec House
Westerham, 4 miles W of Sevenoaks by A25. National Trust. Tel: (01959) 562206. Open April to October Tuesday and Sunday afternoons.

East of St Mary Cray is a Commonwealth War Graves Commission cemetery with 59 war graves. The dead were brought from RAF Biggin Hill, a World War II fighter station seven miles to the south-west, and number 52 British, 1 Canadian, 3 Australian, 1 New Zealand and 2 unidentified. Fourteen died in the raid on Biggin Hill in August 1940. Other graves of the war are in the main cemetery and there are four of men of the German Air Force. At All Saints Church in Orpington is Ontario Cemetery where soldiers who died of wounds

Orpington (St Mary Cray) Cemetery and Ontario Cemetery
Orpington, 16 miles NW of Maidstone by M20 and via Swanley and B258 via St Mary Cray.

at Orpington Hospital in World War I are buried. There are 88 Canadian, 23 British and 5 Australian graves. Other graves of both wars are in the main churchyard.

PORTSMOUTH HARBOUR AND SOUTHSEA

Portsmouth tourist information: The Hard. Tel: (01705) 826722.

The importance of Portsmouth Harbour as a strategic military and commercial feature was recognised by the Romans who built a castle at Portchester on the northern shore. Portsmouth itself, commanding the mouth of the harbour, was established in the 12th century, granted a Royal Charter by Richard I and first fortified by King John. Its supremacy as a naval base dates from the days of Henry VIII who extended the fortifications to Southsea, and its importance led to massive new defences, such as Fort Brockhurst, being built in the 1850s and 1860s.

Portsmouth Historic Dockyard

Information hotline: 0839 407080. By car, in Portsmouth, follow signs to Historic Ships. By rail, Portsmouth Harbour Station. Open daily except Christmas Eve and Day.

There is so much to see at the old Royal Dockyard that a whole day can easily be spent there. While you can buy one ticket at a time, a better deal is to buy a Multiship Saver Ticket to all the attractions at a bargain price. Shore-side support for fighting ships is shown in the Historic Dockyard tour and the skills of a dockyard worker in 1911 are illustrated in the hands-on Dockyard Apprentice and Dockyard 500 features. Warships by Water tours (Easter to October) give a sight of the modern Navy. The history of the Royal Navy is portrayed in the historic ships and the museum.

The Mary Rose *Ship Hall and Museum*
Tel: (01705) 812931.
The *Mary Rose* was Henry VIII's most powerful warship. On 19 July 1545, with the king looking on from Southsea Castle, she sailed against the French and sank almost immediately with great loss of life. The wreck was raised in 1982 and is still in the process of conservation. Visitors can see not only the ship herself, but more than a thousand artefacts that reveal the working and living conditions of the Tudor Navy.

HMS Victory
Tel: (01705) 839766.
Admiral Lord Nelson died on board this 100-gun First Rate Ship-of-the-Line on 21 October 1805. The ship is still in commission in the Royal Navy and, launched as she was on 7 May 1765, she has seen over two centuries of service. The armament and equipment of the time of her active service are in place, giving an unrivalled picture of Nelson's navy.

HMS Warrior
Tel: (01705) 291379.
The Victorian Navy is brought to life in HMS *Warrior* and touching the exhibits is positively encouraged! With steam power added to sail, this iron-hulled armoured frigate was, when launched in 1860, the largest, fastest and most powerful warship in the world.

The Royal Naval Museum
Tel: (01705) 733060.
The serving men and women of the Royal Navy are the focus of the story of
Britain's sea-borne forces from the time of King Alfred to the present day,
arranged in five major galleries. The redeveloped Victory Gallery includes the
vivid Trafalgar Experience, where the sights, sounds and smells of battle convey
what it was like to be there and the hands-on Gundeck display invites visitors to
explore shipboard life. Overseas visitors from the Commonwealth and the USA
will find the World War II sections, including oral history, interesting. The viewing
platform offers unrivalled views over the working dockyard.

Overlooking the narrow entrance to the harbour beyond Broad Street, the Round
and Square Towers are part of the late medieval fortifications and offer excellent
views.

The Round Tower

Henry VIII's defensive measures for the Royal Dockyard at Portsmouth included
the building of this castle in 1544–5. Most of what can be seen today is more
recent, part of the Victorian fortification of the harbour, including an
underground tunnel around the moat. The Time Tunnel Experience is a graphic
presentation of the castle's history.

Southsea Castle
*On the seafront, Clarence
Esplanade. Tel: (01705)
827261. Open daily April to
October, weekends
November to March.*

The massive undertaking of the Allied invasion of Normandy in 1944, Operation
Overlord, is set out in wonderful detail. A unique feature is the modern cousin
of the Bayeux Tapestry, the 272-foot-long Overlord Embroidery. The artificial
port, known as the Mulberry Harbour, that was built for the invasion at
Arromanches was made from prefabricated units. They were manufactured
at Lepe Country Park near Calshot on Southampton Water and on Hayling
Island, to the east of Southsea on the far side of Langstone Harbour, in which
one section of the Mulberry can still be seen.
    A relic of airfield defence measures is also to be seen outside the D-Day
Museum. The Pickett-Hamilton Counterbalance Fort was an underground
pillbox which was buried on the airfield and over which vehicles and aircraft
could drive or taxi. It came into action when compressed air raised the turret.

**The D-Day Museum
and Overlord
Embroidery**
*Clarence Esplanade. Tel:
(01705) 827261. Open
daily.*

As at Chatham and Plymouth, the memorial to the men of the Royal Navy
unveiled here in 1924 is built to give a leading mark, a navigational aid, to
mariners. The names of 9,666 sailors of World War I are recorded and a further
14,921 names from World War II were added on bronze panels in a sunken
garden on the landward side.

**The Portsmouth
Naval Memorial**
*Clarence Esplanade,
Southsea.*

Covering 300 years of history from the early days of sea-borne soldiers to the
elite unit of today, the museum has an audio-visual display on the D-Day landings
and the Falklands War. Hannah Snell, the woman who joined in disguise in
1745, is featured, as are the famous bandsmen. Ticket discount for joint entry
with Submarine Museum, Gosport.

**The Royal Marines
Museum**
*Eastney Esplanade. Tel:
(01705) 819385. Open daily
except Christmas.*

Spitbank Fort

Ferry from Clarence Pier (or from Gosport Pontoon). Tel: (01329) 664286 or (01831) 608383.

Fearing new hostilities with the French, a Royal Commission was set up to examine the defence of Portsmouth and reported in 1860. As a result a ring of forts was constructed, including this one, a mile off-shore. It had a complement of 156 men and massive artillery. Spitbank Fort was bought from the government in 1980 and part is now lived in, but most has been restored to its Victorian fighting form. Allow a minimum of two hours for the ferry trip and tour.

The Royal Armouries Museum of Artillery, Fort Nelson

Down End Road, Fareham. 1 mile N of Fareham off A27 or from junction 11 on M27. Tel: (01329) 233734. Open April to October 10am to 5pm, November to March weekends 10.30am to 4pm.

Fort Nelson was constructed as part of the massive programme of the 1860s. The focus of the Royal Armouries collection is thus on Victorian artillery at the time when rifled breech-loading guns and smooth-bore muzzle loaders existed side by side. A 7-inch Armstrong RBL (rifled breech loader), a 32-pounder SBBL (smooth-bore breech loader) and 13-inch mortar batteries can be seen in their correct emplacements. Victorian field artillery shown includes the 40-pounder RBL and a 9-pounder RML (rifled muzzle loader).

Weapons of World War II include the German Flak 36 88mm gun and the British 3.7-inch AA gun. Captured weapons from Iraq brought back after the Gulf War include the Soviet D-20 152mm howitzer and the infamous 1000mm Iraqi supergun.

It is well worth telephoning some time ahead of your visit to get details of the planned demonstrations of gunnery and other special events. Joint ticket with Submarine World.

Portchester Castle

S of Portchester town, off A27. English Heritage. Tel: 01705 378291. Open April to October 10am to 6pm, November to March Wednesday to Sunday 10am to 4pm.

One of the chain of Roman forts protecting the south-east coast and supporting the *Classis Britannica* (the Channel fleet). The huge outer walls are original and the best preserved in Europe. In the 12th century Henry I built a two-storey keep, the signs of its sloping roof can still be seen, and two further storeys were added later. Henry V set off from here in 1415 on the campaign that culminated in Agincourt and during the Napoleonic Wars it housed over 4,000 prisoners.

Fort Brockhurst

Off the A32, north of Gosport. English Heritage. Tel: 01705 581059. Open daily, April to September.

Fearing attack on Portsmouth Harbour overland from the west, a line of defence from Gosport to Portchester was built, including this fort, begun in 1858. Designed by W D Jervois, it provided for overlapping, supporting artillery fire and had a keep at the gorge (entrance). It was manned by 11 officers and 300 men.

Submarine World – The Royal Navy Submarine Museum

Haslar Jetty Road, Gosport. Tel: 01705 529217. By ferry from Portsmouth Harbour Station, or from M27, junction 11, via A32. South from ferry over Haslar Bridge. Open daily except Christmas/New Year.

The original RN submarine of 1901, *Holland 1*, is here but the story of underwater warfare is told from an even earlier date, the American War of Independence, 1776, through the two World Wars to HMS *Alliance*, in service to 1973, the nuclear-powered submersibles and the Falklands War. Allow two hours for the visit. Joint ticket with Fort Nelson.

RYE

Tourist information: Heritage Centre, Strand Quay (restricted hours). Tel: (01797) 226696.

Under the direction of John Rennie, builder of the Kennet and Avon Canal, this remarkable work was completed in 1805, just as the Battle of Trafalgar destroyed the French fleet and removed the danger. The threat of invasion by Napoleon's forces at Dungeness and over the flat, indefensible marshland had led to the design of this linking fortification between the forts and Martello towers to the east and west. The spoil from the diggings formed a parapet behind which the military road ran inland, while a towpath on the other bank made safe movement of goods and munitions possible rather than running the gauntlet of the open sea. The refortification of the canal in World War II is marked by concrete pillboxes. The canal now supports wildlife and helps control water levels on the Romney and Walland Marshes.

The Royal Military Canal
Waymarked path from Rye to Cliff End westwards and from Rye to Warehorne (near Hamstreet, BR station) eastwards. Further east, from Lympne to Hythe. Planned to be open from end to end eventually.

The central artillery tower was built under Henry VIII in 1512-14 to protect the little harbour and augmented with semicircular bastions 25 years later. The scheme of concentric circles is pretty, but inferior to the angled bastion, already introduced in Italy at the time, which gave a better field of fire and accommodated more cannon.

Camber Castle
1 mile S of Rye. English Heritage. Tel: (01797) 223862. Open July to September Saturday afternoons only.

In World War II, before the installation of radar, incoming enemy aircraft were detected by picking up the sound of their engines. The noise was reflected onto a microphone by a concrete bowl or curved wall and, in calm, quiet conditions, could be heard when the enemy was more than eight miles away. Slab mirrors were shallow dishes in 15-foot square slabs of concrete, bowl mirrors were over 20 feet in diameter and much deeper in their curve, while wall mirrors were curved structures some 200 feet in length. This, the Greatstone group, includes the only wall mirror left standing. The mirrors are now on private land that is part of a gravel-extraction working.

Sound Mirrors
Denge Marsh, SE of Lydd, 8 miles E by A259 and B2075.

Seventy-four towers were built on the south coast between 1805 and 1812 to resist Napoleonic invasion. This is fully restored with a 24-pounder gun on the platform at the top. Open May to July weekends, August daily, 12 noon to 4pm.

Martello Tower 24
Dymchurch on A259 New Romney to Hythe road. English Heritage.

Built at the eastern end of the Dymchurch sea wall, this was part of the extensive works carried out during the Napoleonic Wars. Like the redoubt at Eastbourne, the great circular structure mounted 11 guns. It was sited to protect the drainage sluices of Romney Marsh.

Dymchurch Redoubt
Dymchurch on A259.

A bowl mirror still stands facing France and, alongside, is the fallen ruin of a wall mirror.

Sound Mirror
Near Hythe, may be seen from A259.

Sandgate Castle

Sandgate, near Hythe. Privately owned, open summer.

One of Henry VIII's forts, built at a cost of some £5,000 with a tower and three bastions, to defend Dover from land attack from the south-west. It was modified between 1805 and 1808 to make a Martello tower of the keep.

Lympne Castle

From M20, junction 11, SW on A20 and minor road.

Includes World War II concrete observation post built into the fabric of the castle. Privately owned, it is open in summer.

Brenzett Aeronautical Museum

On the A259 at the junction with the A2070. Tel: (01233) 627911. Open July to September Wednesday to Sunday, Easter weekend and Bank Holidays, afternoons.

This Advanced Landing Ground was completed in September 1943 and first used by Spitfire IXs of 122 Squadron. In 1944 the threat of the V1 (Doodlebug) flying bombs led to the arrival of the Polish Air Force 306 and 315 squadrons, flying Mustang Mk IIIs. Canadian, American and New Zealand pilots also served here. Exhibits include World War II memorabilia, remains recovered from aircraft crash sites and graffiti left by members of the Women's Land Army.

SALISBURY

Tourist information: Fish Row. Tel: (01722) 334956.

Regimental Museum

The Wardrobe, 58 The Close, Salisbury. Tel: (01722) 414536.

The Royal Gloucestershire, Berkshire and Wiltshire is housed in a building dating from the mid-13th century, the museum contains uniforms, weapons and equipment as well as campaign memorabilia.

Old Sarum

2 miles N of Salisbury by A345.

The Iron Age fort was used by the Normans as a strongpoint and a motte was built within its enclosure. Roger of Salisbury, bishop of Salisbury in the 12th century, built a courtyard castle on the Norman mound. The foundations of the 12th century cathedral also lie within the Iron Age work.

The Museum of Army Flying

Middle Wallop, 9 miles NE of Salisbury by A30 and A343. Tel: (01980) 674421. Open daily except week before Christmas.

The Army's use of the air began with kites and balloons and developed into aircraft in World War I with the Royal Flying Corps, gliders in World War II and helicopters in the Falklands War. The American pioneer Samuel Cody is commemorated here and hands-on experience on a helicopter flight simulator is available. Exhibits include over two dozen aircraft and numerous weapons and vehicles, some of which are items captured in the Falklands and Gulf wars.

Old Wardour Castle

Nr Ansty, 12 miles W by A30. English Heritage. Tel: (01747) 870487. Open March to October daily 10am to 6pm, November to March Wednesday to Sunday 10am to 4pm.

By the late 14th century the martial requirements of castles were being overtaken by the domestic needs of the local baron. John, fifth Lord Lovel was granted his licence to crenellate in 1393 and his castle shows French influence as does the keep at Warkworth. It was modernised in the late 16th century so there are features of a northern Renaissance character to be seen, but the original work is not hard to observe. The building is a hexagonal tower-house with a central courtyard and well. The design is sophisticated, one set of apartments intermeshing with the next, to provide a small palace. It was not without serious provision for defence, the entrance has a portcullis and machiolations over the door. Turrets project from the four corners of the castle and the ground floor is lit by loops alone, but above this the character of the building changes. Two huge windows soar above the entrance, dangerous though that may have been, to match the tall windows overlooking the courtyard and light the great hall. A grand staircase ascends from the courtyard to the east end of the hall, near the kitchens, while the Lord's private apartments and chapel are at the other end of the hall. These link with other family rooms by way of a stair in the north tower. Apartments for other members of the household would have occupied the four floors in the south and west sides of the castle. These were destroyed in the Civil War when Old Wardour was besieged.

SHOREHAM-BY-SEA

An earthwork *barbette* (i.e. the guns fire over the breastwork, not through embrasures) battery built in 1856 to defend the harbour entrance. At the rear it had no ditch but a *Carnot Wall*, a wall outside the rampart, with loop-holes, for defence against infantry and within which the garrison could patrol unseen. This was a French invention not usually favoured by English engineers, but perhaps needed here because of the difficulty of making a ditch in shingle.

Shoreham Fort
Soldier's Point, on the W side of harbour entrance. From the roundabout on the A259 W of the River Adur turn S and then E along the beach road. Open site.

The museum is in a World War II blister hangar. Rolls-Royce Merlin engines, which powered the Spitfire and the Hurricane, are on display. A Hawker Typhoon and a Spitfire cockpit are to be seen as is the interior of a Horsa glider. The coverage also includes RAF Fire Engines and an Air Sea Rescue section. Open April to October, November and March weekends, 11am to 5pm.

Museum of D-Day Aviation
Shoreham Airport, off A27. Tel: (01374) 971971.

The remains of a Norman castle gatehouse, walls and earthworks. It is in the care of English Heritage and is an open site

Bramber Castle
4 miles N of Shoreham by A283, on W of village.

Iron Age hill forts are numerous along the high ridge of the South Downs. The fort at Ditchling Beacon has a National Trust car park, and two miles west there is another fort while a further three miles, west of the A23, brings the walker to the complex remains at Devil's Dyke.

Ditchling Beacon
N of Brighton on South Downs Way, by A23 and A273, signed.

The early Iron Age hill fort stands with a late Bronze Age settlement and a pagan Saxon cemetery within its defensive banks.

Highdown Hill
2 miles N of Ferring, 7 miles W of Shoreham. Car park at Highdown Tower, viewpoint, N of A259 and just W of junction with A2032. Footpath to fort.

SOUTHAMPTON

Tourist information: 9 Civic Centre Road. Tel: (01703) 221 1106.
In spite of the fearful damage suffered by the town in World War II, Southampton still has one of the finest stretches of medieval city wall in England. On Western Esplanade Norman merchant houses are an integral part of the defence. God's House Tower in Winkle Street is an early example of artillery fortification.

Southampton Hall of Aviation

Albert Road South. Tel: (01703) 635830. Open Tuesday to Sunday.

This museum is a memorial to R J Mitchell, designer of the Spitfire and Supermarine aircraft. A Spitfire F24 and the Schneider Trophy S6 are on display. The collection also includes a Saunders-Roe SR.A1 jet-fighter–flyingboat, a de Havilland Vampire and a Sea Venom. It is open daily during school holidays.

Calshot Castle

W side of Southampton Water. From M27 junction 2, S by A326 Fawley and B3053. English Heritage. Tel: (01703) 892023. Open daily April to October.

Henry VIII's 'Device' to counter the threat of invasion in 1538 was to have sites surveyed for possible fortification. The Earl of Southampton and Lord St John put to sea to survey how to protect the Solent and decided on forts at Cowes and, at the end of a shingle spit, at Calshot. In the 1890s the simple tower became the western end of the boom defence of Southampton Water with Bungalow Battery securing the eastern end. A barrack room has been restored to its condition at that time. In the 20th century both the Royal Navy and the RAF have used it as a base.

WINCHESTER

Tourist information: The Guildhall, The Broadway. Tel: (01962) 840500.

The Royal Hampshire Regiment Museum

Southgate Street. Tel: (01962) 863658. Open April to October Monday to Friday 10am to 12.30pm and 2pm to 4pm, weekends 12 noon to 4pm.

The 37th Foot was raised in 1702, and other ancestor regiments are the 67th Foot and the Hampshire Regiment. The memorabilia on display also includes relics of the Hampshire Carbiniers Yeomanry. The displays feature the Battle of Minden (1759), World War I, India and Palestine, World War II where the regiment saw service in North Africa, Italy and in the D-Day landings in Normandy, and the post-war period which took them to Malaya. The Home Guard is also given space here.

The Light Infantry Museum

Peninsula Barracks, Romsey Road. Tel: (01962) 828530.

A museum depicting life round the world in a crack infantry regiment, concentrating on recent history such as the Berlin garrison and the Gulf War. Video displays. Open Monday to Saturday, Sundays afternoon only.

The Royal Green Jackets Museum

Peninsula Barracks, Romsey Road. Tel: (01962) 863846. Open Monday to Saturday, Sundays afternoon only.

Regimental mergers mean that the museum covers events from 1741 to the present in the history of the Oxfordshire & Buckinghamshire Light Infantry, the King's Royal Rifle Corps and the Rifle Brigade. There are audio-visual displays on World Wars I and II and a diorama of the Battle of Waterloo.

The Royal Hussars Museum

Peninsula Barracks. Tel: (01962) 828541. Open Tuesday to Friday 10am to 4pm, weekends from 12 noon.

Armoured Fighting Vehicles and other equipment are on display together with other memorabilia. The regiment was formed by the amalgamation of the 10/11th Hussars and the 14/20 King's Hussars and is now the King's Royal Hussars. The displays cover the history of the regiment from 1715 to the present day, including the Charge of the Light Brigade at Balaclava and World Wars I and II.

The Gurkha Museum

Peninsula Barracks, Romsey Road. Tel: (01962) 842832. Open Tuesday to Saturday, Sundays afternoon only.

The history of the Gurkha regiments since 1815 includes action in World Wars I and II and on the North West Frontier. There is also ethnographic material from Nepal, India, Tibet and Afghanistan.

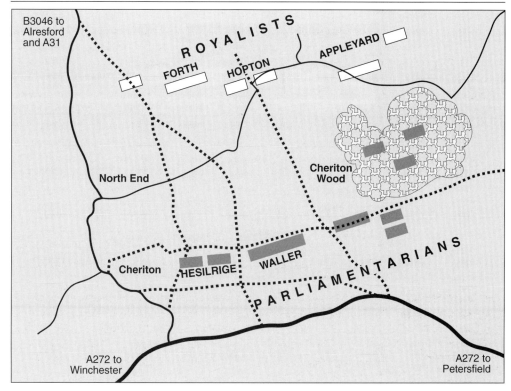

By the spring of 1644 the Royalists had good cause to feel optimistic. They had won the campaign in the west and now, under Lord Hopton, sought to increase their control in the south. Sir William Waller had been successful in regaining Arundel Castle for Parliament and now moved on Winchester with 8,000 men, of whom some 3,500 were cavalry. He evaded the Royalists until caught at Hinton Ampner with the enemy coming south from Alresford with about 6,000 men, including 2,500 horse.

The battle took place between Cheriton village and Cheriton Wood to the east, though the exact site is disputed. The wood itself, probably a little smaller then, played a key role at the meeting-place of two ridges running away to the west. In the morning mist Waller sent 1,000 musketeers to hold the wood while moving his men into line north of the A272, possibly on the more southerly ridge. Hopton was quick to counter the move by having the wood cleared, but did not follow up with an attack from that flank, awaiting Waller's next move against his apparent security on the more northerly ridge. An impulsive charge from the Royalist right was a disaster. Sir Henry Bard's men were killed or captured and the rest of the Royalist cavalry were drawn into confused fighting amongst the hedgerows that covered the terrain at the time.

Hopton withdrew to Alresford, set it afire, and then made for Basing House. The victory was as valuable to Parliament for the boost to morale as it was for ground gained.

The Battle of Cheriton, 29 March 1644

S of New Alresford (on A31 E of Winchester) by B3046, and N of the A272 (Winchester–Petersfield).

THE WEST COUNTRY

Bounded on the north by the mouth of the River Severn and on the south by the Channel, the West Country narrows to the natural fortress of Cornwall. Bristol commands the major routes from the north along the Severn and from London by the ancient routes now followed by the railway and the motorway. Travel is complicated by the succession of hills. South of Bristol the Mendips leave a narrow coast westwards and blend into the austerity of Salisbury Plain eastwards and to the south again the marshy saucer of the Somerset Levels is contained by the Blackdown Hills. The natural exit is by the Vale of Taunton Deane leading to the valley of the River Exe and Exeter, on the southern coast. West of this line Exmoor in the north and Dartmoor in the south bar easy progress to the west. Beyond them steep river valleys challenge the invader; the Tamar separates Devon from Cornwall for all but five miles of the border and Bodmin Moor lies beyond. West of that obstacle the rivers Camel and Fowey come close to cutting the land in two once more before the final, narrow spit of land runs away west to Penzance and Land's End.

This is defensible country. Armies cannot range freely across the land, but are restricted to predictable routes, easily commanded, in early times, by castles. By sea it is a different story. The commerce of the country flows through the Channel to Southampton and London and up the Bristol Channel to Bristol, Avonmouth and the ports of south Wales. The southern coast of Cornwall and Devon is harsh and rocky, but generously provided with welcoming havens. The military interest has thus been maritime, and from the days of the Tudors the

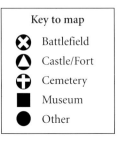

Key to map

- ✖ Battlefield
- ▲ Castle/Fort
- ✚ Cemetery
- ■ Museum
- ● Other

great ports and secure harbours have been fortified for defence and developed as naval bases for aggression. The sea was also an adjunct to war on land. The Spanish Armada passed it by, but the Spanish were back in 1595 to sack and burn Penzance. In the Civil War the Battle of Lostwithiel was governed by the Parliamentarian command of the sea, poorly exercised though it was, and access from the sea led to the last great pitched battle on English soil at Sedgemoor.

The landscape has, all in all, protected the inhabitants from that continuous strife that tormented the Welsh Marches and the northern Border Country. There is, after all, nothing beyond it but the sea itself if it is observed from the east, and coming from the west the sea offers an easier route to power and riches. As a result much has been preserved inland that has been destroyed elsewhere, while the coast bears witness to hundreds of years of naval history.

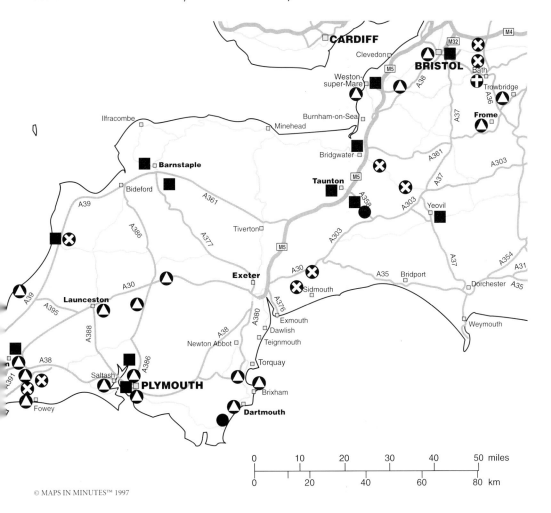

BARNSTAPLE

Tourist information: North Devon Library, Tuly Street. Tel: (01271) 388583.

Museum of North Devon
The Square. Tel: (01271) 46747.

One of the features of this general museum is the display devoted to the Royal Devon Yeomanry which was raised in 1794. Open Tuesday to Saturday.

The Cobbaton Combat Collection
Chittlehampton, Umberleigh, 7 miles SE by A377 and B3227. Tel: (01769) 540740. Open weekdays November to March 10am to 6pm.

A private collection of more than 50 World War II AFVs (armoured fighting vehicles). The bulk of the exhibits are of the British and Canadian forces, but there is some representation of the Warsaw Pact. Other equipment forms part of the Britain at War 1939-45 theme.

BODMIN

Tourist information: Shire House, Mount Folly Square. Tel: (01208) 76616.

Regimental Museum
The Keep, Victoria Barracks. Tel: (01208) 72810. Open Monday to Friday.

The Duke of Cornwall's Light Infantry Regimental Museum covers the history of the regiment from 1702 to 1959. The collection of military small arms is of special interest and there are also uniforms, pictures and other memorabilia.

Castle Kynoch
Castle Camyke, SE of Bodmin.

In 1549 the people of Cornwall and Devon rose in rebellion against the imposition of the Reformed Prayer Book. After the swift capitulation of St Michael's Mount, they gathered under the command of Humphrey Arundell at the Iron Age hill-fort of Castle Kynoch and some 3,000 men marched on Plymouth and Exeter. The Western Rebellion had begun.

Restormel Castle
N of Lostwithiel (5 miles S of Bodmin by B3269) off A390. English Heritage. Tel: (01208) 872687. Open April to October 10am to 6pm.

The Norman motte and bailey castle was built in about 1100 on conventional lines with a shell keep on top of the mound. It became the property of Richard of Cornwall shortly before he died in 1272, and it was probably his son, Edmund of Almaine, who undertook the conversion from the military installation it was to the nobleman's residence it became. The addition of the hall, chapel, chambers and kitchen were normal enough, but what was remarkable was the conversion of the shell keep into a residential tower keep with a central courtyard. His private apartment, between the gatehouse and the hall, soared to the full height of the keep and was serviced by private kitchens. Storerooms at ground level round the rest of the circle had the chapel and bedchambers above as well as the hall which was lit by windows cut out of the original curtain wall on one side and overlooking the courtyard on the other. The lordly estate was completed by the surrounding deer park; a considerable change to the original warlike concept of a castle.

In the summer of 1644 the Earl of Essex marched his Parliamentary army to the relief of Lyme and the subjugation of Royalist Cornwall. Charles I, thus freed of pressure in Oxford and having worsted Waller at Cropredy Bridge on 10 June, moved to attack him. When at Bodmin on 2 August, Essex learned of his peril and moved to Lostwithiel in order to secure supply by sea from Plymouth through Fowey. He occupied Beacon Hill and Fowey with about 10,000 men, but faced 14,000 coming from the east with Charles and a further 2,400 from the west under Sir Richard Grenville. Charles made his headquarters at Bocconoc, east of Beacon Hill. On 21 August Grenville occupied Restormel Castle and Charles's men swept the Parliamentarians off Beacon Hill, trapping Essex on the western bank of the River Fowey. Although some 2,000 Parliamentary horse managed a breakout on 31 August and reached Plymouth, the rest of Essex's force were forced back towards Fowey and by the end of the day were clinging on in their entrenchments at Castle Dore, an ancient earthwork. Essex abandoned the defence to Philip Skippon and reached Plymouth by sea. By 2 September Skippon was forced to acknowledge that the position was hopeless and surrendered his remaining 6,000 men. For the time being the Royalist hold on the west was secure.

The Battle of Lostwithiel, 21 August–2 September 1644
Beacon Hill, S off the A390 just E of Lostwithiel, and Castle Dore, near the Golant turning on the B3269 Fowey road.

Part of the south-coast defence system of Henry VIII, St Catherine's Castle is on the Fowey side of Fowey Haven and was built in about 1520. It is a small two-storey blockhouse, similar to the one at Polruan on the opposite side of the estuary. A chain boom was used to close the river to shipping.

St Catherine's Castle and Polruan Blockhouse
Fowey, 10 miles S by B3268 and B3269.

Hopton's attempt to raise the Cornwall Trained Bands in the Royalist cause failed but he did, with the help of Sir Bevil Grenville, gather a force of 1,500 Cornish volunteers. He then pushed into Devon and the Earl of Stamford, commander of Parliament's Western Army, was sent from Gloucester to oppose him. Meanwhile Lord Ruthin sallied forth from Parliamentarian Plymouth and drove Hopton back across the Tamar. On 19 January, as Ruthin made for Bodmin, he saw what he took to be Royalist stragglers on Braddock Down and charged them. Hopton had the bulk of his men hidden in a hollow and as Ruthin drew near six guns opened up on him. The Royalists scattered Ruthin's men, taking over 1,200 prisoners, and thus secured Cornwall. They were to meet Stamford in May at Stratton.

The Battle of Braddock Down, 19 January 1643
From Lostwithiel, 3 miles E, by A390, minor road through Trewindle towards Boconnoc.

BRISTOL

Tourist information: St Nicholas Church, St Nicholas Street. Tel: (0117) 926 0767.

Little remains of the fortifications of the city, although the traces of the Civil War can be found at Brandon Hill where the most westerly of the forts is now surmounted by the Cabot Tower. (Parking at Canon's Marsh Car Park.) Regrettably the militaria in the collection of the City Museum, relating, for example, to the Civil War, the Crimean War and the Indian Mutiny, are not on display, and can be examined only by appointment.

Bristol Industrial Museum

Princes Wharf, City Docks. Tel: (0117) 925 1470.

Included in the wider spectrum of the collection are a number of important examples of Bristol aero engine technology. It is closed on Mondays.

The Battle of Dyrham, 577

Dyrham, 10 miles E by A420 and A46, or M4 junction 18 and A46, and minor roads.

It is recorded that, in 577, the Saxons Cuthwine and Ceawlin fought and killed three British kings at Dyrham, and captured three of their towns, Gloucester, Cirencester and Bath. It is always a work of conjecture to place such a battle precisely, but assuming that the Saxons had established themselves on the high ground along which the A46 now runs up to the motorway, a possible site has been suggested just north of the village of Dyrham, alongside the road to the A46 that leads from the lane to Hinton. Here the River Boyd runs down a bowl of a valley in the side of the escarpment. The Britons below could not have resisted the force of a Saxon charge from the higher ground.

The Battle of Lansdown Hill, 5 July 1643

N of Lansdown, 9 miles E by A420 and S by minor road from Wick to top of hill. Limited parking.

On 4 July the Royalists under Lord Hopton approached Bath from Marshfield along the ridge that ends at Freezing Hill and begins again at Lansdown Hill to threaten the Parliamentarian strongpoint of Bath. Sir William Waller barred their way with his force of some 6,000 men, about the same number as his enemies but with more infantry and fewer horse. Waller had built positions at the top of the steep, tree-covered slope and the initial attack by the Royalist dragoons failed. The Parliamentarian counter-attack on the men falling back to Freezing Hill also failed when it ran into Sir Bevil Grenville's Cornish infantry. Hopton's next effort used infantry on the flanks in an attempt to enfilade Waller's defence line combined with a frontal attack by cavalry and the Cornishmen. A deadly fire

Brean Down Fort

Weston-super-Mare, S headland of Weston Bay. National Trust.

Overlooking the approaches to the Severn and to Bristol is the fort built in the late 19th century when French invasion was feared. It is surrounded by a nature reserve.

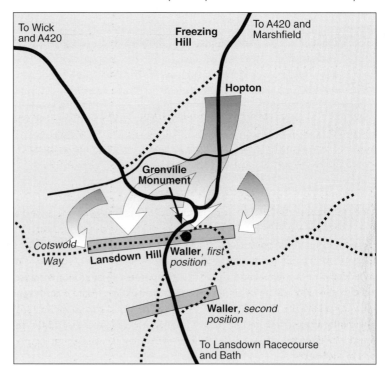

from the hilltop poured upon them, but in spite of that Grenville's men attained the high ground where the monument to their commander now stands. In the face of this expensively purchased success Waller fell back to a stone wall some 300 yards along the road to Lansdown, close to or possibly the same one as the wall there today. Both sides had exhausted themselves and had taken heavy casualties. As darkness fell Waller withdrew to Bath and the Royalists, too weak now to take advantage, fell back the way they had come.

The hill is abrupt enough even when driving up in a car, giving a clear impression of what foot soldiers had to contend with, and looking over the lip of the slope by the Grenville monument shows the strength of Waller's position. The Cotswold Way is routed along the hillside and through Waller's defence line on the top.

The Commonwealth War Graves Commission cemetery has 313 graves of those who died in World War II.

Bath (Haycombe) Cemetery
Englishcombe, 3 miles SW of Bath by minor roads.

Set on the summit of the hill with magnificent views over the Mendips is an Iron Age hill-fort.

Dolebury Warren
Churchill, 12 miles SW of Bristol by A38.

A collection of more than 50 helicopters and autogyros. There are Bristol, Sikorsky and Westland machines in abundance as well as a Czech Mil Mi4 and a Luftwaffe Mil Mi24 gunship. Open daily 10am to 6pm (4pm in winter).

The International Helicopter Museum
Weston Airport, Weston-super-Mare, on A368/371. 18 miles SW of Bristol via M5 junction 21. Tel: (01934) 635227.

DARTMOUTH

Tourist information: The Engine House, Mayor's Avenue. Tel: (01803) 834224.

A fort to protect vessels at the quayside from attack built in the early 16th century. The rectangle of walls had a parapet on top for archers or musketeers and 11 gunports were provided below for cannon. Like the castle, this fortification proved useless when attack came from landward, as it did in the Civil War.

Bayard's Cove Fort
On the riverfront. English Heritage. Open site.

Coastal and harbour raids were more likely than full-scale invasion in the Middle Ages, and Dartmouth Castle is a fine example of the defensive approach of the time. The tower was built in 1481, replacing the original works of 1388 (part of which survive at the car park), and forming the first purpose-built heavy artillery battery in Britain. The guns were mounted at basement level, and the armament was added to with external batteries in the 16th century. The harbour entrance could be closed by a chain boom across to Kingswear, where another castle was built. Open batteries on the headland were added to the complex and in 1861 replaced by a casemated battery (where visitors now enter) for five RMLs. In World War II a pair of 4.7-inch quick-firing guns were installed on the upper level of the battery.

Dartmouth Castle
1m SE by B3205. English Heritage. Tel: (01803) 833588. Open April to October daily 10am to 6pm; November to March Wednesday to Sunday 10am to 1pm and 2pm to 4pm.

Slapton Sands

Torcross, 6 miles SW by A379, on South West Coast path (signed).

Berry Head Batteries

Brixham, 5 miles NE by ferry and A379.

Three batteries of 1779 armed with 20-pounders and secured against attack from the land by an earthwork.

Totnes Castle

Totnes, 13 miles NW by A3122 and A381. Tel: (01803) 864406.

Berry Pomeroy Castle

Berry Pomeroy, 2 miles E of Totnes by A385 and minor road. English Heritage. Tel: (01803) 866618. Open April to October 10am to 6pm.

The D-Day landings in Normandy, a turning-point in World War II, were carefully rehearsed, involving as they did the movement of large bodies of men and machines in and out of landing craft and attacks on heavily defended beaches. The people of this area, some 3,000 of them, were given notice to move out on 13 November 1943 and the Americans took over for their secret preparations. Exercises were carried out, including one in which an amphibious tank, a D-D Sherman, sank. It was recovered in 1984 and remains as a monument. The disaster during Operation Tiger was on a different scale. A massive exercise involving 30,000 troops was undertaken at night, but as the landing craft approached the shore they were attacked by seven German E-boats. Nearly 750 Americans died. The incident was hushed up for obvious security reasons valid at the time. A memorial to the lost of the 4th Infantry Division, the 279th Combat Engineers, and the 70th Tank Battalion, US Army and the men of the US Navy stands close to the tank.

The Norman motte and bailey castle is magnificent to see and appears to be in remarkable repair. The keep, however, was built in the 14th century, inspired by Restormel, more as a residence than as a defence.

When the medieval stone mansion house was fortified the use of artillery was planned. The gatehouse has vertical slits for handguns and the Margaret Tower at the south-east angle of the curtain wall has more elaborate loop-holes for a wider range of weapons. The roof of the gatehouse was also contemplated as an artillery platform, being built to carry a heavy load.

EXETER

Tourist information: Civic Centre, Paris Street. Tel: (01392) 265700. Also at Exeter Services, Sandygate.

In 1549 the rebels protesting the introduction of the Reformed Prayer Book advanced from Bodmin and, on 2 July, laid siege to Exeter. The Cornish miners attempted to undermine the walls, but were repelled by counter-mining which flooded their works and drowned many of them. Parts of the walls survive today. The siege was raised by government forces on 6 August and the last of the rebels were killed or taken prisoner and executed at Sampford Courtenay on 16 August.

The Battle of Fenny Bridges, 27 July 1549

Fenny Bridges, 12 miles E by A30.

There is no memorial to the slain at Bloody Meadow, north of the railway and east of the lane to Feniton. Here Humphrey Arundell, leader of the Western Rebellion, gathered his forces to engage the government troops under Lord Russell. Russell advanced from Honiton by way of Deer Park Hill and had to storm a bridge across a tributary of the River Otter. They succeeded in this, but suffered from the fire of the Cornish longbowmen hidden behind the hedges of the Feniton lane. Reinforcements regained the ground and the rebels fell back towards Exeter.

Lord Russell's forces were supplemented by 1,000 experienced troops under Lord Grey after the success at Fenny Bridges and advanced from Honiton by the valley of the Otter, turning west to the relief of Exeter. They camped overnight on Aylesbeare Common and repulsed the rebels there at what became known as the Battle of Carey's Windmill. The next day the action moved to Clyst St Mary which the rebels had fortified, and a number of actions took place, culminating in a fight at the old bridge over the River Clyst and the causeway over the water meadows, still visible if allowance is made for the banking of the modern B3052. In spite of stout resistance, the Cornishmen were slain in great numbers. The rebels also lost 900 as prisoners and, fearing renewed attack, Lord Grey ordered them to be killed. The survivors, learning of this barbarity the following morning, fell on Grey's forces once again at Heathfield, only to find themselves surrounded when Russell cut off their escape to Exeter. They fought on to the last man.

The Battle of the Clyst, August 1549
Clyst St Mary and Aylesbeare Common, 3 to 7 miles E by B3052.

The original castle was a Norman motte and bailey built by Baldwin of Brionne on the strategically important route to the east. It fell into disuse until Hugh Courtenay became Earl of Devon in 1335 and extended the castle as his residence, building a great hall and accommodation for his retinue. In 1539 Henry VIII had Edward Courtenay executed for treason and plundered the castle, after which it fell into ruin.

Okehampton Castle
Okehampton, 25 miles W by A30. English Heritage. Tel: (01837) 52844. Open April to October daily 10am to 6pm.

Although the motte and bailey is generally thought of as the earliest type of Norman fortification, the newly arrived invaders first made use of whatever natural features offered a position of defence. The solid, square keep of Lydford is a case in point.

Lydford Castle
Lydford, 7 miles SW of Okehampton by A386. Open site.

FALMOUTH

Tourist information: 28 Killigrew Street. Tel: (01326) 312300.

Henry VIII constructed fortifications against French attack along the whole length of the south coast. Here, as at St Mawes across the estuary to the east, the remains of a small blockhouse, Little Dennis, can be seen, pre-dating the larger castle and probably built in 1537 or 1538. The chief structure is a circular gun-tower of 1540 surrounded by a 16-sided curtain wall which is obviously slightly later, as it obstructs the lower gunports on the ground floor of the central tower. The threat of a second Spanish Armada in 1596 led to further, outer, defences, but the enemy fleet was dispersed by storms and they were not put to use. There is an exhibition in the old gun room conveying the sights and sounds of a Tudor battle. The castle also served in World War II, when the Half Moon Battery mounted two 6-inch guns, and there are exhibits illustrating its role. At St. Anthony Head on the eastern side of Carrick Roads, the 19th-century fort and World War II observation post may be seen.

Pendennis Castle
Pendennis Head, 1 mile SE. English Heritage. Tel: (01326) 316594. Open April to October 10am to 6pm, November to March 10am to 4pm.

St Mawes Castle

St Mawes on A3078. English Heritage. Tel: (01326) 270526. Open daily April to October 10am to 6pm, and November to March Wednesday to Sunday 10am to 1pm and 2pm to 4pm.

A three-bastion fort typical of Henry VIII's coastal defence works. His castles were low structures of unlovely appearance, but solid, self-contained and defensible on all sides. This example, with its central tower rising above the bastions, is more pleasing than most. External batteries were added in the 1780s and in 1905 a battery for four 12-pounders was built at the rear. The castle itself, however, is a fine example of early Tudor fortification. It can be visited by foot ferry from Falmouth, Prince of Wales Pier; for timetable tel. (01209) 861020.

Cornwall Aircraft Park

Culdrose Manor, Helston, 13 miles W by A394. Flambards Victorian Village adjacent. Tel: (01326) 573404 and Flambards infoline 564093. Open Easter to October.

Military aircraft and hovercraft are on display, and special features include a reconstruction of a blitzed World War II street, Royal Navy aircrew in the Falklands War, the Gulf War and the Battle of Britain. The D-Day landings are also the subject of a display, as are various aspects of life in Britain during World War II.

FROME

Tourist information: The Round Tower, Justice Lane. Tel: (01373) 467271.

Nunney Castle

Nunney, 4 miles SW of Frome by A361. English Heritage. Open site.

Sir John de la Mare received permission to crenellate, that is, to fortify, his manor house in 1373 and took the opportunity to rebuild it completely. It was, for England, an innovatory building, a tower house with four stout corner towers connected by walls of similar height on top of which ran a continuous fighting gallery in timber (now gone) to encircle the whole. The platform that separates the walls from the moat is a later addition. The inspiration for this design was probably French, and the interior arrangements support this view, being comprehensive in their provision for domestic living on the upper floors. The lower floors, because of the need for defence and thus firing-loops rather than windows, were dark and uncongenial, and therefore were used for kitchens and servants' quarters. The great hall was on the second floor and the lord's apartments on the third and fourth floors, with garderobes in the north-east and south-east towers and a chapel in the south-west tower. The fighting platform was above. Outside the moat there was a curtain wall and perhaps yet more buildings and walls beyond. The castle was damaged by cannonfire in the Civil War, and the north wall fell down in 1910. The design was not followed by later builders as comparison with Farleigh Hungerford reveals.

Farleigh Hungerford Castle

Farleigh Hungerford, 6 miles N by A361, A36 and A366. English Heritage. Tel: (01225) 754026. Open April to October daily 10am to 6pm, November to March Wednesday to Sunday 10am to 1pm and 2pm to 4pm.

Sir Thomas de Hungerford fortified his manor house in the late 1370s on conventional lines, unlike his neighbour at Nunney. The basic plan is square with drum towers at the corners and a gatehouse in the centre of the southern curtain wall. His son, Walter Lord Hungerford, extended the works in the 1420s to convert the house into a castle. He made water defences on the west and a great outer bailey to the south. The parish church was included in the new layout as his personal chapel, as it now survives so impressively, and a replacement built in the village.

ISLES OF SCILLY

St Mary's

The vast scheme to fortify against the French under Henry VIII was extended to the Isles of Scilly after a visit by Lord Admiral Seymour in 1547 when the possibility of their being used as a base for enemy action was recognised. Orders were given for the construction of a fort, later and misleadingly called Harry's Walls, on the latest design from Italy. A length of wall and two *orillon* bastions remain. The orillons stuck out like the barbs of an arrowhead to provide cover for the batteries, the flankers, able to fire along the face of the curtain wall. The fort was never finished, probably because the design was made by someone who had not surveyed the site – it did not fit. Further fortification took place at the end of the century with the building of Garrison Walls, a bastioned position enlarged in the Civil War, later reinforced in stone and added to once more in the 20th century. Star Castle was built in 1593 by Robert Adams. It is essentially a blockhouse.

Tresco

At the same time as Harry's Walls was under construction, 1548–54, a traditional fort now called King Charles's Castle was going up on the northern headland of Tresco to guard the harbour of New Grimsby. A five-sided battery, for one gun a side, overlooks the sea and there is a barrack block to the rear with rather trivial bastions provided in an attempt to give flanking cover. It is, perhaps, the last of the old castle-style structures, its successor rising simultaneously on St Mary's. The headland on which King Charles's Castle stands was also protected by a defence line of which the earthwork remains can be traced, revealing evidence of a curtain wall and two bastions. A blockhouse with a gun platform was also being built to protect Old Grimsby. The protection of New Grimsby was much improved in about 1650 with Cromwell's Castle, a gun-tower later supplemented with a gun battery near the water.

LAUNCESTON

Tourist information: Market House Arcade, Market Street. Tel: (01566) 772321.

Robert of Mortain, William the Conqueror's half-brother, was given the task of overseeing the far west of the newly won kingdom, and was created Earl of Cornwall in 1067. He made Launceston the centre of his administration and erected a motte and bailey castle, probably with a timber stockade, to which a stone shell keep was added later (as at Trematon). In 1227 Henry III bestowed the earldom on his brother Richard who extended and developed the castle. Most notably the shell keep was augmented with a tall central tower, a storey higher than the surrounding wall, to which it was attached by a wide fighting platform. The approach to the summit of the motte was turned into a covered stairway with a gatehouse at its foot. Within the bailey there was a hall and a courthouse, the latter continuing in service until the 17th century. There is no

Launceston Castle

In the town. English Heritage. Tel: (01566) 772365. Open April to October daily 10am to 6pm.

history of sieges or fighting of any significance taking place here; the formidable defences ensured the use of the castle as a centre of government.

Tintagel Castle

Tintagel, 20 miles W by A395 and B roads. English Heritage. Tel: (01840) 770328. Open daily April to September 10am to 6pm, October to March 10am to 4pm.

Legend has it that King Arthur occupied a castle here, but there is no evidence whatsoever to support the claim. The situation on a promontory with high cliffs is characteristic of certain Iron Age fortifications of purely defensive purpose, and the site was further developed in the Dark Ages, possibly as the centre of power of a local chieftain. It is known that Richard, Earl of Cornwall built the castle, of which the ruins remain, in the 13th century. The keep is on the mainland, overcoming to some extent the major disadvantage of the location – the problem of getting out to counter-attack a force besieging the place.

Bude-Stratton Museum

The Castle, Bude, 15 miles NW by B3254. Tel: (01288) 353576.

World Wars I and II displays with special emphasis on the US forces in 1943-44. Archive material includes coverage of the Battle of Stamford Hill or Stratton, a Civil War engagement.

The Battle of Stratton, 16 May 1643

Stamford Hill, Stratton, 2 miles E of Bude.

Lord Hopton had managed to take a grip on Cornwall for the Royalists at Braddock Down in January and the Earl of Stamford with nearly 7,000 men, twice Hopton's strength, moved against him. He took up position outside Stratton off the Poughill road on what is now known as Stamford Hill, where he dug entrenchments, some to be seen today. Hopton took one column, about 600 men, up the south side of the hill, Sir Bevil Grenville two columns up the western slope and Sir John Berkeley took another up the northern side. Stamford stood firm until about 3pm, but was getting low on ammunition when Grenville's

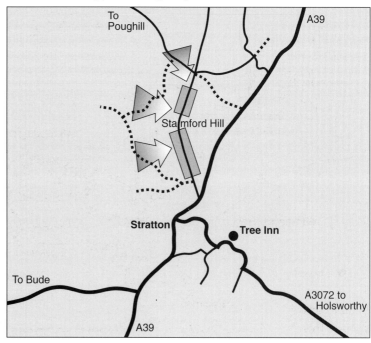

Cornish pikemen gained a hold on the hilltop. The Parliament horse panicked and fled, taking the Earl with them, but Sir James Chudleigh held on and counter-attacked, although he was separated from his men in the confusion. By this time both Hopton and Berkeley had succeeded in pushing up the hillside. The Parliamentarian resistance crumbled and down the eastern slope they went, some 1,700 of them to be taken prisoner, leaving 300 dead. There is a monument on the hill and an earlier plaque is at the Tree Inn in Stratton.

PLYMOUTH

Tourist information: Island House, 9 The Barbican. Tel: (01752) 264849. And Plymouth Discovery Centre, Crabtree.

Plymouth's development as a great naval base dates from 1692, but it had been a noted harbour long before, with defences based on the Hoe and Drake's Island. The town remained a Parliament stronghold throughout the Civil War, and the Royal Citadel was thus built as much to control the town as the sea. Successive rings of fortification to protect the Naval Dockyard were added up to the 20th century, facing both inland and to sea. There are more than those listed below, as the books of Andrew Saunders reveal.

Plymouth and Devonport defences, after Andrew Saunders 'Fortress Britain'.

1. Crownhill Ford
2. Devil's Point Blockhouse
3. Western King Battery
4. Firestone Bay Blockhouse
5. Royal Citadel
6. Mount Batten Tower
7. Staddon Point Battery
8. Bovisand Fort

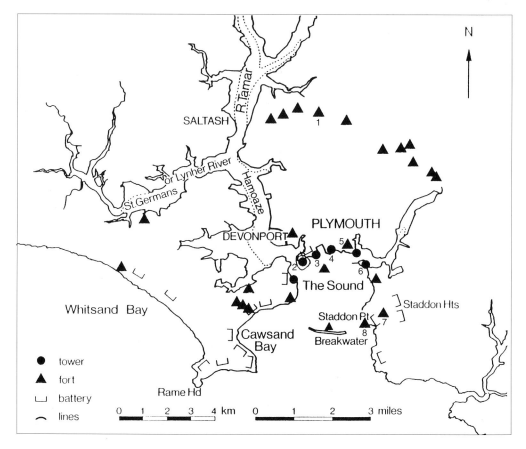

Royal Citadel

At E end of the Hoe. English Heritage. Tel: (01752) 775841. Open May to September, guided tours only, tickets from Plymouth Dome, below Smeaton's Tower on the Hoe.

Construction began in 1665 to the designs of Sir Bernard de Gomme, the wars against the Dutch being part of the reason for its building. It is a huge, bastioned fortress with an interesting baroque gate and some surviving buildings within. The external fortifications, the ravelin and ditch, have succumbed to municipal improvements.

Plymouth Naval Memorial

The Promenade, the Hoe. Commonwealth War Graves Commission.

The memorial to those lost at sea in World War I was unveiled in July 1924 and records the names of 7,256 sailors from Great Britain, Australia and South Africa. After World War II an extension was added in the form of a sunken garden and here there are 15,935 names of sailors from Britain, Australia, South Africa, Newfoundland, India, Pakistan, Sri Lanka, Fiji, Ghana, Hong Kong, Kenya, Malaysia, Nigeria, Sierra Leone and Burma. The statues are of two sailors of the Royal Navy, a Royal Marine and a member of the Maritime Regiment of the Royal Artillery. The register is kept at the Tourist Information Office.

Firestone Bay Blockhouse

The Hoe. Plymouth Corporation.

Part of the earliest fortification of the seaport, and one of a number of block-houses built in about 1500. Like Devil's Point, it is seven-sided.

Devil's Point Blockhouse

Western King, W of the Hoe, overlooking the Hamoaze.

An early Tudor defence work of about 1500, the seven-sided blockhouse has two pairs of rectangular gunports and provision for hand-held guns on the parapet. The small garrison was comforted with a fireplace and a privy.

Western King Battery

Western King, N of Devil's Point.

The western end of the early defence lines was brought up to date in World War I with the construction of two batteries for 12-pounder guns, of which the concrete emplacements remain. In front are the brick-built positions for the armament of World War II, a pair of twin 6-pounder guns. There are searchlight positions in the cliff.

Devonport Naval Base Museum

HM Naval Base, South Yard, Devonport. Tel: (01752) 554582.

The historic buildings are in the process of being converted for the display of dockyard artefacts and the memorabilia of shipbuilding and maritime crafts. It is open by appointment only, telephone to secure pass.

Mount Batten Tower

E side of Sutton Harbour.

A circular gun tower built in the 1650s to protect the approach to Sutton Harbour, with gun embrasures for 10 cannon.

Bovisand Fort

Bovisand Underwater Centre, E side of Plymouth Sound, near Staddon Point.

Part of the fortifications of the 1860s, this single-tier casemated battery was designed to operate in concert with Staddon Point Battery on the cliff above.

Crownhill Fort

Crownhill Fort Road, off A386 to Tavistock. Tel: (01752) 793754. Open daily 10am to 5pm.

The Royal Commission of 1859 encircled Plymouth to landward with a chain of forts, of which this was the centre. The stonework is massive, the gun towers, parade ground and barracks survive, and the earthworks are extensive. The site spreads across 16 acres. There is also a museum.

Because, for students of the evolution of the English castle, this is a fascinating example, the criterion of listing only sites known to be accessible has been bent to get it in. My apologies for any frustration! The basic Norman motte and bailey with its timber palisade was soon upgraded by building in stone. Trematon remains at this next stage of development. The motte is crowned with a shell keep and the bailey is secured with a curtain wall and gatehouse. In this case the motte is not Norman, but was raised in the 12th century and the stonework is 13th century, but the principle is illustrated with a rare purity, marred only by the construction of a fine residence inside the bailey much later.

Trematon Castle
Trematon, 5 miles W by A38 and minor road. Possibly private with no access. Do not trespass; enquire locally.

What was once a Cistercian monastery, and became the home of Sir Richard Grenville and of Sir Francis Drake. Exhibits celebrate these two great heroes of British naval history.

Buckland Abbey
Yelverton, 8 miles N by A386. National Trust. Tel: (01822) 853607. Open April to October daily except Thursday 10.30am to 5.30pm, November to March weekends 2pm to 5pm.

TAUNTON

Tourist information: Paul Street. Tel: (01823) 336344.

A gallery of the museum is devoted to the history of the Somerset Light Infantry and other units associated with the county. There is material on both World War I and World War II. The castle itself was the scene of the Bloody Assize at which Judge Jeffreys condemned to death the rebels vanquished at Sedgemoor.

Somerset Military Museum
County Museum, Taunton Castle. Tel: (01823) 320201. Open Monday to Saturday.

Brigadier A Hamilton-Gault raised Princess Patricia's Canadian Light Infantry Regiment in Canada at the outbreak of World War I. The men were mostly ex-servicemen, of whom only 10 per cent had been born in Canada, and thus an experienced formation. They sailed for England on 27 September 1914 and were the first regiment from the Dominions to arrive. They became part of the British Army's 27th Division and served with great distinction, particularly in the Ypres Salient. Their founder is commemorated here.

Hamilton-Gault and Princess Patricia's Canadian Light Infantry Museum
Hatch Court, Hatch Beauchamp. 5 Miles SE by A358. Tel: (01823) 480120. Open in summer, Thursdays and Bank Holidays, pm only.

Admiral Robert Blake, General-at-Sea under Cromwell's Protectorate is reputed to have been born in this house in 1598. The museum contains personal memorabilia of the great admiral as well as a diorama of the Battle of Santa Cruz, one of his greatest victories. There are also displays on the Monmouth Rebellion and the Battle of Sedgemoor and the Civil War siege of Bridgwater.

Admiral Blake Museum
Blake Street, Bridgwater. 10 miles N by A38 or M5. Tel: (01278) 456127. Open Tuesday to Saturday, 10am to 4pm.

James Scott, Duke of Monmouth and the illegitimate son of Charles II, landed at Lyme Regis on 11 June 1685. His uncle, James II, was a Catholic, and Monmouth, a Protestant, had ambitions to take the throne, while his supporters feared Papist domination. James was aware of the threat of invasion, his spies in the Netherlands having kept him well informed of Monmouth's plans, but did not know where the landing would take place and therefore kept his troops in London. Monmouth moved on Bristol by way of Taunton and Bridgwater, but

The Battle of Sedgemoor, 6 July 1685
Westonzoyland. 4 miles E of Bridgwater by A372. N of village and church via Monmouth Road to Bussex Farm (booklet for sale).

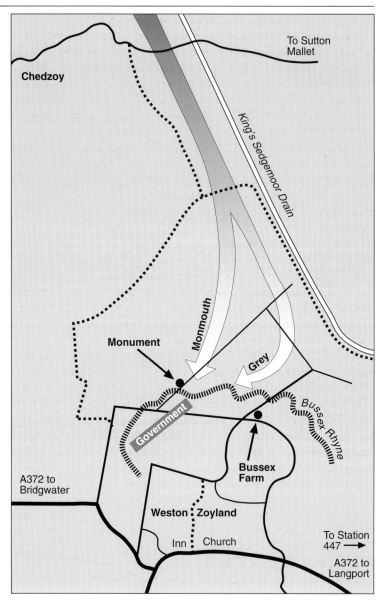

To Sutton
Mallet

Chedzoy

King's Sedgemoor Drain

Monument

Monmouth

Grey

Government

Bussex Rhyne

A372 to
Bridgwater

Bussex
Farm

Weston : Zoyland

Inn : Church

To Station
447 →

A372 to
Langport

The Battle of Sedgemoor

without haste, allowing the king's men to make ready to oppose him. A minor encounter at Keynsham on 26 June caused the rebels to retreat and, after another fight at Norton St Philip, they were back at Bridgwater by 3 July, their force of 7,000 now halved by desertions from the obviously failing cause. Meanwhile Lord Feversham had encamped the government forces at Westonzoyland, south of the Bussex Rhine, a drainage ditch now replaced by the improved drainage channels dug in the late 18th century. It can be seen if you stand with your back to the monument; a shallow dip still runs across the field. It then had two crossings, the Lower and Upper Plungeons, left and right of the government camp which straddled the modern road running west from Bussex Farm.

The government troops had names unfamiliar today, but the regiments still exist. From left to right they were Dumbarton's (now the Royal Scots), the 1st Footguards (Grenadier Guards), 2nd Footguards (Coldstream Guards), Trelawney's (The King's) and the Tangier Regiment (The Queen's). Trelawney's were under the command of the young Colonel Churchill, later the Duke of Marlborough. The last thing they expected was to be attacked; the 17 guns were still back near the road on the extreme left and they did not entrench. Monmouth was informed of their dispositions and, encouraged by a local named Godfrey, conceived the plan of a night attack. In absolute silence the rebels filed out of Bridgwater at 11pm on 5 July to make a long, looping approach north-east up what is now the A39, turning right before Bawdrip and passing east of Chedzoy. On the same day Feversham had taken the precautions of establishing a forward outpost at Chedzoy and sending the King's Horse Guards on patrol towards Bawdrip. The rebels evaded the latter, standing stock still as the horses passed, but alarmed the former at about 1.30am. As the sleeping camp was aroused Monmouth hurried his men forward in the mist and dark.

The idea was to send the rebel horse under Lord Grey over the Upper Plungeon while the infantry would line the space to the Lower Plungeon and shoot their sleepy enemies. In the event all the rebels were concentrated near the Upper Plungeon, near the monument, and trailed back along their approach route. The foremost of them fired at the glowing matches of the government troops and their three cannon did fearful damage to Dumbarton's, but the rest of their opponents were unscathed. As more of the rebels arrived they took position to the east of their comrades. Churchill then took the initiative by moving six guns over to the right, borrowing the Bishop of Winchester's carriage horses for the purpose, and his own Trelawney's and Colonel Kirke's Tangier Regiment with them. At the same time the government cavalry moved over both plungeons to hold the rebel flanks, containing them as an easy, static target for heavy fire as dawn broke. Monmouth fled. The rebels crumbled and fell back, pursued and slaughtered by the professionals they had faced. The Tangiers, known as Kirke's Lambs because of their Agnus Dei insignia, were notable for their ferocity. Across the fields to Chedzoy and along the road to Bridgwater the rebels were hacked to death or strung up on makeshift gallows. Prisoners were taken, and locked up in the church, which is worth a visit.

Monmouth was later captured and executed, and Judge Jeffreys, in the Bloody Assize, sent 250 men to their deaths and 850 to be transported. Nearly 2,000 men lost their lives in this, the last pitched battle on English soil, and its consequences. At nearby Sutton Mallet there is a farm still called Godfrey's Farm. Was it just the residence of Monmouth's guide or, as Godfrey himself was granted a pardon after the battle, was it a reward for an undercover operation successfully completed?

Station 447, Weston Zoyland

Immediately E of Westonzoyland on A372.

The airfield first built in the mid-1920s was used by the RAF in World War II, the A372 being closed and traffic diverted to the south. No 16 Squadron operated first with Lysanders and then with Mustangs until January 1943, after which the airfield was expanded for use by RAF Transport Command. In 1944 it was allocated to the US 9th Air Force and IX Troop Carrier Command operated from here in support of the fighting in Normandy after D-Day. The A372, now following its original route, runs across the old airfield.

The Battle of Langport, 10 July 1646

20 miles E of Taunton by A358, A378 and B3153 to Somerton.

The Parliamentarian victory at Naseby on 14 June 1646 left only two Royalist forces in the field, Lord Byron's at Chester and Lord Goring's besieging Taunton. As Royalist garrisons at Bristol, Bath and Devises barred the New Model Army from marching direct from the Midlands, Fairfax brought it round by a southerly route through Crewkerne. Goring withdrew from Taunton to set up a line between Yeovil and Langport, but when Yeovil fell to Fairfax decided to fall back to Bridgwater. He retained two cannon and sent the barrage and artillery back, placing his 7,000 or so men amongst the hedgerows of the numerous little fields that then covered Ham Down, a mile out of Langport on the Somerton road, overlooking the marshy meadows through which Wagg Rhyne flows. Beyond it to the east Pitney Hill rises, and the roads now designated the B3153 and the A372 offered good going from east to west.

There is now a bridge over the stream, but at that time the narrow road provided the only route, between hedges, across the boggy ground and through a ford. Such a constrained passage was required if Goring was to delay the 10,000-strong army approaching. Fairfax used his artillery to silence the Royalist guns and sent 1,500 musketeers forward to clear the Royalists out of the hedges around the ford, following them with three troops of Cromwell's horse under Major

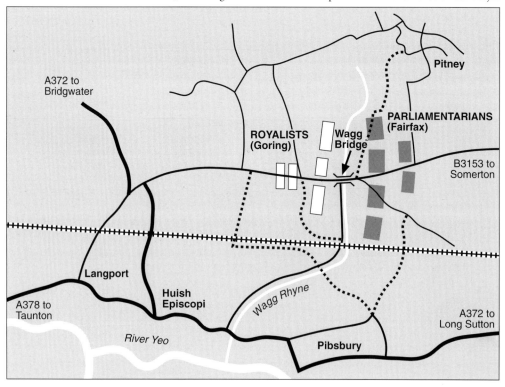

Bethell. The fight was finely balanced when Fairfax took Goring's cavalry in the flank and the Royalists broke and fled, leaving some 300 dead and many prisoners. The survivors garrisoned Bridgwater and Burrow Mump.

This fine, modern museum tells the story of naval aviation from its earliest days, when a Sopwith Pup piloted by Squadron Commander E Dunning landed on HMS *Furious* in August 1917. Early aircraft of World War I on display also include a Sopwith Camel, a Spad XIII, Fokker Triplane, Albatros DVa and a Sopwith Triplane. Among the types representing the inter-war years and World War II are the Tiger Moth, the Gloster Sea Gladiator, the Harvard, the Fairey Swordfish, the Supermarine Walrus, the Fairey Fulmar, the Chance-Vought Corsair and the Grumman Martlet or Wildcat. Among the aircraft of the past 50 years are the Hawker Sea Fury, the Westland-Sikorsky Dragonfly, the Fairey Gannet AEW3 and the Hawker Siddeley Buccaneer.

An outstanding display is the Carrier Exhibition, a re-creation of the flight deck of a working aircraft carrier of the 1970s. Ten aircraft, including the first jet to land on a carrier, a Sea Vampire, are on the flight deck and the control rooms of the carrier's Island are all on show. The last visitors are admitted to the Carrier 90 minutes before closing time; time your visit accordingly. Other special features are the VTOL display including an AV8A Harrier of the US Marines, the prototype 002 Concorde and the Underwater Experience portraying a recovery mission by scuba divers.

Fleet Air Arm Museum
Royal Naval Air Station, Yeovilton, 18 miles E of Taunton, N of Yeovil, by A358, A303, B3151 and minor roads, or via Langport. Tel: (01935) 840565. Open daily April to October 10am to 5.30pm, November to March 10am to 4.30pm.

WALES AND THE MARCHES

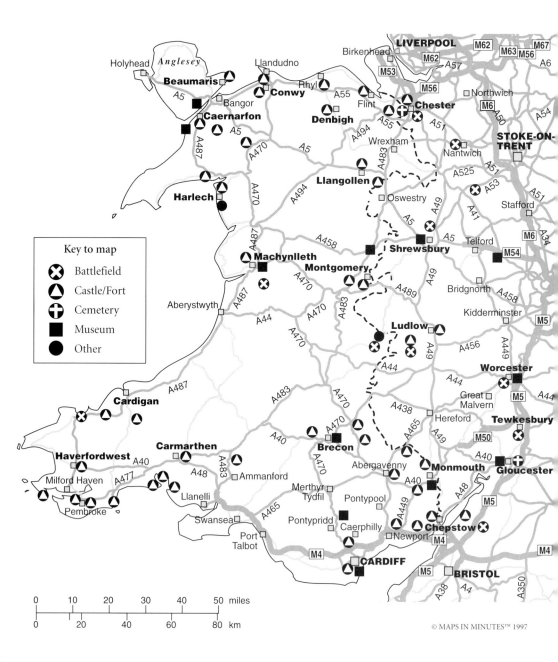

Key to map

- ⊗ Battlefield
- ◭ Castle/Fort
- ✚ Cemetery
- ■ Museum
- ● Other

Holyhead · *Anglesey* · Llandudno · Birkenhead · LIVERPOOL · M62 · M63 M56 · M67

Beaumaris · Rhyl · M62 · A57 · A6

A5 · Conwy · A55 · M53 · M56

Bangor · Flint · Chester · Northwich · M6 · A54

Caernarfon · Denbigh · A55 · A51 · STOKE-ON-TRENT

A487 · A5 · A494 · Wrexham · A483 · Nantwich · A525 · A51

A470 · A5 · Llangollen · Oswestry · A49 · Stafford · A51

Harlech · A494 · A5 · A53 · M6 · A34

A458 · Shrewsbury · A5 · Telford · M54

A487 · Machynlleth · Montgomery · A489 · Bridgnorth · A458

Aberystwyth · A487 · A470 · A483 · Kidderminster · M5

A44 · A470 · Ludlow · A49 · A456 · A449

A470 · A44 · Worcester · M5 · A44

Cardigan · A487 · A483 · A470 · A438 · Great Malvern · M5 · A44

A470 · Hereford · Tewkesbury

Carmarthen · Brecon · A465 · A49 · M50 · A40

Haverfordwest · A40 · A483 · Abergavenny · Monmouth · Gloucester

Milford Haven · A477 · A48 · Ammanford · Merthyr Tydfil · A40 · A48 · M5

Pembroke · Llanelli · Pontypool · A449

Swansea · A465 · Pontypridd · Caerphilly · Chepstow · M4 · M4

Port Talbot · M4 · Newport · M4

CARDIFF · M5 · BRISTOL · A38 · A4 · A350

0 10 20 30 40 50 miles
0 20 40 60 80 km

For military commanders in England, Wales is a danger. For the Welsh it has both advantages and disadvantages. The central and northern mountains provide excellent guerrilla territory for defenders, but the broad approaches across southern Wales gave relatively easy access for invaders from the Romans onwards. The Romans also pioneered the northern route by way of Watling Street to Wroxeter, near Shrewsbury, on to Chester and thence westwards around the coast to Anglesey. The Normans and then Edward I had to use the same route, and Thomas Telford followed much the same line with his Great Holyhead Road to improve travel to Ireland. As each new wave of incomers advanced they built camps, forts and towns along their lines of communication, often superimposing a new structure upon an old one.

Looking down from the fastness of their mountains, the Welsh not only wished to remain independent from Anglo-Norman rule, but also saw rich farmlands and fat cattle begging to be put to better use than the Norman and then the English landowners could make of them. Between the hills and the River Severn the Lords of the Marches established strongpoints for the defence of their lands and for the concentration of forces to strike back. Some of these stand along the line of Offa's Dyke, the great bank and ditch built by the Mercians in the eighth century for exactly the same purpose. The Severn Valley and the Cheshire Plain offer an easy north to south route for forces moving along the western flank of England. Thus armies from the north could link with invaders from Wales or from the south-west to penetrate towards London from Bristol, or into the Midlands north of the Cotswold Edge.

The military legacy is thus easily understood. The great battles took place in the Marches, along the line of the Severn or associated with routes to key crossings of the river. Wales itself is embraced by a ring of fortifications from the extreme south-west, running eastwards before curling north and then west once more along the northern coast. The hills themselves were not entirely impenetrable, and strategically important passes were also fortified, though few battles of any scale could be fought there. Nowhere else in the British Isles is such a magnificent legacy of medieval fortification to be seen; the work of Master James of St George, Edward I's architect, was the last word in castle-building before the age of artillery.

BEAUMARIS

Beaumaris Castle
Beaumaris. Tel: (01248) 810361. Open daily.

The last of Edward I's great castles in Wales, Beaumaris, started in 1295, is Master James of St George's masterpiece. Never finished and soon militarily redundant, it has stood as a supreme example of the concentric fortification of the Middle Ages. The site was a marsh, and lacking any natural defensive feature, so the architect had to create the entire fortification. Within the moat, the curtain wall of the outer ward, punctuated with towers, is octagonal in plan to accommodate the massive defences of the inner ward. The towers at the north-east and north-west corners are more substantial to protect the most vulnerable side. The gates are offset to present attackers with an awkward turn in the approach to the two massive gatehouses that were the ultimate strongpoints of the defences and clearly modelled on the great gatehouse at Harlech. The southern gatehouse was never finished and the towers of the inner ward were not completed to their full height, nor were the great hall and domestic buildings even begun.

The Military Museum, Plas Newydd
8 miles SW of Beaumaris by A545 and A4080. Tel: (01248) 714795. Open daily except Saturday April to September, Friday and Sunday in October.

Home of the Marquess of Anglesey. The military museum is devoted to the first Marquess who commanded the cavalry at the Battle of Waterloo.

BRECON

Tourist information: Tel: (01874) 622485.

The South Wales Borderers and Monmouthshire Regiment Museum
The Barracks, Brecon. Tel: (01874) 613311. Open daily except weekends from October to March.

These regiments are now part of the Royal Regiment of Wales (24th/41st Foot) which has its other museum in Cardiff. The 24th Regiment of Foot was founded on 8 March 1689 and saw service under the Duke of Marlborough and the Duke of Wellington. In 1849 they were in action at Chillianwallah in the 2nd Sikh War. It was in the Zulu War that they achieved undying fame. On 22 January 1879 five companies of the 1st Battalion and one of the 2nd were encamped at Isandhlwana where they were attacked and overwhelmed by a huge Zulu force. Two officers attempted to save the regimental colour, but died doing so. They were awarded VCs posthumously and the colours were later recovered, now to hang in Brecon Cathedral. B Company 2nd/24th was at Rorke's Drift where 4,000 Zulus attacked them that afternoon. The attacks went on into the night, but were beaten off. Seven VCs were awarded for that action, more than have been won in a single day before or since. The regiment also served with distinction in World Wars I and II and in Malaya and Aden. The museum is housed in the old militia armoury building and includes an excellent collection of small arms and an audio-visual display on the Zulu War.

Bronllys Castle
NW of Talgarth. Open site.

A motte and bailey castle with an outer ward to which a stone tower-keep was added in the 13th century.

Y Gaer Roman Fort
W of Brecon, 3 miles by A40 and minor road N to Aberyscir Farm. Open site.

One of the largest inland Roman forts, dating from 80AD. The original earth and timber ramparts were rebuilt in stone in the 2nd century and are well preserved.

Castell Dinas
Near Pengenfford, as the crow flies, 7 miles E of Brecon on A479 Talgarth/ Tretower road. Open site.

A hill fort on the summit of a spur of the Black Mountains with two huge Iron Age ramparts and, within them, an 11th-century Norman motte.

The buildings here evolved over five centuries from the original 11th-century earthwork and timber castle of the Norman Picard. In the next generation the timber structure was replaced in stone and now stands around the tall tower-keep of about 1240. The entrance was on the first floor by a timber porch above the present doorway. In the 14th century more comfortable quarters were built, of which the north range survives. The full development of the castle was undertaken by Sir Robert Vaughan in the 15th century on a courtyard model and fortified with a loop-hole wall and gatehouse after Sir Robert's death in the Wars of the Roses. It is remarkable both for its workmanship in wood and stone, and for the picture it conjures up of the life of a great household in the 15th century.

Tretower Court and Castle
Tretower, off A479, 12 miles SE of Brecon by A40. Tel: (01874) 730279. Open daily, Sunday afternoons November to March.

CAERNARFON

Tourist information: Castle Street. Tel: (01286) 672232.

The Norman motte and bailey of 1073 was taken by the Welsh within 50 years and the area remained theirs until 1283 when, in March, Edward I started his castle-building here and at Conwy and Harlech. Almost immediately the supposed bones of Magnus Maximus, father of Constantine, the first Christian emperor, were found. In 1284 Edward, the first English Prince of Wales, was born here. The significance of the castle as a political and imperial presence was thus at the forefront of the planners' minds, and perhaps explains the deviation of the design from the round-towered structures typical of Edward's programme. The polygonal towers and banded masonry are in the style of what the builders would have believed was Constantine's fortification at Constantinople.

Caernarfon Castle
Tel: (01286) 677617. Open daily.

The castle was built on a scale that far outstripped its military purpose, providing accommodation for government officers and their administrative retinue. The great gatehouse was secured by a drawbridge over a broad moat, five doors and six portcullises with numerous loop-holes for defensive fire. It gives onto the upper ward, formerly the site of the Norman castle, which was separated from the lower ward by a cross-wall. The Eagle Tower at the extreme west of the lower ward was a luxurious residence with a water gate both for supply and, *in extremis*, escape. The Queen's Tower is scarcely less lavish. In spite of all this the castle was taken in the Madog Rebellion of 1294, but it held out against Owain Glyn Dwr in 1403 and 1404. After its surrender to Parliamentarian forces in the Civil War it was allowed to fall into decay, until renovation was begun by Anthony Salvin in the 1840s.

Caernarfon Town Walls
A considerable part of the town wall survives.

The Royal Welch Fusiliers Museum
The Queen's Tower. Tel: (01286) 673362. Open daily.
Raised in 1689, this is the oldest infantry regiment in Wales. It saw service in the Peninsular and the Crimean wars and has a particular association with the US Marines.

The Roman Fort at Segontium was built in 61AD and was the base for Suetonius Paulinus's attack on the druids. The museum sets out the history of the Romans in Wales and the fort itself may be visited.

Segontium Roman Museum
A4085, Beddgelert Road, Caernarfon. Tel: (01286) 675625. Open daily.

Dolbadarn Castle

8 miles E of Caernarfon by A4086. Tel: (01222) 500200. Open daily.

The castle protecting the strategically important Llanberis Pass appears to have been built in two stages. A simple drystone curtain wall encloses a hall with two fireplaces, an unusual feature for a Welsh castle. In about 1230 Llywelyn ap Iorwerth built a circular keep on the lines of English structures. It is entered on the first floor and would have had a stair that could have been drawn up. It was also equipped with a portcullis. The stair within the walls giving access to the upper level has an interesting change of direction to confuse attackers.

Caernarfon Air World

Caernarfon Airport, Dinas Dinlle, 5 miles SW by A487, A499 and minor road. Tel: (01286) 830800.

The low land facing the western end of the Menai Strait was used as an airfield in World War II and the museum here shows aircraft and helicopters, as well as offering hands-on displays and aviation films.

CARDIFF

Tourist information: Central Railway Station. Tel: (01222) 227281.

Cardiff Castle

Tel: (01222) 878100. Open daily.

The Roman fort was the basis for the classic motte and bailey created here by Robert fitzHamon in the 12th century. The existing ditch was excavated and the spoil used to raise the rampart over the crumbling Roman walls and a motte raised in the north-west corner. The Norman keep was strengthened with an octagon gatetower by Richard, Earl of Beauchamp, in the 15th century. In the 19th century the Marquess of Bute had William Burgess build an exotic neo-Gothic residence, The Lodgings, and restored the decaying fort.

1st The Queen's Dragoon Guards Museum

Tel: (01222) 222253. Open daily except Wednesdays and Thursdays.

The regiment was formed in 1959 by the amalgamation of two regiments dating from 1685, the 1st King's and the Queen's Bays. The history thus begins with the aftermath of Monmouth's Rebellion. The regiments saw service in Ireland at the Battle of the Boyne and at Aughrim, under the Duke of Marlborough and in other wars of the 18th century. They were at Waterloo and later in India and China. The Zulu, Boer and Afghan wars are featured as well as World Wars I and II.

The Welch Regiment Museum

The Black and Barbican Towers, Cardiff Castle. Tel: (01222) 229367. Open daily except Tuesdays and Sundays.

The Royal Regiment of Wales has as its ancestors the 41st and 69th Foot, later the Welch Regiment, as well as the 24th Foot with a museum in Brecon. The 69th Foot served as Marines in the 18th century and have two naval battle honours. The history related here also includes the Burma War of 1824–6, the 1st Afghan War, the Crimea, the Egyptian War of 1882–9, the Boer War, World Wars I and II and the Korean War. Volunteer and Territorial forces of the area are also commemorated.

Castell Coch

Tongwynlais, 6 miles N of Cardiff. Tel: (01222) 810101.

As military as Snow White! A Victorian fantasy castle built on the foundations of a real one, but great fun all the same.

By the 13th century the Marcher Lords were extracting sufficient revenues from their holdings in Wales to fund the construction of substantial fortifications not only for defence, but to accommodate their private armies and provide administrative quarters for the governing of the land. Gilbert de Clare, Earl of Gloucester began this fortress in 1268, finishing in 1271. In order both to put his central position out of range of the siege engines and to overawe the beholder, and drawing on his experience of the siege of Kenilworth, he created a great lake. The eastern walls and fighting platforms form a dam, and beyond them over the water stands the gatehouse of the outer ward, overlooked by the huge gatehouse of the inner ward. There is no keep; this is an early example of concentric defence with the keep-gatehouse being capable of all-round resistance to attack. From the inner ward all avenues of approach are overlooked, and within there is provision for all the activities of a great household. The castle has been carefully restored and among the exhibitions is a collection of replica medieval siege engines on the south fighting platform and tournament field.

CARDIGAN

Tourist information: Theatr Mwidan, Bath House Road. Tel: (01239) 613230.

The Welsh castle on this site was taken by William Marshall, Earl of Pembroke in 1204, though it probably fell into the hands of the English for good some 20 years later. It is at the upper navigational limit (at that time) of the River Teifi where the stream passes through a gorge above which the fortification stands. The side lacking natural defence, the south, is protected by two huge drum towers of the inner ward and a strong gatehouse, an arrangement typical of the 13th century. While the twin towers have fireplaces, it is probable that the principal domestic buildings were of timber and on the northern side of the inner ward. By 1258 the castle was derelict, but it was refurbished in 1377 under Edward III who feared a French invasion and it held out against Owain Glyn Dwr in the early 15th century.

The Iron Age hill-fort has been developed to show the daily life of the people 2,400 years ago. The site has been partially excavated to reveal how the fortifications were built and reconstructed thatched round-houses and shelters bring the scene to life.

Although there is little to see, other than the Royal Oak pub where the enemy are said to have surrendered, it is worth noting the last invasion of British soil by the French. In 1797 a French force of some 1,400 men under the American William Tate set out to land near Bristol, but bad weather forced their ships further west. A Welshman keen to rejoin his girlfriend recognised the coast near his native Fishguard and suggested it was an ideal place to land. They were distracted by the plenitude of food and drink prepared in anticipation of a local wedding and, on waking thick-headed the next day, saw what they thought was a platoon of Redcoats advancing. They had mistaken the Welsh women in their

Caerphilly Castle
Caerphilly, 7 miles N of Cardiff by A469, SW of town. Tel: (01222) 833143. Open daily, Sunday afternoons in winter.

Llancaiach Fawr Living History Museum
Gelligaer Road (B4254), Nelson, 7 miles N of Caerphilly by A469 via Ystrad Myach and A472. Tel: (01443) 412248. Open daily October to March, Sundays pm only.

An opportunity to experience life in a Civil War stronghold. The scene is set in 1645.

Cilgerran Castle
Cilgerran, 2 miles S of Cardigan by A478 and minor road E. Tel: (01239) 615007. Open daily.

Castell Henllys
Felindre Farchog, 7 miles SW of Cardigan by A487. Tel: (01239) 891319. Open daily April to October.

The Battle of Fishguard, February 1797.
Fishguard, 18 miles SW of Cardigan by A487.

tall hats and red cloaks for soldiers. Lord Cawdor, a local landowner, had mobilised the Pembrokeshire Yeomanry and some 600 farmworkers to face the invaders who now found themselves abandoned by their sea transport and prudently capitulated. The panic in London caused a run on the Bank of England and thus the first banknotes came to be issued.

CARMARTHEN

Tourist information: Lammas Street. Tel: (01267) 231557.

Carmarthen Castle
Carmarthen. Open site.

The first castle built by the Normans was further down river, and the new one here, built on the edge of the old Roman fort, was taken by Llywelyn the Great in 1215 and destroyed. A yet stronger castle was constructed by the Earl Marshal and the gatehouse dates from that phase. It became the centre of government of south-west Wales in the 14th century. The castle was taken again by the Welsh when Robert Wigmore surrendered to Owain Glyn Dwr on 6 July 1403. On 24 September Henry IV reoccupied it.

Carmarthen was also a Civil War stronghold. One angle bastion of the fortifications survives behind the Police Headquarters.

Carreg Cennan Castle
Near Trapp, 16 miles E of Carmarthen by A40 via Llandeilo, A483 and minor road E. Tel: (01558) 822291. Open daily.

A dramatic fortification on an ancient site, the castle as it stands is the work of the Giffards after its recapture from the forces of Rhys ap Maredudd in 1287. The difficult site precluded classic layout. The curtain wall was strengthened and towers added, and the inner ward was protected with a double-towered barbican typical of Edward I's time, approached by a stepped ramp exposing attackers to fire as it turns twice before facing the drawbridges and portcullis of the triple gatehouses themselves. The ditch was also a reservoir into which rainwater was drained for the water supply. In 1403 John Scudamore held the castle against Owain Glyn Dwr, his future father-in-law.

Kidwelly Castle
Kidwelly, 9 miles S by A484. Tel: (01554) 890104. Open daily, afternoons only on Sundays from November to March.

The original castle Roger, Bishop of Salisbury built after 1106 is gone, leaving only the semicircular ditch based on the riverside cliff. It was destroyed by Llywelyn the Great in 1231 and the de Chaworth family rebuilt it as a square fort with circular corner towers, the cliffside wall including a great hall. When Henry of Lancaster (later Henry VI) married Matilda de Chaworth in 1298, he set in hand the conversion of the castle to a concentric form with a massive gatehouse to furnish a last-ditch stronghold (and a daunting impression when seen from the town) and with a curtain wall to create an outer ward. Owain Glyn Dwr attacked, but failed to take, the castle in 1403 when it was defended by two men-at-arms, six archers and some townsfolk, although he damaged the unfinished gatehouse severely. The rebuilt parts, such as the murder-holes above the entrance, can be recognised by the use of thinner slabs of stone. In 1405 the constable of the castle, Sir John Scudamore, was accused of channelling money to Owain from sympathisers in England. Henry rejected the charge, but Scudamore did marry Owain's daughter Alice, and perhaps gave the defeated Welshman shelter at the end of his life – the truth is not known.

Llansteffan Castle
6 miles S of Carmarthen by B4312. Open site.

On the site of an Iron Age promontory fort the Normans built what is now the inner ward with its square tower. In the 13th century the lower ward was added.

The Norman castle on this site was the scene of the agreement between Henry II and Rhys ap Gruffudd in 1172. After the king's death Rhys took the castle and the Llywelyns also held it in the 13th century. The de Brians built the medieval fort to be seen today, of which two round towers and part of the inner gatehouse stand in reddish stone. In 1464 the Earl of Northumberland added the outer ward and gatehouse in greenish stone. The building was converted to a mansion in the late 16th century, but the Tudor structure appears to have been destroyed after the siege in the Civil War. Dylan Thomas worked on his *Portrait of the Artist as a Young Dog* here.

Laugharne Castle

Laugharne, 10 SW of Carmarthen by A40 to St Clears and A4066. Tel: (01994) 427906. Open daily.

CHEPSTOW

Tourist information: Castle Car Park, Bridge Street. Tel: (01291) 623772 (April to September).

The road to south Wales passes down the western side of the Severn, where the A48 follows the Roman road, and crosses the Wye at Chepstow. Here a rocky ridge offered the opportunity, rare in Britain, to use a promontory for defence and the stone tower raised by William fitzOsbern in 1071 still stands. In the 13th century the successive Marshals, Earls of Pembroke rebuilt the upper part of fitzOsbern's tower, inserting windows on the first floor on the secure northern side and added another floor to make an impressive residence. This was secured by the construction of a bailey with round towers. Their successors, the Bigods, Earls of Norfolk, added to the eastern bailey a large range of domestic buildings, again on the north side, in the 1270s and built Marten's Tower at the south-east, both to defend this vulnerable flank and to give themselves comfortable and impressive personal quarters. The purpose was to create headquarters both for the earl's private army and the administrative requirements of his estates. Efficiency in domestic arrangements is demonstrated by the positioning one above the other, linked by a staircase, of the pantries serving the great and lesser halls. At the east end of each hall is a private (withdrawing) chamber, or drawing room, with a garderobe, that is, a toilet. The halls date from the 1280s. Marten's Tower was finished in the 1290s. It is entered from the bailey but defensible with its portcullis. The helical stair leads to the hall on the first floor and then to a chamber above and the chapel. The workmanship is fine. Evidence of the standing of the occupant and the separation of these personal quarters from the rest of the castle indicates the increasingly hierarchical nature of society at the time and echoes the developments at Windsor 50 years earlier. The castle was besieged in the Civil War as an exhibition records, and modified for cannon and musketry afterwards, remaining a military installation until 1690.

Chepstow Castle

Chepstow. From junction 22 of M4, via A466. Tel: (01291) 624065. Open daily, Sunday afternoons in winter.

A fortified manor house, Penhow consists of three distinct structures. A Norman keep, of three floors, is now entered by a doorway of the 13th century, possibly a modification of a 12th-century building. In the 15th century a hall block was added and a further extension was the house of the 17th century. Privately owned and lived in, the castle demonstrates the evolution of a magnate's dwelling from fortress to house.

Penhow Castle

Penhow, 7 miles W of Chepstow by A48. Tel: (01633) 400800. Open April to September Wednesday to Sunday, October to March Wednesday.

Caerleon Roman Fort

Caerleon, 12 miles W of Chepstow. From junction 25 on M4 by B4596. Tel: (01633) 422518. Open daily, Sunday afternoon only.

One of the largest Roman military sites in Europe, the fort was established in about 75AD. The earth and timber defence works were replaced in stone in the 2nd century, as were the barracks which are a unique survival. The amphitheatre still bears the inscriptions of the units responsible for building the various sections. The substantial baths complex includes athletics and exercise yards. The Roman Legionary Museum displays arms and equipment discovered here and explains the daily life of the soldiers by offering first-hand experience in the Capricorn Centre.

CHESTER

Tourist information: Vicars Lane. Tel: (01244) 351609.

Chester (Blacon) Cemetery

Blacon Avenue, 2 miles W by Malvern Road.

The Commonwealth War Graves Commission graveyard contains 559 graves of servicemen of World War II.

Chester was a Roman town, *Deva Castra*, built in 79AD and has been a place of strategic importance ever since, standing today within the most complete town walls in Britain. Edward I used Chester as a base for his campaign into north Wales and it was a Royalist stronghold in the Civil War. Charles I witnessed the defeat of his army at Rowton Heath from the Phoenix Tower, now known as the King Charles's Tower, on the north-eastern corner of the town wall and there is a small exhibition in the tower recounting those events. In World War II a chain of pillboxes was built, in part to provide a line of resistance in case of invasion, running along the ancient line of the Welsh Marches. Offa's Dyke lives! One pillbox has been preserved in Beech Nursery, Chester.

Deva Roman Experience Museum

Pierpoint Lane, Chester. Tel: (01244) 343407. Open daily.

In addition to showing the considerable discoveries of Roman occupation, the museum offers a voyage in a Roman galley and a walk through the streets of the ancient city.

Cheshire Military Museum

The Castle, Chester. Tel: (01244) 327617. Open daily except 18 December to 2 January.

A museum recording the achievements of the four regiments associated with Cheshire. The Cheshires were raised in 1689 and have served in almost every conflict since. The Cheshire Yeomanry came into existence in 1797 and had the distinction of being the last horsed regiment in service in Syria in 1941. A troop raised by Sir Thomas Grosvenor in 1685 is the ancestor of the 5th Dragoon Guards and the 6th Inniskilling Dragoons, while the amalgamation of the 3rd and 6th Dragoon Guards led to the Carabiniers. Of recent times there is coverage of World Wars I and II and the Bosnian civil war.

The Battle of Rowton Heath, 24 September 1645

Rowton, 4 miles SE by A41.

After the Battle of Naseby Charles I moved north in an attempt to join up with the forces of the Marquis of Montrose in Scotland. On 22 September, when at Chirk, he received an appeal for help from the besieged Royalists in Chester. Charles went to their aid with about 3,000 horse, taking 500 of them under Lord Charles Gerrard to the town and sending the rest under Sir Marmaduke Langdale around the town to take the Parliamentary forces on their flank. However, some 3,000 Parliamentary horse under Colonel-General Sydenham Poyntz were in pursuit and had reached Whitchurch, some 20 miles to the south-east. Langdale had halted for the night of 23 September at Miller's Heath, where the A41 now crosses the railway from Crewe to Chester, and learned of Poyntz's approach. Informed of this, the King decided to send out a relief party the next day.

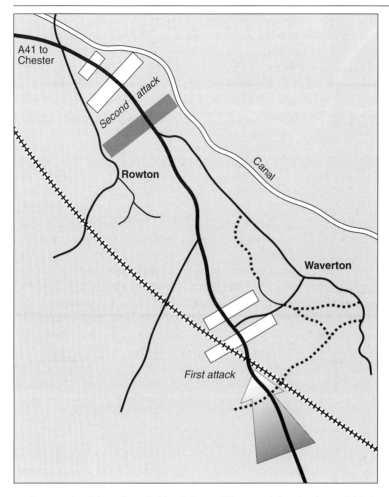

Just south of the railway bridge it is possible to park in a lay-by and this is the centre of the first encounter of the battle. Langdale took up position on the rising ground just north of where the railway now runs, placing his dragoons behind the hedges that edged the sandy track from Whitchurch. Thus, although outnumbered, he repulsed the first attack early in the morning. He then withdrew, doubtless expecting more men from Chester as planned. He next took position on Rowton Heath, to the east of the village across which the bypassing A41 now goes, where the village and the canal now funnel together. The support did not leave Chester until after 3pm, by which time Colonel Michael Jones had brought 900 men from the besiegers' strength to reinforce Poyntz. At about 4pm the Parliamentarians attacked once more, their foot soldiers outflanking the Royalists unseen behind the hedges to shake the cavalry with enfilading musketry. The Royalists broke and a series of confused actions carried both forces back towards Chester under the eyes of the King himself until some of the shattered Royalists made off into Wales or to the north-east. The town was saved for a while, but the King's plan to join Montrose was at an end.

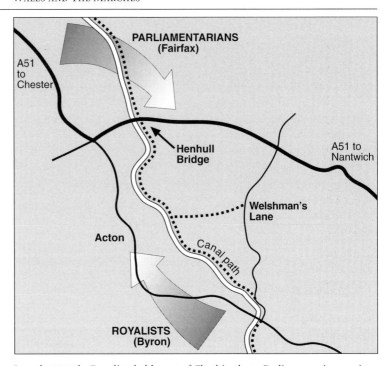

The Battle of Nantwich, 25 January 1644

Acton, NW of Nantwich, 16 miles SE by A51. Canalside path northwards from marina car park to Henhull Bridge.

In early 1644 the Royalists held most of Cheshire, but a Parliamentarian garrison was still firmly ensconced in Nantwich, besieged by Lord John Byron with some 3,500 men. Nantwich was important because, should Charles I decide to bring over Irish troops, Chester would be used and Nantwich commanded routes from that town. Sir Thomas Fairfax and Sir William Brereton set out with 5,000 to raise the siege. Byron was ready for him, but a sudden thaw filled the River Weaver and destroyed the bridge on what is now the A534 to Acton over which his footsoldiers had already passed. The cavalry were obliged to ride south to Shrewbridge before coming up to join them. Byron deployed his troops west to east, just north of Acton, across the low ground over which the canal now passes approximately along the line of the footpath from Acton Bridge to Welshman's Lane. Fairfax, coming from the north-west along the road, now the A51, through Burford, swung eastwards, as the A51 does, though there was no road there at the time, to a position from Henhull Bridge to Welshman's Lane, forcing Byron to turn his troops though 45 degrees to the north-east, and thus expose his right flank to the Parliamentarians in Nantwich. At this point those descriptions of the battle available to me become obscure. A river appears to have run between the armies, but it is said the Parliamentarians broke the foot in Byron's centre and that his right flank was attacked by a force sallying out of Nantwich. In any case, outnumbered and outmanoeuvred, the Royalists fought hard for about two hours before they were beaten, their artillery and ammunition taken and many of their leaders made prisoner. Royalist domination of the north-west was finished. The canal was driven through here in the late 18th century, but has done little to change the landscape and from the bridges and from the junction of the footpath with Welshman's Lane to the east good views may be had.

As a castle built by Edward I, Flint is both the earliest and least typical. It is the only one to have a keep which, in addition, stands separated from the square ward by a moat and drawbridge. It was part of the campaign of 1277 and was, in effect, the principal feature of an armed camp. The original town walls have gone, but the grid layout persists in the modern street plan.

Flint Castle

Flint, 12 miles W by A548. Tel: (01352) 733078.

Little visited, this Welsh castle guarded the approaches to north Wales from Chester. Its early history is unclear but it is recorded that Llywelyn ab Iowerth and his grandson Llywelyn ap Gruffudd both held it. There is a D-shaped tower, typical of Welsh castles, built around 1210, with its entry on the second floor and a stairway up from there within the wall thickness. Grooves to carry a wooden fighting platform can be seen on the southern side. A lower ward and a round tower were added some 50 years later. When the English gained control of the area in 1277 the castle became redundant.

Ewloe Castle

Ewloe, near Hawarden, 8 miles W of Chester by A548, A494 and B5125. Open site.

CONWY

Tourist information: Conwy Castle Visitor Centre. Tel: (01492) 592248.

The castle and town walls were built as a single, coherent unit to provide Edward I with a fortified town to dominate the Welsh. The promontory on which the town is sited was enclosed with walls, 22 towers and 3 gates which may be seen today. The castle itself is arranged as two wards divided by a wall and eight great round towers. There is no keep or gatehouse; the approach was by a ramp and drawbridge to the western barbican and a gateway in the curtain wall. On the east, projecting from the town walls, the inner ward had a watergate and access to the river. The castle was captured by Owain Glyn Dwr's forces in the 15th century and in the Civil War was taken by the Parliamentary army after a three-month siege.

Conwy Castle

Conwy. Tel: (01492) 592358. Open daily.

Deganwy Castles

Deganwy, on A546 Llandudno road. Footpath off York Road.

The remains of a Welsh castle and of an English one crown the hill.

DENBIGH

As a stronghold of the Welsh princes, Denbigh had its first castle built on the site of an Iron Age fort by Llywelyn ab Iorwerth in the early 13th century. Of this the angular tower to the south remains. The castle was slighted to prevent it being of use to the English when Dafydd ap Gruffudd was forced out in 1241 and the rebuilding undertaken by Henry III was itself destroyed by Llywelyn ap Gruffudd in 1263. The victorious Edward I granted it to Henry de Lacy in 1282 and the three-towered gatehouse is probably the work of Master James of St George, Edward's military architect. The polygonal towers and the banded stonework are typical of his work. The gatehouse itself, probably never finished, is a daunting defence with a gate giving onto a restricted killing-ground in front of the third tower of the complex before the inner ward can be entered. Madog ap Llywelyn took the castle in 1294, before the gatehouse was built, and de Lacy regained it only after the uprising had been suppressed. The town walls, of which much survives, were also strengthened at this time.

Denbigh Castle

Denbigh. Tel: (01222) 500200. Open daily.

Rhuddlan Castle

Rhuddlan, 8 miles N of Denbigh by A525. Tel: (01745) 590777. Open daily May to September.

The river crossing at Rhuddlan was a barrier to swift progress across north Wales and was protected as early as 1073 when a Norman motte was raised to the east of the later castle. When Edward I fought Llywelyn ap Gruffudd in 1277 he established Flint further east and chose this as his next site in what was to become a chain of castles around north Wales. As supply by sea was required the meandering Clwyd River was dug out by impressed labour from Lincolnshire to carry deep-water ships. The design of the castle is strictly military, a concentric layout with maximum mobility for defenders within along the curtain walls of the inner and outer wards, and with optimum allowance for sallies to be made against the enemy through one of the four gates. A dry moat surrounds the structure, the dock is overlooked by Gillot's Tower and the outer curtain is dominated by the inner. In March 1284 Edward issued the Great Statute of Wales here, the instrument that laid down the governance of the conquered country, with variable success, until the Act of Union in 1536.

GLOUCESTER

Tourist information: St Michael's Tower, The Cross. Tel: (01452) 421188.

Soldiers of Gloucestershire Museum

Gloucester Docks, follow Historic Docks signs. Tel: (01452) 522682.

The Gloucestershire Regiment and the Royal Gloucester Hussars are celebrated here. Their history includes service in the American Wars, Napoleonic Wars and, in more recent times, World Wars I and II (where the defensive action at Dunkirk was outstanding). A special feature is the coverage of the Korean War in which the 'Glorious Glosters' added to their honours.

Berkeley Castle

Berkeley, 14 miles SW of Gloucester by A38 and B4066. Tel: (01453) 810332.

There may have been a fortification here in Saxon times, and there certainly was a motte and bailey under the lordship of William fitzOsbern, Earl of Hereford, to whom William the Conqueror gave the land. In the 1150s the castle was granted to Robert fitzHarding as a reward by Henry II. The motte was encased in stone at that time and the keep was built. The direct descendants of fitzHarding have lived here ever since, modifying the buildings to suit more comfortable styles of living as time passed. The great hall was built on the site of the former hall in about 1340, although the roof may have been modified in the refurbishment of 1497. The castle is notorious as the place in which Edward II was brutally put to death and his cell and the dungeon may be seen in the keep.

The Battle of Nibley Green, 20 March 1470

North Nibley, 4 miles SE of Berkeley by B4060 to Wotton-under-Edge.

This was a private battle, nothing to do with the Wars of the Roses. The inheritance of Berkeley Castle and its lands was disputed between William, Lord Berkeley and Thomas, Lord Lisle, both of whom were descended from Thomas who died in 1417. In an impassioned and insulting exchange of letters they agreed to fight: 'ffaile not too morrowe to bee at Nybbeleis greene at 8. or 9. of the clocke', wrote William on 19 March. Lisle gathered some 300 men and made his way from Wotton that night, leaving his pregnant wife at home. At daybreak they entered the fields to the south of the church where the edge drops away to the meadows south of Nibley Green, overlooking the stream, beyond which the forest of Michaelwood covered most of the land towards the modern M5.

Berkeley was better prepared, with his own retainers, men from Bristol and others numbering perhaps three times as many as Lisle's force, most of whom remained hidden in the woods.

From the hillside Lisle looked down to the stream where a minor road now leads to Bush Street Farm, south of Upper Wick, over a small bridge. There he saw a small vanguard of Berkeley's men and, possibly mistaking them for a much greater part of the enemy, charged forward to engage them, his men spread out either side of him. As he approached more men came out of the woods, archers. The 19-year-old Lisle rushed on as the arrows started to fly, crashing into the force at the river ford. Berkeley moved forward to meet him, but before he got there Lisle was shot by an arrow in the face and fell to be hacked to death. His forces broke, some fleeing north and some south, past Bassett Court where Berkeley's ancestors had taken themselves while Edward II met his fate. Many others ran back up the hill into the narrow cutting towards the church above. In the confines of this defile half of Lisle's men were slaughtered. Berkeley continued the chase all the way to Wotton to attack Lisle's house. The widow miscarried.

The Berkeleys today write of the peaceable and charitable nature of their forebears, but William pursued power all his life, trading Berkeley itself for preferment and earning himself the name of the Waste-all. He did, however, build the Chantry at North Nibley Church to atone for the deaths of the combatants of Nibley Green.

HARLECH

Tourist information: Gwyddfor House, High Street. Tel: (01766) 780658.

The site at Harlech limited what Master James of St George could achieve for Edward I. The Welsh stronghold of Castell-y-Bere fell to Sir Otto de Grandison in April 1283, during the second of Edward's campaigns. Grandison marched on to Harlech and the rocky outcrop was chosen for fortification, restricted though it was in having virtually no space for an outer bailey. A single, massive structure was the only solution. It is a classic concentric castle, towers and curtain walls surrounding an inner ward containing buildings that could be sacrificed. Within a narrow outer ward the massive gatehouse and eastern corner towers present a daunting sight to attackers from the land while the more vulnerable kitchens and great hall benefit from their position on top of the hill. From the south-western corner a defensible way led to the sea, which washed the foot of the cliff at that time, to ensure supplies in time of siege. It served this function well in 1294 when Madog invested the castle, but its remoteness and the presence of the French fleet under Jean d'Espagne in the autumn of 1403, coupled with the fact that the garrison in January 1404 numbered 5 Englishmen and 16 Welshmen, led to its surrender without resistance to Owain Glyn Dwr later that year. He held it for four years. Harlech next saw action during the Wars of the Roses when the Yorkists took it after a long siege, from which event the song *Men of Harlech* comes. The final conflict was the Civil War when Harlech was the last castle to fall to Parliament.

Gloucester Old Cemetery
Cotteswold Road. Two plots, one on each side.

The Commonwealth War Graves Commission cemetery contains the graves of 162 men of World War I and 203 men of World War II.

Harlech Castle
Harlech. Tel: (01766) 780552. Open daily.

Maes Artro Village
Llanbedr, 3 miles S by A496. Tel: (01341) 241467. Open April to September.

Among other attractions, there is a World War II air raid shelter and memorabilia such as tanks and aircraft.

Criccieth Castle

Criccieth, 7 miles NW across the bay from Harlech, 11 miles by A496 and A497. Tel: (01766) 522227. Open daily, but afternoons only on Sundays from November to March.

Llywelyn ap Iorwerth (the Great) built a castle here in about 1230, but what he built is open to question. His grandson, Llywelyn ap Gruffudd was killed in 1282, after which Edward I took it over. It was refurbished by William of Drogheda who was working on Harlech at the same time, and the similarity of the gatehouse here suggests that the inner ward was added within the confines of the Welsh castle, sharing only the seaward, eastern wall of the existing structure. The great gatehouse faces the town while the gate of the outer ward looks in the opposite direction, forcing attackers to run the gauntlet of fire from the curtain wall of the new castle to enter the inner ward; an economical creation of a concentric design. Supply by sea sustained the castle in 1294, but French naval control led to its fall in 1404 when Owain Glyn Dwr took and burned it.

Dolwyddelan Castle

Dolwyddelan, 20 miles NE of Harlech by A496 and A470. Tel: (01690) 750366. Open daily.

A Welsh castle, guarding the mountain pass, was strengthened by the building of the square tower by Llywelyn ap Iorwerth in about 1210. It was originally two storeys high with a drawbridge in front of a door that could be barred. A trapdoor gave access to the lower floor. A third floor was added later. The castle fell to the English on 18 January 1283 and the outer walls were strengthened by the addition of a second tower. In the 19th century the upper part of the original tower was restored, but the details are not authentic.

HAVERFORDWEST

Tourist information: Old Bridge. Tel: (01437) 763110.
The promontory castle stands above the River Cleddau and is an open site. The outer ward was a prison in Victorian times and now houses a museum. The castle was held against Owain Glyn Dwr and his French allies who had landed at Milford Haven.

Pembroke Castle

Pembroke, 9 miles S by A4076, A477 and A4139. Tel: (01646) 684585. Open daily except Sundays from November to February.

Pembroke was the point of departure for Richard de Clare, known as Strongbow, for Ireland. His daughter married William Marshall in 1189 and the castle to be seen today is almost entirely his work. It is dominated by a mighty, circular, stone keep with a domed roof above four floors. This stands within the inner ward with another stone tower providing a fighting platform over a prison and the principal domestic buildings. Below the hall is a natural cave, the Wogan, which served as a watergate and which can be seen from the quay. The large outer ward is protected by a curtain wall and round towers with one of the earliest gatehouses and barbicans dominating the approach. There were three portcullises, murder-holes and arrow slits to discourage attackers. In 1457 Jasper Tewdwr, Earl of Pembroke had his widowed sister in residence with him and thus, when her son Harri Tudur was born here, the castle became the birthplace of Henry VII and the Tudor dynasty. Pembroke declared for Parliament in the Civil War but the disaffected garrison rebelled against their victorious leaders and Cromwell besieged them. They surrendered at the threat of artillery, and the castle was partially slighted. The damage has since been restored.

Pembroke Dock Towers

Pembroke Dock Martello Tower Visitor Centre, Front Street.

The Martello towers at the north-east and south-west angles of the dockyard wall were built in about 1845 to carry three and one guns respectively. They are cut off at high tide.

In the mid-19th century the defence of Milford Haven was considered for the first time since the Tudors. Pembroke Dock was protected from attack from the landward side by the construction, begun in 1841, of a square, bastioned work embracing barracks around a central courtyard. Both the bastions and the barracks have loop-holes. To the far west on the southern shore of Milford Haven a fort (now an hotel) was built on Thorn Island in 1852. In the next decade two more were added east and west of Angle Bay, Popton Fort and Chapel Bay Battery, as part of a system that included matching positions on the northern side.

Pembroke Defensible Barracks

Pembroke Dock, 2 miles NW of Pembroke.

The ruins on the headland overlooking both the harbour and the sea approaches are those of the castle built in about 1153. The town was taken and sacked by Llywelyn ap Gruffudd in 1260 and the walls were later rebuilt, with a major strengthening taking place in the mid-15th century. One gate and six towers survive of the three gates and twelve towers which originally stood here. The walls are supplied with two rows of loop-holes, one to be used from the wall walkway and, below, a set designed to be fought by men standing on the earth piled up to strengthen the inner base of the wall. The half-rounded towers provide for enfilading fire. The structure known as Five Arches is a D-shaped barbican in front of the South Gate. One arch, at the side, is the entrance; the others are just damage. The archers' positions allow fire both outward and, in case of the enemy having broken into the barbican, inward to frustrate an attempt on the main gate to the town.

Tenby Castle and Town Walls

Tenby, 12 miles E of Pembroke by A4139.

Manorbier Castle

Manorbier, by B4585 off A4139.

A well-preserved 12th to 13th-century castle.

In the 1850s an open battery was built on Dale Point to carry nine guns. To the south, on the next headland, a smaller installation, West Blockhouse Battery, was built on an L-shaped plan to house six 68-pounders. It has a two-storey keep and is protected on the cliff side by a ditch. In 1902 the position was chosen for an open battery on the cliff behind. These batteries, working together with Thorn Island battery on the southern headland of Milford Haven, protected the harbour entrance.

Dale Point Battery

E of Dale, 11 miles SW of Haverfordwest by B4327 and minor road.

LLANGOLLEN

Tourist information: Town Hall, Castle Street. Tel: (01978) 860828.

The ruins of a Welsh castle crown the hill east of Llangollen and a stiff climb faces those who wish to inspect them. An Iron Age fort, of which the bank and ditch can be seen, was the site for Madog of Bromfield's castle of about 1270. The medieval ditch was cut into the rock and survives sufficiently to give a clear idea of the builders' achievement. The square keep on the east may pre-date the rest of the structure which includes a two-towered gatehouse and a D-shaped tower on the southern curtain wall. The most prominent part of the ruin is part of the hall block. Threatened by Edward I's advance in 1277, the garrison burned the castle and fled. It was not reoccupied.

Castell Dinas Brân

Llangollen. Open site.

Chirk Castle

Chirk, 6 miles SE by A5, B5070 and W by B4500. National Trust. Tel: (01691) 777701. Open April to October, phone to check days closed.

Only a vestige of the medieval castle now remains in its exterior appearance. Granted to Roger Mortimer in 1282 by Edward I, this was to be a Marcher Lord's stronghold. The Mortimers fell into an attitude of lordly independence that led to no fewer than six of their number being executed for treason before 1500. It was extensively remodelled in the 18th century and again, by Pugin, in the 19th. Both the interior and the gardens are attractions to today's visitor.

LUDLOW

Tourist information: Castle Street. Tel: (01584) 875053.

Ludlow Castle

Ludlow.

The Laceys, originally from Calvados in Normandy, established a simple ringwork here on the cliff above the River Teme. In the 11th century it was strengthened with wall towers and a rather basic gatehouse, forerunner of the massive gatehouse-keep of the 12th century to which this was converted. The Mortimers had Ludlow as the centre of their Lordship of the Marches in the 14th century and the great hall dates from their time, as does Mortimer's Tower on the west wall. Further changes in the next 200 years were made to adapt the castle to its function as the headquarters of the Council of the Marches.

Offa's Dyke

Knighton, 17 miles W of Ludlow by A4113. Offa's Dyke Heritage Centre, West Street.

Offa became King of Mercia in 757 and is now remembered by the massive fortification he had built to prevent the Welsh raiding his lands. One of the most impressive sections of the wall and ditch that runs along the border of England and Wales is to be seen at Llanfair Hill, some five miles to the north. From the top of the bank to the bottom of the ditch measures 16 feet (5m). A long-distance path traces much of the length of the earthwork, and its history and information on short walks are to be had at the Heritage Centre.

The Battle of Pilleth, 22 June 1402

Pilleth, 18 miles W of Ludlow by A4113 via Knighton and B4357 and B4356.

Successive punitive expeditions by Henry IV failed to quell Owain Glyn Dwr's insurgency and by 1402 Owain had captured his enemy Lord Grey and pillaged his lands. The Welsh moved from the north into Radnorshire and excavations at Bleddfa (on A488 W of Knighton) show that the church was burned about this time. Henry's sheriff, Sir Edmund Mortimer, was at Ludlow and, learning that Owain was at Pilleth, he raised a force of retainers and tenants to move against him. It seems likely that the English camped near Whitton on the night of 21 June.

Mortimer met the Welsh below the hill of Bryn Glas near the church and appeared to be forcing them up the slope. It was, perhaps, a trap. Suddenly Mortimer's archers, themselves Welsh, turned their fire against the English and Owain's force poured off the hill to engulf them. Mortimer was taken prisoner and half of his force was killed. In the 1840s great numbers of bones were found in the churchyard and at the site where four Wellintonias stand under the hill.

The Battle of Mortimer's Cross, 2 February 1461

Mortimer's Cross, 10 miles SW by B4361 and B4362.

The death of the Duke of York and his son at Wakefield on 31 December 1460 left a surviving son, Edward, Earl of March, to maintain the Yorkist cause. While, probably, at Shrewsbury, he learned that the Lancastrian Earls of Wiltshire and of Pembroke had landed in Wales and were marching to the Midlands with Owen Tudor. Edward gathered his forces at his castle at Wigmore. The

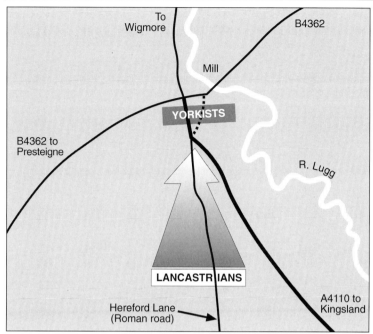

Museum at the Mill (English Heritage) open afternoons, Thursdays, Sundays and Bank Holidays April to September.

details of the battle site have long been based on the idea that the Lancastrians approached along what is now the B4362 from Presteigne, but that is a turnpike road built some 300 years later. Given that Builth and New Radnor were in Yorkist hands, the approach was much more likely to have been from the south, up the Roman road. At Mortimer's Cross (a wayside shrine, not a crossroads) the River Lugg passes through a narrow defile from the north into an open meadow towards Kingsland to the south. Here Edward could oppose the advance on a narrow front with his base at Wigmore to his rear, a position favourable to the 2,000 men he probably had. A position just south of the modern B road anchored on the east on a meander in the river (which could have moved since then) and on the west on a spur of higher land thus seems likely. A public footpath west of the bridge allows access. Details of the action are not known, but the Yorkists prevailed with minimal casualties, the Lancastrians lost many men (chroniclers say 4,000, so maybe 1,500 to 2,000 is a reasonable guess) and Owen Tudor was captured near the monument (to which the footpath goes) a mile south at the junction with Hereford Lane and the road to Kingsland. He was executed in Hereford the next day.

Wigmore Castle

Wigmore, W of A4110. English Heritage. Open on special days only; see local press.

On a site fortified since the 1060s, the remains of 13th- and 14th-century fortifications, in the process of restoration.

MACHYNLLETH

Tourist information: Maengwyn Street. Tel: (01654) 702401.

In September 1400, when it became clear that the law was not to be upheld by Henry IV in the Welshman's dispute with Lord Grey of Ruthin, Owain Glyn Dwr gave practical expression to his claim to the title of Prince of Wales by leading an uprising. He enjoyed considerable success for nine years, but the odds were

Owain Glyn Dwr Centre

Parliament House. Tel: (01654) 702827. Open daily April to September.

against him in the long term and the resistance to the English slowly dwindled away. Owain himself disappeared, possibly taking shelter with his daughter Alice and her husband, Owain's former adversary Sir John Scudamore. The story is told, together with other aspects of life in Wales in the Middle Ages, at the Centre.

The Battle of Hyggden, Summer 1401

Location uncertain, but possibly in the valley of Nant Hyggden, N of Nant-y-Moch reservoir, 8 Miles S of Machynlleth.

The nature of the fighting in Welsh/English conflict was of small bodies of men, moving swiftly and making use of the mountainous country to worst the columns of English travelling between their castles, or raiding the rich pasturelands and making off with their booty before the English could gather their forces. The chronicler Gruffydd Hiraethog reports that Owain brought 120 men to the uplands of Cardigan (probably Plynlimon) and that a force of 1,500 was rallied against him. Despite the odds, Owain defeated them and, on the bank of Afon Hyggden, two white quartz boulders, Owain's Covenant Stones, are said to mark the spot.

Castell-y-Bere

NW of Abergynolwyn, 8 miles NW of Machynlleth, N by A487 and SW by B4405. Open site.

In the 13th century the main route south from Dolgellau ran through the valley dominated by the ruins of the castle Llywelyn ap Iorwerth built in 1221 to secure the southern approaches to his principality. The building followed the triangular shape of the site. The entrance had a barbican and rock-cut ditches before twin towers and a portcullis barred the the way to the ward. At the north and south are two D-shaped towers, typical of Welsh defence works, the latter probably serving as the keep. The decorative carvings (some of which may be seen at Criccieth) bear witness to the prestigious nature of the building. The English took the castle in 1283 and the walls linking the southern tower with the rest of the enclosure may date from their occupation. Madog captured Castell-y-Bere in 1294 and the castle was abandoned.

MONMOUTH

Tourist information: Shire Hall, Agincourt Square. Tel: (01600) 713899 (April to September).

In 1387 Henry V was born in Monmouth Castle, now replaced by Great Castle House which is not open to the public. A massive 13th-century gatehouse stands astride Monnow Bridge and was formerly part of the castle's defences.

The Nelson Museum

Priory Street, Monmouth. Tel: (01600) 713519. Open daily, afternoon only on Sundays.

Horatio Nelson visited Monmouth in 1802 and remarked on the view from the Kymin (the hill east of the town, off the A4136) where a Naval Temple does honour to Britain's maritime heroes. The museum contains an extensive collection of Nelson memorabilia including his fighting sword and some letters to Lady Emma Hamilton, his mistress.

Raglan Castle

Raglan, 7 miles SW of Monmouth by A40. Tel: (01291) 690228. Open daily, afternoon only on Sundays in winter.

The original castle at Raglan was built by William ap Thomas, who had fought with Henry V in France, with funds acquired by two good marriages. The present castle is largely the work of his son, William, Lord Herbert, Earl of Pembroke. He gained favour and wealth as a result of his support of Edward IV in the Wars of the Roses battle at Mortimer's Cross in 1461 and the castle was enlarged to become a stronghold of the Yorkist cause and to demonstrate the eminence of its occupant.

The castle has two courtyards, the northern of which was new and was protected by a great gatehouse with circular gunports at the base, and the hall within was rebuilt with private apartments between the east end and a large six-windowed chamber. The entrance through the old gatehouse to the south was blocked up and the structure became part of the complex of lodgings for the earl's retinue that was built in the inner courtyard. The original castle mound stood separate and on it was built the magnificent Yellow Tower of Gwent. Not only did this tower offer a secure defence combined with a command of the approach to the gatehouse of the castle, it provided self-contained accommodation for the earl with a kitchen, hall and bedchambers. Access was by a drawbridge from the curtain wall of the southern courtyard. The new building was in the French style, with angled towers and substantial machicolations at the top.

The structure was modified in the 16th century with a rebuilt hall and greater domestic comforts but was still a fighting unit. During the Civil War it was besieged by Fairfax for 13 weeks and the great tower withstood artillery bombardment, being taken at last on 19 August 1646 and the tower rendered useless by the undermining of its walls, leaving the shell we see today.

White Castle

NW of Llantilio Crossenny, 9 miles W of Monmouth by B4233 and minor road. On Offa's Dyke footpath. Tel: (01600) 780380. Open daily.

In an isolated position that deterred stone-robbers, this is a wonderful survival of a 13th-century fortification. The first castle here was a Norman earthwork and in the 12th century a stone curtain wall and square keep were added. The approach was from the opposite side to the surviving gatehouse and was protected by a curved outwork, while at the rear there was an outer ward. Together with Grosmont and Skenfreth, it was one of the three castles granted to Hubert de Burgh by King John in 1201, but unlike the others it was not altered by him. In the 1260s, in response to the threat posed by Llywelyn ap Gruffudd, Prince of Wales, Henry III's son Edward rebuilt the castle, placing a gatehouse with staggered cross arrow loops at what was the rear, adding the circular wall-towers and taking down the keep. In short, it was converted from a motte and bailey derivative to a gatehouse and curtain wall model. The whole was rendered in white plaster to add to its imposing visibility.

Skenfrith Castle

Skenfrith, 6 miles NW of Monmouth by B4233, B4347 and B4521. Open site.

Hubert de Burgh rebuilt Skenfrith in stone, finishing between 1228 and 1232; it has not been rebuilt since. It retains the idea of a strong keep and has curtain walls with round towers enclosing space for accommodation for his followers. There is no gatehouse; either it is lost or there never was one, a simple door being overlooked from the towers to discourage attack. The tower-keep was originally whitewashed and can be seen to have been arranged as a residence for the lord of the castle.

Grosmont Castle

Grosmont, 10 miles NW of Monmouth by B4233 and B4347. Open site.

One of the three castles of Hubert de Burgh, it had the timber buildings and Norman earthwork when he acquired it, and he fortified it on much the same design in stone. Hubert fell foul of the king in 1204 and lost his lands, but was reinstated in 1219 when he rebuilt in the early 13th-century style with round towers set in the curtain wall. In the 14th century the Earl of Lancaster knocked down one of the towers to make way for a suite of private apartments.

In 1404 Owain Glyn Dwr was at the height of his powers, dominating all of Wales with the exception of the eight English castles around the northern perimeter of the country. Prince Henry, later Henry V, sent the Earl of Warwick against him and the Welsh suffered a defeat on Campstone (Camstwn) Hill, near Grosmont. Immediate revenge was obtained by the Welsh at Craig y Dorth, a few miles south-west of Monmouth, but the English pressure was starting to erode Welsh manpower. Nonetheless, Owain was now acting as an independent prince, negotiating an alliance with France on 14 July. On 11 March 1405 Owain suffered a major setback when Lord Talbot's swiftly moving companies caught the Welsh in the act of sacking the town and slew 800 or more of them.

MONTGOMERY

A border town since the earliest times, Montgomery is overlooked by the Iron Age hill-fort of Ffridd Faldwyn from the hilltop half a mile to the north-east, and Offa's Dyke runs about a mile east of the town, crossing the B4386 Chirbury road.

Montgomery Castle

By minor roads from town.

In 1223 a reordering of the defences of the Marches led to the conclusion that the old motte at Hen Domen was obsolete: too small to hold a serious force, unsuitable for development in stone and flawed in concept, being purely defensive. A new castle on the rocky ridge with natural defences to the north was begun with timber structures planned for replacement in stone. The inner ward's great gatehouse was built in stone from the outset. Though now a ruin, it is known it rose through four floors with three large rooms running the full width above the entrance. There was a guardroom on the right of the entrance from which the draw-bar of the gate could be worked. A stone-cut ditch stands before it, and the inner ward also has the Well Tower in which a well was sunk to more than 200 feet. The castle was already strong enough to withstand the attack of Llywelyn ap Iorwerth in 1231. The timber works of the middle ward were then rebuilt in stone and finally the southern end was fortified with a ditch and barbican. In a time of concentric castle building this linear layout suited the site. When Owain Glyn Dwr sacked the town in 1401 the castle probably held out.

Dolforwyn Castle

Abermule, 3 miles W by B4385.

A Welsh fortress built by Llywelyn ap Gruffudd in 1273. Excavations may limit access.

Under the Tudors peace permitted the addition of comfortable quarters and the place took on the character of a country house. In the Civil War Lord Herbert of Cherbury came home to Montgomery to avoid becoming involved, but Sir Thomas Middleton had other ideas. He took the castle for Parliament on 4 September 1644 and an attempt by Lord Byron to retake it failed when Sir John Meldrum defeated him at the Battle of Montgomery. The castle was destroyed by the succeeding Herbert soon after his father's death in 1649.

Hen Domen

Montgomery, about 1 mile from the castle, near the Severn.

Soon after the Norman Conquest Roger de Montgomery raised a motte to command the ford over the River Severn here. This was a totally artificial mound, separated from the surrounding bailey by a ditch. Another ditch marks the limits of the bailey itself. A timber fort crowned the motte. The limitations of the castle are clear. If attacked and the bailey was overcome, the defenders were trapped. The design therefore gave way to the curtain layout with defensive towers linked by a wall which, if breached, still had the attackers vulnerable to fire from the remaining towers.

Amongst other exhibits of the history of Montgomeryshire are displays on the Montgomeryshire Yeomanry, World Wars I and II, as well as French prisoners-of-war during the Napoleonic Wars.

Powysland Museum
Canal Wharf, Welshpool, 8 miles N by A483. Tel: (01938) 554656. Open daily except Wednesdays and, October to April, Sundays.

SHREWSBURY

Tourist information: The Music Hall, The Square. Tel: (01743) 350761.

Four regiments are commemorated here: the King's Shropshire Light Infantry, the Shropshire Yeomanry, the Shropshire Royal Horse Artillery and the Territorial 4th Bn Shropshire Light Infantry. Their service dates back to the American Wars of 1776–83 and 1812–15 and the standard of the Harford Dragoons taken from the Americans in 1814 is on display. The Napoleonic Wars and service in India from 1800 to 1939 are covered and World War I exhibits include the Croix de Guerre the 4th Bn KSLI was awarded for their action at Bligny in 1918. Grand Admiral Doenitz's baton forms part of the World War II material and the Korean War is also featured.

The Shropshire Regimental Museum
Shrewsbury Castle, Castle Street. Tel: (01743) 358516. Open Tuesday to Saturday, Bank Holiday Mondays, and Sundays from April to September.

Henry IV had depended on the Percy family for support in overthrowing Richard II and for the defence of the north-east against the Scots. In July 1403 the King set out for the north to assist but discovered that Sir Henry Percy, 'Hotspur', had allied with the Douglas his family had fought at Otterburn and with Owain Glyn Dwr to overthrow him. The rebels were to convene at Shrewsbury where Prince Hal, the future Henry V, was guarding the Welsh Marches. It became a race to the rendezvous. The King managed by forced march to beat Hotspur to the town and Percy retired to the village of Berwick, three miles to the north-west, still hoping the Welsh would join him. In the morning of 21 July it became clear his force was on its own, and he sought a suitable place to fight.

A low ridge runs north and west of the present site of the church and here Hotspur took his stand with his 10,000 men. The King approached from the town, probably along the line of the public footpath that runs south-west from the church, and took position with some 14,000 men between the A49 and the path, with Prince Hal to his left. After attempted mediation, the King's men advanced and the two sides exchanged bow shots; the first longbow versus longbow encounter. Hotspur's archers got the better of it and the rebel force ran forward from their ridge. Percy himself, with Douglas and a small group of followers, thrust for the King's standard in the hope of killing his adversary swiftly and bringing the battle to an end. Meanwhile Hal's men worked round to the west near Albright Hussey (to which another path goes from the church) falling on Percy's flank and rear, and folding up the rebel formation. Hotspur was killed

The Battle of Shrewsbury, 21 July 1403
N of Battlefield, 3 miles N by A5112 and A49. Minor road to W, Battlefield Church (open Sunday afternoons, May to August).

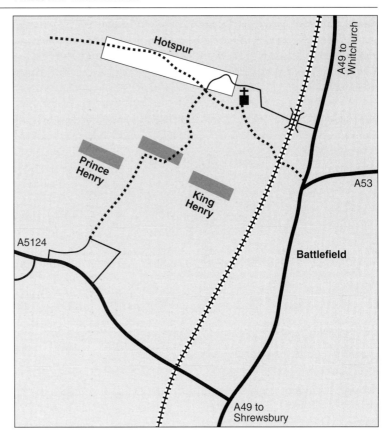

The Battle of Shrewsbury

by an arrow: the last straw for his followers who broke and ran. Casualties were, perhaps, about 3,000 on each side. In 1408 Henry built the church at the burial site.

The Aerospace Museum

Cosford, Shifnal. 16 miles E by A5, M54 junction 3 and S by A41. Tel: (01902) 374112/374872. Open daily.

World War II aircraft from Britain, America, Germany and Japan are on display, including the Spitfire, Hurricane, Liberator and Messerschmitt Me163 and Me262. Post-war aeroplanes include Vulcan and Victor bombers and the Meteor and Buccaneer. V1 and V2 rockets start the range of over 50 missiles on show which ends with Polaris. With the civil aircraft collection as well, more than 80 aircraft can be seen and the research and development section records the innovations of the last 50 years such as the TSR2, Fairy Delta 2 and the stainless-steel Bristol 188.

The Battle of Blore Heath, 23 September 1459

By A53 from Shrewsbury, 20 miles NE via Market Drayton and 2 miles E, after junction with B5415, minor road S to Hales.

After the first Battle of St Albans in 1455 the victor, Richard, Duke of York renewed his oath of allegiance to the defeated Henry VI and assumed the title of Constable of England. Queen Margaret sought to displace him politically and by 1459 armed conflict was inevitable once more. The Yorkists' forces were dispersed and, coming from the north via Newcastle-under-Lyme, Richard Neville, Earl of Salisbury and commander of the Scottish border garrison, desired to join Richard of York at Ludlow. Margaret had canvassed support in the area earlier in the year, passing out Silver Swan tokens and heraldic emblems as symbols of loyalty. Now she called upon James Touchet, Lord Audley, who raised a force of some 10,000 men, largely from local retinues, to bar the passage of Salisbury's 5,000 Yorkists. The Lancastrians took up position where the old road from the north via Manchester running Madeley–Mucklestone–Blore–Wenlock (i.e. Telford) crosses Wemberton Brook (Hemp Mill) and the old road from Nantwich to Lichfield. Many of those old roads can be identified today in footpaths and sunken lanes; the A53 is the line of a much newer turnpike road (1765). The minor road to Hales turns right while Blore bears slightly left; shortly after which a footpath to the left of the Blore road runs down over the brook and up to the A53. This is the line of the old road along which the Yorkists came and the Lancastrians were arrayed along the line of the modern minor road.

When Salisbury's men emerged from the woods that then stood above the valley the sight of Audley's troops must have shaken them. Salisbury wisely decided to establish his own defensive position above the steep bank of the stream with his right a fortified camp on the site of the modern Audley Cross Farm close to where the commemorative Audley's Cross stands on private land two-thirds of the way between the footpath and the A53. His left was near Nether Blore hamlet, now also a farm. The flanking positions had artillery and were linked by a line of archers. How the Lancastrians were provoked to attack is not known, but attack they did. A cavalry charge was shattered by Yorkist archers and panicked by the artillery and a second such attack suffered the same fate, the brook filling with dead and wounded men and horses. Audley then led an infantry attack on the Yorkist right, falling, it is said, where his memorial stands. With the death of their leader, the Lancastrian resolve evaporated and they fled the field. Margaret, according to tradition, saw the defeat of her champions from the tower of Mucklestone Church, which had a spire at that time. There is a memorial window in the church.

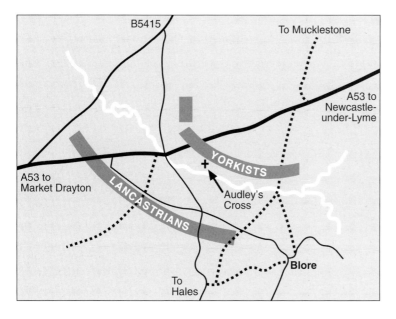

TEWKESBURY

Tourist information: 64 Barton Street. Tel: (01684) 295027. Battle trail leaflet available.

The Battle of Tewkesbury, 4 May 1471
Marked trail S of the town.

Edward IV overcame the Lancastrian army at Barnet on 14 April 1471, the day Queen Margaret and the Prince of Wales landed at Weymouth to restore the captured Henry VI to the throne once more. Margaret made for the Severn in the hope of gaining Welsh support and moving north to gather further strength in Cheshire. Edward moved from Windsor to cut her off, but was tricked into expecting to fight at Sodbury Hill, halfway between Bristol and Malmesbury. The Lancastrians gave him the slip and marched on to Berkeley, making for the Severn crossing at Gloucester, but Edward's messenger arrived there first and she found the town closed against her by 10am on 3 May. Meanwhile Edward was pushing north along the hilltop edge towards Cheltenham. Margaret made for the next crossing at Tewkesbury, arriving there with some 5,000 exhausted troops that afternoon and Edward's force of about 3,000 made it to Tredington that evening.

The Gloucester road of that time ran approximately along the line of the footpath south from the A38 opposite the cemetery, which is part of the battle trail. The Cheltenham road was to the east of the modern road, nearer Swilgate Brook. A low ridge runs at right angles to these across the approach to the town, and this was where the Lancastrians formed up with the Prince of Wales in nominal command of the centre, actually under Lord Wenlock, the Earl of Devonshire on their left and the commander-in-chief, the Duke of Somerset, on the right. The exact position is not certain, though the chroniclers name the Gastons, which is partly built over and may soon be entirely obliterated by housing. Edward was in the centre of his line with his brother, Richard of Gloucester, on his left and Hastings on the right. It seems likely that the left covered the old Gloucester road, the right the old Cheltenham road, and Edward was thus on the ridge along which the modern road runs. Fearing attack from the wooded hill known as the Park south-west of the town and flanking his position, Edward sent 200 spearmen to check it and, if they found it clear, to await developments.

Somerset planned a double stroke with an attack on Edward's left coupled with a frontal assault by Wenlock on the centre. However, when he fell on Gloucester's men the spearmen from the Park took his men in the flank while Wenlock stood still. The Lancastrian right was pushed back and put to the sword in Bloody Meadow along Coln Brook and the banks of the Avon. Somerset, it is said, infuriated by the apparent treachery, rode up to Wenlock and smashed his head in. The Lancastrian army fell apart and the Prince of Wales was killed; ending the Lancastrian line. Edward had Henry VI executed shortly after.

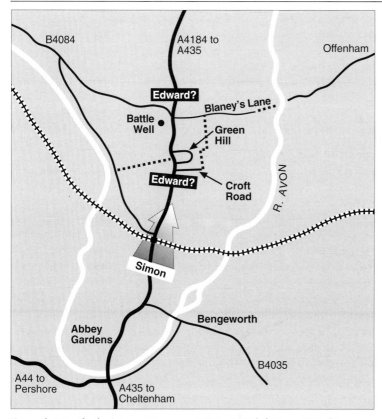

Simon de Montfort's victory at Lewes on 14 May 1264 left Henry III in his power, but he was not without enemies. By the end of May 1265 Prince Edward had escaped and the Earl of Gloucester had defected to the royalists. Edward was gathering his forces at Worcester while Simon, based at Hereford, met Prince Llewellyn of Wales near Hay and made a deal that gave him 5,000 Welsh spearmen to strengthen his army. Simon's attempt to cross the Severn at Newport was frustrated by royalist ships from Gloucester, forcing him to undertake a long march back to Hereford. Edward took this opportunity to attack de Montfort's son, also called Simon, at Kenilworth and neutralise an important element of the de Montfort power before turning south-west towards Evesham.

Meanwhile the elder de Montfort was proceeding towards Kenilworth by way of Pershore and Evesham and here, on the evening of 3 August, he camped, probably near the Abbey. Edward led his men in a night march and, having detached troops to block the Bengeworth Bridge, occupied Green Hill north of the town, trapping de Montfort. The exact deployment of Edward's army is disputed, but it seems clear that the Prince commanded the centre astride the extension of the High Street, Greenhill Road, perhaps just south of the footpath running west of the main road opposite the semicircle of Greenhill Park Road. Other authorities place the royalists on the old saltway from Worcester, now B4084–Blaney's Lane–footpath, which then went over a bridge towards Offenham.

De Montfort's reaction is undisputed. Placing his cavalry in the front, he

The Battle of Evesham, 4 August 1265

Evesham, 15 miles NE by A438, A435 and N through town centre.

formed his men into a broad column along the High Street and tried to smash his way north through Edward's army. The royalists enfolded the column, while the Welsh, whose battle this was not, melted away homewards. Hand-to-hand fighting continued for some hours until some 4,000 of de Montfort's men lay dead, Simon himself and his son Henry with them. Battle Well, where Simon is said to have fallen, is near the B4084, but, even if the initial position of Edward's army was at the more southerly position suggested, the tide of battle could certainly have swept this far north. Although the barons' field army was destroyed, the barons still held their castles and the argument between King and barons was not settled until 1275 when the Statute of Westminster established the role of Parliament. A monument to de Montfort stands in the Abbey gardens in the town.

WORCESTER

Tourist information: The Guidhall, High Street. Tel: (01905) 726923.

After the battle of 1651 the Royalists continued to resist within the town. Castle Mound, south of the cathedral, was one centre of defiance, as was the Earl's Post where Copenhagen Street now runs. On either side of the door to the nearby Guildhall are statues of the two Kings Charles and above it the head of Cromwell, pinned by his ears. In an old alley opposite, now part of a bookshop, is the carving of the death mask of Richard Guise, a traitor to the Royalist cause. He was hanged in Broad Street before the battle.

The Commandery Civil War Centre
Sidbury (leads from Cathedral to London Road A44). Tel: (01905) 355071. Open daily, Sundays afternoon only.

The Commandery was Charles II's headquarters during the Battle of Worcester and now contains a museum dedicated to the Civil War. The London road was protected by an earthwork just outside the city walls, similar to the Queen's Sconce at Newark, and known here as Fort Royal. There is now a park on the site. The Commandery is an excellent introduction to a visit to the battlefield on which there is a video presentation and for which a trail leaflet is published.

The Battle of Worcester, 3 September 1651
Viewpoint off the A422 southern link road at the A38. Ketch Inn overlooks junction of the rivers Teme and Severn.

Charles II and David Leslie left Stirling, where Leslie had been bottled up by Cromwell after the Battle of Dunbar, and set off south in August 1651 with a force of some 16,000 men, crossing the border at Carlisle and brushing aside an attack by Charles Fleetwood at Warrington. They hoped to gather additional English Royalists as they went, but the addiction of the Scots to looting antagonised their potential supporters. Meanwhile Cromwell was hastening south and by 22 August, as Charles entered Worcester, had reached Nottingham. Still hoping to recruit reinforcements, Charles stayed where he was and set about refortifying the city. The Parliamentarian forces were gathering and by the time Cromwell reached Evesham numbered some 30,000. They now had to consider how to destroy the Royalists.

Although outnumbered two to one, the Royalists were in a strong position. The city stood on the east bank of the Severn with Fort Royal and the newly restored walls as protection while the river covered the west flank with the reserve troops stationed in the little suburb of St John's and Leslie's cavalry to the north of the city. Cromwell decided to take the city from the south-west by the

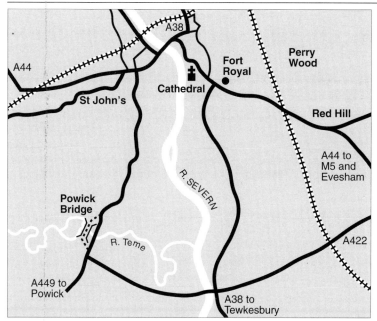

revolutionary expedient of using pontoon bridges to gain access to the flat, hedge-bordered fields between the River Teme and the Severn. The attack would be supported by artillery placed on the hills on the east. Accordingly, at about 5am on the morning of 3 September, Fleetwood and his men set out from Upton-upon-Severn towing 20 boats and ancillary woodwork. They reached the confluence of Teme and Severn at about 2pm and set about stringing five boats across the Teme and 15 across the Severn just upstream of the junction.

At the same time part of Fleetwood's force approached Powick Church and chased off a Royalist picket, leaving the base of the tower scarred for ever by their fire. Powick Bridge (the old one, its repairs obvious, is on the minor road west of the modern A449 crossing) had been partly thrown down but the Parliamentary forces got over here, and by a ford further west, to attack the Royalists deployed in the fields. Cromwell had advanced on the east bank of the Severn and made use of the bridge of boats to throw his men into the battle. This was observed by Charles from the tower of the cathedral and he took the audacious course of mounting an attack on the forces to the east, leading the way out of the Sidbury Gate, up the old London road (now lanes and footpaths to the south of the modern road), taking out the artillery at Perry Wood and turning south to occupy Red Hill (where the roundabout on the A44 is, near the RNIB college) and to attack the Parliamentary foot on the east bank. It was a brilliant stroke and very nearly succeeded. Cromwell had to rush men back over the pontoon bridge to support his militia and a hard, three-hour fight ensued. Leslie, with his cavalry, refused to come to the aid of the Royalists who were slowly pushed back into the city. Charles had to abandon his horse to make his escape into town where it soon became evident that the Scots horse had fled and the day was lost. He left by St Martin's Gate on the start of his tortuous journey to Shoreham where he embarked for France on 15 October. His infantry were all killed or made prisoner.

Powick Bridge, 23 September 1642
The bridge was the scene of a skirmish earlier in the Civil War when Prince Rupert repulsed a Parliamentarian force threatening the Royal treasure caravan on its way to Shrewsbury. The clash was brief and sharp, Rupert's cavalry winning the first action of the war.

CENTRAL SOUTHERN ENGLAND

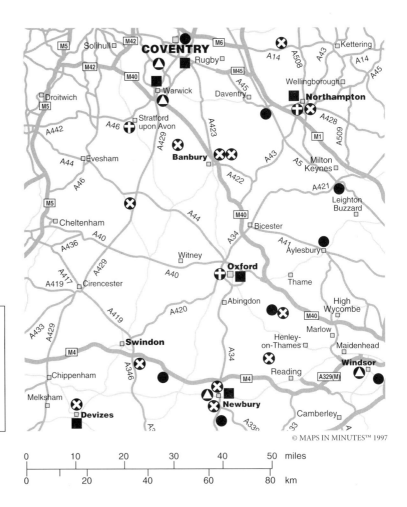

Key to map

- ✪ Battlefield
- ▲ Castle/Fort
- ✛ Cemetery
- ■ Museum
- ● Other

© MAPS IN MINUTES™ 1997

| 0 | 10 | 20 | 30 | 40 | 50 | miles |

| 0 | 20 | 40 | 60 | 80 | km |

The centre of the southern part of the country is a land of through routes. Bounded to the south by the mass of the Berkshire Downs and Salisbury Plain and to the west by the Cotswold Hills, the rivers Kennet and Thames make their way towrds the hub of power, London. The Romans took their westward route to the south of the Kennet valley, using the firmer, higher ground, but the rivers were the key to moving heavy commercial loads and the trade built the great towns such as Oxford and Reading on the rivers. The Cotswolds run in an undulating, fragmented line north-eastwards to end eventually in the Lincolnshire Wolds and presenting successive barriers to easy travel other than along them, as the Romans found when they exploited them as the foundation for the Fosse Way (now the A429 and B4455). The eastern flank of the area carries a major route north from London, the Watling Street of the Romans, which became Thomas Telford's Great Holyhead Road, the way to Ireland. Even now roadsigns display the distance to Hinckley, formerly of great importance on the coach road as a place to change horses. Alongside, bordering the area designated East Anglia in this book, the Great North Road thrusts north from London, also climbing over the Chiltern Hills before descending into the mud.

Routes across the area are few. In the south the Ridgeway runs by Avebury to pass above the Vale of the White Horse and on eventually to Norfolk. To stand on the hill by the church at Braunston, near Daventry, is to view to the south-west the traces of a succession of roads, canals and railways that channelled traffic from the north towards Oxford and Banbury, and droves of cattle and pack-trains of salt from the north-west towards the great markets of the south.

The land is rich and fertile, worth holding and fighting for, and the needs of commerce shaped the country more than military requirements. Castles, therefore, were devices to dominate the local scene and battles, in the main, clashes of armies intending to go somewhere else or prevent others doing so. In only one war, the Civil War, was this a centre of conflict when Charles I, unable to take London, made Oxford his capital.

BANBURY

Tourist information: Banbury Museum, 8 Horsefair. Tel: (01295) 259855.

**The Battle of
Cropredy Bridge, 29
June 1644**

*Cropredy, 4 miles N by A423
or A361 and minor roads.*

After the defeat of the Royalists' southern army at Cheriton, the Parliamentarians moved against Charles I in Oxford. The Earl of Essex, at Aylesbury, was joined by Sir William Waller and forced Royal withdrawal from Reading and Abingdon, but Charles slipped out of Oxford. Essex diverted his attention to the West Country and Waller set off after the King. He was led a merry dance towards the

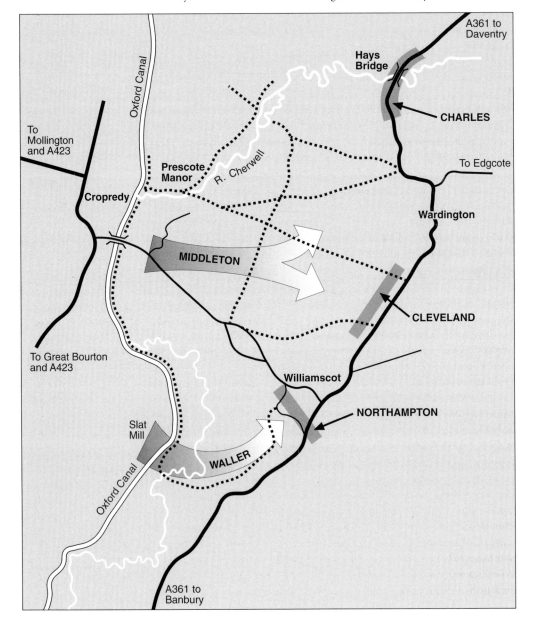

Welsh border before discovering that the King was back in Banbury. Having decided not to attack Waller's well-positioned force of about 5,000 horse and 4,000 foot at Hanwell on the Banbury–Southam road (the modern A423), Charles, with a force of similar size, made for Daventry by the road to the east of the River Cherwill (A361). Waller moved up the western side to Great Bourton and saw that the Royalist forces were strung out along the road. His forward scouts, 300 horse, were seen by Royalist scouts near Hay's Bridge where the Daventry road crosses the river north of Wardington and Charles hurried his forces forward to secure the crossing. A gap of $1^{1}/_{2}$ miles ($2^{1}/_{2}$km) opened between him and the Royalist rearguard.

Waller sent Lt-Gen. Middleton forward through Cropredy and over the bridge, now replaced with a more modern one to cross the Oxford Canal, another more recent feature. He headed towards Wardington and Hay's Bridge with the artillery and most of the men to isolate the King's vanguard, while Waller took the remaining 1,000 men to the right. He crossed the river at Slat Mill Ford, a mile to the south, where a footbridge now leads to a public footpath, and struck up the hill at the Royalist rearguard at Williamscot. The Earl of Northampton's men threw the Parliamentarians back while the other half of the rearguard under the Earl of Cleveland fell on Middleton's flank. Joined by the King's Lifeguards hastening back from Hay's Bridge, Cleveland pushed Middleton back over Cropredy Bridge and captured eleven artillery pieces. Waller took position on the slope above the river in front of Great Bourton and held the west bank through the next day. Learning of the approach of 4,500 Parliamentary reinforcements from London, Charles withdrew to make for Evesham, leaving Waller's force shaken if not shattered. Deserters rendered Waller's demoralised army useless within a week.

After a few years of peace Edward IV was threatened by two rebel armies, one under the Earl of Warwick coming into Kent and another, under Sir John Conyers, marching south from Yorkshire. He sent the Earls of Pembroke and Devon to cut off Conyers's approach and they established their army on Edgcote Hill, where Edgcote Lodge now stands, south of the village. The problem of where to spend the night wrecked the Yorkist army. Pembroke ousted Devon from the inn at Banbury and the offended earl departed, taking his archers with him. The armies faced each other across the shallow valley crossed by a stream on the way from Edgcote to Culworth, the Lancastrians leaving a small body of troops close to the Culworth road while their main force moved further south. On 25 July there was an inconsequential skirmish, but the next day Conyers's archers advanced to lay a heavy fire on Pembroke's men who, being unable to reply in kind, came down off the hill to meet the Lancastrians in the valley bottom, Danes Moor. The fighting was fierce and evenly balanced until the 500 Lancastrians arrived from the Culworth road with all the appearance of the vanguard of a reinforcing army. The Yorkists broke and Pembroke and his brother were taken, to be beheaded in Banbury the following day. Their followers sought to flee, but were obstructed by the hills on three sides and the River Cherwell on the fourth, northern, side. Some 4,000 of them were slain.

The Battle of Edgcote, 26 July 1469

Edgcote, 6 miles NE of Banbury by A361 and minor road from Wardington.

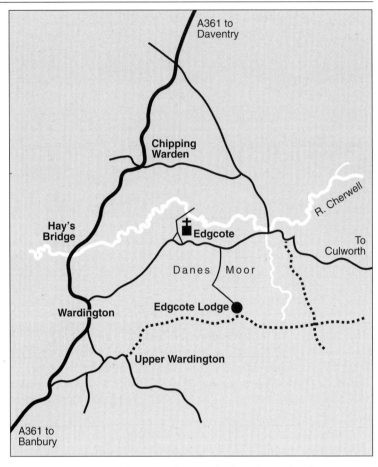

The Battle of Edgecote.

This was the second battle at Edgecote. The first, the Battle of Danes Moor, took place in 914, emphasising the importance of the route through Banbury and Daventry to Rugby and the north.

Sulgrave Manor

Sulgrave, 7 miles NE by B4525 and minor road. Tel: (01295) 76205. Open daily March to December, except Wednesday.

The manor was formerly the residence of the Washington family, ancestors of George Washington, and was presented to the Peoples of Great Britain and the United States of America by a group of subscribers to celebrate the 100 years of peace between the nations in 1914. It is frequently the venue for re-enactments of military interest, such as skirmishes of the Civil War in Britain and of the Civil War in America.

The Battle of Edgehill, 23 October 1642

Radway and Edgehill (Castle Inn, viewpoint), 7 miles NE by A422 and minor road to N.

After raising his standard at Nottingham on 22 August 1642, Charles I went to Chester and to Shrewsbury raising troops before turning for London with some 10,000 men. The Earl of Essex based himself in Northampton and gathered 20,000 men, but of limited experience and low morale. He went to Worcester in search of the King, but Charles had already withdrawn and Prince Rupert won the skirmish just outside the town at Powick Bridge. The Royalists then made their move towards London, and by 22 October were at Edgcote, east of Banbury.

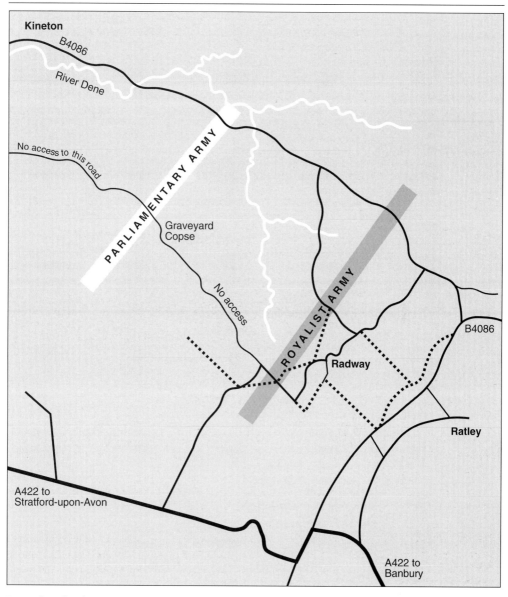

It was then they became aware of Essex's attempt to cut them off, for he was at Kineton on what is now the B4086. It was decided that the Royalists should attack, and by the early afternoon of the next day they had formed a line on the hillside approximately through the modern village of Radway with Rupert and his cavalry on the right, on the road to Kineton. In the centre was the infantry and on the left Lord Wilmot's cavalry. Essex had left garrisons in the various towns he had under control and thus had approximately an equal number of men in the field, drawn up about a mile from the foot of the escarpment of Edgehill. The Royalists attacked, their cavalry rushing down the hill and ploughing through the opposing horse to disappear beyond Kineton. The Royalist

Edgehill Battle Museum

Enquiries to Tourist Office, Stratford-upon-Avon. Tel: (01789) 293127.

The excellent museum formerly at Farnborough Hall was forced to close, but the local council has hopes of finding new premises and to reopen in 1998 or 1999.

Coventry Cathedral

Coventry.

Midland Air Museum

Coventry Airport, Baginton, 3 miles S off A45. Tel: (01203) 301033. Open April to October 10.30am to 5pm, November to March Sunday, Monday, Thursday and Saturday to 4.30pm.

Kenilworth Castle

Kenilworth, 6 miles SW by A429. English Heritage. Tel: (01926) 852078. Open daily April to October daily, 10am to 6pm and November to March 10am to 4pm.

infantry also came down the hill and were soon locked in battle on the plain below. The Parliamentarian cavalry reserves joined the battle and the struggle continued without advantage to either side. When Rupert managed to get his troopers back their horses were exhausted and darkness was about to fall. The fighting abated, Essex withdrawing to Warwick and Charles making for Banbury, leaving some 3,000 dead behind. The poor leadership and feeble control on the Royalist side had deprived them of an early victory in the war, but Essex had failed to block the route to London.

COVENTRY

Tourist information: Bayley Lane. Tel: (01203) 832303.

On the night of 14 November 1940 the manufacturing centre of Coventry was subjected to one of the heaviest air raids of World War II. The city was extensively damaged and the Cathedral Church of St Michael, a jewel of perpendicular Gothic architecture, was reduced to a shell. A new cathedral by Sir Basil Spence has arisen alongside the shell of the old which remains as a memorial, adorned with a cross of damaged timbers and the prayer 'Father forgive'. It was at Coventry that Benjamin Britten's *War Requiem* was first performed, with soloists from Britain, Germany and Russia.

The Sir Frank Whittle Jet Heritage Centre shows a collection of aircraft, engines and other items illustrating the jet age. Aircraft include a DH100 Vampire F1 and a Gloster Meteor F4, as well as such classics as the Vulcan, Hunter, Starfighter and Phantom. Local aviation is the subject of the Wings over Coventry Gallery, and many aircraft associated with local industry are on display such as the Armstrong Whitworth Argosy freighter of 1959.

The original castle at Kenilworth was a Norman motte and bailey built by Geoffrey de Clinton in the early 12th century, modified in the 1170s by Henry II by raising a stone keep which encased the base of the motte and thus provided only two floors of habitable building. As a royal castle it was extended by King John in the 13th century when the great, towerless curtain wall was added and the defences enhanced by the Great Mere, a lake that served both as an obstacle to attackers and as an impressive enhancement. People arriving had to skirt the mere to approach the gatehouse, viewing the castle across an expanse of water that, by reflection, doubled its apparent size. In 1253 the castle was given to Simon de Montfort by Henry III but 13 years later, when the two were at war, the castle was besieged. After nine months disease forced its surrender.

John of Gaunt undertook the transformation of the castle from an essentially military structure to a great house of state in the 1390s. Within the curtain only the keep was preserved and a great hall with lordly apartments adjacent was constructed. The three new towers, the Strong, the Saintlow and Gaunt's, were as much for display as for defence. This was a place designed for the manifestations of the chivalrous ideals of the late Middle Ages. In Tudor times the castle became the property of John Dudley, Duke of Northumberland and in effect ruler of England in the reign of Edward VI. Dudley was executed for his attempt to put Lady Jane Grey on the throne, but his son, Robert, found favour with Elizabeth I for whom elaborate shows were arranged with boats ablaze with lights on the mere.

Warwick Castle

Warwick, 9 miles S by A46. Tel: (01926) 406600. Open daily, except Christmas Day, April to October 10am to 6pm, November to March 10am to 5pm.

Warwick was one of the centres of Norman government and accordingly a castle was built in 1068 to dominate the conquered land, but the fortifications were transformed in the later Middle Ages by Thomas Beauchamp, Earl of Warwick and a founder member of Edward III's Order of the Garter and by his son, also named Thomas. The curtain wall facing the town to the east was given two great corner towers astride the wall, each with a guardroom at the top accessed by a separate stair from the walltop. The floors below were apartments for the Earl's followers and visitors with a main room flanked by a bedchamber and a garderobe for their private use. The names of the towers reflect their role as propaganda: Guy's Tower after the legendary Guy of Warwick, a dragon-slaying hero, and the Caesar Tower after the Roman emperor. Overlooking the river, a less vulnerable flank, were the great hall and stately apartments. The castle has been in continuous occupation since its foundation, and also possesses the characteristics of an English country house with parkland by Capability Brown and flower gardens.

The castle is now one of Britain's most popular tourist attractions with displays evoking life in the medieval stronghold as well as the aristocratic household of the 17th and 18th centuries and the Victorian age.

Royal Regiment of Fusiliers Museum

St John's House, Warwick. Tel: (01926) 491653. Open daily except Mondays and Sundays.

The Royal Regiment of Fusiliers (Royal Warwickshire) was raised in 1674 as the 6th Foot and the museum traces its history to the present day. Of particular interest is the coverage of the Omdurman campaign of 1896–8, of World Wars I and II and of prisoners of war in enemy hands.

Warwickshire Yeomanry Museum

The Court House, Jury Street, Warwick. Tel: (01926) 492212.

The history of the Yeomanry is illustrated with uniforms, swords and firearms, pictures and campaign relics from 1794 to 1968. It is open at weekends and Fridays, April to September

Queen's Own Hussars Regimental Museum

Lord Leycester Hospital, High Street, Warwick. Tel: (01926) 492035. Open daily except Mondays.

The histories of two regiments, the 3rd King's Own Hussars and the 7th Queen's Own Hussars are recorded here through arms, uniforms and other memorabilia. The museum is housed in what was a hospital founded in 1571 for the retired retainers of Robert Dudley, Earl of Leycester in buildings dating from the Middle Ages.

Stratford-upon-Avon Cemetery

Stratford-upon-Avon, 15 miles SW on B439.

The Commonwealth War Graves Commission graveyard contains 22 burials of World War I and 152 graves of World War II.

DEVIZES

Tourist information: 39 St John's Street. Tel: (01380) 729408.

Devizes Museum
41 Long Street. Tel: (01380) 727369. Open Monday to Saturday 10am to 5pm.

The museum has one of the finest prehistoric collections in Europe, including some items of military interest, and Saxon and Roman displays. There is also some coverage of the Civil War.

The Battle of Roundway Down, 13 July 1643
N of Devizes, 3 miles by A361 and left on minor road to Calne, park on left, at entrance to farm track.

Roundway Hill is a ridge running east to west, falling away steeply to the south and more gently to the north. The suggested parking place is at the eastern end with good views to the north from the pedestrian track. At its western extreme it drops very sharply on a line running north to Oliver's Castle.

After the indecisive Battle of Lansdown Hill on 5 July the Royalists moved east, with their commander, Sir Ralph Hopton, suffering from injuries received when an ammunition wagon accidentally exploded. Pursued by Sir William Waller's army from Bath they occupied Devizes Castle and threw barricades across the entrance roads and by 11 July they were surrounded by the Parliamentarians. Prince Maurice and Lord Hertford, with the bulk of the Royalist horse, had escaped to seek reinforcements from Oxford, unaware that a force

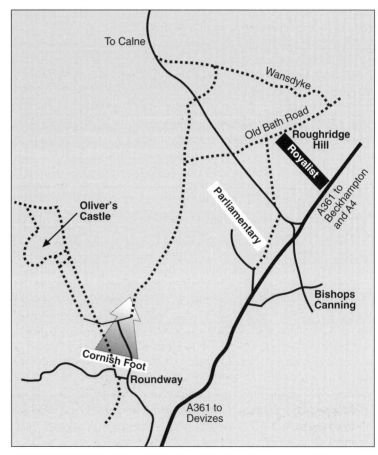

The Churches of Devizes
Civil War artillery damage can be seen on the east wall of St John's which was scarred by canister in Waller's raid in spring 1645, and there is a cannonball hole in the tower of St James, Southbroom, as well as regimental colours laid up within.

under Lord Wilmot was already on the way. They caught up with Wilmot at Marlborough on 12 July and moved on towards Devizes the next day, tired though they were. Waller had been preparing an assault on the town that day but, warned of the Royalist approach, moved his 2,000 horse and 2,500 foot up onto Roundway Hill. The Old Bath Road from Marlborough deviated from the modern A361 just north of the point at which today's road crosses the ancient border ditch of the Wansdyke, and it was along that old road, indicated by a line of trees and hedge, that the Royalists approached to pass through a gap in the dyke and deploy themselves, 1,800 strong, across the face of Roughridge Hill. Waller's horse on the right, Sir Arthur Hesilrige's Lobsters, must have been well forward on Roundway Hill to be able to see them, as walking the ground reveals. Assuming that Waller's foot were in the centre, they would have seen nothing at all until it was too late.

Wilmot charged Hesilrige and broke him, causing a general flight of the Parliamentarian cavalry so uncontrolled that many fell down the western slope into what became known as Bloody Ditch. Meanwhile the Royalists in Devizes overcame their fear that the cannons' sound was an enemy ruse to draw them out and the redoubtable Cornish foot led 3,000 men up Roundway Hill to join Wilmot and Sir John Byron in overpowering Waller's abandoned infantry.

NEWBURY

Tourist information: The Wharf. Tel: (01635) 30267.
Newbury stands at a strategically important crossing of major routes. The Great West Road, now the A4 and replaced by the M4, the Kennet and Avon Canal and the main railway line from London to Bristol run east/west while the main road from Southampton and Winchester to Oxford, the Midlands and the north, now the A34, is at right angles to them.

The museum has a variety of displays on local matters, including the Kennet and Avon Canal, and also extensive coverage of the Civil War including an audio-visual display featuring the two battles of Newbury. There is a portrait of Sir John Boys, who defended Donnington Castle for the Royalists and a model of an injured soldier. Closes 4pm in winter.

Newbury District Museum
The Wharf. Tel: (01635) 30511. Open daily, except Wednesdays, 10am to 5pm and Sundays and Bank Holidays 1pm to 5pm.

When the Earl of Essex, with a force of some 15,000 including men of the London Trained Bands, raised the Royalist siege of Gloucester, Charles I saw a chance to destroy his enemies on the road back to London. His 10,000 men were now the equal of Essex's as the Parliamentarians had left a third of their force to support the Gloucester garrison. Prince Rupert had the better of Essex's horse at Albourne Chase and managed to get to Newbury first where the rest of the Royalist army joined him. They took position roughly along the Andover Road running south-west from the town, where modern housing has covered much of the ground, and with their centre at the crossroads where the Falkland Memorial now stands. The road west from the memorial, Essex Street, has a turning to the north-west and Skinners Green, passing the key position of Round

The First Battle of Newbury, 20 September 1643
Between the A34 bypass and the A343 Andover road.

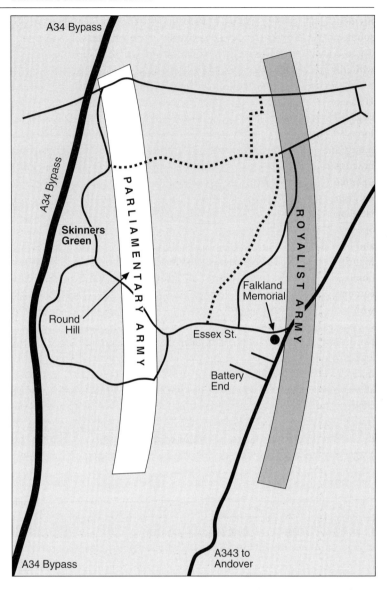

The First Battle of Newbury

Hill which the Parliamentarians occupied and which formed the centre of their north/south line.

At dawn on 20 September Essex's cannon opened fire from Round Hill. The surrounding country was a confusion of little fields and hedges, making the position hard to attack and the Royalists must have regretted their failure to occupy the hill themselves. The Royalist cannon replied from the area of Battery End, two roads south of Essex Street, across Wash Common (now built up), while Colonels Lisle and Wentworth attempted in vain to advance across the ground between the two modern roads. Sir John Byron, from a position just north of the monument, faced a mass of hedges through a gap in which one of his men, Lord Falkland, attempted, fatally, to ride – thus the monument. On the southern flank Rupert's horse could not shake the trained bands of Essex's army. The outcome, as darkness fell, was inconclusive, but the Royalists elected to withdraw towards Oxford, and Essex was free to resume his march to London.

His success at Lostwithiel in August encouraged Charles I to move to relieve the sieges of Donnington Castle, Basing House and Banbury. The Parliamentarian forces were scattered, with the Earl of Manchester at Reading, Essex at Portsmouth and Sir William Waller at Shaftesbury, but they managed to get together near Basingstoke by 20 October, frustrating Charles's aim to relieve Basing House, so he moved to deal with Donnington. The armies were in contact by 25 October between Newbury and Thatcham and Charles took up a position north of Newbury with 10,000 men based on Shaw House in the east and the village of Speen in the west. The Parliamentarian command was by a council of leaders and thus indecisive and confused. Essex fell ill and went to Reading, leaving Manchester and Waller to sort things out. Manchester, it was decided, would bombard Shaw from Clay Hill while Waller would make a march northwards to come at Charles's troops in Speen. On the evening of 26 October Waller set off with some 12,000 men along what is now the B4009 to Hermitage, swung west to Chieveley, north of the modern junction 13 on the M4, and rested briefly at North Heath. Early on the 27th he resumed the march, meeting a Royalist patrol at Boxford and being seen by the garrison of Donnington, but this went unreported so that he still had the advantage of surprise when he attacked Speen at 3pm. The first attack was repulsed, but the second gave him the village. Manchester, meanwhile, was doing nothing. As the Royalists dispersed further attacks from Speen, Manchester belatedly attacked Shaw House with 7,000, only to be thrown back. As night came both sides thought they had lost. Charles took his army towards Oxford while Manchester and Waller had to recognise their failure to take advantage of their greater numbers.

The Second Battle of Newbury, 27 October 1644
Donnington Castle, 1 mile N by B4494.

The manor house for which Sir Richard Abberbury obtained a licence to crenellate on 11 June 1386 was already fortified with a curtain wall and angle towers and what he added was a substantial gatehouse designed as much for comfort and display as for defence. The gatehouse overlooks the Winchester to Oxford road to the east, from which the sight of it would have been impressive. The gate and the ornamental string courses that separate the levels of the tower are clearly intended to show the standing of the occupier.

Donnington Castle
English Heritage. Open site, exterior only.

The Vikings moved west from East Anglia to set up a fort at Reading in 870. Ethelwulf, Ealdorman of Berkshire stopped them at Englefield, north of Theale, and, joined by the Saxon army, attacked their base. Ethelwulf was killed and the Saxons retreated to the high ground to the north-west where their king, Ethelred, and his brother, Alfred, took control. The Vikings came up from Reading on 7 January, taking position in two columns astride the Ridgeway east of its junction with the lane from Aldworth, the two Saxon columns being to the north-west approximately at the junction of the Ridgeway and the lane from Compton. As

The Battle of Ashdown, 8 January 871
The Ridgeway, NW of Aldworth, 10 miles NE of Newbury by B4009. Lane from Aldworth signed to the Downs crosses Ridgeway.

the next day dawned the two sides stood still, and Ethelred decided to hear Mass. As he was at his devotions the Vikings began to move forward and Alfred led a pre-emptive charge to prevent their gaining momentum in a downhill assault. They met near an old thorn tree, probably where the Aldworth Lane crosses the Ridgeway, eventually to be joined by the men of Ethelred's column. The Vikings broke and fled, but victory here did not finish the matter. The Saxons were later beaten at Basing and once more at Reading – nine battles took place that year, at the end of which an uneasy and unstable peace prevailed for four years.

Sandham Memorial Chapel
Burghclere, 3 miles S by old A34. National Trust. Tel: (01635) 278394. Open weekends except December to February.

In the 1920s this memorial to the soldiers of World War I was built overlooking Watership Down. The chapel is unlit, so a visit on a bright day is advised in order to be able to appreciate to the full the amazing paintings by Stanley Spencer. He chose war scenes in Salonika as his theme. It is also open from Wednesday to Friday in summer.

REME Museum
Isaac Newton Road, Arborfield Garrison, Reading. Tel: (01734) 763227. Open weekdays.

The history of the Royal Electrical and Mechanical Engineers is covered up to the Falklands War with dioramas, models, photographs, uniforms and personal papers. The radar and electronic test equipment section is open by appointment only.

Museum of Reading
The Town Hall, Blagrave Street. Tel: (01734) 399800.

The museum is principally concerned with the history of the town from Saxon times to the present day. It also has a faithful replica of the Bayeux Tapestry, the contemporary visual record of William the Conqueror's conquest of England in 1066. Open Tuesday to Saturday, 2pm to 5pm Sunday and Bank Holidays.

Wellington Exhibition
Stratfield Saye House, Stratfield Saye, 6 miles S of Reading by A33. Tel: (01256) 882882. Open May to September daily except Friday.

Personal memorabilia of the Duke of Wellington, victor of Waterloo, include paintings and belongings, books once the property of Napoleon, the Iron Duke's 18-ton funeral carriage and the grave of his horse, Copenhagen.

NORTHAMPTON

Tourist information: Visitor Centre, Mr Grant's House, St Giles Square. Tel: (01604) 22677.

Military Museums
Abington Park Museum, Abington Park. Tel: (01604) 31454. Open occasionally.

The history of the Northamptonshire Regiment and Northamptonshire Yeomanry, from 1741 to 1960, including the 48th and 58th Foot, is displayed with weapons, uniforms, paintings and photographs.

The Battle of Northampton, 10 July 1460
Delapre Park, off A508 London Road, S of town centre and N of A45 ring road.

In June 1640 the Yorkists established a garrison in Sandwich, returning from France to continue their struggle against the Lancastrian King Henry VI. They followed up with an invasion of 2,000 men under Edward, Earl of March and Richard Neville, Earl of Warwick. London fell to them while Henry was in the Midlands organising a defence against an expected landing by York in Wales. The King moved south to Northampton and his men dug in south of the River

Nene in what is now Delapre Park. The Lancastrian lines ran east–west across the modern golf course with the left on the north–south footpath at about the junction with Eagle Drive and the right at the strip of woodland called the Rookery. The Yorkists organised themselves in three 'battles' under March, Warwick and Lord Fauconberg and went into the attack from a line alongside the modern A45, now Delapre Wood, early in the afternoon of 10 July, in pouring rain. The downpour prevented the Lancastrians from firing their guns, but equally left the Yorkists slithering about in the mud and unable to make progress. The commander of the Lancastrian vanguard, Lord Grey, had come to an arrangement with Warwick and treacherously allowed the Yorkists into the defences. Henry's army was defeated in a mere thirty minutes, the King himself captured and countless of his men drowned in the Nene. Richard, Duke of York returned from Ireland on 10 October and was recognised as Henry's heir, a success that was to come to nothing at Wakefield the following December. The Archbishop of Canterbury observed the battle from Queen Eleanor's Cross, a monument raised by Edward I to mark one of the resting places of his dead wife's body on the journey to London in 1290. It stands there still, close by the roundabout at the southern end of London Road.

Towcester Road Cemetery

Northampton, town side of A45 ring road.

The Commonwealth War Graves Commission plot is next to the chapel and contains the graves of the men who doubtless died of wounds in hospital here.

The story of the British Army's Pioneers covers two centuries and is told in detail from 1939. The regiment has seen service all over the world and the collection is thus a broad one. The firearms on display are from the past 150 years and are of particular interest.

Royal Pioneer Corps Museum

Simpson Barracks, Wooton, 3 miles S by B526. Tel: (01604) 762742. Open Monday to Friday.

Watling Street, now the A5, has been a major strategic route for the military since the Romans built it. With the completion of the Grand Junction Canal in 1800 and the Blisworth tunnel in 1805, troops and supplies could be transported to and from London and Liverpool by water. The government then acquired 53 acres of land at Weedon Bec and built the Royal Ordnance Depot, three groups of buildings, the Depot, the Barracks and the Pavilions. The Depot survives (the name by which the buildings are known locally being erroneous), as do the magazine storage buildings within the Cavalry Hill Industrial Park off the Daventry road. The complex was linked to the canal by a waterway spur which, partly, is still there, leading to the East Lodge which acts as a water-gatehouse. The storehouses are now used for a variety of commercial purposes. The Pavilions were pulled down in the 1960s, and had been the residences of the commandant and other officials, and available for the Royal Family in the case of Napoleonic invasion. The Barracks were occupied by cavalry from before World War I to the 1940s. An exercise in the use of the new-fangled motor lorry in autumn 1913 on Blakesley Common, four miles to the south, involved 40,000 troops and was witnessed by Sir John French and Winston Churchill. Aircraft were also involved, flying from a field near Canon's Ashby. In 1995 the Depot was bought by Cavalry Centre Ltd who have applied for permission to establish an integrated heritage, tourist and commercial centre. In the meantime the site may only be viewed from the outside.

Weedon Barracks

Weedon Bec, 8 miles W by A45, SW of junction with A5, W of railway.

The Battle of Naseby, 14 June 1645

Naseby, 14 miles N by A50 and B4036, and minor road (signposted to battlefield) towards Sibbertoft; monument in field on left, lay-by for three cars.

In May 1645 Sir Thomas Fairfax and the New Model Army reinforced the siege of Oxford and to draw him away the Royalists under Charles I attacked Parliamentarian strongholds; Leicester was sacked on 30 May. Fairfax gathered his forces, adding Oliver Cromwell's horse from East Anglia, and moved to Stoney Stratford and then towards the King at Daventry. The Royalists were withdrawing to Market Harborough, leaving a small outpost at Naseby, when they realised they would have to fight. By the early morning of 14 June Fairfax and Cromwell had drawn up their army near Clipston, a couple of miles north of Naseby. They were some 13,000 strong against the King's 9,000 and, although many of their men were fresh recruits, the chance to deal a mortal blow to the Royalists was theirs for the taking. They therefore moved west, leaving a position on a ridge with marshy ground in front, to the Fenny Hill/Mill Hill ridge just north of Naseby, south of the position of the monument, and placed Colonel Okey's dragoons on the western flank, behind Sulby Hedges. Prince Rupert saw this and swung his approaching army to the west, finally to a line running west from the modern Dust Hill Farm. The movement left his artillery lagging behind. Between the armies lay Broadmoor, then a hedgeless, open space.

Fairfax pulled his men back so that most of them were concealed from the Royalists, and also to prevent the inexperienced men becoming demoralised by the sight of the enemy advance. Between 9 and 10am the Royalists advanced, Rupert's cavalry on the west, although enfiladed by fire from Okey's dragoons, more quickly than the rest. They met Henry Ireton's horse and threw them back, pursuing them as far as the baggage train which was west of Naseby, just south of the modern A14, instead of turning on the flank of Sir Philip Skippon's infantry. Skippon's men were soon locked in hand-to-hand fighting with Lord Astley's Royalist infantry and they, too, were pushed back. On the east Cromwell's horse charged and broke Langdale's cavalry and a small detatchment chased them from the field, the rest turning to take Astley on the flank, while Okey's dragoons did likewise from the west. Deprived of cavalry support, Astley was now forced to retreat, making another stand north of the junction with the Sibbertoft/Kelmarsh road. Here they were defeated.

An hour had passed since Rupert's horse had scattered Ireton's troops and taken their commander prisoner, and as they returned to the field up the eastern flank the reformed remnants of Ireton's men fell on them, chasing them north. They joined the King's small force north-east of Sibbertoft and attempted a last attack on Cromwell and Fairfax. It failed and the Royalists scattered, pursued and cut down as they ran to the very gates of Leicester. The Parliamentarian victory was complete and decisive.

At the time of writing the battlefield museum, which has been the work of a generous volunteer for over 20 years, is closed while new premises and support are sought. The obelisk on the Naseby/Cliptson road, built on the site of the old windmill, commemorates the battle, but is well away from the ground fought over. There is a battle plan at the monument.

Civil War Earthworks

Quarrendon, NW of Aylesbury.

A public footpath runs from the Quainton road just north of the junction with the A41 across to the A413, passing the site of St Peter's Church. To the south-east of that point are the remains of entrenchments and gun platforms.

The course of World War II was profoundly influenced by the work of the code-breakers. In the previous war British code-breakers had done excellent work, and to counter their skill the Germans sought ways to create unbreakable codes. Their solution was the Enigma machine, invented by Artur Scherbius. It consisted of a keyboard, a plugboard and a number of rotors which were used according to a set routine to generate coded messages. The French, British and Poles were aware of the invention, and the Poles gave a machine to the British in 1939. It was taken to Bletchley Park. The intricate work of deciphering German secret messages, the creation of electro-mechanical devices and the building of the world's first electronic computer, Colossus, is told here. The foreknowledge of Guderian's Panzer attack in the Ardennes in 1940, the data on German plans in the Battle of Britain and the information that led to the victory in the Battle of the Atlantic are among the successes of Bletchley. Many of the wartime buildings can be seen as well as machines, documents and memorabilia of the secret war. There is also a display of items from the collection of the Military Vehicles Trust and of World War II fire appliances together with other fascinating relics of the war.

Bletchley Park

Wilton Avenue, Bletchley, 20 miles S by A508 and A5 to Bletchley rail station, W by B4034, Buckingham Road, right on Church Green Road and right again. Tel: (01908) 640404. Open alternate weekends 10.30am to 5pm, last tour 3pm.

OXFORD

Tourist information: The Old School, Gloucester Green. Tel: (01865) 726871. Guided walks starting from the Oxford Information Centre include, on occasion, one called Civil War in Oxford.

The museum is devoted to the history of the city and of the university, but has some coverage of the Civil War, during which Oxford was Charles I's capital, including the map of de Gomme's fortifications and Cromwell's death mask. The Royalist Parliaments met in Christ Church Hall near by.

The Museum of Oxford

St Aldates. Tel: (01865) 815559. Open Tueday to Friday 10am to 4pm, Saturday 10am to 5pm.

The County Light Infantry regiment is portrayed together with the militia and territorial battalions, and there are some items relating to the Queen's Own Oxfordshire Hussars. Medals, uniforms, badges pictures and arms are on display. There is a close connection with the Royal Green Jackets. Open most weekdays, but check by telephone.

Oxfordshire and Buckinghamshire Museum

Territorial Army Centre, Slade Park, Headington. Tel: (01865) 716060/778479.

Situated in a fine town house and devoted to the history of the county, the museum has a small display related to the Civil War. It is open Tuesday to Saturday and Sunday afternoon.

Oxfordshire County Museum

Woodstock, 7 miles NW. Tel: (01993) 811456.

Sir John Urry was in the service of the Earl of Essex and Parliament when they came to Thame and took his chance to profit by defecting to the Royalists with news of a baggage train bearing £21,000 pay for Essex's men. Prince Rupert was delighted with the prospect of an enforced subsidy for the Royal coffers and set forth from Oxford with 1,000 horse, 500 foot and 300 dragoons to hijack the money. He attacked a small force at Chinnor, south-east of Thame and,

The Battle of Chalgrove Field, 18 June 1643

Chalgrove, 6 miles SE by B480, and left turn towards Warpsgrove.

although successful, gave the alarm, sending the pay train running for cover. Rupert turned for Oxford through hostile country and as he approached Chisle-hampton to cross the bridge over the River Thame his enemies were too close for comfort. He took up position west of the Warpsgrove road and east of the modern airfield buildings. The Parliamentarian dragoons came forward to a hedge immediately in front of the Royalists and opened fire, precipitating an immediate charge by Rupert's horse who crashed clean through them to engage the cavalry coming up behind them and put them to flight. In the action John Hampden, who had, as a Member of Parliament, been so prominent in his opposition to Ship Money, was seriously wounded. He retired to his home in Thame and, although the King offered the services of his personal surgeon, died six days later. His monument stands at the first crossroads from the main road and the fight took place due north of it.

Station 465, Chalgrove

Chalgrove, see above.

Men of the US 9th Air Force 10th Photographic Group arrived at the newly built airfield in January 1944, the first of several photographic reconnaissance squadrons to be based here, close to RAF Benson, the British PR base. In September IX Troop Carrier Command Pathfinder Group (Provisional) were moved here. They were responsible for marking landing zones for Operation Market and flew on their mission at 1040 hours on 17 September. In March 1945 8th Air Force 7th Reconnaissance Group was stationed here. In 1946 the airfield was leased to the Martin-Baker Aircraft Company for the testing of ejection seats. A memorial to the US Army Air Force men who served here stands near the entrance.

Oxford (Botley) Cemetery

Botley, 3 miles W by A420, near B4017 junction.

The Commonwealth War Graves Commission cemetery contains 165 graves of World War I and 577 of World War II.

The Battle of Stow-on-the-Wold, 21 March 1646

Donnington, 24 miles NW of Oxford by A44, A436 and minor road.

The King's situation in the early months of 1646 was desperate. His advisers encouraged him to seek peace with Parliament, but Charles I, despite the defeats at Rowton Heath and at Philiphaugh the previous September, still had faithful troops in the West Country, at Newark and at Oxford. On 12 March Hopton finally surrendered in the west and the King turned to the aged Sir Jacob Astley to raise fresh troops. Astley managed to gather together some 3,000 men from the Severn valley and was returning to Oxford with them when he was intercepted by Sir William Brereton just north of Stow-on-the-Wold. Astley took a position on a ridge near the minor road through Donnington which connects the modern A424 and A429 which Brereton attacked on the morning of 21 March. The Royalist right did well, but the left wilted under Brereton's pressure and Astley's force fell back towards Stow. The fight spilled into the market place where, finally, Charles's last field army surrendered. The King, hoping to gain from the uneasy relationship between Parliament and the Scots, set off for Newark which was still besieged by the northerners.

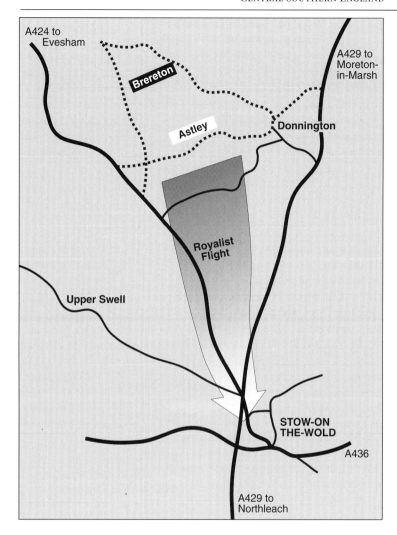

SWINDON

Tourist information: 37 Regent Street. Tel: (01793) 530328.

Amongst other displays there is a room devoted to the Royal Wiltshire Yeomanry where uniforms and other memorabilia are on show.

Swindon Museum and Art Gallery
Bath Road. Tel: (01793) 526161. Open daily.

The battles between the Britons and the Saxons are almost impossible to fix by date or location. Alfred Burne argued for this site in the case of Mount Badon, identifying Liddington Castle as the hill-fort in ancient accounts. The Saxons were pushing westwards from the land already under their control and were opposed by the Britons, commanded by Arthur. Burne suggests the Saxons took their first positions on the edge of hill that runs from Badbury towards

The Battle of Mount Badon, c.495
Liddington Castle, Badbury, 5 miles SE by A419 and minor road E.

Liddington village (now on the north side of the M4 motorway). Here they succeeded in throwing back British attacks all day, retiring across the level land behind them and climbing the hilltop around the Iron Age fort for the night. They defended this new position against Arthur and his cavalry the next day until finally put to flight. In all this there is much conjecture.

Other scholars take the view that Arthur was a member of the Votadini tribe which occupied territory between Edinburgh and Newcastle, that this battle took place near Dumbarton and that Arthur died in the Battle of Camlon in 537, near Birdoswald on Hadrian's Wall.

Membury, Station 466

Membury Services westbound on M4, 10 miles E of Swindon.

The motorway now slices through the north-eastern corner of the airfield built in 1942, and some of the associated buildings are still in use alongside the minor road that crosses the M4 just to the east of the service area. The US Army Ninth Air Force 436th Troop Carrier Group flew from here early on D-Day, 6 June 1944, to drop 1,084 paratroops of the 101st Airborne Division south-east of Ste-Mère-Eglise in Normandy. Elements of the 436th were relocated to Italy in July to take part in Operation Dragoon, the invasion of southern France on 15 August. In September they suffered serious losses while transporting the 101st Airborne to Son, just north of Eindhoven, in Operation Market-Garden, but managed to put 40 C-47s up the next day. Foul weather interfered with the following day's operations, but they flew further missions, towing gliders and dropping supplies up to 23 September. The RAF took over the airfield in July 1945, flying C-47s (Dakotas) to the Far East.

WINDSOR

Tourist information: 24 High Street. Tel: (01753) 852010.

Windsor Castle

Tel: (01753) 383 1118. Open daily 10am to 6pm.

In order to protect his new capital of London, William the Conqueror erected forts in a ring round the city at some 20 miles distance. As the River Thames was a vital waterway the chalky outcrop above the stream in the parish of Clewer was selected for a motte and bailey of unusual layout as the bailey, running along the ridge, was long and thin with the motte in the centre. The royal hunting lodge was at Windlesora, three miles downstream, and when it was abandoned the name was attached to the larger residence. The part of the bailey to the east of the mound is known as the Upper Ward, while that to the west was divided by a dry ditch into the Middle and Lower wards. The original timberwork was first replaced by stone in 1165–71 to build the new royal apartments of Henry II on the northern face of the Upper Ward, still the area reserved to the monarch today. Faced with rebellion by his sons, Henry also refortified the external wall in stone along the line of the original ramparts of the bailey, and replaced the timber structure on the motte with a stone shell keep which now forms the lower part of the Round Tower. The work was suspended when the rebellion ceased.

The fortification of the Lower Ward was completed by Henry III in the 13th century, using round towers in a stout curtain wall, and building accommodation for his courtiers there to replace earlier buildings destroyed by fire. The castle was evolving into an administrative centre while retaining its military importance. In the 14th century Edward III developed the Upper Ward with rebuilt royal apartments on the north and houses for his staff on the east and south, and a new defensive gateway, still there, to secure the area from the rest of the castle. He founded the Order of the Garter, a chivalrous order inspired by the Arthurian Knights of the Round Table, in 1348 and made the Lower Ward its centre with appropriate buildings. A century later St George's Chapel was started and in 1528 it was complete. The gatehouse by which the public now enter was the work of Henry VIII's reign.

The last military activity was in the Civil War, when the castle was taken by the Parliamentarians. With the Restoration new building was undertaken suitable to a royal palace, and from this time forward the extensive changes have been inspired by its function as a royal residence. A severe fire which destroyed a substantial portion of the Royal Apartments led to extensive rebuilding and restoration which was completed in 1997.

A substantial collection covering the history of the regiments since 1660. The regiments represented include the 1st and 2nd Life Guards, the Horse Grenadier Guards, the Royal Horse Guards (the Blues), the 1st Royal Dragoons and the Blues and Royals. Exhibits include regimental standards, firearms, swords, uniforms and equipment, as well as dioramas of battles.

The Household Cavalry Museum
Combermere Barracks. Tel: (01753) 755203. Open weekdays 10am to 12.30pm and 2pm to 4.30pm.

The history of the Berkshire Yeomanry from 1795 to the present is shown through uniforms, medals, pictures and campaign relics and includes personal memorabilia. It is open by appointment only.

Royal Berkshire Cavalry Museum
Territorial Army Centre, Bolton Road. Tel: (01753) 860600.

Overlooking the River Thames and the meadow where King John was obliged to fix his seal to Magna Carta on 15 June 1215 stands the memorial to the airmen of World War II with no known graves. There are 20,401 names recorded here, most of them from the RAF, but a quarter of them from Canada, Australia, New Zealand, South Africa and India.

The Air Forces Memorial
Runnymede, 4 miles SE of Windsor by A308 and A328 (or from junction 13, M25) and E on Coopers Hill Lane. Commonwealth War Graves Commission.

EAST ANGLIA

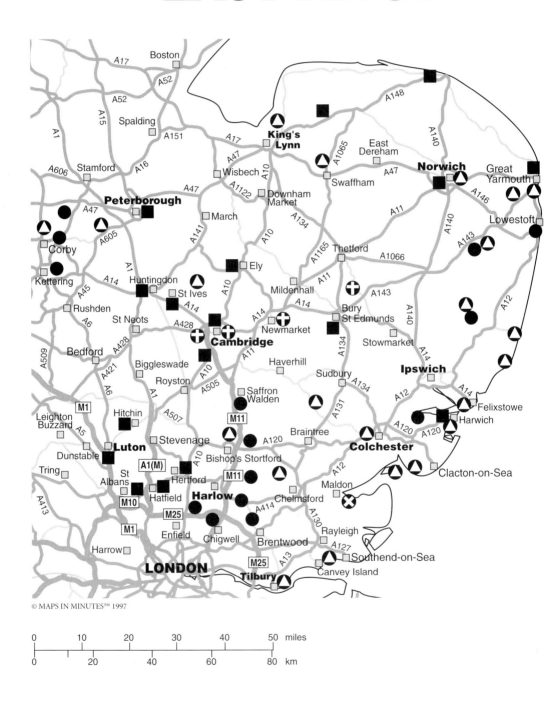

© MAPS IN MINUTES™ 1997

Boston
A17
A52
A52
A15
A16
Spalding
A1
A151
A606
Stamford
A47
Peterborough
A47
A605
Corby
Kettering
A45
Rushden
A6
A509
Bedford
A428
A421
A6
Leighton Buzzard
A5
M1
Hitchin
Dunstable
Tring
St Albans
M10
Harrow
M1
Enfield
LONDON

King's Lynn
Wisbech
A17
A47
A10
A1122
Downham Market
March
A47
A141
Ely
A10
Huntingdon
St Ives
A14
St Neots
A428
Cambridge
Biggleswade
Royston
A10
A505
A507
Stevenage
Saffron Walden
M11
Bishop's Stortford
A10
Hertford
M11
Hatfield
Harlow
A1(M)
Luton
M25
Chigwell
Tilbury
M25

A148
East Dereham
Swaffham
A47
A1065
A11
A134
Thetford
A1165
A1066
Mildenhall
A11
Newmarket
A14
Bury St Edmunds
Haverhill
A134
Sudbury
A131
Braintree
A120
Chelmsford
A414
A130
A127
Rayleigh

Norwich
Great Yarmouth
A146
Lowestoft
A140
A143
A12
Stowmarket
A140
A14
Ipswich
A12
A14
Felixstowe
Harwich
A120
A120
Colchester
A12
Clacton-on-Sea
Maldon
Southend-on-Sea
Canvey Island
A13

0   10   20   30   40   50 miles
0   20   40   60   80 km

The countryside of eastern England is more sky than land, a low landscape of gentle hills and flatlands. Spreading south and west from the Wash in the north, fenland made movement difficult for individuals and impossible for armies. North of Cambridge and east of Peterborough the wetlands were a barrier until the skills imported from the Netherlands in the person of Cornelius Vermuyden at last made efficient drainage possible. On the western flank the rising land carries the road to the north and in the south the Chiltern Hills sweep north of London to curl in a low watershed all the way to the north Norfolk coast, shedding the rainfall into the fen flats on one side and into the short, straight rivers that cut the coast from the Thames up to Ipswich or the meandering web of waterways that reach the sea at Yarmouth.

It is rich land, but it goes nowhere; it was not until the advent of the warplane that the region found itself caught between conflicting power bases. The military legacy is thus more closely associated with the holding and exploitation of the land, or with attempts to wrest from its holders, than with wider power struggles. The battles in the west have to do with the mastery of London, once it had become a capital city, and the battles in the south-east, and only Maldon (991AD) is prominent, with raiders of East Anglian wealth. Before that the Roman conquest disturbed the peace and after that conflict on a large scale was absent until the region became the front line of an aerial war in the 1940s. For the people war was not absent, for the men of the region went elsewhere to fight – Horatio Nelson to sea, Oliver Cromwell west and north, even to Scotland and Ireland – and countless unnamed men and women went with them.

The military installations inland are thus more country house in nature than fortifications. The latter are confined to the coast and the estuaries, notably the Thames. From medieval times to the Cold War, defensive works have been constructed to repel invaders by sea and, more recently, by air and missile.

For all the apparent peacefulness of East Anglia, there is a surprising amount for the military enthusiast to see.

Key to map

Battlefield
Castle/Fort
Cemetery
Museum
Other

CAMBRIDGE

Fitzwilliam Museum

Trumpington Street. Tel: (01223) 332900. Armour Tuesday to Friday 10am to 2pm.

The Fitzwilliam is best known for its outstanding exhibits of art, textiles, ceramics and glass, but it also has a fine collection of armour and early weapons.

Cambridge City Cemetery

2 miles E on the Newmarket, A1303, road. Commonwealth War Graves Commission.

The war graves here are from World Wars I and II. There are 1,010 in all, 145 United Kingdom, 20 Australian, 13 Canadian and 3 South African from World War I. The World War II burials are of Royal Air Force personnel from bases between the Thames and the Humber and number 401 United Kingdom, 252 Australian, 89 Canadian, 81 New Zealand, 1 South African and 1 India and Pakistan. There are four unidentified.

Newmarket Cemetery

Newmarket, 13 miles E by A1303 and A1304, W of town. Commonwealth War Graves Commission.

There are 58 Commonwealth graves here, most of men from the United Kingdom who died in World Wars I and II, as well as 1 Australian, 5 Canadian, 8 New Zealand and 1 South African. There are also the graves of 19 men of the Polish Army who died during the preparations for the invasion of Europe.

Cambridge American Cemetery

Coton, 3 miles W by A1303, near M11 junction 13. Tel: (01954) 210350. Open daily.

The American Cemetery at Madingley, as it is known, is the last resting-place of servicemen who gave their lives in World War II. There is a reception building and a memorial chapel.

Imperial War Museum, Duxford

Duxford, 8 miles S by A10 and M11 at junction 10. Tel: (01223) 835000.

Spigot Mortar Pit

Wendens Ambo, 8 miles S of Duxford by A1301 and B1383.

An anti-tank weapon of World War II, the 29mm spigot mortar or Blacker Bombard had a range of some 400 yards. It was mounted on a concrete thimble some five feet high, with a stainless-steel mounting pin on the top, placed in a gun pit. An example is said to be hereabouts, part of the GHQ Stop Line.

The former Battle of Britain fighter station and American 8th Air Force base is now home to the massive collection of the Imperial War Museum. The collection includes the World War I Bristol fighter, Spitfires, Mustangs, Harriers and numerous other aircraft. The World War II Operations room is preserved as it was during the Battle of Britain and a simulator gives the visitor the chance to experience a dog-fight between a Spitfire and a Messerschmitt. The American Air Museum has Europe's finest collection of American combat aircraft, 21 of them, including a B-52 bomber, a Grumman Avenger painted in the colours of the aircraft former President George Bush flew in the South Pacific and numerous exhibits portraying the two World Wars, the Korean War, the Vietnam War, the Cold War and the Gulf War.

The Land Warfare Exhibition presents an impressive display of tanks, military vehicles and artillery from World War I to the Gulf War. Special events include a number of flying display days and vehicle displays. The Royal Anglian Regiment Museum is part of the display. The research into World War II defences, the Defence of Britain Project, is based here and acquired its first historic object in 1995 – an Alan-Williams steel turret in need of restoration and preservation retrieved from Nazeing Common. Open daily, mid-March to October 10am to 6pm; winter 10am to 4pm. Special events information, tel. 0891 516816.

Oliver Cromwell was born in Huntingdon in 1599 and went to school in this building. The museum is devoted to the life of Cromwell and the Parliamentary side in the Civil War of 1642–60. There are portraits of the leading figures of the time and various of Cromwell's possessions including a surgeon's chest made by Kolb of Augsburg. The exhibits also include coins and medals.

Cromwell Museum
Grammar School Walk, High Street, Huntingdon, 15 miles NW by A604. Tel: (01480) 425830. Open April to October Tuesday to Sunday.

The museum of Huntingdonshire, it deals with the broad history of the county but also includes special displays on the Civil War and French prisoner-of-war work from the prison camp that was at Norman Cross.

Norris Museum
The Broadway, St Ives, 12 miles NW by A604 and A1096. Tel: (01480) 465101. Open Monday to Saturday.

To guard Ely from a Royalist advance from the west in the Civil War, Parliamentarian forces built a fort at Earith, between the New and the Old Bedford rivers. The square earthwork has angle bastions at each corner and a covered way and a glacis, a sloping parapet, beyond the ditch.

The Bulwark
Earith, 10 miles N by A604 and B1050, on A1123. Conditions of access not known; do not trespass.

The Isle of Ely rises above the surrounding fen, formerly a maze of creeks and bogs which gave shelter to Anglo-Saxon dissidents, such as the legendary Hereward the Wake, to the Norman regime. The museum is devoted to the history of the area from the earliest times and includes coverage of the Cambridgeshire Regiment.

Ely Museum
28C High Street, Ely, 15 miles NE by A10. Tel: (01353) 666655. Open daily 10.30am to 5pm.

This was the family home of Oliver Cromwell, Lord Protector of England, and the museum deals not only with the man himself but with the broader context of 17th-century life. There is a large exhibition on the Civil War. The Tourist Information Office is in the same building.

Oliver Cromwell's House
29 St Mary's Street, Ely. Tel: (01353) 662062. Open daily 10am to 6pm; closes 5.15pm and Sunday October to March.

COLCHESTER

Tourist information: 1 Queen Street. Tel: (01206) 282920.
Before London even existed, Colchester was the thriving capital of Roman Britain. Considerable portions of the city walls remain and a fine gate, the Balkerne Gate, demonstrates the size of the city with its broad entranceways in the 107-foot wide façade. The city was sacked by Boudica and the Iceni when they rose against the Romans, and was later rebuilt.

The Roman temple of Claudius stood here long before the largest Norman keep in England was built, using the foundations laid by the earlier invaders and recycling materials from the ruins of their works. It was built by William the Conqueror at much the same time as the White Tower in London and for a similar purpose – as a fortified palace. The apse of the chapel projecting from the south-east wall was clearly an essential part of the original design, demonstrating its residential role in addition to its military importance. The Roman temple vaults still support the structure. The upper levels of the keep were demolished in the 17th century and the entrance, now at ground level, was repositioned a century after the castle was built.

Colchester Castle
Tel: (01206) 282931. Open Monday to Saturday 10am to 5pm and also March to November Sunday 2pm to 5pm.

The castle now has a number of interesting displays for visitors. The early history of the town, including the destruction by Boudica and the Roman occupation, are featured, as are life in Norman and medieval times.

Lexden Earthworks and Bluebottle Grove
2 miles W off A604. Open site.

The Iron Age earthworks were the centre of power in pre-Roman East Anglia where Cunobelinus, known to the Romans as the King of the Britons, ruled. The Romans took over what was, in effect, the capital city of Britain in 43AD.

Essex Secret Bunker
Crown Building, Shrublands Road, Mistley, 9 miles NE by A137 and B1352. Tel: (01206) 392271. Open April to September 10am to 4.30pm.

This was Furze Hill, the Essex County Nuclear War HQ bunker, from which the administration would have continued, though what would have been left to administer may be questioned. It remains as it was when decommissioned. The communications rooms and operations rooms are to be seen together with the offices and accommodation for staff, 27 rooms in all. The original equipment is in place in the radio room and command centre. Two cinemas show formerly secret archive film.

Harwich Maritime Museum
Low Lighthouse, the Green. Tel: (01255) 503429.

Part of the exhibits cover the Royal Navy. Those with a special interest in the sea may also like to visit the Lifeboat Museum at Timberfields, off Wellington Road, which opens at the same times daily June to August.

Harwich Redoubt
Main Road, Harwich, 18 miles E by A120. Tel: (01255) 503429. Open daily June to August 10am to 1pm and 2pm to 5pm; September to May Sundays same hours.

Fear of invasion during the Napoleonic Wars led to the construction of the Martello tower system along the south coast. This eleven-gun redoubt was built as part of the programme, to defend the naval installation, always a fairly small one, at Harwich. The defences at Harwich also included the Bathside Bay Battery which is an open site.

Point Clear Martello Tower
Point Clear, St Ostyth, 9 miles SE by B1027. Tel: (01255) 423604.

The coastal defences of the Napoleonic Wars made great use of Martello towers as far north as Aldeburgh and all along the channel coast. This example houses the East Essex Aviation and Forties Museum. It is open on Sundays and Mondays, limited hours, and other days in summer.

Mersea Island Defences
Mersea Island, 8 miles S by B1025.

In World War II the defences against invasion consisted of coastal installations and three stop lines in Essex, the Colchester Stop Line, approximately north–south through the town, the GHQ Line, which ran east of Basildon and Chelmsford as far north as Saffron Walden, and the Outer London Defence Ring, south of Harlow. On Mersea Island the beaches were protected with scaffolding erected at low tide and with barbed-wire entanglements. Anti-tank obstacles were positioned to impede exit from the beaches and pillboxes built. At Cudmore County Park, East Mersea, a hexagonal pillbox can be seen and on the beach the fragments of concrete which are the only remains of two 4.7-inch gun casemates destroyed by the sea. At West Mersea on the southern end of the island a similar casemate survives, now in service as the Two Sugars beach café. Cudmore also contains a 16th-century blockhouse.

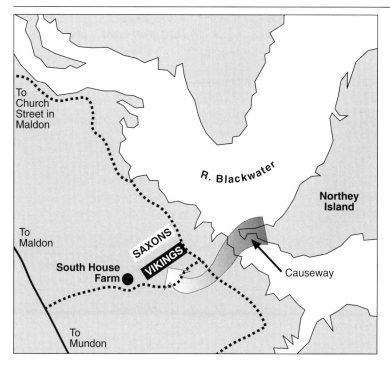

The Viking raids reached a new height of ferocity in 991, 93 ships being involved in raids along the Suffolk, Essex and Kent coasts under the leadership of the Norwegian Olaf Tryggvasson and the Danes Guthmund and Jostein. The Saxons opposed them under the command of Ealdorman Brithnoth, but the problem was catching the sea-borne plunderers. A party of the Vikings camped on Northey Island, now a National Trust bird sanctuary, even then connected to the mainland by a causeway. Brithnoth managed to occupy the land to the south and, it being high tide and the causeway covered, exchanged remarks with the foe. The Vikings demanded tribute, the Saxons refused. As the tide fell three Saxon warriors took position to contest the attempt to cross to the mainland and were so successful that the Danes proposed that Brithnoth allow them to come over for a proper fight. The opportunity to inflict a comprehensive defeat on the Danes was too good to resist; the Vikings were granted their request and drew up facing Maldon just north-west of the modern road. An exchange of spears followed and then the armies met hand-to-hand. After the first shock the Vikings withdrew a little and then a Dane advanced alone, offering single combat. Brithnoth went to meet him, but was soon wounded and as the armies clashed once more the Saxon leader fell. Many of his dismayed followers broke and fled while the remainder fought doggedly until they were cut down. The Viking victory encouraged them to settle in the land and extract the first payment of tribute, what was to become known as the Danegeld.

The sea level has risen since that time, when a clear-cut channel of half the width separated the island from the shore. Later flooding was dealt with by the building of the sea-wall and much silting-up has taken place.

The Battle of Maldon, 11 August 991

Maldon, 13 miles SW by B1022. On foot on S bank of Blackwater from Church Street, or via South House Farm off B1018 to S.

USAAF Memorial

Chelmsford Cathedral

A porch forms a memorial to the men of the US Army Air Force who lost their lives in World War II.

Essex Regiment Museum

Chelmsford and Essex Museum, Oaklands Park, Moulsham Street, Chelmsford, 19 miles SW. Tel: (01245) 353066.

The museum covers the service of the 44th (East Essex) and 56th (West Essex) regiments from 1741 to 1881, and of the Essex Regiment and its successors to the present day. The exhibits relating to the Napoleonic Wars include an eagle captured at Salamanca. Other major conflicts in which the regiments served are recorded: the Crimean War, the China War, the Afghan Wars, the Boer War and World Wars I and II. Open Monday to Saturday and Sunday afternoon.

Earls Colne, Station 358

10 Miles W by A120 and B1024.

The first heavy bomber airfield to be built in Essex, Earls Colne was started in January 1942 and virtually ready by September. It was occupied briefly by the 94th Group, 8th Air Force with B-17s in 1943 before 323rd Bomb Group, then 8th, later 9th Air Force moved in with B-26 Marauders. They commenced operations on 16 July 1943. They bombed bridges in the preparation for the D-Day landings and flew in support of the landings themselves before being transferred to Hampshire. The RAF's 296 and 297 Squadrons then took over the field, flying in support of the Market-Garden and Rhine crossing operations. The airfield lost operation status in 1946 and permission to build a golf course was granted in 1990.

Hedingham Castle

Castle Hedingham, 17 miles NW by A604. Tel: (01787) 460261. Open at times available by telephone.

Although there are few traces of the other buildings on the site, the superb tower keep, similar to Rochester, stands as a reminder of the wealth and power of the de Veres, Earls of Oxford, and the trust reposed in them by Henry I. A remarkable feature of the internal design is the height of the second floor, making a galleried living space, a great hall which is more appropriate to the domestic and formal requirements of the family than military need. Already, in 1140, wider considerations than war were influencing castle planning.

HARLOW

Stansted Mountfitchet, Station 169

London (Stansted) Airport, 9 miles NE, M11 junction 8.

Little remains of the World War II airfield now overlain by the modern airport. The field was allocated to the US 8th Air Force in August 1942 and was opened for operation a year later. The 9th Air Force took it over in October and the 344 Bomb Group arrived in February 1944. They flew over 100 missions from here, including leading the support of the D-Day landings in Normandy on 6 June, attacking targets to the rear of Utah Beach and bombing the St Lô area in July, for which they received a Distinguished Unit Citation. In September they moved to France after which the airfield was used for repair and overhaul work. The runway was extended to 10,000 feet in the 1950s, during the Cold War, as a reserve base. It was developed as a civil airport in the 1980s and opened as London's third airport in 1990.

Mountfitchet Castle

Stansted Mountfitchet, 10 miles N by A1184 and B1383. Tel: (01279) 813237. Open daily mid-March to mid-November 10am to 5pm.

A reconstructed motte and bailey castle, complete with Norman village. There are reproduction weapons, a siege tower and numerous other features of life in Norman times.

391 Bomb Group, 9th Air Force came to the airfield a mile north-east of the village in January 1944. They flew B-26 Marauders on over 150 missions before being moved France in September 1944. The road east to Abbess Roding uses part of the runway. There is a roadside memorial to the fallen of the 391st and a plaque to their memory in Matching church.

Matching, Station 166
Matching Green, 5 miles E by minor road.

A classic motte and bailey castle with only one modification from its original state, the erection of a permanent bridge over the motte ditch. The early use of these structures involved a portable palisade which was put together on top of the motte by the visiting force to secure their temporary residence, and the appearance of Pleshey enables the visitor to visualise the process. Permanent timberwork later took its place and yet later stone might be used for a more established stronghold.

Pleshey Castle
Pleshey, 12 miles E by B183, A1060 and minor roads. Open site.

North Weald Aerodrome was bombed in 1940 and the RAF operations centre for Sector E was set up at Blake Hall. The operations room was left untouched after the war and has now been opened as a museum. It boasts a full-size model of a V1 flying bomb amongst other memorabilia. The gardens of Blake Hall are open to the public.

Blake Hall
Nr Ongar, 6 miles SE, via junction 7 on M11, by A414. Tel: (01277) 362502. Open April to September Sundays, Bank Holidays.

Fears of possible French invasion in the 1880s led to the construction of mobilisation centres for the volunteer force. They were to contain arms and ammunition in magazines set within a rampart and ditch with some limited barrack space. In the event they were not required for use. North Weald was in use by British Telecom until 1996 and its fate is not known at the time of writing.

North Weald Mobilisation Centre
North Weald, 5 miles SE by A414. Not open at time of writing.

The last-ditch stand to protect London, had England been invaded in World War II, against German troops advancing from the east would have been here. It consisted of a 20-foot-wide anti-tank ditch up to 12 feet deep across the countryside, running north of Bumble's Green and curving south to the east of Copped Hill, then south of the modern M25 to Jack's Hill and on through Loughton to Rolls Park and Chigwell Row. The line was supported by octagonal Type FW3/27A pillboxes with 42-inch-thick concrete walls to be manned by 10 defenders, some of which can still be seen near Nazeing. Less sophisticated was the Alan-Williams turret, a steel dome for a machine-gun which was rotated by one member of the gun crew while the other fired the gun. A rare survival on Nazeing Common was removed to the Imperial War Museum, Duxford, for restoration and preservation in 1995. The ditch itself has largely been obliterated since the war, but a length can be found off the B172 at Jack's Hill, west of Theydon Bois. A wide path called Centenary Walk runs south from the road and a few yards further west is a narrower path down which you go for 100 yards to view the anti-tank ditch on the left side.

The Outer London Defence Ring
4 miles SW, from Lower Nazeing to Loughton.

Pickett-Hamilton Elevating Fort
North Weald airfield.

Used exclusively for airfield defence in World War II, this was a four-man underground pillbox, flush with the surface when not in use, but raised above it by compressed air to go into action. A restored example is here.

Kelvedon Hatch Nuclear Bunker

Kelvedon Hall Lane, Kelvedon Hatch, 10 miles SE by A414 and A128. Tel: (01277) 364883. Open daily.

A Cold War installation, this bunker was still in active service in 1992. It is a three-storey regional headquarters 100 feet below ground with a canteen, BBC studio, dormitories, plotting floor and communication and scientific centres. From such bunkers the country was to be controlled in the aftermath of nuclear attack.

The Royal Gunpowder Mills

Waltham Abbey, 9 miles SW by A414, A10 and A121, or M25 junction 26. Accessibility unknown at time of writing.

On the banks of the River Lee, the gunpowder mills at Waltham Abbey had access to water transport for the (relatively) safe carriage of the product to the Royal Arsenal at Woolwich. Gunpowder manufacture is thought to have been taking place here as early as 1560 and was certainly being undertaken by the 1660s. The mills were nationalised in 1787 as the government was determined to standardise the quality of gunpowder and thus the reliability of the artillery and musketry in warfare.

Power for the production process was also supplied by the river until the introduction of steam engines in the 1850s. The skills of the Waltham men were used in the American Civil War when one individual emigrated to Tennessee to advise the South while employees of the Du Pont company visited here in order to improve the munitions of the North. The mills were of immense importance in World War I, producing all the cordite required and thus employing over 5,000 people, more than half of them women. The last of the water-powered machinery was destroyed in 1941. After World War II the site was used for research and testing until it closed in 1991. At the time of writing plans have been made for the development of the site as a mixture of historical preservation, commercial development and housing use so that the old buildings, interesting both from architectural and industrial archaeological points of view, can be seen and enjoyed, but the site is closed in the meantime.

Hertford Castle

Hertford, 10 miles E by A414. Tel: (01992) 552885. Museum, 18 Bull Plain, Tuesday to Saturday 10am to 5pm.

Only a small portion of the castle remains as such and the gatehouse, built in the mid-15th century, may be visited on certain Sundays in summer. There was a Norman motte and bailey here to which curtain walls were added under Henry II. The offices of the tourist information centre are here. A small museum devoted to the Hertford Regiment forms part of the displays at the Hertford Museum.

Hatfield House

Hatfield Park, E of Hatfield, 15 miles W of Harlow by A414. Tel: (01707) 262823.

The magnificent house is open to visitors on a guided-tour basis, but the park and gardens are less restricted in access, open daily 11am to 5.30pm, and one of the buildings holds the National Collection of Model Soldiers.

IPSWICH

Tourist information: St Stephens Church, St Stephens Lane. Tel: (01473) 258070.

Landguard Fort

1 mile S of Felixstowe, near docks, 9 miles SE by A45. English Heritage. Tel: (01394) 286403 (evenings).

The fort is in course of restoration at the time of writing, and visiting is limited until work is finished. The original fort overlooking the mouth of the Orwell Estuary was built in the 1740s on classic pentagonal lines. In the 1870s it was rebuilt as a casemated fort at the end of the programme of works for defence against the French. The development of shore defences continued in the 1880s and a submarine mining establishment can be seen here. Landguard was further modified in World Wars I and II. Open only on special days.

A unique four-in-one tower that was the northern end of the east coast line built in 1808–12. It is quatrefoil in plan to carry four guns, and a further gun-platform on the seaward side carried additional armament, but it has now been lost to the sea.

Aldeburgh Martello Tower

Aldeburgh, 24 miles NE by A12 and A1094. Landmark Trust. By appointment only.

The superb tower-keep overlooking the sea at Orford was built as much for domination of followers of doubtful loyalty, such as the Earl of Norfolk at Framlingham, as it was for coastal defence. It was built by Henry II in 1165–7 and was in stone, a material the king preferred to deny to lesser men for their fortifications. The tower comprises three rectangular turrets joined to the central cylindrical structure, leading to a highly complex building within. The residential floors are planned to be quite separate, a helical stair connecting the kitchen level with the royal apartments above. The chapel is contained in the largest of the turrets, the forebuilding, over the entrance. The surrounding buildings and curtain wall have gone, only earthworks marking their place. The coastline has altered considerably since the castle was built, and it now commands the narrow creek of the River Alde where once there was a harbour, with Orford Ness beyond.

Orford Castle

Orford, 20 miles E by A12, A1152 and B1078. English Heritage. Tel: (01394) 450472. Open April to October daily 10am to 6pm, November to March Wednesday to Sunday 10am to 4pm.

The control tower of the former USAAF Station 153, Parham has been converted into a memorial to 390th BG, US 8th Air Force, by local volunteers funded from their own resources to honour the 140,000 airmen who gave their lives in operations from East Anglian airfields in World War II. The exhibits include a rare collection of recovered aircraft engines and parts of Allied and German aircraft, uniforms, photographs, documents, combat records, paintings and memorabilia. Entry is free, but donations to maintain the collection are welcome and vital.

Station 153 Air Museum

Parham Airfield, near Framlingham. 16 miles N by A12, B1116 and minor road E from Parham. Open March to October Sundays and Bank Holiday Mondays 11am to 6pm, June to August Wednesday to 4pm.

The stone castle was built by the Roger, Earl of Norfolk in about 1190 on the site of a castle destroyed by Henry II when the previous earl's rebellion had been defeated. It consists of 13 towers linked by a curtain wall to form the inner ward. The remains of the earlier castle and of 13th-century domestic buildings are within. The outer ward was still an earthwork with a timber palisade and may never have been fortified in stone. The building has served many purposes over the years, with consequent alteration within.

Framlingham Castle

Framlingham, 18 miles N by A12 and B1116. English Heritage. Tel: (01728) 724189. Open April to October daily 10am to 5pm, November to March to 4pm.

The burials of World War II are from the RAF station near the village. There are 48 Commonwealth graves, including 1 Australian, 13 Canadian and 4 New Zealand. There are also the graves of men from Czechoslovakia and Poland in the plot at the northern boundary of the churchyard.

Honington (All Saints) Churchyard

Honington, 27 miles NW by A14 and A1088. Commonwealth War Graves Commission.

Suffolk Regiment Museum

The Keep, Gibraltar Barracks, Bury St Edmunds, 28 miles NE by A14. Tel: (01284) 752394. Open weekdays.

The regiments, militia, volunteer and territorial units associated with the county regiment are the subject of the museum in a collection that goes back to 1685.

KING'S LYNN

Tourist information: The Old Gaol House, Saturday Market Place. Tel: (01553) 763044.

The town was first fortified with a rampart and ditch in the 13th century. The South Gate, built in 1437–40, has circular gunports. During the Civil War bastioned earthworks were constructed.

Castle Rising

Castle Rising, 4 miles NE by A149 and minor road. English Heritage. Tel: (01553) 631330. Open April to October daily 10am to 6pm, November to March Wednesday to Sunday 10am to 4pm.

William d'Aubigny, a faithful servant of Henry I, was created Earl of Arundel in 1139 and allowed to build in stone. He sited his hall-keep within an earthen ringwork of Norman construction, adding a stone keep to the inner defence of an existing castle. The two-floored building has a substantial and decorative forebuilding to protect the entrance and the upper, residential floor has a kitchen, hall, chapel and gallery. The design was not a true forerunner of the concentric castle and not particularly effective in military terms, given its single entrance.

Houghton Hall

11 miles W by A148. Tel: (01485) 528569. Open April to November Saturday to Wednesday.

In the house built for Sir Robert Walpole in the early 18th century there is, amongst other items of interest, a collection of over 20,000 model soldiers as well as other militaria. Open afternoons only.

Castle Acre Castle

Castle Acre, 10 miles SE by A47, via Swaffham, and A1065. English Heritage. Open site.

The impressive earthworks at Castle Acre suggest an early fort supplemented by later building in stone. The opposite is the case. The early castle was an 11th-century hall on two floors built by William de Warenne as a residence rather than as a military work. The entrance was at ground level through a wide, ceremonial door and the defences appear to have consisted of a modest earthen bank and timber palisade. A century later his heirs extended the earthworks on a great scale and rebuilt the castle as a tower. The village itself lies on the Peddar's Way, a Saxon route based on the Roman road from Colchester via Ixworth to the Wash at Holme-next-the-Sea. A Roman camp was situated here and the road to the sea can still be followed.

Fenland Aviation Museum

63 St Leonards Road, Leverington, Wisbech, 12 miles SW by A47 and W by B1169. Tel: (01945) 585808.

The collection includes aircraft engines, uniforms, models, photographs and parachutes. There are a number of early British military jet aircraft, some under restoration and three on view. Open weekends in summer.

LUTON

Tourist information: 65–67 Bude Street. Tel: (01582) 401579.

Luton Museum

Wardown Park, off A6 Bedford road. Tel: (01582) 746722/746723. Open daily, Sunday 1pm to 5pm only.

The museum is concerned with various aspects of local history and also devotes a gallery to the history of the Bedfordshire and Hertfordshire Regiment. This includes Marlborough's campaigns, the Boer War and World Wars I and II. War as experienced by civilians is portrayed in the Luton During the Wars exhibit.

A gallery of the museum is devoted to the mounted and artillery units of the Hertfordshire Yeomanry raised in the county since 1794. Uniforms, weapons and other memorabilia are on display.

Hitchin Museum
Paynes Park, Hitchin, 7 miles NE by A505. Tel: (01462) 434476.

The 1930s aerodrome that is now a memorial to Pilot Officer Richard Shuttleworth RAFVR houses one of the most exciting collections of historic aircraft in Europe. Some 40 aircraft are on display, of which about half are the only examples in flying condition still in existence. The collection includes World War I aircraft such as the Sopwith Pup, a Hawker Hind, a Gloster Gladiator and a Supermarine Spitfire of World War II, as well as civil aircraft starting with a 1909 Bleriot. In addition to the regular flying displays there are special events and rallies of classic motor vehicles.

The Shuttleworth Collection
Old Warden Aerodrome, 2 miles W of Biggleswade, 15 miles NE off A1. Tel: (01767) 627288. Open daily 10am to 4pm. Flying displays May to October first Sunday of the month.

The principal exhibits in this collection of de Havilland aircraft are the prototype Mosquito W4050 and three other Mosquitos, but there are also a Tiger Moth, a DH100 Vampire, three DH112 Venoms, three DH115 Vampires and parts of other aircraft. There is also the fuselage of a Horsa glider as used in airborne operations in World War II.

Mosquito Aircraft Museum
Salisbury Hall, London Colney, St Albans, 13 miles S by M1, M10 and A414. Tel: (01727) 822051. Open March to October Tuesday, Thursday, Saturday, Sunday and Bank Holidays.

NORWICH

Tourist information: The Guildhall, Gaol Hill. Tel: (01603) 666071.

The Anglo-Norman King Henry I built the great keep in stone at Falaise in Normandy in the 1120s and his hall-keep at Norwich is very similar. Like William the Conqueror's White Tower in London and Colchester Castle, it was both a military structure and a palatial residence. Here the exterior is enhanced with blind arcading and pierced with windows. The windows do not, however, admit light to the interior but serve as the outward-facing apertures to a fighting gallery that, within the thickness of the wall, runs right round the castle and formed a key feature of its defensive design. The king had his apartments on the upper level.

Norwich Castle and Castle Museum
City centre. Tel: (01603) 223624. Open April to September daily 10am to 5pm, October to March same except Sunday 2pm to 5pm only.

The museum is not principally devoted to matters of military interest, but does offer a tour of the battlements and dungeons.

Raised in 1685, the regiment has served in almost every theatre and conflict since and the collection is thus of wide interest. The record includes the Battle of the Boyne, the American War of Independence, the Peninsular War, the Crimean War, Tibet, India, the Boer War, World Wars I and II and the Korean War. There is an extensive collection of photographs. The museum is linked by the old prisoners' tunnel to the keep of the castle and the Castle Museum.

Royal Norfolk Regimental Museum
Shirehall, Castle Meadow. Tel: (01603) 223649. Open April to September daily 10am to 5pm, October to March same except Sunday 2pm to 5pm only.

This isolated fortification on the river bank is one of the earliest specifically designed for the use of guns. It was built in 1398–9 and the records show that a payment was made to one Robert Snape, a mason, at the rate of 9 pence per

Cow Tower
N of Bishopgate, on banks of the River Wensum. English Heritage. Open site.

City of Norwich Aviation Museum
Horsham St Faith. Tel: (01603) 625309.
8 aircraft, all post 1945.

shothole for 12 holes. Without this evidence one might doubt that the small cross-loops were, indeed, for guns. The weapons might have been handguns or, more probably, devices mounted on flat boards which were placed on the sills of the loop-holes. The holes are too close to the floor to have been for crossbows. Gunners had been recorded in Norwich as early as 1365.

The Muckleburgh Collection
Weybourne Military Camp, Weybourne, W of Sheringham, 20 miles N by A140 and W by A149. Tel: (01263) 588210. Open mid-February to November, 10am to 5pm.

Claimed to be the largest privately owned military museum in Britain, the collection includes over 60 armoured vehicles. Sixteen tanks are in full working order and there are SPGs (self-propelled guns), armoured cars and other heavy vehicles. A model ship display includes one of HMS *Vanguard*, the nuclear submarine. The Royal Air Force is also represented with a Battle of Britain exhibition. The Royal Flying Corps is commemorated in a collection of photographs of VII Wing, RFC Norwich discovered in 1997. On Sundays and Bank Holidays, and daily during the summer, tanks are demonstrated on the move and rides are given in the American 6-wheel personnel carrier, the Gama Goat.

The Suffolk and Norfolk Yeomanry Museum
The history of the famous Territorial regiment is told from its raising in 1782. There are over 400 exhibits on show.

Great Yarmouth and the Town Walls
16 miles E by A47. North West Tower, tel: (01493) 332095 for opening times.

The medieval town walls and towers were strengthened with an internal rampart in 1544 and further reinforced in the late 1580s, when the Spanish Armada threatened, with earthworks. Great Yarmouth was the location of the Royal Navy Hospital built to serve the Eastern Squadron in 1809. The work of Sir Henry Pilkington, it was constructed on reclaimed sand dunes. After the Napoleonic Wars it became a cavalry barracks and then a hospital once more until 1993. At the time of writing it has been acquired for conversion into dwellings and there are plans to open a museum in the former clock tower showing what a 19th-century medical ward was like and memorabilia of Lord Nelson.

Maritime Museum
Marine Parade, Great Yarmouth. Tel: (01493) 842267. Open daily June to September 10am to 5pm.

The museum is concerned with Norfolk's maritime tradition, including fishing and the Norfolk wherry. There is also a section on World War II and the experience of civilians in the war. It is closed on Saturdays.

Burgh Castle
Burgh Castle, 15 miles E by A47 and 3 miles W of Great Yarmouth, S of Breydon Water. English Heritage. Open site.

A Roman fort of the late 3rd century of which the bastioned walls still stand. It was one of a number of forts such as Richborough and Pevensey built for coastal defence against the threat of Saxon invasion. The Roman settlement of this area appears to have been substantial. There is another English Heritage site three miles north of Great Yarmouth near Caister-on-Sea. The Caister Roman Site is apparently that of a fortified town, and is also an open site.

Bungay Castle
Bungay, 20 miles SE by A146 and A143. Tel: (01986) 893148. Key must be collected.

The Norman castle built by the Bigods, Earls of Norfolk, in 1165 was further developed in 1294. The impressive gatehouse and curtain walls are of the later date. The problems associated with the defence of a keep, and which were particularly severe with a square structure, are illustrated by the mine tunnel to be seen here. The driving of a tunnel beneath the corner of the keep at Rochester in 1215 brought down the whole corner turret and it was only the existence of the internal cross-wall that allowed the defence to continue. Round towers were less vulnerable. The polygonal tower at Orford was a less than perfect attempt to combat the problem. Open daily 9am to 6pm.

The museum shows a collection of 23 aircraft or parts of aircraft from World War I to the present. On the same site there is a Royal Observer Corps display and a museum and memorial to the US 466th Bomb Group.

Lowestoft was bombarded by the German Navy in World War I and in World War II suffered heavy attack from the air when it was the headquarters of the Royal Naval Patrol Service. The service was, at the outbreak of the war, manned by fishermen in trawlers and drifters requisitioned for patrol duties. They were later joined by men from other professions and the vessels used were equally varied. The memorial carries the names of 2,401 men of the Service who lost their lives at sea and have no known grave.

In what was the control tower of Station 139 memorabilia of the US 8th Air Force and 100th Bomb Group are preserved. The collection includes photographs and documents. Occasional special events and reunions take place.

A Norman motte and bailey with a chapel and various later alterations. The keep is robust and the earthwork of the bailey rises to 40 feet.

PETERBOROUGH

Tourist information: 45 Bridge Street. Tel: (01733) 317336.

There was a prisoner-of-war camp near by at Norman Cross during the Napoleonic Wars, and the museum has a large collection of ships and military models made by the prisoners out of bone. There are also items of military interest as part of the other displays.

Of a castle with two outstanding historical associations there remains only a series of grassy mounds. Here Richard III was born and Mary, Queen of Scots was executed.

A Norman motte and bailey was built overlooking the crossing of the River Nene in the 12th century and the remains of the motte still stand here. The original moat was filled in when the inner bailey was extended in the 14th century and the keep rebuilt in stone. The new bailey was protected on the south-west by the river from which a moat was cut, starting some 150 yards from the modern bridge and curving anti-clockwise within the space between the river and the modern farm track. The great hall stood in the south-eastern corner. At much the same time an outer bailey was added, with a moat running from the modern bridge to the right of the road into the village, and then turning right north-east

Norfolk and Suffolk Aviation Museum
The Street, Flixton. Tel: (01986) 896644.

Lowestoft Naval Memorial
Belle Vue Gardens, Lowestoft, 25 miles SE by A146.

100th Bomb Group Memorial Museum
Common Road, Dickleburgh, nr Diss. Tel: (01379) 740708.

New Buckenham Castle
New Buckenham, 15 miles SW by B1113. Tel: (01953) 860374. Open Monday to Saturday 8am to 5.30pm. Key from garage opposite.

Peterborough Museum
Priestgate. Tel: (01733) 343329. Open Tuesday to Saturday.

Fotheringhay Castle
Fotheringhay, 7 miles E by A605 and minor road. Open site.

of the farm track and broadening into a lake before turning back to the river by joining the mill stream. Much of this can be worked out on the ground.

North-west of the castle stands the curiously proportioned parish church. It is all that remains of the buildings of the College of St Mary and All Saints which was a Chantry college. With the help of the booklet (which also has details of the castle) on sale within, a visit is rewarding. The noble buildings of Fotheringhay were falling into ruin by the early 17th century and in 1635 the castle was entirely demolished.

Spanhoe Airfield, Station 493

Harringworth, 14 miles E by A47, A43 and minor road via Laxton.

Originally called Wakerley when built in 1943, 315th Troop Carrier Group of the US 9th Air Force were stationed here from February 1944. They were reinforced by 309th and 340th Troop Carrier Squadrons and by April there were 60 C-47s (Dakotas) on station. On D-Day 48 C-47s carried men of the US 82nd Airborne Division into action at Ste-Mère-Eglise. The 315th were in continuous action during Operation Market-Garden, the airborne element of the offensive directed towards Arnhem in September 1944. Two serials of 45 C-47s delivered 664 and 690 men of the 82nd Airborne to the area of the River Maas and the next day 27 aircraft carried British troops to Ginkel Heath. The attempt to drop men of the 1st Polish Paratroop Brigade on 21 September resulted in the loss of five aircraft and the damage of many others, but the next sortie two days later achieved the delivery of 565 men of the 1st Polish to Overasselt. In Operation Varsity, the crossing of the Rhine, the 315th lost 19 C-47s when carrying the British 6th Airborne Division. A memorial obelisk to the 315th stands on the approach road to the airfield. A mid-air collision of two C-47s on 8 July 1944 resulted in the loss of 8 US airmen and 26 Polish troops. The wreckage fell at Tinwell, just east of Stamford, and there is a memorial to them in Tinwell Church.

Memorial window

Weldon Church, on A43 E of Corby.

The 401st Bombardment Group (Heavy) of the US 8th Air Force flew B-17s out of Deenthorpe in World War II and a memorial window to them is in the church. The 20th Fighter Group of the 8th Air Force was stationed at King's Cliffe airfield, eight miles north-east on the Wansford road. The 351st Bombardment Group were at Polebrook, east of Oundle by the A427.

Rockingham Castle

Rockingham, N of Corby on A6003, 17 miles E by A605, A427 and A6116. Tel: (01536) 770240. Open April to September Sunday, Thursday, Bank Holiday Mondays and Tuesday in August 1.30pm to 5.30pm.

The relic of the original motte and bailey can still be discerned here, though the castle has been much changed as it has been in continuous occupation from the time of William the Conqueror to the present day. The most striking addition is the magnificent gatehouse with its huge drum towers, built in the late 13th century. It was a royal castle from its foundation until 1530, when Henry VIII granted it to Edward Watson whose family is still in residence. The castle was stormed by Parliamentarian troops in 1643 and starred in the television serial about that conflict, *By the Sword Divided*.

Grafton Underwood Airfield

Geddington to Grafton Underwood road, 18 miles SE by A605, A427 and A43.

The 384th Bombardment Group (Heavy) of the US 8th Air Force was based at Grafton Underwood. The first and last bombing missions flown in World War II by the USAAF were from here in 1943 and 1945, and a granite memorial stands at the side of the main runway along this road. There is also a memorial window in the church.

TILBURY

Tourist information: Granada Motorway Service Area, M25 Thurrock. Tel: (01708) 863733.

A magnificent example, the largest and best preserved, of a 17th-century fort. The Dutch raid on the Medway in 1667 led to a huge programme of coastal fortification. Here the old West Tilbury Blockhouse was replaced in the 1670s and 1680s by a substantial fort built by Sir Bernard de Gomme. It is a classic pentagonal bastioned structure with a covered way and double wet moats. It faced New Tavern Fort across the river at Gravesend to which a ferry can be taken across the river.

Tilbury Fort
E, off A126. English Heritage. Tel: (01375) 858489. Open April to October 10am to 6pm, November to March Wednesday to Sunday 10am to 4pm.

The defences of the Thames were supplemented with new forts downstream during the Napoleonic Wars and Tilbury was strengthened in the 1860s by modification of the riverside bastions to take RMLs and, later, 12-pounder quick-firers which can be seen today. The barracks, powder magazines and casemates are open to visitors and a World War II anti-aircraft gun is also to be seen and, on occasion, fired.

During the war scare of the 1860s, when the possibility of a French invasion seemed serious, the defence lines of the Thames were moved eastwards to form the Thames Advanced Line with new fortifications around Chatham and the construction of new forts east of Tilbury. This casemated fortress is a fine example of Victorian military architecture. It later had 6-inch and 12-pounder guns mounted on the roof. In World War II controlled minefields were adopted as part of the defensive system, operated from reinforced concrete towers (XDOs) such as the example here. Guided tours take visitors to the magazines and the roof. Displays include (telephone to check) a World War II display team, Thameside Aviation Museum and military vehicles.

Coalhouse Fort
Princess Margaret Road, East Tilbury, 3 miles E by minor roads. Tel: (01375) 859673. Open February to November last Sunday in the month and Bank Holidays 12 noon to 4pm (1pm to 5pm summer time).

The defence of the Thames was not a concern exclusive to more recent times. Edward III in the Hundred Years War was equally fearful of French incursion and built here and at Queenborough on the Isle of Sheppey across the river. When work began in 1361 there was already a modest castle on the site which was massively modified by the construction of the east curtain wall with two huge drum towers to dominate the outlook over the river and strike fear into any approaching invader. The circular castle was given a new main gate on the north with a barbican before it and a half-round tower to one side. The domestic arrangements catered for the King's comfort as this was a favourite residence. Edward's chamber was well heated and glazed and a new chapel was built alongside, both of these buildings being battlemented to add to the castle's daunting bulk when viewed from the south. The eastern curtain and the remains of the drum towers still stand, the rest requires imagination.

Hadleigh Castle
S of Hadleigh, 14 miles NE by A13. English Heritage. Tel: (01760) 755161. Open site.

HMS *Lobstersmack*
Holehaven Creek, Canvey Island

A River Emergency Service base was established by the Port of London Authority in the Lobstersmack pub in 1939. In 1940 the Royal Navy took over and most of the men entered the Royal Navy Patrol Service. The pub survives.

NORTH MIDLANDS

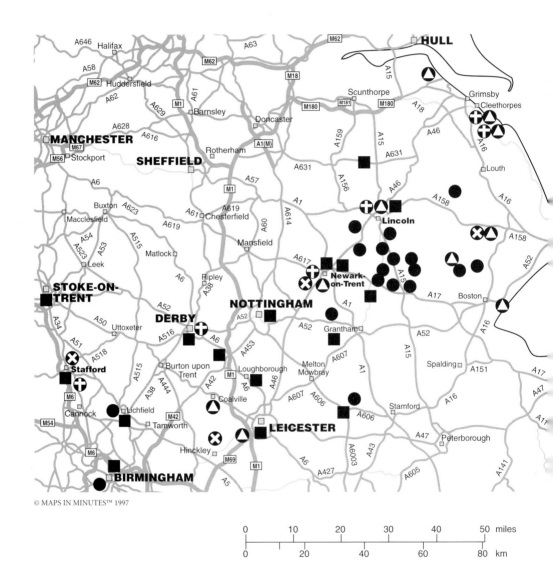

© MAPS IN MINUTES™ 1997

0	10	20	30	40	50 miles
0	20	40	60	80	km

The mighty waterway of the River Trent hooks around the south of the daunting hills of the Pennines and alongside the high land occupied by Birmingham and Leicester to flow north to the Humber through wide, flat country, the mountainous spine of England to the west and the plains of Lincolnshire to the east. The Roman Fosse Way had to descend from the hills after passing Leicester as it made its way to Newark-on-Trent and towards Lincoln where it met Ermine Street, which had made use of the last finger of higher land coming north from Grantham. From Lincoln the Roman route to York lay across the Humber, acceptable for low-volume traffic in dry weather, but when winter floods swelled the rivers, an inland route by Doncaster was used. The line of the modern A1 follows close to the latter, and more practical, route. The region was thus, for centuries, a crossroads. Traffic from the north and north-east chose here the line for London or the line for Bristol. The country was too open to encourage laying traps for enemies in the east and too difficult for manoeuvre in the west, so battles were few. The castles built here, as further south, were more for local control than for defence against outsiders.

It was not until Lincolnshire became the front line in World War II that military installations proliferated. The number of airfields here is staggering. The massive aerial assault on Germany was mounted largely from this region and neighbouring East Anglia. It is rich in historical associations for Americans, Canadians and other Commonwealth people as well as for the British. This landscape also witnessed the departure of the airborne forces for the great gamble of Operation Market-Garden. Equally, it lies between Germany and tempting targets for their bombers in Britain, requiring the construction of fighter stations to resist them. The graveyards bear witness to the cost.

Key to map
✕ Battlefield
⬢ Castle/Fort
✚ Cemetery
■ Museum
● Other

DERBY

Tourist information: Assembly Rooms, Market Place. Tel: (01332) 255802.

Regimental Museum of the 9th/12th Lancers
Derby City Museum and Art Gallery, Strand. Tel: (01332) 255581. Open daily.

The museum contains a section devoted to the 9th/12th Lancers (Prince of Wales's), relating, with the help of audio aids, their history from 1715. The story of the local Yeomanry, Militia and Volunteer units since 1689 is also covered. Items in the Imperial German collection are to be seen by appointment only.

Derby (Nottingham Road) Cemetery
In the eastern suburbs, between Nottingham Road and the canal.

The Commonwealth War Graves Commission plot is in the south-west of the cemetery. From World War I there are 1 Australian, 4 Canadian, 1 India/Pakistan and 187 United Kingdom graves, while from World War II there are 134 United Kingdom graves. Many of those who lie here died of wounds, and alongside them are men of the Home Guard and of the RAF.

East Midlands Aeropark
East Midlands International Airport. 9 miles SE by A6. Tel: (01332) 810621.

The overall objective of the museum is to tell the story of the science of flight and the development of civil aircraft, but there are also some post-World War II military jet aircraft, including an Avro Vulcan B2.

Hanbury Crater
Hanbury, 10 miles SW by A516, A515 and minor road E.

One of the major hazards to civilians in World War II was the vast quantity of ammunition and explosives stored for military use. The workings of the gypsum mines south and east of Hanbury were used for storage of bombs. The store was managed by RAF Fauld. In November 1944 there were 14,975 tons of explosive in store and work was in hand to repair damaged bombs, extracting exploder charges. For this bronze chisels were used – except when someone broke the rules. On 27 November the whole store exploded.

The blast hurled earth, rock and trees into the sky, leaving a crater 900 feet long, 700 feet wide and 80 feet deep. It destroyed a 6 million-gallon reservoir and released a wave of mud and water, creating a landscape reminiscent of a World War I battlefield. The buildings of Hanbury were largely destroyed, including the Cock Inn (now rebuilt). Seventy people died, of whom only 26 were working at RAF Fauld, and about 20 more were injured. The crater, although fenced off, may be seen today with a memorial next to it.

LEICESTER

Tourist information: 7/9 Every Street, Town Hall Square. Tel: (0116) 265 0555.

Jewry Wall Museum and Site
St Nicholas Circle, city centre, A47. Tel: (0116) 544766. Open Monday to Saturday 10am to 5.30pm, Sunday 2pm to 5.30pm.

The great Roman road of the Fosse Way can still be traced in modern roads from Cirencester running up through High Cross (Venonis) and Leicester (Ratae) to Lincoln (Lindum). One of the largest sections of Roman wall surviving is here, standing more than 30 feet high. It used to form one side of the exercise hall of the civic baths. The museum presents the archaeology and history of the county up to 1485.

The museum of the Royal Leicestershire Regiment is housed in a 15th-century gatehouse and displays memorabilia of the regiment, the 17th Foot, from 1688 to 1964.

The museum includes a gallery devoted to the history of the volunteer soldier in Leicestershire and Rutland, including the Yeomanry and the Rifle Volunteers. Of particular interest to New Zealand visitors is the 58th (Rutlandshire) Regiment exhibit in the 18th-century riding school. Open daily.

In February 1944 the USAAF 52nd Troop Carrier Wing moved here from Sicily and set up its HQ in Exton Hall, two miles south-east as 316th Troop Carrier Group started to arrive. By the end of the month 52 C-47s and C-53s were on station, as were men of the US 82nd Airborne Division. On the night of 5 June 72 aircraft of the 316th carried 1,256 paratroops of the 82nd on their mission just west of Ste-Mère-Eglise as part of the D-Day operations. The 316th was also active in Operation Market-Garden, the thrust for Arnhem. On 17 September 1944 87 C-47s and 3 C-53s flew 1,453 paratroops and 540 para-packs to the drop area near Nijmegen and the following day they towed 82 CG-4A gliders to the battle area. On 23 September 89 gliders were towed to Overasselt and three days later 72 aircraft flew troops and supplies to an airstrip near Grave. Cottesmore was handed back to the RAF in July 1945 and Lancasters of 1668 Heavy Conversion Unit moved in from Bottesford. In March 1948 No 7 Flying Training School took over, until disbanded in 1954. Canberras of 15, 44, 57 and 149 Squadrons were briefly in occupation before the station was developed for V-bombers. The Victors of 10 and 15 Squadrons were here from 1958 to 1964 when the Vulcans of 9, 12 and 35 Squadrons took over until 1969. Between 1981 and 1992 the Tri-National Tornado Training Unit trained over 2,500 aircrew here. A memorial plaque to the USAAF Troop Carrier units stands outside the station.

It is interesting to compare this work with the castle at Ashby-de-la-Zouch as both were built by the same man and the difference between them illustrates the changing ideas of the time. Kirby Muxloe was a new castle started by William, Lord Hastings in the last week of October 1480. The old manor house was there, and was probably intended for replacement as work proceeded, but Hastings was executed in 1483 and building stopped.

The plan is clear, a symmetrical enclave within a broad moat, with substantial corner turrets and a solid gatehouse. There was no intention to build a tower-keep. Artillery was to be an essential element of the defence and gunports were built into the walls. Their field of fire, however, was very limited and their positioning meant that some of them were directed at other parts of the castle rather than any attackers, showing how new the concept was to the designer. The castle is also one of the earliest to be constructed in brick as well as stone, and the master mason who had worked on Tattershall, John Couper, was engaged on the job. By October 1481 the site had been cleared and foundations dug, and in the winter of 1481–2 the work was covered with straw against the frost. Only

The Magazine

Oxford Street, city centre, A47/A50. Tel: (0116) 555889.

Rutland County Museum

Catmos Street, Oakham, 18 miles E by A47 and A6003. Tel: (01572) 723654.

Cottesmore Airfield

Cottesmore, 4 miles NE of Oakham by B668.

Kirby Muxloe Castle

Kirby Muxloe, 4 miles W by A47 and B5380. English Heritage. Tel: (01533) 386886. Open April to October weekends and Bank Holidays 10am to 1pm and 2pm to 6pm.

the stonemasons worked on in a shed on the site. Building continued the next year and started once more in spring 1483 when the tower and gatehouse reached their present state.

Ashby-de-la-Zouch Castle

Ashby-de-la-Zouch, 12 miles NW by A50. English Heritage. Tel: (01530) 413343. Open April to October 10am to 6pm, November to March Wednesday to Sunday 10am to 1pm and 2pm to 4pm.

William, Lord Hastings was a supporter of the House of York in the Wars of the Roses and was rewarded in 1474 with the ownership of this castle which, at the time, was a large manor house with a hall, chamber block and vaulted kitchen (recently rebuilt). To this he added a substantial tower-keep at the centre of the south-facing wall. The keep had its own well and the ground floor was window-less and used for storage. The kitchens were on the first floor and also had the apparatus for raising the portcullis which closed the entrance to the courtyard. Next came the great hall with a chapel off it and above that the lord's chamber. Rooms for others were in an annex on the east side, seven storeys high and each room with its own garderobe (toilet). The top of the tower was a fighting platform with complex machiolation. Hastings's followers were accommodated in buildings, now gone, around the south court and the final proof of his success and wealth was the large chapel in the north-eastern corner of the court.

The Battle of Bosworth Field, 22 August 1485

Bosworth Battlefield Visitor Centre, Sutton Cheney, near Market Bosworth, 9 miles W by A47, B582, B585 and A447. Open April to October daily 1pm to 6pm, July and August opens at 11am.

As is inevitable when considering events which took place over 500 years ago, there are differing views about the exact location of the battle. The presentation and trails so well made by the Leicestershire County Council favour a site on the north-west of Ambion Hill while others suggest it took place to the south-west. What is not in doubt is the historical significance of the battle.

Richard III was expecting a rival for the throne to land in England, but did not know where. The claimant, Henry Tudor, could have chosen south Wales where he enjoyed local support, or the Hampshire coast which was close to London, so Richard based himself at Nottingham. Henry landed at Milford Haven in Wales on 7 August 1485 and Richard summoned the Duke of Norfolk from East Anglia, the Earl of Northumberland and the Earl of Surrey to meet him at Leicester. Henry had been joined by the Earl of Oxford and moved by way of Shrewsbury and then down Watling Street (the A5) before turning up the old Roman road through Fenny Drayton. The unknown factor in all this was the loyalty of Lord Stanley and his brother Sir William Stanley. Henry had good reason to hope they would join him and Richard attempted to ensure their adherence by holding Lord Stanley's son, Lord Strange, hostage. In the days before the battle Sir William shadowed Henry's progress but did not interfere.

On the evening of 21 August Richard with, perhaps, some 8,000 men encamped on Ambion Hill and Henry with about 6,000 was at White Moors to the south-west. The Stanleys were either both together to the north of Ambion Hill or in two parties at Market Bosworth to the north and Dadlington to the south, numbering some 4,000. On the morning of 22 August Richard's army occupied the western crest of the hill and Henry moved north-east towards him. At that time the area to the south of the hill between it and the modern canal was marsh, so Henry had to file off to his left to come at the King and as he reformed his line Richard's archers opened fire. Norfolk's vanguard held and pushed back Oxford's charge, but failed to break them and in the ensuing hand-to-hand fighting Norfolk fell. Henry's men continued to press forward, but Richard was denied reinforcement from Northumberland who kept his men back. It is said that Richard was unhorsed and that Stanley's men slew him. What is certain is that, with his death, his army lost what little heart they may have had for battle. Henry was crowned in the field and the naked corpse of the last English king to be killed in battle was displayed to the populace of Leicester before burial.

Loughborough War Memorial Museum

A display of medals, badges and other items associated with the local Yeomanry, British and US Airborne forces and with Parachute and Glider Pilot units. The exhibits are shown on three floors of the tower that houses the carillon created as a war memorial by this town, famous for its bell foundry.

Loughborough Carillon, Queen's Park, Loughborough, 9 miles N by A6. Tel: (01509) 263151, ext 2652. Open April to September 2pm to 6pm.

LINCOLN

Tourist information: 9 Castle Hill. Tel: (01522) 529828.
Lincoln was an important Roman town of which relics, such as Newport Arch, are to be seen. It continued in influence thereafter as a Norman stronghold and was the scene of a battle in 1217 when the supporters of the 10-year-old Henry III defeated an army of rebels reinforced with a party of 611 knights and 1,000 foot from France. In World War I the first tanks were made here.

Lincoln Castle

The site of the Roman fort was converted into a castle in 1068. The Norman shell keep survives together with the complete curtain wall with three towers, the eastern gatehouse and part of the barbican.

Castle Hill. Tel: (01522) 511068. Open daily.

Lincoln Cathedral Airman's Chapel

The chapel houses the memorial books of 1 and 5 Groups, Bomber Command, recording the names of the 25,611 personnel who died in World War II. They include 1,140 Australians and 1,233 Canadians. The Bomber Command Memorial consists of stained-glass windows as do the Flying Training Command Memorial and the New Zealand Memorial. A service is held each Thursday at 10.30am in memory of those who gave their lives.

Royal Lincolnshire Regiment Museum

Part of the museum is devoted to the history of the Royal Lincolnshire Regiment and to the Lincolnshire Yeomanry, displaying medals, weapons, pictures and *Flirt*, a World War I Mark IV tank. The regiments have seen service in the American War of Independence, India, the Sudan, the Boer War, World Wars I and II and the Malaya Emergency.

Museum of Lincolnshire Life, The Old Barracks, Burton Road. Tel: (01522) 528448. Open daily.

50 & 61 Squadrons' Museum

The museum commemorates 50 and 61 Squadrons' operations from RAF Skellingthorpe with photographs and other memorabilia. The Squadrons' Book of Remembrance is here.

The Lawn, Union Road. Tel: (01522) 560330. Open Easter to October 10am to 5pm, November to Easter 10am to 4pm.

Lincoln (Newport) Cemetery

North of the Cathedral. Commonwealth War Graves Commission.

There are 260 Commonwealth graves here. From World War I, 5 Australian, 9 Canadian and 126 United Kingdom; from World War II 1 Australian, 18 Canadian, 1 New Zealand, 98 United Kingdom and 1 unidentified. The WWI graves are those of men of the Royal Flying Corps and RAF who were killed in accidents and soldiers who died of wounds. The WWII RAF graves are of men who died in battle or accident in the air.

North Kesteven Airfield Trail

Free guide from Sleaford Tourist Information Centre, The Mill, Money's Yard, Sleaford, Lincs NG34 7TW. Tel: (01529) 414294.

The wide, flat countryside of Lincolnshire made it ideal for the development of heavier-than-air machines in the early years of aviation and for operational use in World Wars I and II. The Trail has been created to enable visitors to locate the active RAF stations and the sites of former airfields. Lincoln itself was a manufacturing centre in the first war, Robey's works producing Sopwiths, Ruston, Proctor & Co BE2 biplanes and Clayton & Shuttleworth also made Sopwiths. The airfields are given below as a circular tour from Lincoln and their locations are described accordingly.

RFC Bracebridge Heath

Bracebridge Heath, 3 miles S by A15.

The Robey's airfield lay to the east of the road. Six Belfast-type hangers were built here by the Royal Flying Corps in 1917, of which four survive. In World War II A V Roe used the hangers to repair Lancasters and the A15 south of the village was used as a taxiway. The prototype Avro 707A and 707C were built here.

RAF Waddington

3 miles S by A15. Parking in public viewing area.

The airfield was first established as a training station for the Royal Flying Corps in 1916. 503 County of Lincoln Squadron, Royal Auxiliary Air Force was based here on its formation in 1926. In the expansion of the RAF in the 1930s 44 and 50 Squadrons were stationed here with Hawker Hinds and then with Handley Page Hampdens which they flew in the early part of World War II. 44 Squadron was equipped with Lancasters in 1941. Near the church is a memorial to the Australian Squadrons 463 and 467. During the Cold War 50 and 83 Squadron operated with Vulcans. Since 1985 AWACS (Airborne Warning and Command Systems) have operated from Waddington and the first Boeing E-3D *Sentry* AEW1 arrived on 4 July 1990 to be operated by 8 Squadron. 51 Squadron, with the Nimrod R, arrived in April 1995. The annual airshow is an event of international importance (information: The Airshow Office, RAF Waddington, Lincoln, LN5 9NB. Tel: (01522) 720271).

RAF Coleby Grange

Boundary Café, 2 miles S by A15.

In 1940 Hurricanes and Defiants operated from the airfield east of the junction with the B1202 (Metheringham) road. The watch tower (private property) of the airfield still stands behind the café. 409 Squadron, Royal Canadian Air Force moved in during the summer of 1941 for nightfighter operations in Beaufighters. In February 1943 410 (RCAF) Squadron took over flying Mosquitos. 307 (Polish) Squadron also operated out of Colby Grange. Between 1958 and 1963 Thor Intermediate Range Ballistic Missiles were sited here in the care of 142 Squadron.

RAF Metheringham
Visitor Centre, West Moor Farm, Martin Moor, 5 miles E of A15 W of junction of B1191 and B1189. Tel: (01526) 378270. Open Easter to October Wednesdays 12 noon to 4pm, weekends and Bank Holidays 12 noon to 5pm.

The airfield opened in October 1943 and the minor road to the east from the B1189 just north of the Visitor Centre is part of a runway, while the first right (opposite which there is a memorial) is part of the perimeter track, leading back towards the Centre. The Lancasters of 106 Squadron arrived in November 1943 to fly their first raid on Berlin a week later. In the next four months the RAF lost 492 aircraft attacking that target. A Book of Remembrance is in Holy Trinity Church in nearby Martin, recording the names of those lost in 57 Lancasters that failed to return to base. The fog dispersal system known as FIDO was installed in 1944. It worked by burning petrol pumped through perforated pipes.

RAF Digby
Scopwick, 4 miles E by B1191. Ops Room visits, tel: (01526) 327200.

In Scopwick village, off Vicarage Lane, the graveyard has the remains of British, American and Canadian flyers, as well as some German. Beyond the village is what was once RAF Scopwick, the new name being adopted in 1920. This was a training establishment until 1937 when 12 Group Fighter Command took over and 46 and 73 Squadrons flew Gloster Gauntlets and Gloster Gladiators here. They re-equipped with Hurricanes before the war. 402 Squadron, Royal Canadian Air Force arrived in December 1940 and flew Hurricanes, Spitfires and Defiants from Digby which became RCAF Digby and still has a maple leaf in its badge. The Lima Sector Ops Room Museum is open on special days.

RFC Anwick
Near Ruskington, 5 miles SE by B1188, then 2 miles E by minor road.

Anwick was the home of 38 Squadron under the command of Major L J E Twisleton-Wykeham-Fiennes in World War I and an important element in the fight against Zeppelins. None were shot down. In World War II Anwick served as a decoy for Digby, with a flare path and beacon at the ready in case of the approach of enemy bombers.

Cranwell Aviation Heritage Centre
Heath Farm, 6 miles W off A17 on minor road to North Rauceby. Tel: (01529) 488490. Open daily April to September 10am to 4.30pm.

The Royal Air Force College at Cranwell, a couple of miles to the north, is celebrated here with an account of its growth from a Royal Naval Air Service Station to become the first Military Air Academy in the world, and its continuing importance today. The history of the airfield is also told. There, for example, Britain's first jet aircraft, the Gloster E28/39, flew.

Cranwell Primary School
4 Bagdad Road, Cranwell. Tel: (01400) 261271. Open mid-April to mid-July, Sunday, 2pm to 4.30pm.

A former RAF house presents a picture of life on the home front in World War II.

Zeppelin Raid Memorial
Washingborough, 3 miles E by B1190.

Eight stained-glass windows commemorate a Zeppelin raid on the village in September 1916.

RFC Leadenham

NE of Leadenham, 4 miles W by A17 and N by minor road to E of and parallel to A607.

Just after the turn to Brauncewell one brick building is all that remains of this World War I airfield. Four BE2e biplanes of 38 Squadron were based here to counter Zeppelin raids and from August 1918 90 Squadron operated from here with Avro 504 Night Fighters.

RAF Wellingore

Near picnic site S of Wellingore, 2 miles N on minor road.

If, after locating the picnic site, you turn right (signed Temple Bruer) and right again onto Ermine Street (the Roman road to Lincoln) the old RAF field can be found on the right. It was used in 1914–18, but it was in World War II that it was important as a satellite to RAF Digby, when the main field was under attack.

RAF Swinderby

Between Thurlby and A46, 9 miles NW by minor roads.

The airfield closed in 1993, having opened in 1940 when 300 (Polish) and 301 (Polish) Squadrons arrived with Fairey Battles. They were replaced with Wellington bombers in late 1940. There are plaques in Norton Disney church, to the south, in memory of these flyers. In 1941 50 Squadron arrived and the Australians of 455 Squadron soon followed, both with Hampden bombers. Manchesters and Lancasters then appeared on the scene. After the war 8 Flying Training School was set up here with Vampires and Varsitys. The exhibition in the Methodist Hall, Swinderby, is open daily from 10am to 4pm.

Coastal Defences
South of R. Humber.

World War I gun towers at North Killingholme, Haile Sand Fort, Cleethorpes and pillbox at Humberston.

RAF Skellingthorpe

Skellingthorpe Heritage Room, Community Centre, Lincoln Road, Skellingthorpe, 6 miles NE by A46 and NW by minor road. Open daily April to October 10am to 5pm, November to March 10am to 4pm.

The airfield lay on the other side of the A43 where the Birchwood development now stands. In 1941 50 Squadron and 455 Squadron, Royal Australian Air Force flew Hampdens here. 50 Squadron then acquired Manchesters and Lancasters. In 1943 1485 (Bomber) Gunnery Flight arrived with Wellington and Martinet aircraft. 61 Squadron came in late 1943. There is a memorial near Birchwood Leisure Centre, Birchwood Avenue.

Grimsby (Scartho Road) Cemetery
South side of Grimsby, 28 miles NE by A46. Commonwealth War Graves Commission.

Grimsby suffered severely from enemy bombing in World War II and both service and civilian casualties are buried here. To the graves of naval personnel of both wars were added those of men of RAF Bomber Command in World War II. In the southern part of the cemetery there are 274 United Kingdom graves of 1914–18 and 1 Australian, 5 Canadian, 3 New Zealand and 244 United Kingdom of World War II in the south-east.

Cleethorpes Cemetery
Near Beacon Hill, W of Cleethorpes, S of Grimsby.

At the south-western boundary, in a single grave, are 24 men of the Manchester Regiment who were killed on 1 April 1916 in an air-raid by a Zeppelin. There are 77 United Kingdom graves of that war, and 79 of World War II, as well as 1 New Zealand grave, in the south corner. There are men of the Royal Navy, the Merchant Navy and the Fishing Fleet who were killed in action. There are also servicemen's graves in the main cemetery.

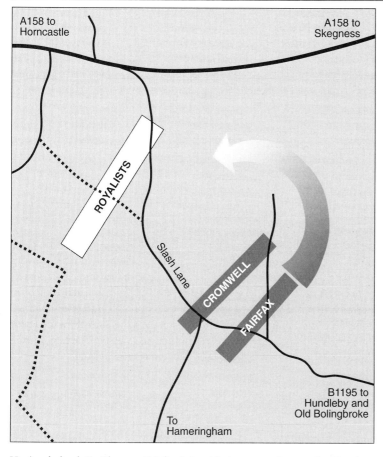

Chain Home Radar Station

Stenigot, 15 miles E, by A158 to Wragby and minor roads via Market Stainton.

In World War II Radio Direction Finding (RDF), now known as radar, stations were organised in the Chain Home network. The tower, listed, survives here, but not the ACE HIGH disk array – destroyed by official vandals.

Having helped Sir Thomas Fairfax bring his horse south over the Humber, Oliver Cromwell went with him to join the Earl of Manchester who was besieging a Royalist force at Bolingbroke Castle. The Governor of Newark, Sir John Henderson, and Sir William Widdrington were on their way to raise the siege and ran into elements of Manchester's horse at Horncastle on 10 October, putting them to flight, and the next day they continued for Bolingbroke. As they turned south off what is now the A158 Cromwell and Fairfax were coming up from Bolingbroke to Winceby, each side with some 2,500 horsemen, one-fifth of the Royalists being dragoons. From the Winceby ridge, probably where a lane now runs south to Hameringham, the poor organisation of the Royalists was evident. Cromwell was quick to charge and pushed back the dragoons into the Royalist second line, though at the cost of losing his horse. Fairfax seized the initiative and passed round Cromwell's right before veering to the left to meet the Royalist right wing which was to the left of the road, just about where it kinks northwards. On the southern edge of the field to the south of this road and in the woods to the west there are the remains of ancient hedgerows, and it is said that Fairfax caught and destroyed his adversaries in just such an enclosure. The road is called Slash Lane and the shallow valley Slash Hollow.

The Battle of Winceby, 11 October 1643

30 miles E via Horncastle by A158 and S by B1195 Spilsby road.

Bolingbroke Castle

Old Bolingbroke, 3 miles SE of Winceby. English Heritage. Open daily April to September 9am to 9pm, October to March to 7pm.

In the 13th century the Earl of Chester built both at Beeston and here, following the new style of creating a strong curtain wall with flanking turrets rather than a Norman-style keep or motte and bailey. This hexagonal castle has suffered much damage, not least at the hands of the Parliamentarians in the Civil War. It was the birthplace of Henry IV in 1367.

Tattershall Castle

Tattershall, 15 miles SE on A153. National Trust. Tel: (01526) 342543. Open April to October Saturday to Wednesday and Bank Holiday Mondays 10.30am to 5.30pm, November and December weekends 10.30am to 4pm.

Ralph Lord Cromwell had served under Henry V at Agincourt (1415) and became treasurer of England for a decade from 1433. He was experienced in war and also wealthy. His great tower-house at Tattershall was not, therefore, just a house, for the outer defences of the castle were enhanced with the addition of a second outer moat and the approach was secured by three bridges, all commanded from the tower, and each with its own gatehouse. The tower itself was, however, something entirely new to England. It was built, in about 1440, in brick, an expensive material, and finished in lavish decorative style. There were already the usual buildings of a medieval castle here, a great hall, chambers, kitchens and a chapel. In the tower he made luxurious apartments for himself. On the ground floor there was a court-room with a fine fireplace and above it a hall, connected to the kitchen in the building to the south, with closets in the turrets and a garderobe (toilet) on the north. On the second floor an audience chamber is approached by a ceremonial corridor and above this again is the Lord's personal bedchamber. Here Cromwell could not only be secure from such enemies as William Tailboys, a local squire, but also live in a style that displayed his standing.

Freiston Shore

E of Boston.

World War II battery for two 6-inch guns.

RAF Battle of Britain Memorial Flight

RAF Coningsby, nr Tattershall. Tel: (01526) 344041. Open weekdays.

The collection has nine historic aircraft, all in flying condition. There are five Spitfires, a Hurricane IIc and the Lancaster bomber *City of Lincoln*. Guided tours are given and there is a Visitor Centre.

Lincolnshire Aviation Heritage Centre

East Kirkby, 7 miles E of Coningsby by A155. Tel: (01790) 763207.

The Centre is on the former airfield of 5 Group Bomber Command. The control tower has been restored to its original condition and there is a wealth of historical material, including an Avro Lancaster bomber and a Bison mobile pillbox. Closed Sundays.

Bomber County Aviation Museum

Caenby Corner Estate, Hemswell Cliff, 12 miles N of Lincoln by A15 and A631. Tel: (01472) 240744. Open Sundays 10am to 5pm.

Established on the former bomber airfield, the museum has a Canberra T19, a Hunter, a Vampire, a Mystere and a Sycamore helicopter. There are also engines, equipment and clothing on display.

NEWARK-ON-TRENT

Tourist information: Castlegate. Tel: (01636) 78962.

Newark was a Royalist stronghold in the Civil War and there are many sites of interest, including the Governor's House and the Millgate Museum. Details from the tourist information centre. Less than a mile south of the railway station, on London Road, is Newark-on-Trent Cemetery where the Commonwealth War Graves Commission plot has 49 graves of World War I and 484 of World War II.

The castle was an important element of the Royalist defence of the town in the Civil War and was therefore substantially decommissioned by Parliament after their victory. The North Gate of 1170 survives, as do other features, such as the curtain wall overlooking the River Trent, that still make it worthy of a visit.

Newark was besieged by Parliamentarian forces three times in the Civil War, first in February 1643 and again from 29 February to 21 March 1644. On that occasion Prince Rupert relieved the defenders in a typically dashing action against the 6,000 men of Sir John Meldrum. The defence was commanded by Lord Loughborough who harried Meldrum with some success while persuading Rupert to join him to repel the besiegers. On 20 March Rupert and Loughborough started a night march around the south of the town to catch Meldrum in a trap between the river and the northern flank of Newark and force his surrender. The defences of the town have mostly disappeared, but the Queen's Sconce survives. It is a huge earthwork gun platform with bastions at each corner and surrounded by a ditch. It is a magnificent example of 17th-century work. It stood outside the town walls alongside the River Devon, as did another, the King's Sconce, north-east of the town next to the Trent. For a good idea of both the defensive works and the trenches surrounding the town built by the attackers, the maps in the Newark Museum in Appletongate are very informative. The final siege ended on 5 May 1646 with the King's surrender to the Scots at Kelham, having previously taken dinner at the Saracen's Head in Southwell, seven miles to the west of Newark.

The museum is located around the World War II aircraft dispersal point of RAF Winthorpe, from which Lancaster, Halifax and Sterling bombers operated. Half of the collection is shown over cover and it includes aircraft of the RAF, the Fleet Air Arm, the US Air Force, the French Air Force, the Royal Norwegian Air Force and the Royal Danish Air Force. In addition to aircraft of World War II there is a Hastings as used in the Berlin Airlift, a Canberra, a Mystere and a Sea Hawk of the Suez Crisis, a Shackelton that took part in the aerial surveillance carried out by the Beirra Patrols in the Rhodesian UDI, a Falklands War Vulcan and aircraft that took part in the Gulf War. Special event days give visitors the opportunity to inspect some of the aircraft from inside.

Although the victory at Bosworth Field was complete, Henry VII's grip on the throne was not entirely secure. A Yorkist group commanded by the Earl of Lincoln had Lambert Simnel crowned as Edward VI in Dublin in May 1487 and landed in Lancashire with 2,000 Swiss and German mercenaries under Martin Schwartz and 4,000 Irish troops. They made for York which they failed to take, but forced Henry's followers to stay there as they turned south with their numbers grown to some 8,000 men. Henry met George Stanley, Lord Strange, near Nottingham and moved to meet Lincoln. The Yorkists crossed the Trent at Fiskerton, by a ford now long gone, and took position on a ridge. From the road off the A46 towards St Oswald's church, Humber Lane runs to the left towards the ridge, and from the road after it turns left beyond the church a footpath goes to the

Newark Castle

Castlegate. Tel: (01636) 79403. Open April to October daily except Monday and Thursday 1pm to 5pm.

The Queen's Sconce

Devon Park, SW of town, off A46.

Fulbeck

10 miles E by A17 and A607.

Fulbeck Hall, HQ of British 1st Airborne, has a display about Operation Market-Garden. The airfield was base to US 434 and 442 Troop Carrier Group.

Newark Air Museum

The Airfield, Winthorpe, 3 miles NE off A46. Tel: (01636) 707170. Open March to September daily 10am to 5pm, 6pm weekends, October to February daily 10am to 4pm.

The Battle of Stoke Field, 16 June 1487

East Stoke, 3 miles SW by A46, and W by minor road.

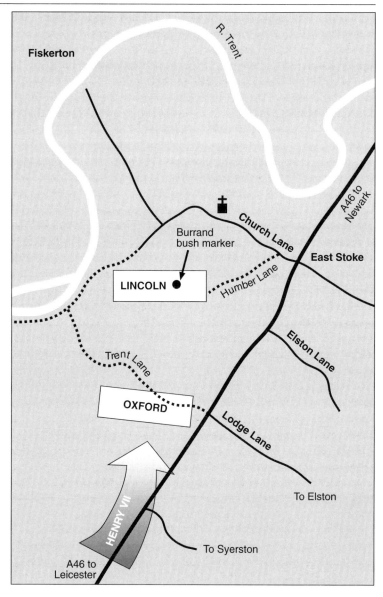

The Battle of Stoke Field

western end of the high ground, with a view to the river crossing to the north-west. Trent Lane, a track opposite Lodge Lane, off the A46 south of East Stoke, is roughly the position reached by Henry's army.

The Earl of Oxford, leading the royal vanguard, was coming up the Fosse Way (now A46) when he saw the Yorkist force off to his left. He hurried his men to face them and Lincoln seized the opportunity to attack. Oxford's men were pushed back and suffered high casualties, but the rest of Henry's army eventually came up and the balance swung in their favour. In the centre the Swiss and German soldiers fought on doggedly, but the rest of the Yorkist force turned tail, pursued by the victors. As they made their way back to the river they were cut down in such numbers (4,000 died) that the gully that runs through the wood is now called the Red Gutter. Schwartz fell, the King's standard was planted in a burrand bush on the ridge, where a memorial stone stands, and the Tudor dynasty was secure. Lord Lovell, who had been with Lincoln, escaped across the river and hid in a concealed cellar at his home at Minster Lovell, near Burford in Oxfordshire. In 1728, when building a chimney, workmen found a skeleton sitting at a table in a vault, possibly the refugee rebel. Memorials of the battle are at the church.

Bottesford Airfield, Station 481

Between Bottesford and Normanton, 9 miles S by A1 and minor road from Long Bennington.

The airfield lies immediately to the east of the road between the villages. It opened in the autumn of 1941 when 207 Squadron, Bomber Command, arrived with Manchesters. In March 1942 they were re-equipped with Lancasters and flew bombing raids over Germany. In November the Australian-manned 467 Squadron replaced them, training with Lancasters before making their first raid in January 1943. In August US Troop Carrier Command took over the field for use as a reception base for C-47 (Dakota) groups arriving from the USA. 436th and 440th Troop Carrier Groups trained here with paratroops of the 82nd Airborne Division in preparation for D-Day. RAF No 5 Group took over in July 1944 and 1668 Heavy Conversion Unit was re-formed. The airfield closed in August 1945. The property was sold for commercial use in 1962 and the Roseland Group Ltd has its offices in the restored control tower, on the staircase of which are memorial plaques to the units that served here. The building is private property.

The Queen's Royal Lancers Regimental Museum

Belvoir Castle, nr Grantham, 16 miles S by A1, A52 and minor roads. Tel: (0115) 957 3295. Limited opening April to October.

Housed in the castle, which was rebuilt in the 19th century after destruction in war and by accidental fire, the museum tells the story of the 16th/5th The Queen's Royal Lancers and the 17th/21st Lancers cavalry regiments. Battles and campaigns covered include the American War of Independence, the Battle of Waterloo, the charge of the Light Brigade at Balaclava, the Battle of Omdurman, the Boer War and World Wars I and II. Amongst the other attractions offered by the castle are medieval jousting tournaments on certain weekends.

Sherwood Foresters' Regimental Museum

The Castle, Nottingham, 21 miles SW by A612. Tel: (0115) 948 3504/946 5415. Open daily.

Part of the Nottingham Castle Museum, the museum of the Nottinghamshire and Derbyshire Regiment, the 45th and 95th Foot, contains shakos, medals, uniforms, weapons and campaign memorabilia.

STAFFORD

Tourist information: The Ancient High House, Greengate Street. Tel: (01785) 240204.

Museum of the Staffordshire Yeomanry

The Ancient High House, Greengate Street. Tel: (01785) 240204.

The Staffordshire Yeomanry (Queen's Own Royal Regiment) was raised in 1794. The museum contains audio-visual displays, uniforms, medals and other memorabilia. There is an important photograph collection. The building in which the museum is housed is said to be the largest timber-framed townhouse in England. Open Monday to Saturday.

The Battle of Hopton Heath, 19 March 1643

Hopton, 2 miles NE by B5066 and minor road to E or A518 and minor road to NW.

After his failure at Brentford, Charles I sought to secure the centre of the country by establishing garrisons at Newark, Ashby-de-la-Zouche, Wolverhampton and Stafford, where Henry Hastings was in command. At the end of February 1643 Lord Brooke was on his way to attack Stafford, but he was shot while inspecting the fieldworks around Lichfield. Sir John Gell took over the command and, with Brooke's Purplecoats, took Lichfield and then planned to meet up with Sir William Brereton to invest Stafford. For the Royalists, the Earl of Northampton moved to Hastings's support from Warwickshire.

Brereton moved south along the line of the A51 and turned at Sandon towards Stafford on what is now the B5066 while Gell moved up the A51 route to Weston before turning along the line of the A518. Within Lane runs between these two roads just north-east of Hopton, and a footpath goes north-east alongside the RAF Stafford Depot a little way south-east of the junction with Wilmorehill Lane. On the morning of 19 March Gell arrived and drew up his force along the ridge up to which the footpath runs, with his west flank at the edge of the woods and the left, his dragoons, on the A518 to the east. Brereton arrived by 2pm and placed his dragoons on Gell's right. It was a Sunday and Northampton and Hastings were, at 11 o'clock, in church when the news of the

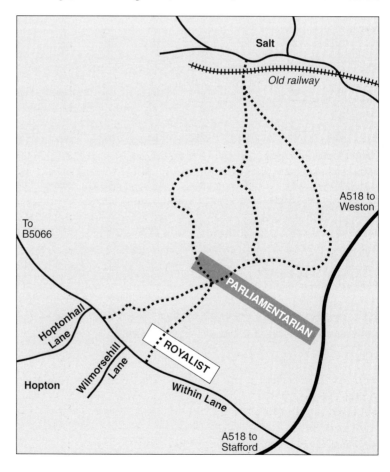

enemy's approach was brought to them. They were galvanised into action, rushing off with about 1,000 men, the horse in front and the footmen trailing along behind.

At 3pm the Royalist dragoons were attacking the dragoons on the Parliamentary flanks and succeeded in routing them, leaving Gell's centre to continue the fight. After a few shots from his great cannon, Roaring Meg, Northampton led a charge which disposed of the remaining cavalry opposition, but the foot, on their ridge, held on, protected by the rise of ground pitted, as it was, with rabbit holes. The Royalist horse fell back to Within Lane once more, regrouped and charged again. The musketeers, covered by pikemen, held them off and Northampton's horse, putting a hoof in a rabbit hole, pitched the Earl off amongst the enemy where he was killed. Hastings gathered the Royalists for yet another charge but that, too, was thrown back in the failing light. No more attacks were made. Gell withdrew his gallant band under cover of darkness. Stafford was saved and the Royalists had a victory, but at the price of a general's life.

Wall Roman Site
Off A5 at Wall, S of Lichfield. English Heritage. Open daily April to October 10am to 1pm, 2pm to 6pm.

The foundations of an inn and a bath-house remain of this staging-post on Roman Watling Street. Finds are to be seen in the museum.

Reginald Mitchell, the designer of the Spitfire, is commemorated here by the exhibition of a late model, a Mark XVIE. Apart from that there is little of military interest except for some archive memoirs of factory workers' experiences in World War II.

Stoke City Museum
Warner Street, Hanley, Stoke-on-Trent, 21 miles N by A34 and A500. Tel: (01782) 202173. Open daily.

The Commonwealth War Graves Commission graveyard has the substantial number of 355 graves of World War I. Such concentrations usually occur near hospitals to which the wounded were evacuated. There are also 33 graves of World War II.

Cannock Chase War Cemetery
On the moor near Brocton, 4 miles SE by A34 and minor road.

The Staffordshire Regiment (the Prince of Wales's) was formed by the amalgamation of the South and North Staffordshires in 1959. The former was raised as the 38th Foot in 1705 and the North Staffs as the 64th Foot in 1758. The campaigns and battles represented include the American War of Independence, the Sikh Wars, the Crimean War, the Zulu War, Egypt, Sudan, the Boer War, World Wars I and II and the Gulf War. The 2nd South Staffords fought with distinction at Arnhem. The old regimental colours can be seen in Lichfield Cathedral and the King's Head pub in Bird Street is the place in which the 38th Foot was founded.

Museum of the Staffordshire Regiment
Whittington Barracks, Lichfield, 18 miles SE by A51 and 3 miles on towards Tamworth. Tel: (0121) 311 3229. Open Monday to Friday 9am to 4.30pm.

While the scope of the museum is wider, there are items of military interest, including weapons, engines and two aircraft, a Hurricane IV and a Spitfire LF.IXC.

Museum of Science and History
Newhall Street, Birmingham. Tel: (0121) 235 1661.

From 1914-18 there are 53 Australian, 31 Canadian, 8 New Zealand, 1 South African and 405 United Kingdom graves in the south part of the cemetery, the memorial stones being laid flat. From 1939–45, in the east part of the cemetery, there are 1 New Zealand and 124 United Kingdom graves with a further 48 United Kingdom names recorded on the Cremation Memorial.

Birmingham (Lodge Hill) Cemetery
Selly Oak, Birmingham. Commonwealth War Graves Commission.

THE NORTH

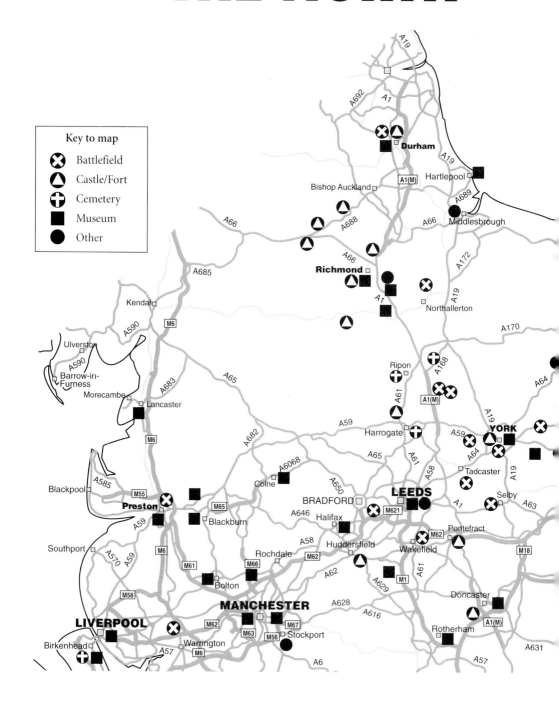

Key to map

⊗	Battlefield
◭	Castle/Fort
✚	Cemetery
■	Museum
●	Other

A19

A692

A1

Durham

A1(M)

Bishop Auckland

Hartlepool

A19

A689

A66

Middlesbrough

A66

A688

A172

Richmond

A66

A1

Northallerton

A19

A170

A685

Kendal

A590

M6

Ripon

A168

A64

Ulverston

A590

Barrow-in-Furness

A683

A65

A61

A1(M)

Morecambe

Lancaster

M6

A59

Harrogate

YORK

A19

A59

Blackpool

A585

A682

A59

A65

A61

A58

Tadcaster

A64

A19

M55

A6068

Colne

A650

BRADFORD

LEEDS

Selby

A1

A63

Preston

M65

M621

Pontefract

A59

Blackburn

A646

Halifax

Wakefield

M62

M18

Southport

M6

A58

Huddersfield

M62

A61

A570

A59

M61

Rochdale

M62

A62

M1

M58

Bolton

A629

Doncaster

A1(M)

MANCHESTER

A628

A616

LIVERPOOL

M62

M67

Rotherham

Birkenhead

M63

M56

Stockport

A631

Warrington

A57

M6

A6

A57

North of the line between the Mersey and the Humber, England is divided in two by the mass of the Pennines. The hills flank the sea on the west, leaving only a narrow litoral over which armies might move freely until the Cumbrian Hills block the way. Invaders, of either England or Scotland as the case might be, found it easier going in the east where the Vale of York runs north from the confluence of the Trent, Ouse, Aire and Don at the western end of the Humber estuary. Indeed, the rivers themselves eased the passage of the water-borne Vikings who established themselves in York. The Romans drove their roads to York and beyond for the same reasons that medieval kings passed this way.

The incidence of battlefields attests to the importance of the route in the east, as does the generous sprinkling of castles. The north was not compliant to the Norman invasion and William the Conqueror laid waste this land, leaving characteristic motte and bailey fortifications from which his vassals could dominate the territory. Far from London, these lords begat families that held the capital in small respect and themselves became a source of trouble for centralised power.

In the west the Mersey forms one of the finest harbours in the country around which the industrial power of Lancashire grew. Liverpool became the life-line on which Britain depended in both World Wars, and suffered fearfully as a result when air power had developed sufficiently to make long-distance bombing raids effective. The convoys that brought supplies across the Atlantic were subject to constant danger and thus it was from Liverpool that the Battle of the Atlantic was controlled.

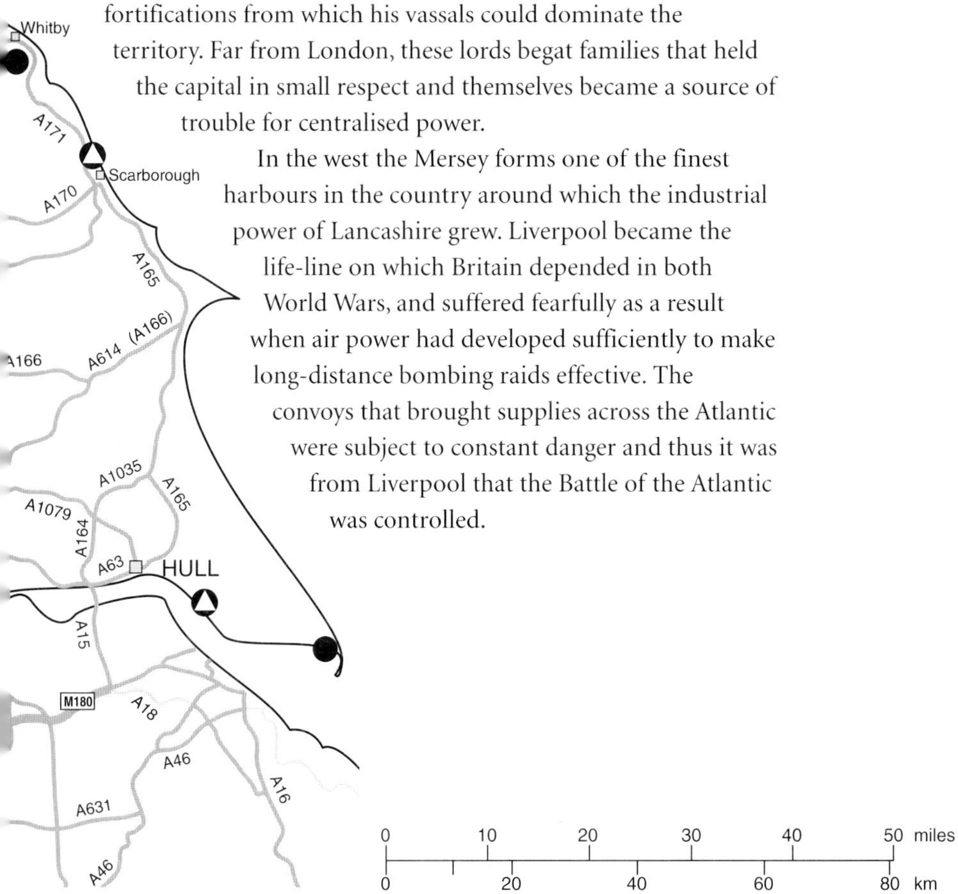

Whitby

A171

Scarborough

A170

A165

A614 (A166)

A166

A1035

A165

A1079

A164

A63 □ HULL

A15

M180

A18

A46

A16

A631

A46

0   10   20   30   40   50 miles

0   20   40   60   80 km

DURHAM

Tourist information: Market Place. Tel: (0191) 384 3720.

Durham Castle

Tel: (0191) 374 3800. Open, guided tours, July to September weekdays 10am to noon and 2pm to 4.30pm, Sundays 2pm to 4.30pm, October to June Mondays, Wednesdays and Saturdays 2pm to 4.30pm.

Together with the cathedral on the promontory formed by a meander in the River Wear, the castle is part of a World Heritage site. It represents a fusion of sacred and secular power, for it was, until 1836, the seat of the Prince Bishops of Durham. In 1072 a motte and bailey castle was built. The timber structure was rebuilt in stone and hugely elaborated under Hugh de Puiset, bishop in the late 12th century. It is now one of the greatest surviving Romanesque palaces in England.

The Durham Light Infantry Museum

Aykley Heads, Framwellgate. Tel: (0191) 384 2214. Open Tuesday to Saturday 10am to 5pm, Sunday 2pm to 5pm.

The regiment was raised as the 68th Foot in 1758. It saw service in the Peninsular War, the Crimean War and New Zealand and became the 1st Battalion DLI in 1881. The 2nd Bombay European Infantry, which served in India and Persia, became the 2nd Battalion DLI. The DLI saw action in Egypt and in the Boer War and took part in every great action of World War I on the Western Front. In World War II the regiment was on active service in Europe, North Africa and India, notably at Kohima. Their last active postings were in Korea and Borneo before, in 1968, they became part of the new Light Infantry. The Volunteer and Militia units also have their place in the museum.

The Battle of Neville's Cross, 17 October 1346

Junction of A167 and A690 W of city, N over railway and up onto footbridge over A167. Walk leaflet from Tourist Office.

After Edward III's victory at Crécy, the French king asked David II of Scotland to distract the English from their siege of Calais by invading the north. David complied, crossing the border at Carlisle and marching by way of Hexham. By 16 October he was encamped at Beaurepaire (Bearpark) Abbey, north of Durham. The English gathered at Bishop Auckland and moved north on the 17th, routing a raiding party led by Sir William Douglas who took the news of their approach to David.

Neville's Cross was one of the ancient shrines around the city and may be seen just east of the A167/A690 junction, in St John's Road. To the north (of the junction and the railway) the English took position on Crossgate Moor on the summit of the north–south ridge with Sir Thomas Rokeby on the left, his flank protected by the steep slope to the River Browney, Ralph Neville in the centre and Henry Percy on the right. The reserve, mainly horse, were to the rear. The Scots had David in the centre with Douglas on the right and Robert the High Steward on the left, but as they advanced up the slope Douglas's men encountered the ravine to be seen north of Toll House Road. Some descended and attempted to get at Rokeby, whose archers shot them down, while others veered left, colliding with David's men and offering the English bowmen another solid target. On the other flank the Steward pushed Percy back, but the English line bent rather than broke and the new north–south alignment exposed the Scots flank to the English reserves. With Douglas beaten and the Steward's men scattered by cavalry, the English wings closed round David in the centre and the Scots were defeated.

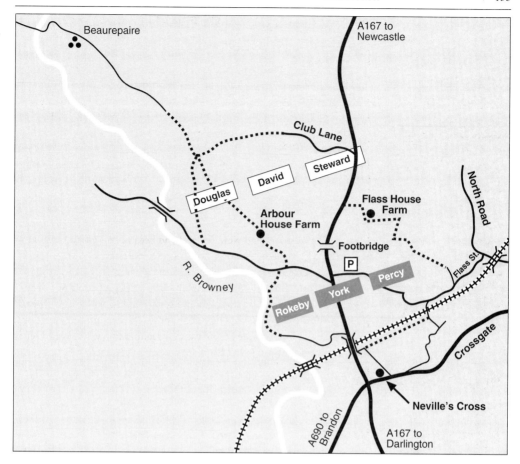

A collection of civil and military aircraft, the majority British and post-World War II. Among more than 30 aircraft on view there are an Avro Vulcan B.2 bomber, De Havilland and Westland helicopters and a Bensen autogyro. One of only three remaining Vickers Valettas was destroyed by vandals here in January 1997. The Royal Observer Corps Northern Area Collection is also housed here.

North East Aircraft Museum

Old Washington Road, Usworth, Sunderland, 12 miles NE by A690. Tel: (0191) 5190662. Open daily.

The Historic Quay is a replica of an 18th-century naval quayside, with gaol, naval tailor, shops, swordsmith and naval officer's home. The galleries devoted to fighting ships, pressgangs and sea power have audio commentaries. The frigate HMS *Trincomalee* has been under restoration here. She was built in Bombay in 1817, one of 47 copies of the French ship, the *Hebe*, ordered by the Admiralty in the first 30 years of the 19th century. Telephone to check access.

Hartlepool Historic Quay

Maritime Avenue, Hartlepool Marina, Hartlepool, 15 miles SE by A181, A19 and A179. Tel: (01429) 86006. Open daily.

Human Torpedo

Middlesbrough, 20 miles SE by A181 and A19. Tel: (01642) 243425 – Tourist Information.

In World War II human torpedos or chariots, devices ridden by two men, were used in attacks on enemy ships. The warhead could be detached to explode under the target. An attempt to destroy the *Tirpitz* in Norway was made in October 1942 and attacks on Sicilian harbours in December of that year accounted for an Italian cruiser and a troop ship. In June 1944 the operation at La Spezia in northern Italy led to the sinking of another cruiser and damage to other vessels. The machines were also used for the transportation of operatives on clandestine coastal missions. A Mark II model has been restored here through the work of the Chariots Trust, but at the time of writing no display location has been found. It is hoped to show it in the town in which it was restored. The Trust has also masterminded the construction of a facsimile Mark I which is displayed at various locations by arrangement.

Leeds City Art Gallery

Tel: (0113) 247 8248.

World War I paintings of Stanley Wilson, who served with the 10th Duke of Wellington's Regiment (West Riding) in Italy.

LEEDS

Tourist information: The Arcade, City Station. Tel: (0113) 242 5242.

The Liddle Collection

Brotherton Library, University of Leeds. Tel: (0113) 233 5566. Entry by appointment with the Keeper.

For some 25 years the historian Peter Liddle built up a collection of letters, diaries, maps, photographs, books and many other items relating to World War I. Material documenting the experience of almost 6,000 men and women is held here, including items relating to French and German people, and it is stored by individual so that photos, letters and other material relating to a given person are kept together. A sophisticated reference system allows research by topic. Of Commonwealth countries, Australia, Canada, South Africa and New Zealand are well represented. There is also coverage of the Boer War and World War II, the latter including a growing collection of tape recordings.

The Royal Armouries

The Waterfront. Tel: (0990) 106666 or (0113) 245 6456. Open April to August 10am to 5pm, 6pm at weekends and in school holidays, September to March until 4pm, 5pm weekends.

The collection of the Royal Armouries, the exhibition of which was formerly limited to what could be shown at the Tower of London, is now the basis of a museum that makes use of the most modern techniques of presentation. Three thousand years of warfare, hunting, self-defence and tournament can be experienced here, including live displays of jousting, Wild West gun fighting, Oriental swordsmanship and duelling. The global development of arms and armour is presented using film, computer interactive technology, object handling sessions and live demonstrations. A leather-worker, gunsmith and armourer have workshops on site.

Harrogate (Wetherby Road) Cemetery

Harrogate, 13 miles N by A61 and A658, 2 miles out of town on A661. Commonwealth War Graves Commission.

There are 15 United Kingdom graves from World War I, but the great majority of the fallen are from World War II. In 1943 an area was designated for an RAF regional cemetery which can be entered through iron gates on York-stone pillars from a side road. The majority of the buried are Canadian airmen, 666 of them in all, and maple trees from their native land are set in avenues to form a cross in their memory. Australian graves number 97, New Zealand 23, United Kingdom 200 and there is 1 East African and 1 unidentified grave. Some are scattered amongst the other burials in the cemetery and beside the north wall. A shelter of Bolton Wood stone with a Westmorland slate roof has a bronze plaque with the names of those cremated at Harrogate, and the Register in a bronze box is in a side wall.

An 11th-century castle which was the scene of Richard II's death and a Royalist stronghold in the Civil War. It was an early candidate for preservation when, in the early 17th century, it was described as a monument of antiquity and goodly building. A painting of the castle at that time may be seen in the museum in Salter Row in the town.

Pontefract Castle
Castle Chain, Pontefract. 10 miles SE by M62 and A639, off A645 to Knottingley. Tel: (01977) 600208. Open daily.

With the defeat of the Royal army at Northampton in July, the Duke of York was able to obtain an Act of Settlement that declared him and his issue heirs to Henry VI. Queen Margaret reacted at once to the exclusion of her son, Edward, from the throne and gathered the Lancastrian forces in the north. York hastened from London to his castle of Sandal, two miles south of Wakefield and at the time in a landscape of field and forest. The Yorkists were outnumbered by the Lancastrian army, which may have had as many as 12,000 men, and doubtless welcomed the proposal of a truce over Christmas. The reinforcements so gladly received at Sandal were actually enemy infiltrators, and when Sir Andrew Trollope turned up on 30 December with more men near the bend in the River Calder north-west of the castle, York may well have thought them further troops coming to aid him. In any case, he unwisely sallied forth from the security of the castle to find himself beset not only by the new arrivals he could see, but by additional Lancastrian soldiers hidden in the woods to the north-east and south-west. More than 2,000 Yorkists fell, including York himself and his younger son Edmund. The Duke of York's head was displayed on Micklegate Bar in York so that York might overlook York.

The Battle of Wakefield, 30 December 1460
Sandal Castle, off A61 S of Wakefield, 9 miles S of Leeds.

Ripley Castle
Ripley, 3 miles N of Harrogate by A61. Tel: (01423) 770152. Open daily July and August, limited in other months.

The 15th- and 16th-century home of the Ingilby family has a display of English Civil War arms and armour.

The KOYLI was formed in 1881 by the merging of the 51st Foot and the 105th Foot, formerly the 2nd Madras European Light Infantry. Their history dates back to the Battle of Minden in 1759, and includes service in Minorca, the Peninsular War, the Battle of Waterloo, the Boer War and World Wars I and II. The museum also houses memorabilia of the 1st West Yorkshire Militia and the Volunteer Rifle Corps. Open daily, Sundays afternoon.

King's Own Yorkshire Light Infantry Regimental Gallery
Doncaster Museum and Art Gallery, Chequer Road, Doncaster, 25 miles SE by M1, M62 and A1. Tel: (01302) 734293.

The castle was built for Hamelin, the illegitimate brother of Henry II in the 1180s and was, at that time, in the most modern style. On an earlier earthwork, which had doubtless boasted a timber structure of strictly military purpose, a magnificent circular stone tower-keep was built as a residence. Above the storage rooms are the apartments of the lord on the second and third floors, where a substantial fireplace may be seen and a chapel provided for the comfort of the soul, as did garderobes (toilets) for the easement of the body. The keep was surrounded with a curtain wall from which turrets rose to give defenders a good field of fire. There is a visitor centre, exhibition and audio-visual presentation.

Conisborough Castle
Conisborough, 4 miles SW of Doncaster by A630. English Heritage. Tel: (01709) 863329. Open April to September 10am to 5pm, October to March 10am to 4pm.

Central Library

*Walker Place, Rotherham,
10 miles SW of Doncaster by
A630. Tel: (01709) 382121.*

The York and Lancaster regiment was formed from the 65th and 84th Foot and the history dates back to 1758. The story is told chronologically, and includes coverage of the Militia, Volunteers and Territorials. There is a case devoted to Field Marshal Plumer. Closed Sunday and Monday.

Cannon Hall Museum

*Cawthorne, 6 miles NW of
Barnsley by A635 and 15
miles S of Leeds. Tel: (01226)
790270.*

The display of uniforms and equipment from the Peninsular War to 1992 is housed in the local museum as the 13th/18th Royal Hussars (Queen Mary's Own) drew most of its manpower from the locality. The regiment served at Waterloo, Balaclava, in the Boer War, World Wars I and II and Malaya. Coverage includes the regiment of today, the Light Dragoons. Closed Monday.

Almondbury Hill Fort

*Castle Hill, Almondbury, 2
miles SE of Huddersfield, 13
miles SW of Leeds by A62.*

The hill-fort dates from 300BC, and was modified some 200 years later by adding banks and ditches and the creation of a narrow entranceway on the south-western side, some way down the hill, to force attackers to endure enfilading resistance.

**The Battle of
Adwalton Moor, 30
June 1643**

*Drighlington, 9 miles SW of
Leeds by A58 on open land
crossed by A58 and A650 E
of Birkenshaw and N of
Adwalton.*

The Parliamentary cause in the north was led by the Fairfax family who drew their strength from the cloth towns. Fearing an attack on Bradford when the Duke of Newcastle led 10,000 Royalists against them, the Fairfaxes advanced along the line of the present A650 with only about 3,500 men and found Newcastle ready for them on Adwalton Moor. Sir Thomas Fairfax commanded the Parliamentary right, Lord Fairfax the centre and General Gifford the left which was on the A650. The moor in the centre was sound land while the right

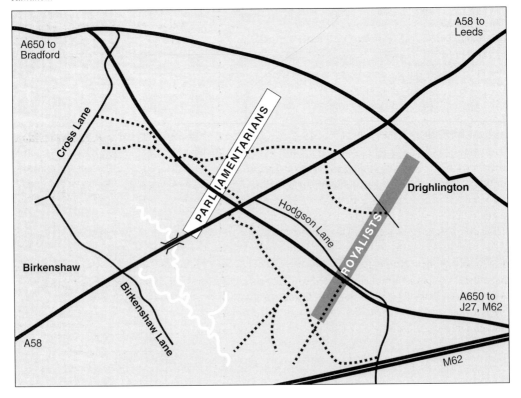

flank was in amongst coal pits, fine for infantry but poor for horse. A number of hedgerows, of which some survive, cross the battlefield and at first the Parliamentarians were able to advance and harry the Royalists by taking advantage of this cover. The lie of the land hampered the Fairfaxes; a ridge carrying the Bradford road prevented their seeing each other and Newcastle's men were able to split the Parliamentarians in two. Sir Thomas fell back to Halifax before he could attempt to return to Bradford while the rest of the Parliamentarians tried to retreat the way they had come, only to find the enemy had got round behind them. Newcastle was able to occupy Bradford and the Fairfaxes led their force away to Hull. The Royalists had achieved a hold on the north that was to last until Marston Moor.

The regiment was formed by the amalgamation of the 33rd Foot, raised in 1702, and the 76th Foot, formed in 1787. The uniforms and equipment are, in part, shown in period tableaux. There is coverage of militia and volunteer forces and some memorabilia of the first Duke of Wellington.

The Duke of Wellington's Regiment (West Riding) Museum
Bankfield Museum, Boothtown Road, Halifax. 14 miles SW of Leeds by A58. Tel: (01422) 354823. Open Tuesday to Saturday 10am to 5pm, Sunday 2pm to 5pm.

LIVERPOOL

Tourist information: Merseyside Welcome Centre, Clayton Square Shopping Centre. Tel: (0151) 709 3631. Atlantic Pavilion, Albert Dock. Tel: (0151) 708 8129.

The importance of Liverpool as a supply port in World War II cannot be overstated. In the course of the war 1,285 convoys of merchant vessels were escorted past the marauding U-boat packs of the German Navy to bring food, fuel and munitions to Britain. From early 1941 the operations in the Battle of the Atlantic were controlled from this bunker beneath the streets of Liverpool where the plotting tables and apparatus of command can be seen.

Western Approaches
1 Rumford Street (near Town Hall). Tel: (0151) 227 2008. Open daily.

As part of an extensive coverage of Liverpool's maritime history, the Battle of the Atlantic gallery occupies a central position. Audio and video presentations enliven the story of the struggle against attack from the air and beneath the sea in World War II. ASDIC and radar equipment are shown as well as a 22-foot torpedo, a German magnetic mine and an Enigma machine. Pictures and memorabilia illustrate the German viewpoint in addition to that of the Allies. The gallery forms a memorial both to the Royal Navy and to the Merchant Navy.

Merseyside Maritime Museum
Albert Dock. Tel: (0151) 478 4499. Open daily 10am to 5pm (last admission 4pm).

The history of the regiment covers 300 years of service to the Crown and the presentation emphasises the experience of battle. Also to be seen are the Native American artefacts collected in Canada by Colonel de Peister. Modern service is given its place in sections devoted to the Korean War and Northern Ireland. The museum includes the service of the Volunteer and Pals battalions.

The King's (Liverpool) Regiment Gallery
Museum of Liverpool Life, Albert Dock. Tel: (0151) 478 4499. From early 1999, open daily 10am to 5pm (last admission 4pm).

The Battle of Winwick Pass, 19 August 1648

Winwick, 16 miles E by M62 to junction 9 and N on A49.

In the Second Civil War, after the defeat of his forces at Preston by Cromwell, the Marquis of Hamilton set off south to catch up with his horse which Middleton was leading towards Warrington. Hamilton took his foot by the Standish road (now A49) but Middleton, becoming aware of something amiss to his rear, had turned back using the Chorley road (A6). They missed each other on the night of 17–18 August but met on Wigan Moor the next day. Cromwell left 4,000 men at Preston lest Scottish reinforcements came south and set off in pursuit of Hamilton, who hoped to make it to Warrington and hold the crossing of the Mersey and wait for Lord Byron to reinforce him. Several thousand Scots were detached to block Cromwell's advance at Winwick Pass, also known as Red Bank, to the south of Newton where a tributary of Newton Brook runs across the southern edge of Newton Park and the road to Winwick Green. The modern road now runs about 100 yards west of the road line at that time. The Scots occupied the southern bank over the little valley with their left flank protected by Newton Brook.

When Cromwell's men came up they ran into fierce resistance from the Scots, and though they came to push of pike (literally pike-to-pike contact), were held back. Colonel Pride's crack troops were brought forward and the Parliamentarian horse explored a possible flanking manoeuvre east via Hermitage Green (to which the road has since been improved and raised). Now threatened by cavalry and hard-pressed by Pride, the Scots fell back to Winwick Green where they made a last stand north of the church. They lost some 2,000 killed and 1,000 as prisoners in their final collapse. Most of the rest of the Scots, soaking wet, exhausted from the overnight march and without food, surrendered at Warrington later in the day. Charles I's last hope was gone.

Historic Warships

East Float Dock, Birkenhead, via Wallasey Tunnel and first exit. Tel: (0151) 650 1573. Open daily from 10am.

The frigate HMS *Plymouth* served in the Falklands War. The surrender of South Georgia was signed in her wardroom and she led the invasion fleet into San Carlos Water. She was severely damaged by bombs, but there were no serious casualties. In the same conflict the submarine HMS *Onyx* operated close to the shore transporting men of the SAS and SBS who, in honour of the cramped conditions, named her The Sardine's Revenge. A unique attraction is the German U-boat U534, sunk on 5 May 1945 and raised to be shown here.

Birkenhead (Landican) Cemetery

Landican Cemetery and Crematorium, 4 miles from Birkenhead.

The war graves are in the north-west corner of the cemetery where the Cross of Sacrifice is flanked by silver birch trees. There are 124 UK graves, 1 New Zealand and 3 unidentified. The names of those cremated are carved on the wall facing the cross and include one Australian. Soldiers of the Cheshire Regiment killed by land mines on 12 March 1941 lie here.

MANCHESTER

Tourist information: Town Hall Extension, Lloyd Street. Tel: (0161) 234 3157.

Little remains to bear witness to the importance of Manchester in Roman Britain except the restored fragments of the walls of the fort at Castlefield.

Castlefield Roman Fort
Castlefield.

Commissioned as a minesweeper in 1954, HMS *Bronington* was later converted to a mine hunter, using sonar and divers. In 1976 she was commanded by HRH The Prince of Wales. She was decommissioned and brought to Manchester in 1988. Open April to September Friday to Monday 1pm to 5pm.

HMS *Bronington*
Quay West, Trafford Wharf Road, Wharfside, Trafford Park. Tel: (0161) 877 7778.

A collection of arms and armour, mainly dating from the Civil War. The house itself was built in the 15th century, but much restored in the 19th.

Turton Tower
Tower Drive, Chapeltown Road, Turton, Bolton. Tel: (01204) 852203.

The museum presents the history of the Lancashire Fusiliers and includes material relating to the American War of Independence, the War of 1812 and the burning of the White House. World War I service was seen at Gallipoli and on the Western Front. There are personal relics of Major Generals Wolfe and Ross of Bladensburg and of Napoleon on St Helena.

The Fusilier Museum Lancashire
Wellington Barracks, Bury, 9 miles N by A56 and 1 mile W on A58. Tel: (0161) 764 2208. Open daily except Wednesday and Sunday.

Unusual in presenting the history of the regiment in the context of the community, the story starts with the 63rd and 96th Foot which amalgamated to form the Manchester Regiment in 1881. Active service recounted includes the Boer War, World War I, Palestine, World War II and Malaya. There is a section dealing with medals and one on Women at War.

Museum of the Manchesters
Ashton Town Hall, Market Place, Ashton-under-Lyne, 6 miles E by A635. Tel: (0161) 342 3078. Open Monday to Saturday 10am to 4pm.

Work on air raid shelters in anticipation of bomber attack by the Germans began in 1938. The sandstone beneath Stockport lent itself to tunnelling and extensive shelters were dug, equipped with electric light, toilets and first-aid facilities and fitted out with bunks. The Surviving the Blitz tours start with an audio-visual presentation and visitors are then issued with hard hats and guided through the shelters.

Air Raid Shelter Tours
61 Chestergate, Stockport, 6 miles S by A6. Tel: (0161) 474 1940. Tour times: Tuesday to Friday 3pm, Saturday and Sunday 2pm and 3.30pm and Wednesday 7pm.

PRESTON

Tourist information: The Guildhall, Lancaster Road. Tel: (01772) 253731. Preston lies on the western route from Scotland to England and has been the scene of conflict as a result. The battlefields are now lost under subsequent building. After the failure of negotiations between King Charles I and Parliament and the King's escape on 8 November 1647, Charles reached agreement with the Scots. The Marquis of Hamilton entered Carlisle on 8 July and made leisurely progress southwards. Cromwell, once he had dealt with Pembroke Castle, met General John Lambert at Wetherby and they crossed the Pennines with some 9,000 men to reach Clitheroe, in Hamilton's rear, and catching him with some 20,000 men in a long straggle from Preston southwards. On 17 August 1648, on the outskirts of the town at Ribbleton on the Longridge (B6243) road, the Scots faced their pursuers and in a long, bloody fight were eventually killed or put to flight. They were chased out of the town over the old bridge on what is now the A6 crossing of the river, having lost about 4,000 killed and a similar number as prisoners in the Battle of Preston.

Preston was again in the wars on 12 November 1715, the first Jacobite rising. A force of some 3,000 rebels under Thomas Foster, Tory MP for Northumberland, occupied the town on 10 November. Two Hanoverian armies were approaching, so barricades were set up and the attack of the 12th was held off. Lacking hope of relief, as well as strong leadership, the Jacobites surrendered two days later and the rebellion in England was over. In Scotland it had been put down the previous day at Sherrifmuir.

Lancashire County and Regimental Museum

Stanley Street. Tel: (01772) 264075. Open daily except Thursday and Sunday 10am to 5pm.

The museum records the histories of many of the county's regiments in addition to the Queen's Lancashire Regiment. The East, South and Loyal North Lancashire and the 30th, 40th, 47th, 59th, 81st and 82nd Foot and the Duke of Lancaster's Own Yeomanry are all covered as well as the 14th/20th King's Hussars. There are also recreated scenes including a World War I trench complete with sound and smell effects.

The Queen's Lancashire Regiment Museum

Fulwood Barracks, Watling Street Road (B6242) off A6 north. Tel: (01772) 260362. Open Tuesday to Thursday.

The displays cover uniforms, weapons, medals and memorabilia and the archives (by appointment) of the regiments of Lancashire: the East Lancashire, the South Lancashire, the Loyal North Lancashire, the Lanchashire and the Queen's Lancashire as well as the Militia, Rifle Volunteers, Home Guard, Territorials and Cadets.

The King's Own Royal Regiment Museum

City Museum, Market Square, Lancaster, 17 miles N. Tel: (01524) 64637.

The history of the King's Own Royal Regiment (Lancaster) is portrayed from its foundation in 1680 to its amalgamation with the Border Regiment in 1959. Displays include memorabilia of the 1868 Abyssinian Campaign. It is closed on Sundays.

Ribchester Museum of Roman Antiquities

Riverside, Ribchester, 9 miles NE by B6243 and B6245. Open Monday to Friday 9am to 5pm, Saturday and Sunday afternoons.

Ribchester, Roman Bremetenacum, was at the junction of the road to Carlisle from Manchester and the road east to York (the route of Cromwell's approach in 1648). The fort was built in the 1st century and had a garrison of 500 horsemen. The country hereabouts became a favoured place for retired soldiers. The museum contains many Roman objects, including a cavalryman's tombstone.

The East Lancashire Regiment is recorded here from the founding of its predecessors, the 30th and 59th Foot, to its amalgamation with the Prince of Wales's Volunteers in 1958. Exhibits include a drum from the field of Waterloo and an eagle of the 22nd Line taken at Salamanca in the Peninsular War. Also represented are the Benin Expedition and the retreat from Dunkirk in World War II.

Blackburn Museum and Art Gallery
Museum Street, Blackburn, 9 miles E by A59 and A677. Tel: (01254) 667130. Open Monday to Saturday 10am to 5pm.

Comprehensive coverage of British rule in India. The substantial photograph collection includes those of R B Holmes of the 1919 Afghan War. There is also a collection of handmade model soldiers. Other memorabilia include the uniform of Field Marshal Sir Claude Auchinleck. There is a diorama of the Last Stand of the 44th at Gandamak.

British in India Museum
Newtown Street, Colne, 12 miles NE of Blackburn by M65. Tel: (01282) 613129. Open daily, except Sunday, February to November 10am to 4pm.

RICHMOND

Tourist information: Friary Gardens, Victoria Road. Tel: (01748) 850252.

A rare survival of a Norman promontory castle. William the Conqueror bestowed the lands hereabouts on Alan the Red, Count of Penthièvre. He chose this place for its natural defensive potential, building, in the 1070s, a walled enclosure on the triangular eminence above the River Swale. It was for the protection of the settlers in times of trouble, with a curtain wall punctuated with towers and a gatehouse at the northern corner. These walls, and Scolland's Hall in the southeastern corner, are unchanged. In 1171 Alan's son Conan the Little died, his improvement to the castle being left to Henry II to complete. This was the replacement of the gatehouse with a substantial gatehouse-keep. At much the same time the next generation of castle was being started at Middleham.

Richmond Castle
Richmond. English Heritage. Tel: (01748) 822493. Open April to October 10am to 6pm, November to March 10am to 1pm and 2pm to 4pm.

The regiment was raised in November 1688 for service under William of Orange and is now named the Green Howards (Alexandra, Princess of Wales's Own Yorkshire Regiment). In 1744 Colonel the Hon. Charles Howard was in command and the regiment was thus known as Howard's, but on being brigaded with another also commanded by a Colonel Howard, the colour of the facings of their uniforms was added to distinguish them from the Buff Howards, and so they became the Green Howards. The association with Yorkshire dates from 1782, when they were the 19th Foot. Their service record includes Fontenoy, Ceylon, the Crimea, Egypt, the North-West Frontier, the Boer War, World Wars I and II and Malaya. The museum also displays memorabilia of the Volunteers and the Militia. Audio and interactive video are utilised.

The Green Howards Regimental Museum
Trinity Church Square, Richmond. Tel: (01748) 822133. Open April to October Monday to Saturday 9.30am to 4.30pm, Sunday 2pm to 4.30pm, November the same but closed Sunday, February the same but closed weekends. Closed December and January.

The original castle was much modified by the Victorian restoration of William Burn, but the legacy of the Nevilles can be appreciated. In 1334 Ralph Neville and Henry Percy were appointed joint wardens of the Marches. The centre of the Neville power was Raby where John, who died in 1388, built the great gateway on which the family heraldry is prominent. Of the medieval interior only the magnificent kitchen survives.

Raby Castle
Staindrop, 13 miles N by B6274. Tel: (01833) 60202. Open Easter weekend, May and June Wednesdays and Sundays, July to September daily except Saturdays. 1pm to 5pm.

Piercebridge Roman Fort

Piercebridge, 10 miles N by A1 and B6275 and NE on A67. Open site.

The East Gate, barrack blocks and part of an internal road are visible. It is here that Dere Street (now the route of B6275), the Roman road, crossed the River Tees and the remains of the Roman bridge can also be seen.

The Battle of the Standard, 22 August 1138

Oaktree Hill, 9 miles E by B6271 to Northallerton and N on A167. Monument on E of road 1 mile S of Oaktree Hill.

Henry I had extracted an oath of loyalty to his daughter Matilda from his barons before his death in 1135, but his nephew Stephen managed to seize the throne. David I of Scotland took advantage of the confusion to invade and occupy Carlisle, Wark, Alnwick, Norham and Newcastle. Repeated truces and invasions followed, and in 1138, while Stephen was putting down rebellion in the south, David once more ravaged the northern counties. The Archbishop of York gathered the English barons, who were heartily tired of the Scots' depredations, and with the standards of St Peter of York, St John of Beverley and St Wilfred of Ripon at their head they moved from York to Thirsk. David declined to negotiate and the two armies met north of Northallerton.

The road north from Brompton joins the Northallerton–Darlington road at Oaktree Hill and the Scots took position on a small hill just south of the junction. King David was in the rear, his son, Prince Henry, was on the right (astride the A167) north of Malt Shovel Farm and the Highlanders were on the

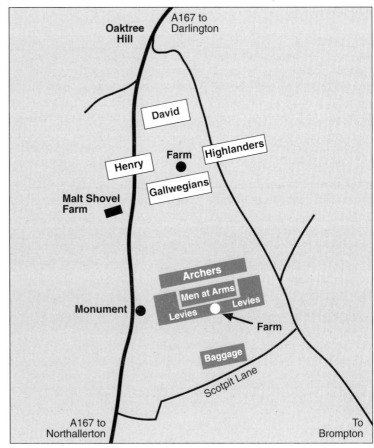

Scorton Airfield

Scorton, 5 miles E by B6271 and B1263.

The airfield opened in 1939 and saw action in the Battle of Britain. It is reported that a number of bunkers, gun positions and a gymnasium survive in the village and that there are Nissen huts and air raid shelters at Bolton on Swale.

left. At their insistence the men of Galloway were in the fore, unarmoured though they were. Facing them on the hillock to the south, north of Standard Hill Farm, were the English, with knights around the standards on the hilltop, men-at-arms and archers before them and shire-levies on each flank and at the rear. Further south, on the lane between the two larger roads, were the baggage and horses. Fierce and brave though their charge was, the Gallwegians suffered fearfully from the archers – they were said to have been stuck so full of arrows they looked like hedgehogs. They broke through the front rank of the English nonetheless, but were soon pushed back. Prince Henry charged and his cavalry passed clean through the English lines, only to become surrounded by the reserves with the baggage, there to be cut down or, throwing away their identifying badges, hoping to go undiscovered until they could escape. The rest of the Scots quietly left the field. Although defeated here, the Scots continued to go much where they wished in the north thereafter, stimulating the building of bigger and better castles from which the English could attempt to control the countryside.

Royal Corps of Signals Outstation Museum

Helles Barracks, Catterick Garrison, 5 miles SE by A1. Tel: (01748) 873778. Open Monday to Friday.

The museum shows items relating to the function of the Royal Corps of Signals.

A private collection with over 60 mannequins dressed in uniforms and equipment dating from 1900 to the present. Included are the Royal Navy, WRNS, Army, ATS, Home Guard, RAF, WRAF, Land Army, Red Cross, ARP and Civil Defence. It is open Easter to September Tuesday to Friday and weekend afternoons.

The Museum of Badges and Battledress

The Green, Crakehall, nr Bedale, 8 miles S by A1 and A684. Tel: (01677) 424444.

There are 78 Commonwealth graves here, 20 United Kingdom, 57 Canadian and 1 Australian. The Canadians served with No.6 Bomber Group and many of the RAF men flew with No.51 Squadron, both based at Dishforth. Other graves are of men stationed at Topcliffe which was a heavy bomber station throughout World War II. While the burials are of Royal Canadian and Royal Air Forces personnel, some of the men themselves came from New Zealand, South Africa and the USA. There are two graves of German airmen.

Dishforth Cemetery

Dishforth, 20 miles S by A1 and E on A168 towards Topcliffe.

In World War I there was a military hospital at Ripon and soldiers who died of their wounds were brought here for burial. There are 100 United Kingdom and 22 Canadian graves from that war, and a further 31 United Kingdom, 27 Canadian and 1 Australian grave from World War II. Most of the burials in the little plot in the north-west of the cemetery are Canadian airmen who flew from Leeming Bar, a heavy bomber base. Other graves are scattered about the cemetery.

Ripon Cemetery

On the Kirkby Road, Ripon, 18 miles S by A1 and A61.

Alan the Red granted Middleham to his brother Ribald in 1086 and the first castle, now an earthwork in Sunskew Park some 500 yards south-west of the present castle, was a motte and bailey. In the 1170s Robert fitzRalph started the work on the construction of a great rectangular stone keep on two floors, rather than the three that were usual a little later. The public rooms on the first floor are approached by a long stairway on the eastern side, the first-floor entrance giving onto the great hall. A central spine wall divides it from the great chamber and a chamber of presence on the west. A circular stair from the great hall leads down to the kitchen and cellars. The original chapel in the north-eastern corner

Middleham Castle

Middleham, 12 miles SW by A6108. English Heritage. Tel: (01969) 623899. Open April to October 10am to 6pm, November to March Wednesday to Sunday 10am to 1pm and 2pm to 4pm.

Barnard Castle

NW 12 miles by A66 and B6277. English Heritage. Tel: (01833) 638212. Open same as Middleham.

The 12th-century keep is round, in the French style. The great hall dates from the 14th century.

Bowes Castle

Bowes, 15 miles NE by A66. English Heritage. Open site.

Kohima Museum

Imphal Barracks, Fulford Road, York YO1 4AU. Tel: (01904) 662381. By prior appointment in writing only.

Memorabilia of the Second Infantry Division which fought at Kohima in 1944.

Clifford's Tower

Tower Street. Tel: (01904) 646940. English Heritage. Open April to October 9.30am to 6pm, November to March 10am to 4pm.

of the first floor was replaced with a chapel in a tower added in the 13th century, and in the next century the whole was heightened and a new window added as outer defences lessened the military role of the keep. The remaining outer walls are those of the 14th century strengthened by the Nevilles. The three-floor gatehouse was given diagonal corner turrets and a crenellated parapet projecting on corbels as a fighting platform. Sanitary provision was made with the construction of the garderobe tower with several privies (toilets) on each floor. Middleham was a centre of power in the north under the Nevilles who held it from the late 13th century until 1471, when Richard, Earl of Warwick, known as the Kingmaker, was killed at Barnet and the castle was forfeit to the Crown. Edward IV gave it to his brother who was to become Richard III.

The Roman road from York ran, as much of the modern road now does as the A1, to Scotch Corner where it divided, the modern A66 being the route first constructed by the occupiers towards the north-west and the forts at Brough and Brougham. The first on the route was at Bowes where the earthworks can still be seen, and within them a massive three-floor tower-keep built under Henry II.

YORK

Tourist information: TIC Travel Office, 6 Rougier Street, tel: (01904) 620557. Railway Station, tel: (01904) 621756.

The city of York holds a key strategic position in the north of England, commanding the road to Scotland and standing on the River Ouse up which ships came from the North Sea, thus offering an alternative line of supply. Its importance was recognised by the Romans and it retained its military significance to the end of the Civil War.

The great motte on which the tower stands was raised in 1069–70 as one of two strongholds to dominate the town. It was surmounted by a wooden structure which burned down in 1190 when the Jews of the city took shelter in it during a terrible pogrom which wiped them all out; a lasting stain on the honour of York and of England. The stone tower-keep was started by Henry III and is of an interesting quatrefoil design by Master Henry of Reyns (probably Reims) following, perhaps, the French inclination to round keeps. Before it stood the bailey, entered by Castle Gate and developed to have a curtain wall and cylindrical turrets. Its name is said to come from Roger Clifford, a Lancastrian defeated at Boroughbridge in 1322 and whose corpse was hung in chains from the tower. In the Civil War it fell to the Parliamentarians after Marston Moor in 1644 and was partially destroyed by fire in 1648.

This fascinating museum of everyday life includes a military gallery with medieval and Civil War weapons: armour, swords, pole-arms and firearms. It also houses the Thornley Collection of orders and decorations.

The Royal Dragoon Guards and the Prince of Wales's Own Regiment of Yorkshire were raised in 1685 by James II to take part in the defeat of the rebellion by the Duke of Monmouth. They saw service in Canada, America, India and the North-West Frontier, the Napoleonic Wars, New Zealand, Egypt and the Sudan, the Boer War and in World Wars I and II. The 4/7th Royal Dragoon Guards were involved in the first engagement of World War I near Mons on 22 August 1914 when they encountered a patrol of Uhlans.

The Regimental Museum
3 Tower Street. Tel: (01904) 662310. Open Monday to Saturday 9am to 4.30pm.

The World War II prisoner-of-war camp is the basis of a wide-ranging museum of civilian and military life of the time. There are a number of military vehicles and replica aircraft. The sights, sounds and even the smells of World War II are to be experienced here. It is closed 24 December to 13 February.

Eden Camp
Old Malton, Malton, 17 miles NE by A64, near junction A169. Tel: (01653) 697777. Open 10am to 5pm.

A classic Norman motte and bailey castle of the 11th century. The original motte and its ditch are unchanged, the only modification being the stone shell keep, probably dating from the 1180s, that replaced the timber structure that first crowned the mound. There was little provision for comfortable residential use. The surrounding bailey was first a simple earthwork with a timber palisade, and strengthened with a stone wall early in the 13th century. Even the modifications of the 1320s left the essential plan unchanged.

Pickering Castle
Pickering, 24 miles NE by A64 and A169. English Heritage. Tel: (01751) 474989. Open April to October 10am to 1pm and 2pm to 6pm, November to March Wednesday to Sunday.

In World War II attempts were made to confuse enemy bombers by setting up dummy airfields. The K sites were daylight decoys with dummy aircraft and buildings while the Q sites were either lights, QLs, or fires, QFs, the scheme being known by the name of Starfish. A QF has been identified on Sneaton Moor, three miles from the coast on an approach route to Middlesbrough. Trenches and bunkers in decayed state have been found, and a number of shallow ditches forming circles 100 yards across appear to have been used as fire-breaks to prevent the decoy fires burning out of control. The area is Forestry Commission controlled, and access is thus unlikely, but this seems too interesting to leave out! The personnel are said to have been accommodated in Nissen huts on the site of what is now the Sneaton Low Moor Caravan Park.

Starfish Decoy
Sneaton Moor, 5 miles S of Whitby, 42 miles NE by A169. Access uncertain.

The headland was used as a Roman signal station and offers a natural defensive promontory on which the castle was built in the 1160s. The great keep is of the usual three-floor type to provide residential facilities in addition to its military purpose. The fighting design of the keep was becoming redundant at this time given the increasing sophistication of the curtain defences and the growing importance of the gatehouse. The castle was bombarded in the Civil War and, most recently, in World War I when the German Navy shelled the town.

Scarborough Castle
Scarborough, 38 miles NE by A64. English Heritage. Tel: (01723) 372451. Open April to October 10am to 6pm, November to March Wednesday to Sunday 10am to 1pm and 2pm to 4pm.

The Battle of Stamford Bridge, 25 September 1066

Stamford Bridge, 8 miles NE by A166.

The Battle of Fulford, 20 September 1066

Fulford, 2 miles S by A19

Morcar of Northumbria and Edwin of Mercia deployed their forces between the River Ouse and a marsh near Heslington to stop the Vikings. After a long fight Hardrada rolled up the English line from west to east, killing more than 1,000 men.

The uneasy summer of 1066 passed with King Harold's forces guarding the Channel, watching for the approach of William (the Conqueror), but by 8 September the strain of supplying them led to their dispersal to their homes. Just then Harold Hardrada and King Harold's brother, Tostig, struck the north-eastern coast with a force of 300 ships and perhaps as many as 12,000 men, ravaging Cleveland and sacking Scarborough before sailing up the Ouse to Ricall, only nine miles from York. Having overcome the English at Fulford on 20 September they started negotiations for the surrender of York and arranged to meet at Stamford Bridge.

The King gathered what forces he could and was now on his way north from London, reaching Tadcaster by 24 September, an astounding feat. Early the next day Harold pushed on through York and along the Roman road to Stamford Bridge. The A166 now turns sharp right to cross the River Derwent, but the bridge at that time was much closer to the continuous line of the road either side of the town. Roused by the cloud of dust approaching from York, Hardrada hastily formed a shield wall half a mile south-east of the bridge between the modern dismantled railway line, across the Minster Way to Winchmore, and the public footpath round Burton Fields, leaving a small force to delay Harold at the bridge. In spite of an heroic defence the bridge soon fell and the English swarmed across to attack, perhaps and unusually entering battle on horseback. The conflict was not brief, but it was decisive. Hardrada and Tostig were killed, reinforcements from the Viking bridgehead fought off, and Harold's victory was complete. The way was open, however, for William to cross the Channel and land unopposed at Pevensey, consolidate and meet Harold at Hastings.

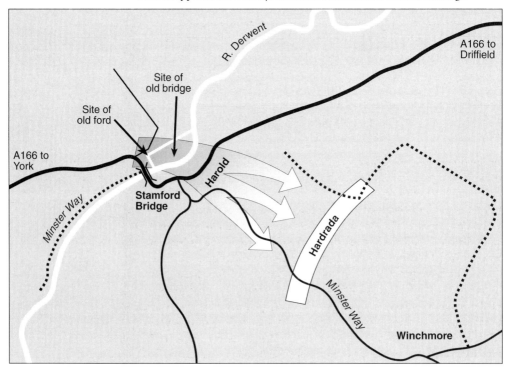

There is some World War I material here, but the emphasis is on the bombing missions of World War II when this was an operational airfield. There are some 20 aircraft, several in the process of restoration, including a Halifax and a Mosquito. The signals office and radio room are to be seen as well as a room devoted to 609 Squadron. The Barnes Wallis Collection is here, as is the Allied Airforces Memorial. The airfield was a Free French base during part of the war.

Pocklington RAF Station was a heavy bomber base in World War II from which bombing and mine-laying operations were flown. The men who lie here served in the Royal Canadian Air Force or the RAF, the latter including men from other countries. There are 27 United Kingdom, 21 Canadian, 3 Australian and 3 New Zealand graves here. Near by is one United Kingdom grave from World War I and there is one German burial.

With the Humber cutting into the land eastwards, Selby occupies a strategically important position on the north/south route through York. As Parliamentarian strategy in the Civil War owed so much to sea power and as they held Hull, the tenure of Selby was vital. The Royalists had attempted to cut off Lord Fairfax here on his retreat to Hull after Adwalton Moor, but were driven off by the unexpected appearance of Sir Thomas Fairfax in the Market Place.

By 1644 the Royalists were in occupation of the town and in April Fairfax moved against them, meeting Sir Thomas at Ferrybridge and advancing by way of Thorpe Willoughby (now on the A63). The waterways had been adapted to defence; Dam Fields was flooded. Millgate, leading to Cawood (by B1223) was left open. Barricades were built at the east end of Ousegate, Brayton Lane and the west end of Gowthorpe and all three were attacked by the Parliamentarians. Sir Thomas – Black Tom – broke through the Ousegate barrier and was able to take the remaining Royalists in the rear. Some 1,600 of them were captured and the rest fled towards Cawood, leaving 500 horses, 4 brass guns, 2,000 arms, 7 barrels of powder, 16 bundles of match and all the baggage. What was worse, the Royalists had lost the approaches to York that would prove a vital factor at Marston Moor.

The importance of the Humber as a trade route and fishing centre required a system of defence. The relics are not made much of. There is a Victorian fort at Paull, south-west of Hedon, on the north bank of the estuary. It was built in 1856 and rebuilt in 1899 for three 6-inch guns, quick-firers and machine-guns. In World War I Spurn Point, the extreme tip of the northern shore of the Humber, was fortified with batteries and two Sea Forts and they were brought back into service in World War II. The complementary Haile Sand Fort on the southern side was purchased privately in 1997 for renovation, though for what eventual purpose is not known. At Kilnsea, the last village before Spurn Head hooks off into the estuary, a sound mirror survives. This is an upright, concrete slab some 15 feet square with a concave hollow dish in its face. In front of the curved surface a post stands to hold a microphone at the focus of the curved surface in order to detect the sound of approaching World War II aircraft – a precursor to

Yorkshire Air Museum

Elvington Airfield, 5 miles SE by B1228. Tel: (01904) 608595. Open Monday to Friday 10.30am to 4pm, weekends 10.30am to 5pm. Phone to confirm in winter.

Barmby-on-the-Moor (St Catherine) Churchyard

Barmby Moor, 10 miles E by A1079.

The Battle of Selby, 10 April 1644

Dam Fields/War Memorial Fields, near the Abbey, Selby, 15 miles S by A19.

Humber Defences

East of Kingston-upon-Hull, 36 miles SE by A1079 and on by A1033, B1445 and minor road.

radar. These devices worked well in good conditions, being able to detect aircraft at a range of 8 to 15 miles, but wind and extraneous noise reduced efficiency, and increasing aircraft speeds the time available to act on the warning.

The peninsula is owned by the Yorkshire Wildlife Trust, and the Spurn Heritage Coast Project is investigating the defensive installations.

The Battle of Towton, 29 March 1461

Towton, 10 miles SW by A64, A162 and B1217 to Battlefield Cross (viewpoint).

The Wars of the Roses were finely balanced in early 1461. The Lancastrians had won a close contest at the Second Battle of St Albans, but were too weak to attempt to take London and retired north. Meanwhile Edward IV had gained a clear victory at Mortimer's Cross and, having had himself proclaimed king in London, was determined to make his position secure. He gathered his forces

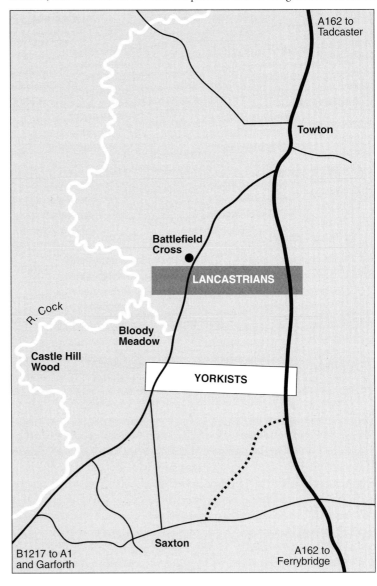

and set off to Pontefract and thence to Ferrybridge where, on Saturday, 28 March, a fierce engagement took place in which Lord Clifford prevented the Yorkist Lord Fauconberg from crossing the River Aire. Edward sent Fauconberg in again to cross the river higher up successfully, and Clifford was caught and killed at Dintingdale.

Palm Sunday dawned in snow and wind. The Lancastrians, under the Duke of Somerset, had taken up position south of Towton with their right near the Battlefield Cross, the flank protected by the deep valley of the River Cock, and the left on the Ferrybridge road (A162). South of the valley they faced is another ridge, with Castle Hill Wood standing above the river and the village of Saxton south of it. The Yorkists occupied this ridge with their left just north of the junction with the lane to Saxton and their right straddling the Ferrybridge road, the wind at their backs blowing the snow into the faces of their enemies. The Yorkists advanced briefly to loose a volley of arrows and as swiftly retired, allowing the answering fire to fall short. A Lancastrian advance was assisted by a flanking force concealed in Castle Hill Wood, but the two sides locked together in a long, murderous mass. For three hours the slaughter continued. At last the Duke of Norfolk's men came up from Ferrybridge to turn the Lancastrian left flank and force Somerset's men back towards the river over which they attempted to flee to York by way of Tadcaster. The Yorkist cavalry pursued and cut them down. Some 20,000 Lancastrians died and about 8,000 Yorkists lost their lives – the costliest battle on English soil. As recently as 1997 yet another mass grave was discovered near Tadcaster.

The Battle of Marston Moor, 2 July 1644

Long Marston, 7 miles W by B1224 and minor road to Tockwith.

In September 1643 the English Parliament made, by the Solemn League and Covenant, an alliance with the Scots against King Charles I, and his commander in the north, the Marquis of Newcastle, had a fight on two fronts. By the end of April he was besieged in York. Prince Rupert moved to his relief, fighting his way into Lancashire and then advancing by way of Skipton. The Allied armies fell back from York southwards and westwards, occupying the ridge at Long Marston to keep Rupert at a distance. The Prince immediately cut round to the north and entered York on 1 July. Had he been content to bide his time the alliance might have fallen apart, but he believed his orders were to engage the enemy and he overcame Newcastle's reservations – in spite of the fact that the alliance's 28,000 men were double the Royalist numbers.

The Allied army was falling back towards Tadcaster on the morning of 2 July, and the arrival of Rupert's cavalry on the moor north of the Long Marston–Tockwith road was a surprise. The Royalist army was slow to gather; indeed the last of the foot got there around 4pm. In the early stages cavalry skirmishes drove the Royalists back, leaving the Allies in command of the ridge south of the road. Through the afternoon the troops gathered, the Royalists being pushed into a line that ran partially behind a broken line of ditch and hedge, deepest at their left, the eastern end, shallow in the middle and deepening once more near Tockwith where rabbit warrens in front gave added protection. As supply waggons brought food to the hungry Royalists at about 7pm the Parliamentary cannon opened fire.

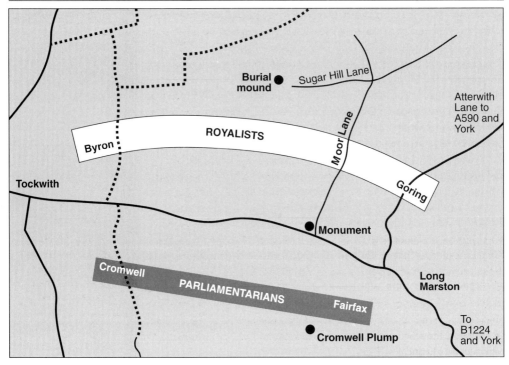

The Battle of Marston Moor

Lord Byron, on the Royalist right, became impatient and, forsaking the protection the broken ground gave him, advanced only to be shattered by Cromwell's horse which swept on to smash the reserves to Byron's rear. On the other flank Sir Thomas Fairfax had to use Atterwith Lane (running north from the western end of Long Marston) to try to penetrate Lord Goring's position. He failed, his men being struck down by Royalist fire, and Goring's cavalry pounded forward, driving the Allies back to the summit of the ridge at Cromwell's Plump. Fairfax and those still with him rode clean round the Royalist rear to meet Cromwell and join him on the return trip to where Goring had been at the start.

In the centre a dogged infantry battle was in progress. The Allied infantry had advanced at a run as a rainshower passed and were soon in amongst the Royalist forces. Rupert's attempt to counter Cromwell's thrust had failed, and Allied cavalry beset the Royalist right while the remains of Goring's cavalry under Sir Charles Lucas pushed against the Allied right. Briefly Newcastle's infantry, supported by Blakiston's cavalry, broke through to reach the top of the ridge, but their numbers were now too few and Lucas could not exert enough strength to save them. Goring now found himself attacking Cromwell in the same situation as Fairfax had attacked Goring at the outset, and though his men did better in spite of their fatigue, he failed. Only Newcastle's crack infantry, including the Whitecoats, remained in the enclosures west of the Moor Lane. Here they fought on for more than an hour before, their ammunition exhausted, they died where they stood, and there they were buried. The north was lost to the Royalists.

After the success of Bannockburn the Scots continued the war against the English, taking Berwick-on-Tweed in 1318. Edward II laid siege to the town in the following year and the Scots, to create a diversion, set about raiding and pillaging Yorkshire. A scratch force under William de Melton, Archbishop of York, set out to oppose them. They swarmed across the bridge over the River Swale at Myton in disorder to get at the Scots. The Scots were to the north-west with their left at about Clot House Farm and their right near Ellerthorpe Lodge. The Scots had no difficulty in stopping the English and then enveloping their flanks, thrusting them back, slaughtering them and chasing many to drown in the Swale. The Archbishop was lucky to get away. Today a footpath runs north from the bridge and turns west towards Clot House Farm, on the way to which it gives a good view of the field of battle. There is a riverside walk to Boroughbridge.

Edward II's association with Hugh Despenser and his son completed the estrangement of Thomas, Earl of Lancaster who led an uprising against the King. Lancaster failed to defeat him at Burton-on-Trent and withdrew to seek the security of Northumberland, only to find his way barred by Sir Andrew de Harcla, Warden of Carlisle, on the River Ure at Boroughbridge. Lancaster's men tried to cross the bridge, probably a wooden structure on the same site as the modern bridge, and at a ford a little way to the east. Harcla held them off and, discouraged, the rebel force dispersed. Lancaster and his fellow rebel leaders were later caught and executed.

The Battle of Myton, 1319

Myton-on-Swale, E of Boroughbridge, 13 miles NW by A19 and minor roads.

The Battle of Boroughbridge, 1322

Boroughbridge, 15 miles NW by A59 and B6265 (the Roman Dere Street).

BORDERS

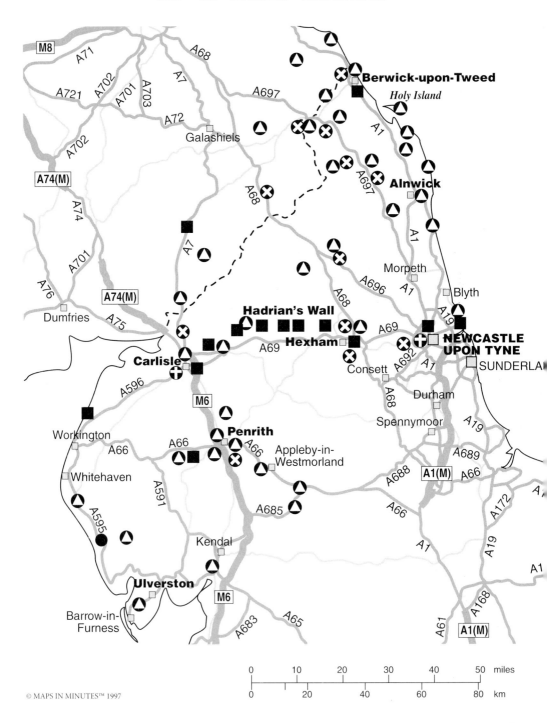

© MAPS IN MINUTES™ 1997

It was not until the Act of Union between England and Scotland in 1707 that things became quieter here. The present position of the border is simply where it happened to be at that time, in as much as it was anywhere, for it meant little except at the eastern and western extremes. The hills dominate the border country, the heights of the Pennines running into the Cheviots and Southern Uplands of Scotland with the River Eden cutting into them in the west, to offer the Romans an easy start to their road over the tops to Scotch Corner. In the east a number of rivers slice into hills that lean against the sea, from north to south: the Tweed, the Aln, the Coquet, the Wansbeck, the Blythe, the Tyne and the Wear. Each presents a barrier to the traveller, but on the west the bulk of the Lake District's mountains bars the way to the north, demanding the ascent of Shap Fell, and thus the easterly route is the favoured one.

From prehistoric times this has been a region of conflict, first between the various small tribal groups and then between the Romans and the indigenous inhabitants. Here the Roman solution, Hadrian's Wall, still strides its amazing way across the hills. When the Romans had gone, new arguments fuelled fresh mayhem, sometimes between the English and the Scots, sometimes between families or between settled peoples and bandits of one kind or another, Vikings or reivers. The fortifications that resulted are too numerous to list in their entirety, ranging from fortified farmhouses through pele towers and castles to whole towns. The battlefields are also numerous, some the sites of skirmishes and ambushes, others the places in which massive armies slaughtered each other on an horrific scale. A countryside of wonderful beauty is haunted by the memory of death.

ALNWICK

Tourist information: The Shambles. Tel: (01665) 510665.

The town was a strategic centre in the troubled history of the Borders. It was repeatedly attacked and sacked by the Scots, and Henry VI granted a licence to enclose the town in 1433. Of the fortifications only the Bondgate Tower, known as the Hotspur Tower, remains.

Alnwick Castle

Tel: (01665) 510777 (weekdays) 603942 (weekends). Open Easter to mid-October 11am to 5pm.

The Percy family acquired Alnwick in 1309 and were to add nearby Warkworth Castle a generation later as their power as Marcher Lords increased, to be recognised in the grant of the earldom of Northumberland in 1377. When Henry Percy first came here he found a shell keep standing in an enclosure with an outer bailey on the west, towards the town, and an inner bailey to the east. The keep was reinforced with seven semicircular towers, interval towers were added to the curtain wall and the division between the inner and outer baileys fortified with a great gateway. The second baron, also called Henry, succeeded in 1315 and added to the keep the twin polygonal towers and also lengthened the entrance passage. His most remarkable work was on the western curtain where he built a double-tower barbican and a gatehouse flanked by polygonal towers. The surrounding landscape owes its appearance to Capability Brown's work in 1765 while the castle was much altered and restored in the 19th century by Anthony Salvin, the medieval context and content becoming obscured as it took on the character of a fine country house. The armoury shows the weapons of the Percy Tenantry Volunteer Cavalry.

The Fusiliers Museum of Northumberland
The Abbot's Tower, Alnwick Castle.
The history of the regiment is traced from 1674 to the present day. The Royal Northumberland Fusiliers became part of the Royal Regiment of Fusiliers in 1968.

Preston Tower

Preston, 8 Miles N by A1 and minor roads NE from North Charlton. Open daily daylight hours.

Pele towers were vital to the survival of Border communities from Norman times to 1603, when England and Scotland were united (so far, so good). This example was built by Robert Harbottle in the 1390s. The walls are seven feet thick and the rooms tunnel vaulted. After 1603 half the tower was pulled down and the northern wall is a later repair while the clock dates from 1864. The guardroom and prison are on the ground floor while the first floor is furnished as it might have been in 1400. On the second floor is a room devoted to memorabilia of the Battle of Flodden.

Bamburgh Castle

Bamburgh, 13 miles N by A1 and B1341. Tel: (01668) 214515. Open April to October 11am to 5pm.

The naturally strong site was the location of a fortification of the kings of Bernicia in AD547 and was used for a Norman castle soon after the conquest. It was a strongpoint even before the birth of Christ. The rectangular keep is said, given records of expenditure in 1164, to be Henry II's work and the inner bailey was furnished with two halls and a kitchen in the 13th century. Since its completion as a military installation in about 1250 it has undergone numerous alterations and modernisations. Unlike Alnwick and Dunstanburgh, which capitulated,

Bamburgh was taken by artillery attack in 1464 in the Wars of the Roses. The Earl of Warwick was sweeping up the remains of Lancastrian resistance, using the royal siege train which included the bombards *Newcastle*, *London* and *Dijon*. A message was sent to Sir Ralph Grey asking him to yield: *The King our most dread Sovereign Lord, specially desires to have this jewel whole and unbroke by artillery, particularly because it stands so close to his ancient enemies the Scots and if you are the cause that great guns have to be fired against its walls then it will cost you your head and for every shot that has to be fired another head down to the humblest person within the place.* Sir Ralph refused, the castle fell and he paid the penalty.

Thomas of Lancaster incurred the enmity of Edward II because of the leading part he played in the death of the king's lover, Piers Gavaston, in 1312. At the same time the Scots, who had suffered severely at the hands of Edward I, were threateneing the security of the borders once more. These are the influences that led Thomas, in 1313, to start the construction of a purely defensive stronghold where he and his extended household might be secure on a lonely headland, protected on two sides by the sea. There are two principal elements to the castle, the massive gatehouse and the huge outer ward. Within the curtain walls Lancaster's retinue, army and tenants, their livestock and their families could shelter from attack by Scots or by the king. The gatehouse-keep was both a defensive and a residential building. The result was a viable defence at minimal expense.

Dunstanburgh Castle

Craster, 7 miles NE by B1340 and minor roads. English Heritage. Tel: (01665) 576231. Open April to October 10am to 6pm, November to March Wednsday to Sunday 10am to 4pm.

The castle passed to John of Gaunt, Duke of Lancaster who, in 1372, repaired and altered it, adding a new gatehouse just west of the old one, and a mantlet, a wall confining the approach to the new gate and thus exposing arriving men to dangerous fire from the defenders. Possibly as a result of using poor materials, little of these additions remains. An inner ward was also built behind the original gatehouse to produce a more conventional succession of defensive works to frustrate attackers who managed to enter the castle. The other towers are lookouts which also served as quarters for the garrison, with the exception of the Constable's Tower in the southern curtain, a fine residential building. To the south there was a small port for supply by sea, and the footpath inland past Craster Steads to the minor road from Craster to Embleton still bears the signs of paving – it is the road to the castle for heavy carts. In 1940, in World War II, a detachment of the Royal Armoured Corps was stationed here for a short time to fend off invasion.

On a promontory above the town and the river, Warkworth Castle is in a position of command and defence. The first castle here was Norman and when the property passed to the Percy family – the second baron was rewarded with it for service to the Crown – their improvements were limited to the south bailey's curtain wall and corner towers. It was the fourth baron who, in 1377 when he became the Earl of Northumberland, built the great tower-house in the most modern style of the time; it provided all the accommodation a great lord and his household required. The restorations and new windows of Anthony Salvin have, happily, allowed much of the original to survive.

Warkworth Castle

Warkworth, 7 miles SE by A1068. English Heritage. Tel: (01665) 711423. Open April to October 10am to 6pm, November to March 10am to 1pm and 2pm to 4pm.

Edlingham Castle

Edlingham, 5 miles SW by B6341. English Heritage. Open site.

The ruins consist of a 13th-century hall-house, a 14th-century defended courtyard and a 15th-century tower-house.

The Battle of Otterburn, 19 August 1388

Otterburn, 21 miles SW by B6341. Location disputed.

The great keep has a lantern or light-well at its centre which provides almost the only light to the ground-floor guardrooms and stores. The northern store-room gives access to a system of ducts for flushing the garderobes (toilets). Above, the layout is that of a residence, even the apparently thick walls are hollowed to provide stairs and storage. Here are the Great Hall and the Chapel, a solar and an inner chamber, these last with fine views towards the sea. At the west end of the Great Hall are the buttery, pantry and a huge kitchen. Above all this are various private apartments. In considering the military situation of the castle it is interesting to cross the bridge over the river on the north of the town and look back as well as to examine the castle from the more obvious southern approach.

The weight of authority places the Battle of Otterburn to the north-west of the village of that name and descriptions of what is supposed to have happened are readily available. They are hard to believe, but may be correct. A more credible alternative proposed by C F Wesencraft (1988) is the basis of this account.

Taking advantage of the dispute between Richard II and his lords, the Scots mounted an attack on England, the main force making for Carlisle while James, Earl of Douglas led a decoy raid in the east. The Earl of Northumberland had prepared for the onslaught by securing Alnwick and Warkworth himself and sending his two sons, Sir Ralph and Sir Henry (Hotspur) Percy, to hold Newcastle, which Douglas then passed by in an advance that took him to the gates of Durham, whence he fell back to besiege Newcastle. The defenders assumed Douglas was the vanguard of a larger force and, despite the three to

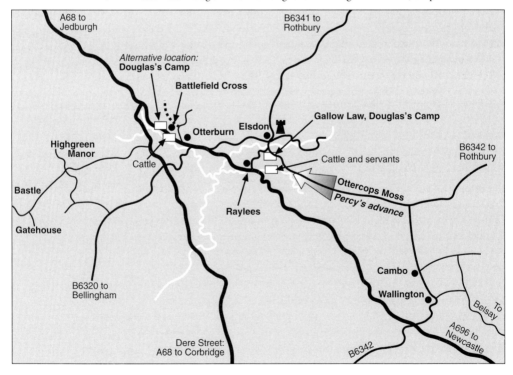

one advantage of numbers, let the 2,500 Scots bottle them up there for three days, from Saturday 15 August until Monday. Douglas and Hotspur fought in single combat and the Scot won the Englishman's pennon – his personal banner – a slight Percy was hot to avenge.

On the Tuesday morning the Scots were gone. They sacked and burned Ponteland and took their booty, including the livestock, north by the old drove road through Belsay to encamp at Wallington that night (the road is now the B6342). The next day they passed through Cambo where they attempted to take the tower (misnamed Otterburn Tower in many accounts; there was no tower at Otterburn before 1415) but, finding it too hard, pushed on towards Elsdon and Otterburn over Ottercops Moss. As evening drew on Douglas chose the first suitable campsite, putting the animals and their attendants down on Raylees Burn and his own camp on the hill to the north, Gallow Law, a mile south of Elsdon.

Hotspur, in the meanwhile, had been gathering his men for the pursuit, but it took time to get 8,500 troops previously engaged in a siege ready to take the road. By late afternoon on 19 August they were at Cambo and, presumably having had a report of Douglas's presence there that morning, decided to press on. The long column set off in the evening light and, seven miles on, the advance guard saw the campfires down on Raylees Burn to their left as darkness was coming on. Hotspur hurriedly deployed for a surprise attack, although three-quarters of his force had not yet come up. He hurled forward, hitting the cattle camp by the stream, unaware of Douglas's main force on the hill above. The Scots reinforced the camp below, but also attacked the exposed flank of the English descending from the road. As more men came up in the moonlight the English rallied and pressed their enemy back. Douglas led a charge and fell, but Sir Ralph Percy was wounded and captured and the Scots thrust forward to retake Douglas's fallen banner and capture Hotspur himself. The English broke and fled. Off the A696 north-west of Otterburn is a monument marking the alternative site of the battle, complete with interpretative panels. The visitor can decide which account best explains the victory of the Scots.

After the Wars of the Roses' Battle of Towton (1461), the Lancastrians needed some years to regather their strength. In June 1462 Queen Margaret obtained help from Louis XI of France and then attempted to dominate Northumberland, but with small success. In spring 1464 they managed to capture Skipton Castle and they tried to ambush John Neville, Marquis of Montagu who was riding north to meet ambassadors of the Scots. Montagu heard that Lord Roos, Lord Hungerford and Sir Ralph Percy were in the field and diverted to meet them at Hedgeley Moor. Roos and Hungerford soon left Percy to face Montagu's 2,000 men alone. Percy urged his horse forward to make a huge bound at the enemy but was fatally wounded. The place of his death is marked by a cross in a garden further south and Percy's Leap by two boulders.

Elsdon Tower

Elsdon, 18 miles SW by B6341. Visits by arrangement.

The 14th-century pele tower is lived in and is private property. A Norman motte and bailey castle's earthworks can be seen north-west of the village.

Black Midden's Bastle House

Gatehouse, 8 miles SW of Otterburn by minor roads (see Otterburn map). English Heritage. Open site.

A stone-built fortified farmhouse of the 16th century. The livestock were stabled on the ground floor and the living quarters are above.

The Battle of Hedgeley Moor, 25 April 1464

Battle Park, Hedgeley Moor, 11 miles NW by B6346 and S on A697. Two miles N of Powburn, lay-by on W of road.

Chillingham Castle

Chillingham, 10 miles NW by B6346 and minor roads. Tel: (01668) 215359. Open May to September 1.30pm to 5pm.

A great, square 14th-century courtyard keep, fully equipped as a residence as well as a defensive work, was based on an earlier, 12th-century castle. It has been in the ownership of the same family for over 700 years and has been continuously altered to suit its domestic purpose. It contains a wonderfully eccentric collection of arms and armour. It is also known for its gardens and the herd of wild cattle.

The Battle of Homildon Hill, 14 September 1402

Humbleton, 15 miles NW by B6346 and A697, 1 mile NW of Wooler.

While the English were distracted by the campaigns against Owain Glyn Dwr in Wales, the Scots, under Archibald Douglas, made a foray into the north as far as Newcastle. Lord Percy and his son, Hotspur, had gathered a force at Dunstanburgh Castle and moved to Wooler to block the Scottish retreat. Douglas deployed his troops, some 10,000 men, on the slopes of what is now called Humbleton Hill, west of the village where a public footpath now runs, expecting to enjoy the advantage of height and numbers in the ensuing battle. Percy was positioned between the modern A697 and the old railway to its north, between Humbleton and Akeld, with his right near the Bendor Stone, at the junction of the A697 with a minor road to the north-west. It was clear to him the Scots were proof against assault by footsoldiers or cavalry, so he depended on his archers. They moved along the stream below the hill to the west and began a steady fire from the flank of Harehope Hill. This the Scots endured as long as they could, steadily losing men. Eventually a small band under Sir John Swinton and Adam Gordon broke away and charged Percy, who cut them down without difficulty. Douglas then moved forward and against the bowmen, but the hail of arrows persisted even as the archers fell back towards the main English force. Douglas suffered five arrow wounds in spite of his chain mail and was captured, as were more than 80 of his barons and knights, while his broken force was pursued as far as

Yeavering Bell Hill-Fort

2 miles W of Akeld, S of B6351.

The capital of the Votadini tribe is said to have been this hill-fort, from which their leader, King Arthur, held sway over the surrounding country and resisted the incursions of the Saxons.

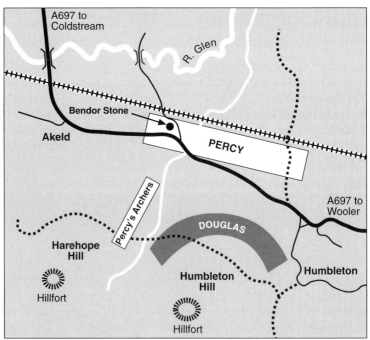

the River Tweed. The demonstration of the power of the longbow was convincing. After the battle Henry IV demanded that Percy hand over the valuable prisoners, an imposition that further soured Hotspur's relations with the king and contributed to his decision to join the revolt the following year in which he was to die at Shrewsbury.

BERWICK-UPON-TWEED

Tourist information: Castlegate Car Park. Tel: (01289) 330733.

The fortifications of Berwick today are principally Elizabethan and are one of the outstanding examples of town fortification in Europe. The medieval castle was down by the river (near the railway station) and the town walls ran from it towards the Bell Tower and Lord's Mount, where they turned along a line that joins the present walls to King's Mount. From King's Mount along the waterside and back towards the road bridge the medieval walls survive. In 1558, towards the end of Mary's reign, Sir Richard Lee was sent to fortify the border town against land attack by the Scots and their allies, the French. The work overtook the building of a small fortress that Lee had started eight years before, sited between the more recent Windmill and King's Mount bastions. As the work proceeded under Elizabeth I, technical disputes slowed progress, for this was the age of the new artillery defences. The Italian engineer Giovanni Portinari was called in as a consultant in 1560 and four years later another Italian, Iacopo Contio, and the Englishman William Pelham offered their views. They said that the flankers, the batteries in the protected angles, the orillons, of the arrow-head bastions, designed to fire along the face of the walls, were too small and that the earth banks and walls too steep to stand up to artillery fire. The building of forts had become the province of the professional military engineer.

Berwick-upon-Tweed Castle
Near railway station and river bank. English Heritage. Open site.

The remains of the castle date from the 12th century.

The Jacobite Rising of 1715 led to military works in the Borders and in Scotland, roads and forts were built to assist the suppression of future rebellion. In 1717 the Board of Ordnance gave instructions for the construction of a barracks for 36 officers and 600 men at Berwick at a cost of £4,937 10s 7d. It is thought that the design is by Nicholas Hawksmoor rather than Sir John Vanbrugh. This was the first such structure built for the Board in Britain. Two blocks face each other across the parade ground with a screen wall joining them on the north, pierced by a gate, and with a guardhouse and storeroom. Each block has three stairways with four rooms off on each of the three floors. Each room was for eight men, with four double cots, a table and two benches. There were no latrines or washrooms. The officers were housed in pavilions projecting from the northern end of each block. By 1740 it was recognised that the barracks was too small and the Clock Block was built along the south side. It now houses the Borough Museum and Art Gallery.

Berwick-upon-Tweed Barracks
The Barracks. Tel: (01289) 304493. English Heritage. Open April to October 10am to 6pm, November to March Wednesday to Sunday 10am to 1pm and 2pm to 4pm.

By Beat of Drum
The Clock Block.
An exhibition of three centuries of the British soldier's life, with reconstructions of everyday scenes.

The King's Own Scottish Borders Regimental Museum
The Barracks. Tel: (01289) 307426.
The history of the regiment dates back to 1689, and the museum also gives
account of Leven's Regiment, the Edinburgh Regiment, the 25th Foot and the
King's Own Borderers. The extensive service of the regiment includes the
World War I Battle of Loos and Field Marshal Haig's original 'backs to the
wall' message and the World War II Battle of Arnhem. There is a collection of
German, Russian, Japanese and Chinese weapons. Use is made of audio-visual
displays and dioramas.

Lindisfarne Castle

*Holy Island, 10 miles SE by
A1 and minor roads. Check
tides. National Trust. Tel:
(01289) 389244.*

As part of the Tudor fortification against the Scots this little castle was built in
1549 on a high rock from which it could protect the harbour. It was in a ruined
state when Sir Edwin Lutyens converted it into a residence in 1902. It is open
April to October daily except Friday 1pm to 5pm.

Etal Castle

*Etal, 10 miles SW by B6354.
English Heritage. Tel:
(01890) 820332. Open April
to October 10am to 6pm.*

The four-storey keep dates from the 14th century and there are the remains of
part of the curtain wall, a corner tower and the gatehouse. The building houses
an exhibition about the castle, warfare in the Borders and the Battle of Flodden
which took place near by. Visitors are guided by personal stereo.

The Battle of Flodden, 9 September 1513

*Branxton, 12 miles SW by
B6354, A697 and minor
road. Monument W of
village, Piper's Hill. Leaflet
from church.*

In 1513 Henry VIII, in his early twenties, was in belligerent mood. He invaded
France in May and Louis XII called upon his ally, James IV of Scotland, to invade
northern England in retaliation. Henry had left the north in the care of the Earl
of Surrey who was 70 years old, but not lacking in vigour. The force James raised
numbered some 40,000 men, including 5,000 French troops under the Comte
d'Aussi and five great cannon, capable of firing shot weighing 60lb, commanded
by Robin Borthwick. The Scots invested and took Norham Castle and went on
to attack Wark, Etal and Ford castles.

Surrey gathered his force of 25,000 men at Newcastle and marched to Alnwick
where he met his son, Thomas Howard, the Lord Admiral with 1,200 men from
the fleet. A challenge was issued to James to give battle at Milfield, south of
Flodden, on 7 September and the Scottish king accepted. To Surrey's dismay
intelligence arrived of James's deployment on Flodden Edge, north of the village,
a strong position protected by marshy land on the west and a steep slope on the
east. The daring decision was taken to outflank the Scots and take them in the
rear, so on 8 and 9 September Surrey marched north to the east of the River Till,
passing Ford and Etal which were held by the Scots, the vanguard under the
Lord Admiral crossing the river at Twizel Bridge (on modern A698) and the
main body at Heaton Mill ford, near Castle Heaton. They made for Branxton,
negotiating a bog at Pallinsburn (junction of A697 and B6353), Surrey and the
artillery getting over at Sandyfords and the Admiral at Branx Brig to the west,
and gained the ridge. The Admiral could see the Scots to the south.

When he got news of the English movement James decided to move his
force from Flodden Edge to occupy Branxton Hill, a mile to the north. As they
arrived in the new position the English were appearing opposite, and for two
hours the Scots watched the enemy deploy. The Admiral was just south of the

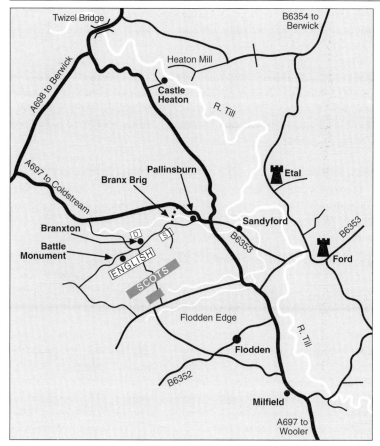

Wark Castle

Wark, 13 miles SW by A698 and B6350.

Only the ruins of the castle remain. It was one of a line of border castles of strategic importance in the wars between the Scots and the English. It fell to James IV in 1513 and was rebuilt with a polygonal keep four storeys high and on each floor 'fyve grete murdour holes, shot with grete voultes of stone, except one stage wich is with Tymbre, so that grete bumbardes may be shot out at icheon them'. Trap doors were made in the floors to lift the cannon into place. It held out against an attack by the Scots in 1523, but the days of tall towers, even armed with cannon, were over; they could not stand against improved artillery.

monument with his brother, Sir Edmund Howard, on his right, a mounted reserve under Lord Dacre north of the church, and his father, Surrey, on his left astride the road running south from the village. King James was astride that same road, to the south of the dog-leg, with the Highlanders and Islanders under the Earls of Argyll and Lennox to his right, the men of Earls Erroll, Crawford and Montrose immediately to his left and the Borderers and Highlanders of Lord Home and the Earl of Huntley on the far left. The French and Bothwell's Lothians were in reserve.

The battle started with artillery fire in which, by chance, Robin Borthwick was killed. Home's Borderers were the first to move, charging Sir Edmund's Cheshire levies and pushing them back. Erroll advanced in support and James also moved forward. The Admiral's men held against Erroll's, but Surrey recoiled under the force of James's charge. Dacre's reserves fell on the Borderers as they plundered the dead and thus Home's men were thrust from the field and the English right was steadied. On the left the last of the English were still coming up under Sir Edward Stanley. He deployed part of his force to face the Highlanders on the Scottish right, while the rest passed west of Mardon in the dead ground east of Pace Hill to appear suddenly on the Highlanders' flank to loose a hail of arrows on them. Bothwell and d'Aussi had moved forward in support of James, and Stanley's men, having put the Highlanders to flight, fell on their rear. The English enfolded and destroyed their adversaries, killing James, two dozen Scottish lords and some 10,000 men.

The Battles of Carham, 1016 and 1370

Wark, 13 miles SW by A698 and B6350.

The River Tweed became a recognised border as a result of the battle that took place here in 1016. The likely site is just to the east of the village of Wark and here Earl Uhtred was killed, yielding control of the Borders as far south as the Tweed to the Scots. A second battle took place here in 1370, probably to the west of the village on the way to Carham. Again the Scots won.

The Battle of Ancrum Moor, 27 February 1545

Ancrum, 25 miles SW by A698 and NW by A68, 2 miles N of village towards Melrose.

The 'rough wooing' began when the betrothal of the child Mary, Queen of Scots to Henry VIII's son Edward was repudiated by the Scots; the marriage would, if the English had their way, be imposed by force. Henry's troops ravaged the Border country, burning, raping and looting. On 27 February 1545 an English band under Sir Ralph Evers and Sir Brian Latoun was returning to base at Jedburgh after a raid on Melrose during which they had desecrated the tombs of the Douglases. Lying in wait for them as evening drew on was Archibald Douglas, Earl of Angus. The English were probably following the route of Dere Street, the Roman road that ran north-east of the modern road, and can be detected in a line of trees. As the English approached, Angus withdrew his vanguard over the summit of Gersit Law, the highest point of the NE/SW ridge over which the A68 passes, now crowned with a 19th-century mausoleum. The English pursued, but as they crested the hill and the evening sun shone full in their eyes, the Scots

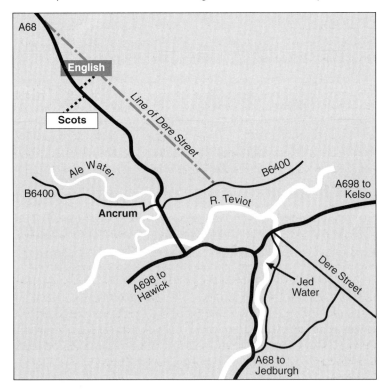

struck. The English were driven back down the hill, eastwards onto Ancrum Moor. A troop of 700 Borderers who had been pressed into English service changed sides and added their efforts to the destruction of the invaders. Some 800 men, including Evers and Latoun, fell and a still greater number were taken prisoner, while the losses of the Scots were trivial. An old monument of red sandstone is said to stand on the line of Dere Street, accessible by a footpath to the north-east a little way up the A68 from the south-west running path to the mausoleum. It marks the grave of Lilliard, a Scottish heroine who died in the battle avenging the killing of her lover by the English.

High on a rocky outcrop stands this small, rectangular tower with a stone wall around it. This stern border fort is said to have aroused the imagination of the young Walter Scott. It is open April to September 9.30am to 6.30pm and opens 2pm Sunday.

Smailholm Tower

22 miles SW by A698 to Kelso then 6 miles NW by B6397 and minor road. Historic Scotland. Tel: (01573) 460365.

The castle on a promontory overlooking the River Tweed is based on a Norman motte and bailey which is clear to see. The great tower-keep with its three floors is the work of Hugh du Puiset, Bishop of Durham in about 1160. It was severely damaged in 1513 when James IV invaded England before his defeat at Flodden and the then Bishop of Durham set about repairing and strengthening it. Clapham's Tower was built to mount artillery with a casemated gun position covering the approach to the inner ward and with an unusual angular front. The corner towers were also given angular faces, for what purpose is obscure. They did not offer the opportunity to act as caponiers, that is as fighting galleries to cover the ditch. Plans were made to replace the curtain wall with a four-pointed bastion, better suited to artillery warfare, but they were never carried out.

Norham Castle

Norham, 7 miles SW by A698, B6470 and minor road. English Heritage. Tel: (01289) 382329. Open April to October 10am to 6pm.

This is one of a very few Iron Age brochs found this far south. The broch is a hollow-walled tower with only a single doorway as an opening to the exterior, designed for defence and shelter. The top of the wall served as a fighting gallery, but the purpose was to give people and livestock an impregnable stronghold against attackers rather than a base from which to fight them off. This example is in a fort defended by ramparts and ditches which have been obscured, in part, by later works.

Edin's Hall Broch

N of Preston, 13 miles NW by A6105, B6355 and N on A6112. About 1 mile from road. Historic Scotland. Open site.

Robert the Bruce died in 1329 and his infant son David II was crowned in 1331, at the age of 7, together with his queen, Joan, sister of Edward III. Edward Balliol, son of the Scottish king who had died in 1296, invaded Scotland and had himself crowned in 1332, but was overthrown and sought Edward III's help. The English King revoked the Treaty of Northampton and together the two Edwards besieged Berwick. The Scottish Regent, Archibald Douglas, attempted to distract them with border raids, but had to act directly because of the treaty reached with the defenders of Berwick that the town would yield if not relieved before 20 July. He drew up his force on the southern slope of Witches Knowe, facing Edward's army on Halidon Hill to the south-east. A farm in the valley is still called Bogend, though the land has been drained since that time, and the low moor was boggy

The Battle of Halidon Hill, 19 July 1333

Off A6105, 1 mile NW of Berwick, to NE by minor road.

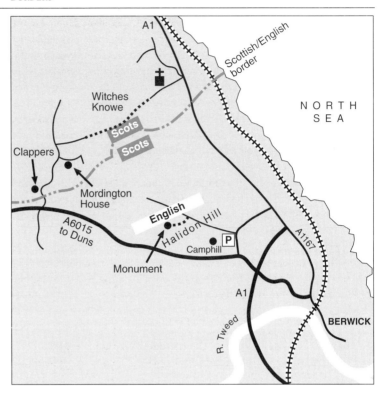

The Battle of Halidon Hill

indeed. As the Scots struggled forward Edward's archers loosed a torrent of arrows and those that survived had to climb the hill to get at Edward's men-at-arms. The battle lasted all afternoon, but eventually the Scots broke and were ruthlessly pursued and put to the sword, losing perhaps as many as 10,000 men for an English loss of 100. Douglas was killed and Berwick fell.

Eyemouth Forts

Eyemouth, 7 miles N by A1 and A1107.

The Duke of Somerset invaded Scotland to enforce the betrothal of Mary, Queen of Scots to Edward VI in 1547 in the campaign known as the 'rough wooing'. As part of the operation some of the earliest bastion fortifications in England and Scotland were built here. Thomas Petit constructed a massive bastion earthwork across the promontory. Another, beyond this, was built by French engineers after the English had withdrawn in 1557, with a bastion at either end of an earthen rampart.

CARLISLE

Tourist information: Carlisle Visitor Centre, Old Town Hall, Green Market. Tel: (01228) 512444.

Carlisle commands the only easy route on the west between England and Scotland and thus was, for centuries, of major strategic importance. The Romans were here for 300 years. In addition to its formal military function as a fortified defensive position, it was a base from which attempts could be made to hold in check, if not pacify, the raiders and outlaws of the Borders.

With the establishment of Norman power here in 1092, William II built the first castle, and a square keep and curtain wall were built after the town had been restored to Henry II by the Scots in 1157. It was extended and improved over the years, notably by John Lewyn, whose contract for the work was signed in 1378 fixing a price of £333 6s. 8d. for the construction of the outer gatehouse. Henry VIII had major modifications carried out to make it suitable for artillery. The parapets were levelled off, wide gun embrasures made and the walkways strengthened in 1541 by Stephen von Haschenperg, a Bohemian engineer.

As a fighting installation its record is less than perfect. It fell quickly to Marmaduke Langdale when the Scots invaded England in 1648, but it did not fall easily to Cromwell, the siege lasting nine months. It was bypassed in the Jacobite uprising of 1715, but had fallen into such neglect that it was surrendered after a short siege to Bonnie Prince Charlie's forces in 1745 and his men soon yielded it up when the Duke of Cumberland had cannon brought from Whitehaven on 27 December. It is said that over 1,100 shots were fired the next day and the castle was surrendered on the 30th. An exhibition devoted to the Jacobite risings can be seen. The castle also served as a prison and the graffiti made by the unfortunates held here survive.

Carlisle Castle
Castle Way. English Heritage. Tel: (01228) 591922. Open daily April to October 9.30am to 6pm, November to March 10am to 4pm.

The Border Regiment and King's Own Border Regiment Museum
Queen Mary's Tower, Carlisle Castle. Open as castle.
The regiment was raised in 1702 and, through amalgamation, became the King's Own Border Regiment in 1959. The regiment has seen service against the Jacobites, in the American War of Independence, the Peninsular War, China, India, Burma, the North-West Frontier, Egypt, the Boer War and World Wars I and II. In 1944 they fought with great distinction at Arnhem in Operation Market-Garden. The displays include dioramas and video presentations.

The role of Carlisle in the history of the Borders is told here in thrilling style. The Romans have their place, but most fascinating is the coverage of the reivers – the lawless raiders who number amongst their descendants two Presidents of the United States, Nixon and Johnson. A car-trail leaflet to guide visitors to the reiver country is available.

Tullie House
Castle Street. Tel: (01228) 34781. Open Monday to Saturday from 10am, Sunday from 12 noon.

The Commonwealth War Graves Commission plot lies in the southern part of the cemetery, and there is another small group of graves, which includes those of men of the Polish Army and Air Force, a little way to the north-west. From World War I there are 124 United Kingdom graves, 2 Australian and 8 Canadian. The World War II burials are of 108 men from the United Kingdom, 2 Australian, 12 Canadian and 7 New Zealand. Many of the airmen flew from Crosby-on-Eden where the Solway Aviation Museum is sited.

Carlisle (Dalston Road) Cemetery
Dalston Road (B5299) on SW of city.

Henry VIII's disputes with the Scots, who were allies of his enemies, the French, flamed up once again in 1542 and, in October, he sent the Duke of Norfolk on an expedition to burn Roxborough and Kelso. The organisation of the invaders was faulty, even to the extent of failing to provide the troops with their beer, and it withdrew to England. James V then sent 17,000 troops on a similar raid into

The Battle of Solway Moss, 24 November 1542
Longtown, 8 miles N by A7. Just S of the town.

Hollows Tower

N of Canonbie off A7. Tel: (013873) 71876. Open by appointment, entry by donation.

A stone tower-house typical of the Borders. The poverty of the region prevented the building of more lavish defences, while the instability of the times demanded at least some basic security.

England. A force of only 3,000 was sent to oppose them. The two major roads to Longtown from the south and east are more recent. The A7 follows the route of the new road of the 1850s, while the A6071 from Brampton is the turnpike of 1817 and the countryside has been enclosed since the time of the battle. The Scots saw the English flags on the hill where a minor road now branches north-west on the edge of the woodland and drew themselves up halfway between the English and the town with their left on the A6071 and their right near Arthuret House, near St Michael's Church on the minor road running due south. At first they moved to attack but, fearing they were going into action against the advance party of a much larger force, they hesitated and then attempted to retreat. The English cavalry fell on them and, although the Scots made a stand at the ford across the Esk, they were soon killed or put to flight into the marshes of Solway Moss north-west of the river. James V was in any case unwell, but the news of this shameful defeat hastened his death, leaving the infant Mary to become Queen of Scots.

Hermitage Castle

Hermitage, 26 miles N by A7 to Canonbie and B6357, then minor road NW. Historic Scotland. Tel: (013873) 76222. Open April to September Monday to Saturday 9.30am to 6.30pm, Sunday 2pm to 6.30pm, October to March weekends only.

Liddlesdale was reiver country, and the forbidding bulk of Hermitage Castle fits the history of brutality, theft and murder that characterised the region for so many years. The original manor house of the Dacre family was built between 1358 and 1365 with a block on either side of a small court. It was then converted into a tower-house and, in about 1400, projecting square towers were added. Above them and linking them is a continuous parapet. Mid-16th-century earthworks can be detected; a bastion on the northern side and a redan-shaped (pointed) work on the west, possibly for artillery.

The castle controlled the route through the southern uplands of Scotland both for defence against the English and as a centre from which an attempt to control the reivers could be made. The Earl of Bothwell, husband of Mary Queen of Scots, was based here as Lieutenant of the Marches.

Museum of Border Arms and Armour

Teviothead, 32 miles N by A7. Tel: (01450) 850237.

A display of civilian weapons and equipment from the 16th century is to be seen here. There is also a craft gallery specialising in Celtic jewellery in gold and silver.

The Solway Aviation Museum

Carlisle Airport, Crosby-on-Eden, 8 miles NE by B6264 and A689. Tel: (01228) 75517. Open Sunday 10am to 5pm.

This operational civil airport was, in World War II, RAF Crosby-on-Eden. The museum is being developed and opening times will be extended. The entrance is through a bomb shelter. The Blue Streak rocket was tested in Cumbria and an exhibit is devoted to it here. There is also a small collection of post-war civil and military aircraft.

Naworth Castle

Brampton, 12 miles E by A69. Tel: (016977) 41156. Open by appointment to groups of 15 or more.

Lord Dacre received a licence to crenellate (fortify) his house on a promontory above the River Irthing in 1335. Many of his successors served as Wardens of the March, and the castle became a headquarters for the policing of the area, beset as it was with reivers. The east wing, now a picture gallery, was previously a barracks for 120 men. In the 17th and later centuries the castle was modified to become a fine country house.

A minor road from Naworth to Lanercost passes the ruined abbey from which, turning east, it joins the line of Hadrian's Wall and the B6318 which runs along much of the wall's length.

The Romans surrounded rather than penetrated the Lake District, with the exception of the Ambleside-Hardknott-Ravenglass and the High Street routes. The A595 follows the Roman road to Egremont, and Maryport was reached by a side road over which the A594 passes south-east of Dearham. The Roman fort lies immediately inland of the museum which is housed in a former Naval Reserve Battery of 1885. It has information on the fort as well as a large collection of Roman altars, religious sculptures and the mysterious serpent stone.

Senhouse Roman Museum

The Battery, Sea Brows, Maryport, 27 miles SW by A596. Tel: (01900) 816168. Open April to June and October Tuesday and Thursday to Sunday, July to September daily 10am to 5pm, November to March Friday to Sunday 10.30am to 4pm.

HADRIAN'S WALL

Public transport information: Cumbria Travel Link, tel: (01228) 81128112. Northumberland Public Transport Helpline, tel: (01670) 533128. Train services: Carlisle, tel: (01228) 44711, Tyneside, tel: (0191) 232 6262. Entries below are centred on Carlisle and on Hexham.

The greatest Roman monument in Britain is the 74-mile long wall built on the order of the Emperor Hadrian in AD122. It took six years to build and runs from Bowness-on-Solway in the west to Wallsend-on-Tyne in the east. It was as much an exhibition of dominance as a defensive line, for there was already a line of forts along Stanegate, the Roman road from Carlisle to Newcastle immediately to the south. The basic arrangement was a ditch on the northern side behind which the wall, in stone or turf, ran up to 15 feet high with a walkway in the rear of a parapet. Behind that there was a military road and to the rear of that, to offer protection from the south and create a military area, a vallum, a ditch 20 feet wide and 10 feet deep with mounds 20 feet high on each side. At intervals of a Roman mile were milecastles garrisoned by eight men, and between them two turrets for sentries. A number of large forts were also built at which there were crossing points for civilian traffic.

There is little evidence that fighting took place along the wall. Indeed, it was rendered redundant for a time when, from AD140 to 163 the Antonine Wall further north across the narrowest part of Scotland became the forward position. By the 3rd century Roman power was declining and the wall's function ceased. In the east and west the materials were plundered for local building, but in the sparsely populated centre it survived. It was declared a World Heritage Site in 1987.

Walking

In the summer the Hadrian's Wall Bus calls at all the major sites between Carlisle, Haltwhistle and Hexham and connects with local bus services. It can provide an easy return to the car after walking a length of the wall.

Hadrian's Wall from Carlisle

From Banks to Walltown, N of Haltwhistle on A69.

From Brampton, off the A69, minor roads lead to Lanercost, with its fine, ruined abbey, to Banks and then along the wall eastwards towards the junction with the B6318, the Military Road attributed to General Wade, much of which was created by building with or on top of the wall itself. The road was part of the provision made for the swift movement of troops after the defeat of the Jacobites in 1746.

Banks East Turret
Minor road E of Banks, NE of Brampton off A69. Open site.
A well-preserved turf wall turret. Two other turrets, Leahill and Piper Sike, are near by.

Birdoswald Roman Fort
Near Gilsland on B6318, N of A69. English Heritage. Tel: (016977) 47602. Open April to October 10am to 5.30pm.
All the components of the wall can be seen on this site. There is a length of turf wall between the fort and Harrow's Scar milecastle and the granaries and east gate, which is well preserved, can be seen. There is also a visitor centre.

The Battle of Camlon in 537 took place near by. Here King Arthur is said to have fallen, and the tribe he led, the Votadini, were forced to migrate to north Wales, taking with them Arthur's battle name, Red Dragon – now the national emblem of Wales.

Poltross Burn Milecastle
Gilsland, near railway station. Open site.
One of the best-preserved milecastles. There are steps that led to the top of the wall, remains of the gates and barrack blocks. Nearby Willowford Bridge has 1,000 yards of the wall with a turret and the remains of the bridge abutments; a small charge is made by Willowford Farm for access to visitors.

The Roman Army Museum
N of Greenhead. Tel: (016977) 47485. Open March to October daily.
The museum is in the former Carvoran farm steading next to the fort of Magna and Walltown Crags. Here one can gain an insight into the life of the serving Roman soldier through models and reconstructions.

Walltown Crags
NE of Greenhead off B6318. Open site.
A well-preserved section of the wall with a turret that pre-dates the wall itself.

Hadrian's Wall from Hexham

From Cawfields to Heddon-on-the-Wall.

Cawfields Roman Wall
Cawfields, 1 mile N of Haltwhistle on A69.
A fine stretch of wall and vallum with camps, turrets, a fortlet and Milecastle 42 perched on the crags of Whin Sill.

National Park Centre
Once Brewed, on B6318 N of Bardon Mill. Tel: (01434) 344396. April to October.
Information and interpretation on the central section of the wall, and also on the National Park.

Vindolanda Fort and Museum
N of Bardon Mill on A69. Tel: (01434) 344277. Open daily 10am to 6pm (closes later in summer, earlier in winter).
An open-air museum has reconstructions of the wall in both turf and stone, a Roman temple, house, shop and remains of eight successive Roman forts and civilian settlements. The museum has many unusual artefacts from everyday Roman life including writing tablets, leather goods, textiles, pottery and wooden objects.

Housesteads Roman Fort and Museum
3 miles NE of Bardon Mill on B6318. English Heritage. Tel: (01434) 344363. Open April to October 10am to 6pm, November to March 10am to 4pm.
Built on a dramatic site on Whin Sill in about AD124, this is the most complete Roman fort to be seen in Britain. The full curtain walls with the foundations of the towers and gates are here, together with remains of all the principal buildings that constituted a typical fort, including a hospital and flushing latrines. Here also are the remains of the civilian settlement that sprang up next to so many forts. Artefacts discovered show that cavalry from Fresia, in the north-west of what is now the Netherlands, were stationed here in the 3rd century.

Sewingshields Milecastle
Off B6318 E of Housesteads.
The stretch of wall running east of the fort is largely unexcavated and includes Milecastle 35, which has been excavated, and a number of turrets.

Carrawburgh and Mithras Temple
4 miles W of Chollerford on B6318. Open site.
There are traces of a fort built astride the vallum and the remains of a temple dedicated to the sun-god Mithras.

Black Carts Turret
2 miles W of Chollerford. Open site.
A 500-yard length of wall with a turret.

Chesters Roman Fort and Museum
2 miles W of Chollerford on B6318. English Heritage. Tel: (01434) 681379. Open April to October 9.30am to 6pm, November to March 10am to 4pm.
Chesters was built astride the wall above the crossing of the River Tyne. It was one of the earliest sites on the wall to be excavated and the finds made in the mid-19th century are still displayed in the museum in the fashion of the time. The layout of the fort can be seen and a short walk leads to the well-preserved bath-house and the abutments of the Roman bridge over the river.

Brunton Turret
Between Low Brunton and Wall on A6079. Open site.
The turret rises to a height of 8 feet and there is a length of wall of some 65 yards.

Heddon-on-the-Wall
E of Heddon village, S of A69. Open site.
A good stretch of wall up to 10 feet thick. There is a medieval kiln near the west end.

HEXHAM

Tourist information: The Manor Office, Hallgate. Tel: (01434) 605225.

Border History Museum

The Old Gaol, Hallgate. Tel: (01434) 652349. Open mid-April to October daily, and November and February Saturday to Tuesday.

The Border country was not under any steady official control until the Union with Scotland in 1603. Until then local lords and bands of reivers made life precarious, though the worst period was in the 15th and 16th centuries. The story of those troubled times is told here, as is the history of the Jacobite Rebellion of 1715.

The Battle of Heavenfield, 635.

Chollerford, 6 miles N by A6079 and 2 miles E by B6318.

This is where King Oswald is said to have defeated Cadwallon, King of North Wales in a battle that restored Christianity to Northumbria. A tall wooden cross stands at the roadside and St Oswald's Church marks the place on which the saint erected a cross before the battle. Information is available at the church and the council have provided a lay-by and information board.

Corbridge Roman Site and Museum

Corbridge, 4 miles E by A695 and NW by minor road. English Heritage. Tel: (01434) 632349. Open April to October 10am to 6pm.

The fort on the road from York to Scotland developed into a major settlement which endured until the 5th century. Outside the fort itself are the foundations of barracks and workshops, temples, houses and granaries. The museum is a good place to start a visit to Hadrian's Wall and has displays of weapons and armour. Open Wednesday to Sunday in winter.

Aydon Castle

Aydon, 1 mile NE of Corbridge off B6321. English Heritage. Tel: (01434) 632450.

A fine example of a fortified manor house. It was built in the late 13th century and fortified against the Scots. Nonetheless, the Scots took and pillaged it in 1315. It was converted into a farmhouse in the 17th century. Open daily April to October.

The Battle of Hexham, 15 May 1464

Hexham Levels, 2 miles SE by B6306.

The Duke of Somerset, with Lords Roos and Hungerford who had escaped from the fight at Hedgeley Moor, gathered what Lancastrian strength he could at Hexham. The Marquess of Montagu attacked him with a superiority of about eight to one and put him to flight. The Yorkists captured the leaders and executed them, thus ending Henry VI's and Queen Margaret's attempt to establish a power base in the north.

NEWCASTLE-UPON-TYNE

Tourist information: Central Library, Princess Square. Tel: (0191) 261 0610. Also Central Station. Tel: (0191) 230 0030.

Museum of Antiquities

University of Newcastle-upon-Tyne. Tel: (0191) 222 7846. Open daily.

A full-length model of Hadrian's Wall is to be seen together with numerous Roman artefacts in this outstanding archaeological collection. There is also a reconstruction of a temple to Mithras.

This is a museum of local history, but it also has material relating to the 15th/ 19th The King's Royal Hussars and the Northumberland Hussars forming the award-winning display 'A Soldier's Life'. There are audio-visual and interactive displays of army life in peace and war, including the experience of soldiers' wives and children.

Newcastle Discovery

Blandford House, Blandford Square. Tel: (0191) 232 6789. Open 10am to 5pm, Sunday 2pm to 5pm.

The museum was established in 1983 by members of the North East Military Vehicle Club and many of the exhibits are on loan from them. There are some 50 British, American and Canadian vehicles on show, most dating from before 1945. They include staff cars, jeeps, trucks, tractors, a water carrier and a field workshop. Fighting machines include a 25-pounder field gun, the Mobat anti-tank gun, the German 2-cm Flak 38 gun, a Vickers 3.7 anti-aircraft gun and Ferret and Saracen armoured cars. There is also a mock-up of a World War I trench and an Anderson air raid shelter. The three searchlights are in working order. The building itself is the last surviving structure of the 1929 North East Coast Exhibition, a steel-framed listed building.

Military Vehicle Museum

Exhibition Park, N of University, car park on B6388 Claremont Road. Tel: (0191) 281 7222. Open daily 10am to 4pm.

Hadrian's Wall ran to this military settlement on the banks of the Tyne. Fragments of the fort and a length of wall are there, and a section of wall has been reconstructed.

Wallsend

Wallsend, 3 miles E of Tyne Tunnel on A187. Tourist information tel: (0191) 200 8535. Open site.

The priory which the castle surrounds was founded in about 1090, but the site has been the burial place of the kings of Northumbria since the 7th century in a former religious house that was destroyed by the Danes. The importance of the site, commanding the entrance to the river, led to the construction of the medieval castle. It was later strengthened with an Italian-style bastion, and the Spanish Battery was added lower down the cliff in the mid-16th century. Until the end of the Napoleonic Wars there was a matching battery on the south shore. In 1893 the Spanish Battery was equipped with one 6-inch barrel-loader (BL) and two 6-pounder quick-firing (QF) guns, and another 6-inch BL was added before World War I.

At the castle itself the armament had increased to 20 guns, of which six were rifled, by 1881. By 1905 there were two 6-inch Mark VII BLs, one 9.2-inch Mark X BL and two 12-pounder QFs, the positions of which can be seen today.

Tynemouth Castle

Tynemouth, 9 miles E by A1058. English Heritage. Tel: (0191) 257 1090. Open April to September 10am to 6pm, November to March Wednesday to Sunday 10am to 1pm and 2pm to 4pm. Gun Battery April to September weekends and Bank Holidays.

It is a striking experience to see the full-size reconstruction of the West Gate of the 3rd-century supply base built by the Romans. The excavation of the remains continues and the museum displays the finds. There is a reconstruction of the house of a Roman volunteer and Timequest, a hands-on demonstration of an archaeological dig.

Arbeia Roman Fort and Museum

Baring Street, South Shields, 8 miles E, S of river, by A194. Tel: (0191) 456 8740. Open daily.

In World War II Newcastle endured heavy bombing in which many civilians were killed. The servicemen killed are buried here in a plot in the south-east of the cemetery. There are 69 United Kingdom graves, 1 Canadian and 1 South African. On the cremation memorial there are 120 United Kingdom names, one Canadian, 1 from India and Pakistan and 1 West African.

Newcastle-upon-Tyne (West Road) Cemetery

Denton Bank.

The Battle of Newburn Ford, 1640
Newburn, 5 miles W by A6085, bridge to Ryton over River Tyne.

In 1637 Charles I's attempt to impose a new Prayer Book on the Scots led to a rising that was eventually settled, or appeared to be settled, by the Pacification of Berwick in June 1639 by which the Scottish army under Alexander Leslie would disperse and Charles agreed to summon a Parliament after 11 years of personal rule. Parliament met on 13 April 1640 and showed itself as opposed to the King as ever; it was dissolved on 5 May. The Scots moved south once more to threaten Newcastle, which they decided to take from the more vulnerable southern side. Their intended crossing of the Tyne was opposed by Lord Conway who built fortifications to cover both fords, one of which was where Newburn Bridge now crosses the river and another at Ryton Haugh, to the east. A public footpath runs west along the southern side of the building towards which the road south from the bridge leads, and fortification earthworks are said to be visible there.

Scottish artillery pounded the forts and the Scots were able to get across the river, their cavalry soon putting the unpaid and unenthusiastic English troops to flight, although some retreated to the higher ground and fought on for a time before capitulating. With that the Scots occupied Newcastle and, in order to buy them off, Charles was forced to summon a fresh Parliament. The resulting disputes were to build towards the Civil War. The tide of industrial development has obscured much to the area, but the positions of the Scots on the high ground at Newburn Grange, north-west of the bridge, and of the English on the south bank, south and east of the bridge, can be appreciated.

PENRITH

Tourist information: Robinson's School, Middlegate. Tel: (01768) 867466.
The town stands at the crossroads of the roads to Carlisle in the north and the trans-Pennine road from Scotch Corner, now the A66 and once a Roman road, which continues to Keswick. Penrith Castle was built in the 14th century and its ruins may be visited (open site) in the park on the edge of the town. It was clearly built to provide accommodation as well as security, as it was arranged in a great square of buildings with a central courtyard. It is similar in many aspects to Bolton Castle in Wensleydale, except that it has only two towers, one on the east and one on the north side, next to the gateway. The gatehouse was strengthened and provided with forebuildings in the 1470s when a number of other alterations were made to make it more comfortable as a residence, such as adding bigger windows.

Kirkoswald Castle
Kirkoswald, 7 miles NE by A6 and B6413. Access by permission of landowner.

The ruins of a castle of the 13th century, overlooking the Eden valley. Three towers and the gatehouse remain. The moat was added in the 15th century.

Appleby Castle
Appleby-in-Westmorland, 13 miles SE by A66. Tel: (017683) 51402. Open April to October daily 10am to 5pm, 4pm in October.

The Norman grip on the region was secured by the construction of the great square keep here, rather than the development of the Roman fort at Brougham. Completed in 1170, the castle is a simple keep and bailey development of the motte and bailey concept which was possibly the first Norman fortification. The house which occupies one end of the bailey is a later addition. The keep houses a museum with replicas of Roman armour and insignia, medieval and 17th-century furniture and a collection of 19th-century bicycles!

The Roman fort of Veteris was taken over by the Normans in about 1100 as part of their attempt to prevent the Scots invading either from the north or from the west of Brough. The northern third of the fort provided the new castle while the southern part was converted into a bailey. A great square keep was built at the western side over the Roman barracks on a foundation of herringbone masonry, an example of which can be seen at the north-eastern end of the curtain wall. The keep was burned down by William the Lion, King of Scotland, when he invaded in 1174. The keep was rebuilt, possibly by Robert de Vipont, to whom King John granted the barony in 1203. The ground-floor doorway was added by Lady Anne Clifford in about 1660, when the keep was converted as a guest house and given fireplaces. The first floor was a barrack room and the room above was the residence of the castle commander and originally had a pitched roof, later replaced by a fighting platform. The north curtain has twice been repaired, the central section by Robert Clifford in about 1300 and a short length to the west of that, including a latrine, by Lady Anne. The kitchen, brewhouse and bakehouse at the eastern end are also Lady Anne's work. The eastern curtain wall once had a hall against it which was demolished by Robert Clifford when he built Clifford's Tower at the south-east corner and the hall over the storerooms between that and the gatehouse in the south curtain. His grandson, Roger (died 1389) remodelled the hall block, adding, above the hall, the Great Chamber, used by the lord as a private dining and reception room and connected to the sleeping apartment in Clifford's Tower. The building was damaged by fire in 1521 after a Christmas feast and the remains to be seen today owe much to the restoration undertaken by Lady Anne. After her death in 1676 the castle fell into decay. The keep was gutted in 1695 and the stone from the domestic wing plundered to repair Brough Mill in 1763.

The site of the Roman fort, one of a chain of forts including Kirkby Thore, Brough and Bowes, is alongside the castle, suggesting that the theory that the Normans converted it to their use is incorrect. The first documentary evidence dates from the death of Robert de Vipont in 1228. The square keep and the basis of the curtain wall probably date from Robert's time and the modification of the ditches suggests that the fort was adapted as an outer bailey. Robert Clifford succeeded to the lordship of Brougham in 1283 and strengthened the castle, turning the keep into a gatehouse-keep by adding the inner and outer gates with a court between them, and adding another floor to the keep itself as accom-modation, with a chapel attached. Clifford died at Bannockburn (1314) and it was his grandson, Roger, who undertook the next phase of development up to his death in 1389. The buildings against the east and south curtain walls, with storerooms below, gave him a great hall, kitchen and chapel of a size and convenience suited to a Warden of the Marches. After the Civil War Lady Anne Clifford restored the castle, adding fireplaces and doorways in the Tudor style. The castle was partly demolished in 1691 and any usable materials were sold off in 1714.

Brough Castle
Brough, 21 miles SE by A66. English Heritage. Open site.

Pendragon Castle
Near Kirkby Stephen, 4 miles S of Brough. Access by permission of landowner.

A 12th-century castle, pillaged by the Scots and burned down twice, in the 14th and 16th centuries. It was restored by Lady Anne Clifford. Legend has it that it was the home of Uther Pendragon, father of King Arthur.

Brougham Castle
Eamont Bridge, 1 mile S by A6 and E by B5320. English Heritage. Tel: (01768) 862488. Open daily April to October 10am to 6pm.

Mayburgh Earthwork

Eamont Bridge, 1 mile S by A6 and W B5320. English Heritage. Open site.

The ancient importance of the location on the crossing of the River Eamont is shown by the prehistoric earthwork. It has banks up to 15 feet high and covers an area of one and a half acres. A solitary stone stands within.

The Battle of Clifton Moor, 18 December 1745

Clifton, 2 miles south by A6.

As Bonnie Prince Charlie and the Jacobites withdrew from Derby, the Duke of Cumberland commanded the pursuit. On 17 December the Prince slept at the inn at Shap, spending £4 17s on food and 2 guineas on lodging for himself and his party. Lord George Murray arrived from Kendal the next day about noon, the Scots having had a terrible journey in heavy rain up the tortuous old road, losing carts and cannon in the streams which were inadequately bridged. The Hanoverians followed, equally impeded by the terrain.

As Murray approached Clifton he saw a group of light horse who fled before them. He gave chase towards Lowther and caught a few from whom he learned that the Hanoverians were close behind, so he sent the cannon and carriages on to Penrith. As the Scots debated what to do, the Duke of Perth observed men appearing to the south, drawn up in two lines. They were Bland's Regiment, Kerr's Dragoons and part of Ligonier's Horse. Perth made for Penrith to seek reinforcements while, in the setting sun, Murray deployed his troops, from right to left, Glengarry men, Col. Roy Stewart's, Stewarts of Appin and Cluny's Macphersons, about 1,000 men in all. He made the most of their numbers by having flags carried back and forth, first unfurled then furled, to give the impression of substantial troop movements. The trap was set with the Glengarry men concealed on the west behind a stone wall, ready to fire, Roy Stewart on the edge of the village near the church and the rest along the hedges and embankments of the lane heading south-east to Cliburn. No reinforcements arrived; indeed, the Prince sent an order to retreat which was wisely ignored.

Dacre Castle

Dacre, 5 miles SW on minor road between A66 and A592. Not open.

The 14th-century pele tower can be seen from the road, standing guard over the little settlement to give shelter to the inhabitants when raiders threatened.

Some 500 dragoons advanced dismounted, cautiously working through the little enclosures. In the fitful moonlight they could see little of the Scots, but were themselves easy to see. Murray ordered Cluny forward to a hedge running north/south which turned out to be lined with dragoons and concealed a ditch. There was an exchange of fire, followed by a charge to Murray's cry of 'Claymore!' The dragoons were thrown back into the flanking fire of the Glengarrys and tried no more. Under the cover of darkness the Jacobites withdrew safely to Penrith and thence, without trouble, to Carlisle. The last battle on English soil had left something above two dozen dead. A monument to Bland's Regiment stands in the churchyard.

Westmorland and Cumberland Yeomanry Museum

Dalemain, 3 miles SW by A66 and A592. Tel: (017684) 86450. Open April to mid-October Sunday to Thursday 11am to 5pm.

The museum is located in a country house on the site of the property acquired by Sir Edward Hasell, steward of Lady Anne Clifford, in 1680. The history of the yeomanry from 1819 to 1919 is portrayed in displays of uniforms, prints, photographs and weaponry.

ULVERSTON

Tourist information: Coronation Hall, County Square. Tel: (01229) 587120.

The property has been in the possession of the Strickland family since 1239, but the pele tower dates from about 1340. It varies from the usual defensive border work in its great size. The basement is tunnel-vaulted as is usual but it also has an added tower in the western side, originally to provide garderobes (toilets), and a staircase turret. The range alongside was probably built quite soon after the pele tower but, as is to be expected of a residence in use over the centuries, most of the features to be seen are of later date, notably of the 16th century. The gardens are open from 12.30pm.

Sizergh Castle

Sizergh, near Kendal, 15 miles E by A590 and A591. National Trust. Open April to October Sunday to Thursday 1.30pm to 5.30pm.

A pele tower built between 1315 and 1360 for the protection of the lands of Furness Abbey. It could have been a replacement for an earlier tower destroyed in the raid of 1322 by Robert the Bruce. It appears to have been used as a prison and courthouse. The entrance to the cellar dungeon is now in the ladies' lavatory. It originally had four floors connected by a helical staircase, but two floors have been removed and a new stair added.

Dalton Castle

Market Place, Dalton-in-Furness, 5 miles SW by A590. National Trust. Open April to September Saturday 2pm to 5pm.

The Romans contained the Lake District in a circle of roads and forts, the southern side having a fort at Ambleside from which a road ran over the Wrynose and Hardknott passes down to the sea at Ravenglass. The coast was overlooked from the Hardknott Pass, where a fort and a parade ground were built in what must be the most stirring location in Britain. If approaching from the east the road through Wrynose Bottom passes through a gate and over a bridge and a side road to the left leads to a hostel. This track runs precisely along the line of the Roman road which later made a right turn up to Hardknott; the modern road follows a different route.

Hardknott Roman Fort

Hardknott Pass, 15 miles N, but longer drive, on minor road from Ravenglass to Ambleside. Caution – narrow, difficult road.

The layout of the fort can be seen quite clearly. The track to the entrance passes the bath-house, through the main gate to lead directly to the administrative headquarters. To the left is the commander's house and to the right the granary. The other three gates were flanked by towers and towers were positioned at each corner. Rocky outcrops would have prevented adherence to the rigid layout usual in Roman forts, and the barrack buildings, doubtless of timber, do not survive. The parade ground can be detected as an artificially flattened area further up the spur on which the fort stands. In clear weather the view is stunning. In murky weather a visitor may, as the author did, get spooked. While standing in the main gate, I heard a horse approaching at speed from behind. It passed as I leaped aside, but nothing was to be seen as the sounds of the animal being pulled up at the HQ building continued.

Ravenglass Roman Bath-House

Ravenglass, off minor road to A595. English Heritage. Open site.

Of the sea fort little survives, but the bath-house walls stand to a height of more than 12 feet and are among the most complete Roman remains in Britain.

The motte of a early Norman castle stands to the north of the surviving structure, and was strengthened with a stone tower and presumably a curtain wall. The Great Hall was on the division between the missing inner bailey and the surviving outer bailey, the curtain wall and gatehouse of which can be seen. The ruins are of the castle built by William de Meschines in about 1130.

Egremont Castle

Egremont, 26 miles NW by A595. In public park.

SCOTLAND

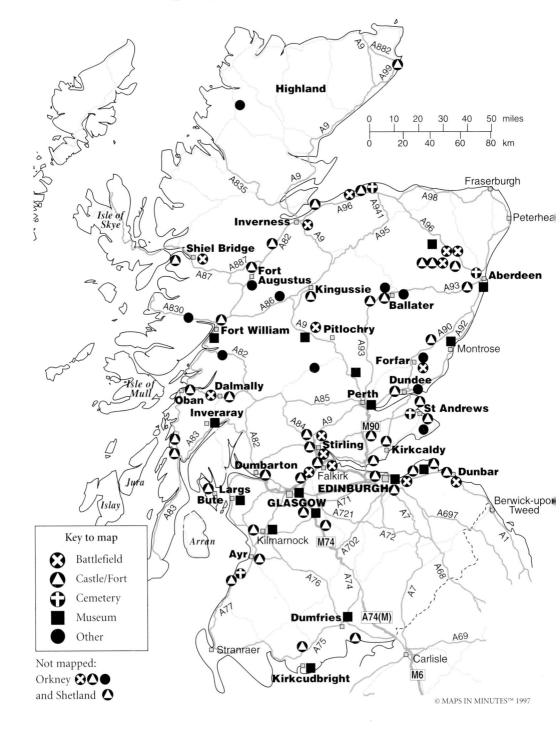

Highland

Fraserburgh

Peterhea

Isle of
Skye

Inverness

Shiel Bridge

Fort
Augustus

Kingussie

Aberdeen

Ballater

Fort William

Pitlochry

Montrose

Forfar

Dundee

Dalmally

Perth

St Andrews

Oban

Inveraray

Stirling

Kirkcaldy

Isle of
Mull

Dumbarton

Falkirk

Dunbar

Jura

Largs

EDINBURGH

Bute

Berwick-upo
Tweed

Islay

GLASGOW

Kilmarnock

Arran

Ayr

Dumfries

Stranraer

Carlisle

Kirkcudbright

Key to map

⊗	Battlefield
▲	Castle/Fort
✚	Cemetery
■	Museum
●	Other

Not mapped:
Orkney ⊗▲●
and Shetland ▲

© MAPS IN MINUTES™ 1997

Scotland presents an interesting puzzle to the military. The mountains of the North-West Highlands are cut abruptly by the geological fault of the Great Glen and the country beyond is difficult; the Grampian Mountains sitting hard against the west coast and providing only a narrow area of less daunting country on the east, widening the further south one goes. To control such country sea power and roads are required. In the far north, in Orkney and Shetland, the Norsemen ruled and it is said they still do today. The brochs and castles of the north and west stand witness to fear of the sea raider.

Narrow glens, boggy uplands and steep hillsides favour the guerrilla fighter and devalue the worth of mere numbers of troops. First the fighting between the clans and then the struggle against the English show the importance of skill and valour over brute numerical superiority. The building of the military roads and the use of the sea were the keys to the subjugation of the Highlands in the 18th century.

Further south again Scotland is almost cut in two by the Firth of Clyde on the west and the Firth of Forth on the east. The narrow neck of land is dominated by Stirling and was the location chosen for the most northerly of the Roman walls. Between here and the Southern Uplands a great number of battles were fought and castles built to control the rich farmlands.

The Southern Uplands bar the road south, or north, depending on which side you regard as home. On the west they run close to the coast, which is cut deep by the Solway Firth leaving a little, marshy flatness round Carlisle. On the east, near Berwick, the going is a little easier and it was on this side of the country that Scots and English slew one another with such regularity. Being of divided loyalties, I have given the much fought-over Borders a chapter of their own, and Hadrian's view of where the dividing line was is in that section.

ABERDEEN

Tourist information: St Nicholas House, Broad Street. Tel: (01224) 632727.

The Gordon Highlanders Museum
St Lukes, Viewfield Road. Tel: (01224) 311200. Open March to October.

The history of 'the finest regiment in the world' (Winston Churchill) spans 200 years. There is a Victoria Cross room, interactive displays with touch screens and an audio-visual theatre. Closed Sunday morning and Monday.

Dyce Old Churchyard
Overlooking the River Don at Dyce, 6 miles NW of Aberdeen by A96 and A947. Commonwealth War Graves Commission.

The World War II burials are mainly of men stationed at RAF Dyce; 23 UK, 13 Canada, 4 Australia, 4 New Zealand and 1 unidentified in a plot to the west of the old church. One of the RAF men was from Czechoslovakia and there is a member of the Polish Air Force. There are ten German graves by the south wall and a World War I grave north-west of the church.

Drum Castle
10 miles W of Aberdeen via Peterculter on the A93. Tel: (01330) 811204. Open daily May to September and weekends in October afternoons only.

Drum, one of the three oldest tower-houses in Scotland, was built by Richard Cementarius in the late 13th century and bestowed on the Irvines by Robert the Bruce in 1323. The keep offers an opportunity to appreciate the working of the medieval fortification, and later domestic additions are interesting. The castle was sacked by Covenanters in May 1644. The Drum Stone, marking the place where Sir Alexander Irvine of Drum looked back on his home and forward on the field of Harlaw where he was to die, is by the roadside at Auchronie, Skene.

The Battle of Harlaw, 24 July 1411
2 miles N of Inverurie (18 miles NW of Aberdeen by A96) left off the B9001.

Reid Harlaw Memorial
Besides the battlefield monument, the gravestone of Sir Gilbert de Greenlaw, showing his armour, is in Kinkell Churchyard near Inverurie.

The rise of the house of Stewart as rulers of all Scotland was not unresisted. The Lord of the Isles attempted to gain lands and titles he held to be his and led a force of some 10,000 men from Ardtornish on the Sound of Mull, fighting as they went. He set Inverness on fire, and advanced towards Aberdeen, reaching the plateau of Harlaw on 23 July. In this fine defensive position, secured to the south-west by the River Urie, and unaware of the approach of the Earl of Mar's hastily assembled forces, he camped. Mar was already at Inverurie with 6,000 men and moved north at dawn, crossing Howford Bridge just west of Lochter Burn. The Highlanders were taken by surprise and the first clash of 'Reid Harlaw' took place roughly on the site of the modern monument. The Lowlanders were pushed back, but reinforcements arrived through the hard-fought day and the battle ended in stalemate. Nearly 1,000 died on each side and few survived unscathed. Both armies retreated, each claiming victory, but Aberdeen had been saved.

The Skirmish at Inverurie, 23 December 1745
The Bass of Inverurie, S of town on B993, around the old churchyard.

With the intention of taking Aberdeen from the Jacobites Macleod of Macleod led 700 men south from Inverness in mid-December 1745. They halted at Inverurie, uncertain as to the situation in Aberdeen, and during the delay the Jacobites organised an attack. A column under Gordon of Avochie moved up the main road while Lord Lewis Gordon took 900 men to the east. The Macleods had men around the churchyard and the Bass (the ruins of a motte and bailey castle) but the fords over the Don and the Urie were unguarded. In the late afternoon the Jacobites attacked from east and west, putting the Macleods to flight with ease.

Agricola's advance from the Forth–Cyde line he had secured in AD81 depended on the establishment of a series of camps up the east coast to allow supply by sea. The native Celtic tribes, lumped together by the Roman narrator Tacitus under the name of Caledonians, cooperated to resist with a series of raids and guerrilla actions. In the face of Agricola's determination to destroy, plunder and enslave them, the Caledonians gathered together in AD84 at Mons Graupius, a site for which the great hill of Bennachie is favoured. The Romans were north of the hill on the far side of the River Urie at Durno.

Agricola kept his legions in camp and used 8,000 auxiliaries as his fighting line, flanked with some 3,000 horse. The Caledonian front line was across the foot of the hill (where Pittodrie car park now is) with further fighters in support on the slopes above; they numbered perhaps fifteen to twenty thousand. Chariots manoeuvred in front of their line, but were dealt with by the cavalry as the Roman line crashed into the Caledonians. As the invaders gained the upper hand, the Caledonians forsook their dominant positions on the hill and were drawn into the fight only to be cut down while those attempting to outflank the Romans were mopped up by the horse. They broke and fled, pursued by Agricola's horsemen; the slaughter continued until dark. The error of offering the Romans pitched battle was not repeated and the conquest of the Caledonians was abandoned two years later.

After the Battle of Auldearn the Royalist forces under the Marquess of Montrose were short of cavalry and attempting to recruit troops to go to the aid of Charles I while hunted by General William Baillie in command of the Covenanters. Baillie followed Montrose south to Alford where there was a ford across the Don, and

The Battle of Mons Graupius, AD84

Bennachie (probable site), 6 miles W of Inverurie. Durno Roman camp: by minor road from Pitcaple on A96 to point between Easterton and Westerton steadings. Forestry Commission car park at Pittodrie signed from the B9002.

Leith Hall

W of Kennethmont 22 miles NW of Inverurie by B9002. National Trust for Scotland. Open May to September. Tel: (01464) 831216.

Exhibition: For Crown and Country: the Military Lairds of Leith Hall.

The Battle of Alford, 2 July 1646

27 miles NW of Aberdeen by the A944 at junction with A980.

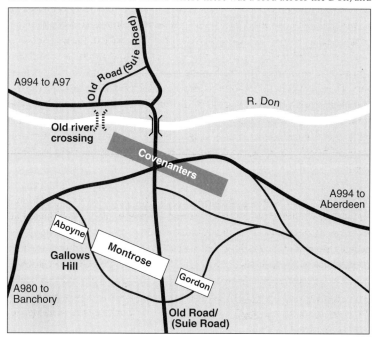

Castle Fraser

4 miles N of Dunnecht on A944. National Trust for Scotland. Open in summer. Tel: (01330) 833463.

One of the Castles of Mar and a superb example of the evolution of the tower-house to castle in Scotland.

discovered Montrose overlooking the ford and the boggy ground from Gallowhill Ridge (between the modern A980 and the minor road running south from the A944 from the river). As soon as Baillie was over the river Lord Gordon led the cavalry on the Royalist right against him. The Covenanter cavalry fought well but support from Nathaniel Gordon's infantry, who hamstrung the enemy horses, tipped the balance and as Baillie's left fell back the rest of Montrose's forces came into action, turning retreat into a rout.

Kildrummy Castle

34 miles NW of Aberdeen, on A97 S of junction with A944. Open April to September Monday to Saturday, Sunday pm only. Tel: (019755) 71331.

At first a plain polygonal enclosure erected in the first half of the 13th century, it was modified by the addition of a chapel in the eastern curtain, set askew to make it run true east to west. This was pulled down in the 1290s to make way for a large keep, never completed, and a solid gatehouse was added as well, following the design of Harlech. The airy hall looks north over a ravine, and on the west is a donjon (keep). The presence of both donjon and gatehouse marks the castle as transitional from the earlier keep and bailey layout. In 1306 Robert Bruce, harried by Edward I's armies, gave his wife and daughter into the care of his brother Neil at Kildrummy but they fled as the English approached. The siege was ended by the treachery of Osborne the blacksmith who set fire to the stores beneath the great hall. The castle became the seat of the Earls of Mar and was destroyed after the 1715 uprising.

Glenbuchat Castle

7 miles W of Kildrummy. Historic Scotland.

An excellent example of a Z-plan tower-house, built in 1590.

AYR

Tourist information: Burns House, Burns Statue Square. Tel: (01292) 288688.

The Ayrshire Yeomanry Museum

Rozelle House, Monument Road. Tel: (01292) 445447.

The regiment was originally formed to help meet the threat of Napoleonic invasion in 1793. It served as cavalry in South Africa, infantry in World War I and field artillery in World War II. It is now a long-range reconnaissance unit. Open daily, Sunday afternoon in summer only.

Ayr Citadel

Near the harbour.

In 1654, after the victory of the Parliamentary forces, the great castles of Scotland were broken with cannon and mortars and army bases were established in purpose-built citadels. Of the Cromwellian fortresses little remains except here, where part of a bastion with a corbelled angle turret can be seen.

Dundonald Castle

10 miles N of Ayr by A78 and A759 to Kilmarnock. Historic Scotland. Tel: (01563) 850201 for details of opening.

The castle hill was originally the site of prehistoric and Dark Age forts before the Stewarts built their castle. This was rebuilt by Robert II in the second half of the 14th century, changing the keep-gatehouse into a tower-house by blocking up the old gateway and erecting two great barrel-vaults. The use of structurally unnecessary ribs suggests a wish to enhance the appearance of the vault.

Dean Castle

Dean Road, Kilmarnock. 12 miles NE of Ayr by A77. Tel: (01563) 522702. Open daily afternoons only.

Amongst other things the displays include the Howard de Walden Collection of European arms and armour.

From a hilltop the visitor looks out over the Firth of Clyde and Ailsa Craig. The burials are from RAF Turnberry and of bodies recovered from the sea in World War II; 16 UK, 16 Canada, 10 Australia, 5 New Zealand and 1 unidentified.

The West Lowland Fencible Regiment armoury is housed in this 18th-century house. The house itself was designed by Robert Adam.

BALLATER

Tourist information (summer): Station Square. Tel: (01339) 755306.

A tower-house where the Earl of Mar raised his standard in 1715, it was forfeit on the failure of the rising. It was leased for 99 years for a rent of £14 a year to the Hanoverian government in 1748 and converted to a barracks for occupying troops, as was Corgarff Castle. The star-shaped outer wall was added at that time. The castle secured part of the military road, now approximating to the A93, from Blairgowrie.

Major William Caulfield succeeded General Wade as road builder, though with the purpose of promoting commerce rather than providing troop routes. For 100 years after it was built in 1753 this fine bridge carried travellers across the River Dee.

The military road from Blairgowrie to Fort George, built between 1749 and 1754 and now approximating to the A93 and A939, swings up into the hills from Braemar, tight against the mass of the Grampians to the west, towards Tomintoul – a route of vital strategic importance. Just to the south of the castle a length of it can be walked. The 16th-century tower-house at Corgarff, which had been used by the Jacobites in both the '15 and the '45 rebellion, was converted to a fortified barracks by 1750. The lofty hall was made into two storeys to give a five-floored building and surrounded by a star-shaped wall with musket loops. Forty-six regular soldiers were based here to patrol the country and their living quarters and a whisky still are to be seen today. The castle remained in government service until 1831 to control, not rebels, but the illicit whisky trade.

BUTE

This favourite residence of the Stewart kings is of particular interest, although its history is not certain. In 1230 the Norsemen besieged and took a castle in Bute by hewing through the stone walls, protected with 'flakes of wood' from boiling pitch and lead hurled upon them by the defenders. It seems probable that the original, circular shell keep was that castle. The four towers were added in the 13th century when the castle was repaired, and the curtain wall was strengthened at the base with stone instead of the former earth bank as the section to be seen in the chamber of the later forework east of the entrance reveals. The entrance was secured with provision for a portcullis and gate, and

Dunure Cemetery
Dunure, Maybole, 8 miles SW of Ayr by A719. Commonwealth War Graves Commission.

Culzean Castle
4 miles W of Maybole on the A719. National Trust for Scotland. Tel: (01655) 760274. Open daily April to October.

Braemar Castle
N of the A93 just E of Braemar.

Invercauld Bridge
Off the A93, just N of Braemar

Corgarff Castle
14 miles N of Ballater on the A939 Grantown-on-Spey road. Historic Scotland. Open daily in summer, weekends in winter. Tel (opening times): (0131) 668 8800.

Well of the Lecht
Just N of Corgarff.

A memorial erected by the builders of the military road is at the roadside.

Rothesay Castle
Historic Scotland. Tel: (01700) 502691. Open daily, Sunday afternoon only.

the curtain wall raised adding the earliest surviving crenellation in Scotland. A barbican was added in the late 15th century, projecting well into the moat and providing a great hall. The outworks were rebuilt as a Cromwellian defence in 1650, to carry guns.

DALMALLY

Kilchurn Castle

W of Dalmally on the A85, on shore of Loch Awe. Historic Scotland. Open summer only. Tel (info on opening): (0131) 668 8800.

The ruins of the ancestral home of the Campbells of Glenorchy stand at the head of Loch Awe. The 15th-century castle was extended in the 1690s by the Campbell of the time, Lord Breadalbane, to provide headquarters for about 200 men, possibly for a militia to preserve peace in the Highlands, but perhaps for his private army. The three-storey block is probably the earliest surviving barrack in Britain.

Battle of Brander, 1309

9 miles W of Dalmally on the A85, near the Bridge of Awe.

Robert the Bruce had started his bid to become king with the murder of John Comyn, nephew of Alexander Macdougall, an act for which Macdougall and his son, John of Lorne, did not forgive him. While accepted as king throughout almost all Scotland, Bruce had to deal with the opposition of his victim's uncle and moved against him in the late summer of 1309. John of Lorne sought to ambush Bruce in the narrow pass, taking up position on the lower slopes of Ben Cruachan overlooking the road as it neared the bridge, but Bruce had foreseen the tactic and sent James Douglas with his archers on a flanking movement yet higher up the mountain to the north. The Macdougalls attacked the main body of Bruce's force as it approached the bridge, only to be shot down by arrows from above. They broke and attempted to flee across the bridge or through the torrential river. In the flat valley bottom they were cut to ribbons. The cairns south of the river at the south-eastern end of the valley bottom are said to mark their graves. John of Lorne escaped to join Edward III and continue his fight against the Scots whom he saw as rebels.

DUMBARTON

Tourist information: Milton. Tel: (01389) 742306.

The name Dumbarton translates, it is held, as the Fort of the British and was formerly known as Kaer Alclyd – the fort on the Clyde. This is where the chronicler Monmouth relates that the Battle of Mount Badon took place, King Arthur's great victory over the invading Saxons. Others hold that it took place near Swindon in Wiltshire.

Dumbarton Castle

Historic Scotland. Tel: (01389) 32167. Open all year except Thursday pm and Friday in winter.

The volcanic rock on which the castle stands is the site of the ancient capital of Strathclyde. Mons Meg, the massive cannon now in Edinburgh Castle, was dragged to the siege of Dumbarton in 1489. Today the features of greatest interest are the 17th- and 18th-century fortifications, including King George's Battery by John Romer.

DUMFRIES

Tourist information: Whitesands. Tel: (01387) 253862.

The collection is grouped around the control tower of the old airfield, RAF Tinwald Downs, and includes early jet aircraft, the remains of a couple of Spitfires and parts of other aircraft. It includes a number of 'firsts': the first jet-powered aircraft to enter service with the RAF, the first capable of supersonic speeds in level flight and the first British-built helicopter to enter service with the RAF. The ground floor houses one of the best collections of aero engines in Britain, ranging from the Wasp radial to a Bristol Hercules from a Wellington bomber.

Dumfries and Galloway Aviation Museum
Heathhall Industrial Estate, Tinwald Downs. 4 miles NE of Dumfries by A701. Tel: (01387) 256680. Open weekends April to October 10am to 5pm.

A magnificent castle, triangular in plan, with Scotland's earliest keep-gatehouse dominating the approach and two circular towers at the base of the triangle, built about 1290–1300. It is surrounded by a moat that, at the siege of 1300, was only 2 feet deep when filled to the brim. By 1640, when it was subjected to an artillery siege, the bank had been raised to its present height and the approach changed. By that time it had also been modified by the addition of the superb Renaissance Nithsdale Lodging. On the south side the surrounding bank angles away from the line of the curtain wall, possibly to provide standing for stone-throwing machines that could not operate from within the walls. To the south appear the traces of an earlier castle.

Caerlaverock Castle
8 miles SE by B725, via Glencaple. Historic Scotland. Tel: (01387) 77244. Open all year, Sundays pm only.

DUNBAR

Tourist information: 143 High Street. Tel: (01368) 863353.

The medieval castle, slighted in 1488, was rebuilt for James IV in 1496–1501. By 1517 there were five French gunners stationed here, which suggests that the great outer blockhouse built on an island and linked to the castle was built about this time. It has four casemates at ground level.

Dunbar Castle
In the town.

After the execution of Charles I the Scots accepted Charles II as their king and he was so proclaimed in July 1650. In the same month Cromwell moved north with 10,000 foot and 5,000 horse to Dunbar where he was resupplied by sea. Finding David Leslie with 20,000 men well established near Edinburgh, Cromwell fell back under pressure from Leslie and was again in Dunbar on 1 September. The Scots took up position with their left on the forward slope of Doon Hill, three miles south of the town, looking north over the valley of Brox Burn (Spott Burn). The Parliament forces took up position along the northern side of the burn. On 2 September Leslie moved his force down the hill and extended his right to a position just north of the monument where a minor road now turns round the cement works. The road south was blocked.

Cromwell and John Lambert reconnoitred the Scots position and found that, between Broxmouth and the sea, the burn offered no obstacle. On the morning of 4 September Lambert's horse and George Monck's foot moved along what is

The Battle of Dunbar, 4 September 1650
2 miles SE of the town, near Broxburn.

Dunbar Battery
Near the harbour.
A fortification of the 1780s war with America.

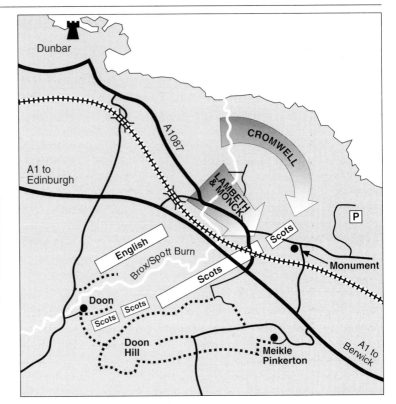

The Battle of Dunbar

Chesters Hill Fort

1 mile S of Drem (3 miles W of East Fortune).
Historic Scotland.

A well-preserved Iron Age hill-fort with an elaborate system of ramparts and ditches.

now the A1087 to crash against Leslie's right and centre while Cromwell moved close to the sea to take the Scots on the flank. Their right collapsed and the left fled. Three thousand Scots were slain and 10,000 made prisoner by the time the pursuit was over.

Museum of Flight

East Fortune Airfield. 10 miles W by A1 and B1377. Open April to September daily, October, November and February Monday to Friday. Tel: (01620) 880308.

Flying took place here in World War I when airships patrolled the Firth of Forth and East Fortune was an important RAF base in World War II. The museum covers the history of flight from the 100-year-old Hawk, a hang-glider, to the Blue Streak rocket. A Spitfire, a Soviet MiG, a Lightning and a Vulcan bomber may be seen.

Tantallon Castle

Auldhame, near North Berwick, 8 miles NW of Dunbar by A1 and A198. Historic Scotland. Open daily all year, Sundays pm only and closed October to March Thursday pm and Friday. Tel: (01620) 892727.

Probably built in 1350, Tantallon represents the ultimate in the development of the keep-gatehouse concept of castle design. A huge curtain wall, 50 feet high, cuts across the seashore promontory. A tower at each end and a massive gatehouse in the centre complete the defence. Later, possibly connected with the siege of 1528, outer defensive earthworks were added to the landward side to deal with the threat of the artillery of James V. Additional works done ten years later gave Cromwell's besiegers problems. Displays here include replica guns.

DUNDEE

Tourist information: 4 City Square. Tel: (01382) 434664.

The oldest British-built warship afloat, HMS *Unicorn* was launched in 1824. Originally a 46-gun frigate, a curious roof was fitted when she ceased sea-going service.

HMS *Unicorn*
Victoria Dock. Tel: (01382) 200900. Open daily April to October.

This 15th-century tower-house was strengthened by Protector Somerset during the War of Rough Wooing when he was attempting to enforce the marriage of Edward VI with Mary, Queen of Scots. The Italian engineer Giovanni di Rossetti carried out the work. It was further modified in 1860 to form a coastal defence battery with two 68-pounders and five 10-inch guns.

Broughty Castle
Broughty Ferry, 3 miles E by A930. Historic Scotland and Dundee Museums. Tel: (01382) 76121. Open all year, Sundays pm only.

EDINBURGH

Tourist information: Edinburgh and Scotland Information Centre, 3 Princes Street. Tel: (0131) 557 1700.

Dominating the city from the height of a volcanic outcrop, the castle has been modified and extended since Norman times. The threat of artillery attack, and its use for defence, led to the works of 1650–1750, including the Dry Ditch, the perimeter wall and the zigzag defences, fine examples of early 18th-century fortification. The pepper-pot corner turrets, sentinel boxes, are the hallmark of military architect John Romer who worked under the direction of General Wade. Mons Meg is a massive gun probably made in Flanders in the 15th century.

Edinburgh Castle
In city. Historic Scotland. Open all year (for hours, tel: 0131 668 8800). Parking limited to two hours, winter only.

The castle first became a royal residence in the 11th century when Malcolm III and Queen Margaret lived here. After her death in 1093 it was unsuccessfully besieged for the first time on record. In 1174 it was forfeited to the English King Henry II, then restored to the Scots and was to be taken by force by Edward I in 1296. The Earl of Moray took it back in 1313. The next English occupation ended in 1341. The conflict surrounding the succession of the youthful James VI led to the long siege of 1573 when great destruction was done by artillery, leading to the extensive rebuilding including the Half Moon Battery. Cromwell took it in 1650 and its refortification continued under Charles II. The last siege was in 1689 when starvation led to surrender. The Jacobite uprisings of 1715 and 1745 saw it remain in Hanoverian hands, surrounded but not seriously threatened, and it then became a military base for the victors as the great barracks attest.

Claypotts Castle
Near Broughty Ferry, Dundee.

Although only the exterior can be viewed, this is a very early (1569) Z-plan tower-house. Unaltered, it is worth seeing. Defence was from the wide gun-ports of the round towers; one looking out from the kitchen fireplace and another necessitating a groove in a stairtower to let the shot pass.

Scottish National War Memorial
The Castle. Open daily. Tel: (0131) 226 7393.
Built in 1927 to commemorate the fallen of World War I, the memorial also houses the rolls of honour of World War II and of conflicts of more recent date.

Leith Citadel

Nr junction of Dock Street and Commercial Street, Leith.

The gateway of the Cromwellian citadel survives, the rest having been destroyed after the Restoration.

Scottish United Services Museum

The Castle, Crown Square and Museum Square. Open all year, Sundays pm only. Tel: (0131) 225 7534.

Scotland's national museum of the armed services includes Royal Navy and Royal Air Force coverage in the Crown Square building and the special relationship with Poland in World War II in the Museum Square building.

The Royal Scots Dragoon Guards Museum (Carabiners and Greys)

The Castle. Open daily April to September, Monday to Friday October to March. Tel: (0131) 310 5102.

An amalgamation of regiments dating back to 1678, the modern regiment is an active tank-equipped unit which served in the Gulf War. Amongst the memorabilia of more than 300 years past are the eagle and standard of the 45th French Infantry taken in the charge of the Scots Greys at Waterloo and dioramas of the Scots Greys in Italy in 1943 and the 3rd Carabiners in Burma in 1944.

The Regimental Museum of the Royal Scots (The Royal Regiment)

The Castle. Open daily April to September, Monday to Friday October to March. Tel: (0131) 310 5016.

The Royal Regiment was raised in 1633 by Sir John Hepburn and its first battle honour is Tangier 1680. It can therefore lay claim to being one of the oldest regiments in the British Army. It has seen service in Europe, Asia, the Middle East, Africa and the Americas.

Royal Museum of Scotland

Tel: (0131) 2257534. Open daily.

Both museums (Chambers Street and the Museum of Antiquities, Queen Street) include amongst their exhibits collections of arms and armour, including specifically Scottish items.

Craigmillar Castle

2.5 miles SE of Edinburgh centre by A7 Dalkeith road. Historic Scotland. Tel: (0131) 661 4445.

The core of the castle is an L-plan tower-house built about 1374 which, with the exception of the stair, is virtually unchanged and an excellent example of a Scottish fortified dwelling. A curtain wall was added in about 1427, possibly the earliest artillery fortification in Scotland, although the gunports are probably a later modification. Open daily except Thursday afternoon and Friday in winter.

Blackness Castle

2 miles NE of junction 3 on the M9 on the shore of the Forth. Historic Scotland. Tel: (01506) 834807. Open all year except Thursday pm and Friday in winter.

The 15th-century castle, modified with a casemented reinforcement to the south in 1537, was converted into an artillery fortress by John Slezer in the 1690s. He built the upper part of the Spur, a battery covering the entrance, with square gun embrasures and a cylindrical sentry turret. The North Tower was lowered at the same time to make a platform for three heavy guns to command the waters of the Forth.

Inchcolm

Historic Scotland has the Abbey (tel: 01383 823332) in its care. Ferries from South Queensferry (tel: 0131 331 4857) and North Queensferry (tel: 0131 554 6881). Summer only.

To protect the Firth of Forth and its anchorages in World War I batteries were set up on shore and on the islands. On Inchcolm there were four 4.7-inch guns and four 4-inch QFs by 1917, and two 6-inch guns were added soon after. The guns were mounted in concrete emplacements with magazines below and protected with trenches and pillboxes.

In 1543 Henry VIII, in an attempt to resolve the centuries-old conflict with Scotland to his advantage, forced the betrothal of the infant Scottish heir, Mary, Queen of Scots, to his son. After the boy came to the throne as Edward VI, the Protector, the Duke of Somerset, sought to have the engagement reinstated in the War of Rough Wooing. On 1 September he invaded Scotland with 16,000 men. He found the Earl of Arran with 25,000 on the west bank of the Esk at Musselburgh. Although outnumbered, Somerset had artillery support from his fleet and the lucky chance of a foolish foray by the Scottish cavalry which was destroyed by his knights. He rejected Arran's offer of safe passage home and moved to attack at 8am on the 10th. Unaccountably, the Scots crossed the river to meet them, exposing themselves to fire from the English fleet, the superior English artillery and the unopposed English cavalry. 10,000 Scots were massacred and the English lost only about 500 men.

The Battle of Pinkie, 10 September 1547

S of Musselburgh (7 miles E of Edinburgh) in the triangle between the A6124, the A6094 and the A199.

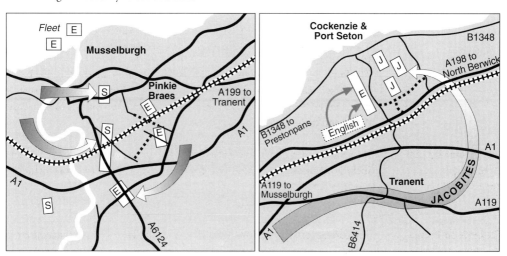

The raising of Prince Charles Edward's standard in August 1745 found the Hanoverian forces ill prepared. Sir John Cope led a makeshift army north, but failed to make contact with the Jacobites and returned to Dunbar by sea. He found his enemies in possession of Edinburgh and both armies converged on Tranent. Cope deployed his men along the present line of the railway, east of the station, facing across the boggy land towards the Jacobites in Tranent. Lord George Murray declined to attack in the circumstances and during the night led his men around to the east, past Seton House. Cope swung his line to form along the present B6371, but as the sun rose the Jacobites charged. Cope's artillerymen fled without firing a shot and the disorganised Hanoverians had the rabid Highlanders amongst them before they knew what was happening. They broke and ran, as Prince Charles remarked, 'like rabets'. Some 300 government troops died and 1,600 were taken prisoner. The '45 was off to a good start.

The Battle of Prestonpans, 21 September 1745

N of Tranent (10 miles E of Edinburgh) on the B6371 N of the junction with the A198.

FORFAR

Tourist information: The Library, 40 East High Street. Tel: (01307) 467876.

The Battle of Nechtansmere, 20 May 685

Near Dunnichen, S of the Forfar to Arbroath A932 road which passes over Dunnichen (Dun Nechtan) Hill.

In the year 676 the Picts attempted to throw off the yoke of the kingdom of Northumbria which held the country as far north as the Firth of Forth and dominated the client Pictish kingdom of Fortriu to the north. The rising was bloodily supressed. In 682 Bridei became King of Fortriu and, with his brother, Owen of Strathclyde, sought to consolidate an independent Pictish kingdom. Egfrith of Northumbria mounted punitive expeditions, laying waste the land and, in 685, venturing into the hilly, boggy country north of the Tay.

It seems probable that Egfrith's army approached from the north-west, passing between Dunnichen Hill and the hill to the south-west. Between Dunnichen and the modern village of Letham lay Nechtansmere, a bog-bordered loch now drained, but skirted by today's roads, forcing Egfrith to turn left between the hill and the bog – into a trap. The Picts poured down the hill with axe and sword to do immense slaughter, ending the power of Northumbria north of the Tay for ever. A monument to the battle is at Dunnichen Church.

The Dunnichen Stone

Meffan Institute, Forfar

Reputed to be a memorial of the Battle of Nechtansmere, this Pictish stone was removed from Dunnichen House to which it had been moved as an adornment. It was returned to the area of its origin in 1997.

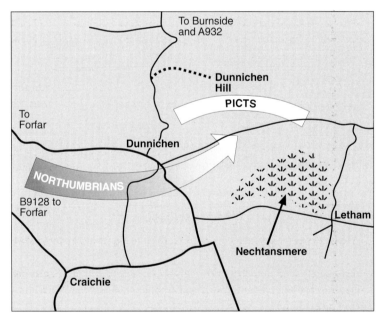

The Aberlemno Stone

By the west porch of the church at Aberlemno, 6 miles from Forfar on the B9134 Brechin road.

Four sculptured stones are to be found in the area, three by the roadside (covered in winter) and one in the churchyard. The latter has warlike figures on one side, which may be a depiction of the Battle of Nechtansmere. Some of the warriors have noseguards, as the Northumbrians did, and it is suggested that the figure being pecked by a bird is Egfrith of Northumbria who was slain by the Picts.

Two large hill-forts, the Brown Caterthun with four ramparts and ditches, the White with a huge stone rampart, a ditch and outer ramparts. They are near Menmuir, 5 miles NW of Brechin via Little Brechin by minor road.

The Brown and the White Caterthuns
Historic Scotland.

This was Britain's first operational air base. The Royal Flying Corps No II (AC) Squadron took up residence on 26 February 1913. It then became a major training base for British, American and Canadian pilots. World War II saw the RAF here both operationally and for training, and Commonwealth, Polish, Czech, American, Russian, Turkish and Free French airmen trained and served at Montrose. In addition to memorabilia, the museum has a Seahawk 131, a Commer airfield control van and a Whirlwind XJ723.

Montrose Air Station Museum
Waldron Road, Broomfield, Montrose. Tel: (01674) 672035/675401/673107. Open May to October Sunday pm.

FORT AUGUSTUS

Tourist information (summer): Car Park. Tel: (01320) 366367.

To secure the Highlands after the failure of the 1715 uprising four great barracks were built (see Ruthven) in key locations. The arrangements of the buildings were broadly similar, but Kiliwhimen was the largest, housing six companies (360 men). General Wade declared himself dissatisfied with it in 1724 when it was scarcely finished; too small and too far from the loch itself. He built a new fortress close to the water and thus accessible for waterborne supplies. John Romer's design was for a square fort with huge corner bastions, only one of which survives at the abbey which was founded when Lord Lovat gave the fort to the Benedictines in 1876. The barracks, too, have gone, leaving just one stretch of musket-looped wall behind the hotel.

Fort Augustus and Kiliwhimen Barracks
The Benedictine Abbey and the Lovat Arms Hotel.

Two examples of the military road-building of the 18th century can be seen, one in regular use along the south-eastern side of Loch Ness, the other the route over the Corrieyairack Pass.

The Military Road
B862 to Whitebridge. 1 mile S of Fort Augustus, off the A82 to Fort William, minor road running SE on the SW side of Glen Tarff.

FORT WILLIAM

Tourist information: Cameron Centre, Cameron Square. Tel: (01397) 703781.

Until the family's decline in the 14th century the Comyns were lords of Lochaber, ruling from one of Scotland's earliest stone castles, built in the 13th century. Access limited during repairs.

Inverlochy Castle
2 miles NE of Fort William. Historic Scotland. Tel: (0131) 668 8800.

Commanding the route from the west to the Great Glen, the strategic importance of the site was evident to General Hugh Mackay, commander of William of Orange's Scottish Army in 1689. Cromwell had built a citadel at Inverlochy which was torn down on the restoration of Charles II and the new fort was based on the old, close to the River Nevis and Loch Linnhe and thus protected on two sides, with the most extensive fortification on the south and east. It had a garrison of 1,200 men and 12 guns.

Fort William
Behind the railway station on the N of the town and at Craigs Burial Ground.

By 1715, the first Jacobite uprising, only 340 men were based here but they were partly dispersed to other, lesser forts. General George Wade repaired it in the 1720s, and in the '45 rebellion it was blockaded, but played little active part except as a barracks in the aftermath. It was abandoned in 1864 and largely destroyed in 1889 to make way for the railway station. Parts of the north and west bastion, including the sallyport, are to be found behind the station and the burial ground boasts the old main gate as well as soldiers' headstones.

The West Highland Museum

Cameron Square. Tel: (01397) 702169

Information on the fort is to be found here and the panelling from the Governor's house is on display. The Jacobite risings from Glencoe to the '45 and Montrose's campaigns as far as they affected Lochaber clan battles are the military interests of the museum.

Glencoe

17 miles S by A82. National Trust for Scotland Visitor Centre Tel: (01855) 811307.

The Massacre of Glencoe on 13 February 1692 has become legendary. The truth is more complicated and can be explored here. The visitor centre is open in summer only.

Glenfinnan

18 miles W of Fort William by A830. National Trust for Scotland Monument (open site) and Visitor Centre, open April to October daily. Tel: (01397) 722250.

Here Prince Charles Edward, the Young Pretender, raised his standard on 19 August 1745. The passion that convinced Charles and his followers that they could succeed in taking the English throne can well be understood by the visitor to this wild and lovely place. The story of the '45 rebellion is told in full at the Visitor Centre.

GLASGOW

Tourist information: 35 St Vincent Place. Tel: (0141) 204 4400.

Hunterian Museum and Art Gallery

University Avenue, Hillhead. Tel: (0141) 330 4221. Open Monday to Saturday. Admission free (donations welcome).

The archaeological collection includes Iron and Bronze Age relics such as spearheads and extensive coverage of Roman relics; the Antonine Wall ran to the north of the city. The coins and medals collection includes items of military interest and, of course, the Hunterian has many other fascinating exhibits in other fields. It is closed on certain public holidays.

Glasgow Art Gallery and Museum

Kelvingrove. Tel: (0141) 221 9600. Open daily.

Arms and armour form part of the collections held here. There are medieval and Scottish weapons as well as European armour and firearms. The Scottish Volunteer units are also recorded.

The Royal Highland Fusiliers Museum

518 Sauchiehall Street. Tel: (0141) 332 0961.

Housed in a building designed in part by Charles Rennie Mackintosh, the history of the regiment from 1678 is displayed in a mix of artefacts, pictures and videos. It is open Monday to Friday.

The Antonine Wall

Shortly after the completion of Hadrian's Wall the new Emperor Antoninus Pius ordered the construction of a new wall from the Forth to the Clyde. It was built of turf with a wooden walkway on top, taking it to a height of 14 feet, and was completed in AD142. The vallum, the ditch, was some 40 feet wide and 12 feet deep, leaving traces that can be seen today.

Bar Hill Fort

Historic Scotland. NE of Glasgow by the A803, and then by B8023 to Twechar and follow signs to the fort, half a mile E. See map below.

This was the highest fort on the line of the wall and the foundations of the headquarters building and the bath-house can be seen. The vallum passes both the Roman fort and a small Iron Age fort to the east.

Croy Hill

Historic Scotland. From Twechar continue E and then S by B802 to Croy and E towards Dullatur.

Between Croy and Dullatur the wall ditch can be seen as well as two beacon platforms. Half a mile east of Dullatur is another section of ditch.

Bearsden Bath-house

Historic Scotland. NW of Glasgow by the A82, near Grange Road.

The remains of a bath-house and latrine of a small fort.

After the Battle of Alford Montrose moved south and chose to meet General Baillie, who was pursuing him from Stirling, at Kilsyth before reinforcements could get to him. The lake now covers some of the low ground of the battlefield. Baillie was a little higher to the east and both armies' lines ran north to south. Baillie attempted an outflanking move on his right, up the hill, and was set upon by the Royalists under Alasdair Macdonald. He soon needed support and

The Battle of Kilsyth, 15 August 1645

E of Kilsyth (14 miles NE of Glasgow) by A803 at Colzium-Lennox Park. Take a walk round the lake.

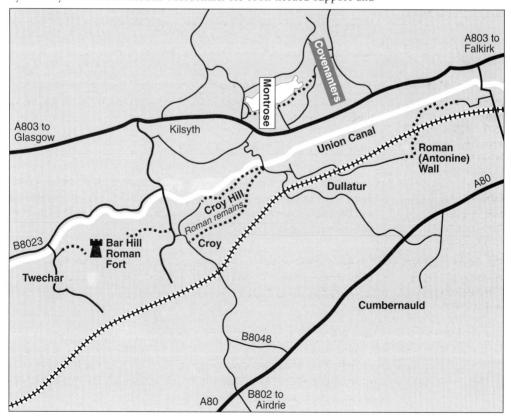

Montrose had to send in his cavalry both to counter the flanking movement and to help Macdonald nearer the centre, where Baillie's line was then cut in two. This was the chance for Montrose; his advance scattered the Covenanters and the fugitives were cut to ribbons.

Montrose occupied Glasgow but his force dwindled as the Highlanders drifted away home. His weakened army was surprised and beaten at Philiphaugh, just west of Selkirk, on 3 September.

Bothwell Castle

Bothwell via Uddingston, 9 miles SE of Glasgow by A74. Tel: (01698) 816894. Historic Scotland. Open daily except Sunday am, and Thursday pm and Friday October to March.

The 13th-century castle was dominated by a huge, round keep at the rear of the enclosure, which is one of the chief items of interest. In 1314 1,600 English soldiers retreating from the defeat at Bannockburn were caught here and most of them died at the hands of the Scottish cavalry. Half of the keep was demolished in 1337 to deny it to the English; it had twice been held by them before. The castle was rebuilt and extended in the 14th and 15th centuries.

The Cameronians (Scottish Rifles) Regimental Museum

129 Muir Street, Hamilton. Tel: (01698) 283981. Open daily all year, Sunday pm only, except Christmas and New Year public holidays.

The regiment was raised on 14 May 1689 and named after Richard Cameron, a covenanting minister. Charles I's attempt to impose the English Prayer Book on the Scots led to the declaration of the National Covenant in 1638 and the raising of an army to which Charles yielded without a fight then, and again in the following year. The Covenanters were Presbyterians and thus supported William of Orange against James II. The museum, recently renovated, covers the history of the Cameronians until their disbanding in 1968.

Craignethan Castle

5 miles NW of Lanark (25 miles SE of Glasgow) by A72. Tel: (01555) 86364. Historic Scotland. Open March to October daily, Sundays pm only, and closed Thursday pm and Friday in March and October.

Built in about 1530, this is a tower-house built broad, like two of them side by side, on a promontory with an artillery wall closing the vulnerable side. Some of the gunports are angled down, but in general it would have been hard to fire on close attackers. It has the earliest example in Britain of a *caponier*, a loop-holed stone defence work that runs across the ditch to enfilade the enemy.

HIGHLAND

Tourist information: Argyll Street, Ullapool. Tel: (01854) 612135.

The Inchnadamph Memorial

25 miles N of Ullapool by A835 and A837.

On 13 April 1941 an Anson bomber from No 19 OTU, Kinloss crashed on Ben More. The bodies of the crew were buried where they fell and the spot marked with a cairn. A memorial is set into the south-east wall of the old churchyard.

Castle of Old Wick

1 mile S of Wick. Historic Scotland.

An early Norse tower, now ruined, in a spectacular setting above the sea. *Visitors must take great care.*

INVERARAY

Tourist information: Front Street. Tel: (01499) 302063.

From small-scale commando raids to the massive D-Day operations that took the Allies back into mainland Europe, the effective management of combined operations was crucial. Thousands of men and women passed through the CTC at Inverary during World War II. The Armoury Hall in the castle itself has a major collection of early armour.

Combined Operations Museum
Cherry Park, Inveraray Castle. Tel: (01499) 500218. Open April to mid-October daily except Fridays, Sundays pm only, July and August, Fridays as well.

INVERNESS

Tourist information: Castle Wynd. Tel: (01463) 234353.

The original fort of this name was built by John Romer on the site of Inverness Castle on which Cromwell had built a citadel. It was taken by the Jacobites in 1746 and blown up. A new fort was built some 11 miles north-east on the southern shore of the Moray Firth to plans drawn up by William Skinner in 1747. The contract went to the builder William Adam and was carried out after his death by his sons Robert, John and James over the next 20 years.

Fort George
4 miles N of the A96 Inverness–Nairn road, via Ardersier. Tel: (01667) 462777. Historic Scotland. Open all year.

The result is one of the finest, and largest, fortresses in Britain. Built on a narrow peninsula, there is a bastion for the seaward gun battery and a bastion on each of the sides, as well as a ravelin covering a sallyport. The landward defences are massive: two huge bastions and, in front, a gigantic ravelin protecting the main gate. The buildings and barracks within were extensive as the complement of two battalions (1,600 men) required. Virtually unaltered to this day, it is a superb example of the 18th-century artillery fort.

Reconstructed barrack rooms portray the life of the Hanoverian soldier and the Seafield Collection of arms completes the picture.

Brodie Castle
24 miles E of Inverness by 96. Tel: (01309) 641371. National Trust for Scotland. Open April to October.

The 16th-century part of the castle is an example of Z-plan tower-house design, a square tower with round towers at diagonally opposite corners.

The Queen's Own Highlanders (Seaforth and Camerons) Museum
Fort George. Open Monday to Saturday and Sunday pm, April to September, and Monday to Friday October to March. Closed on Bank Holidays. Free admission (donations welcome).
The earliest antecedent regiment of the Highlanders was raised in 1778 and thus India, South Africa, Afghanistan, Egypt, the Crimea and the Sudan, amongst other foreign fields, figure in their history as well as service in two World Wars and the numerous combat zones since. Allied regiments are the Lovat Scouts, the Liverpool Scottish, three Canadian Highland regiments, battalions from Australia and New Zealand and the 7th Duke of Edinburgh's Own Gurkha Rifles.

In the nine months since he had been joined by Alasdair Macdonald and his Irish Macdonalds, the Marquess of Montrose had gained a series of victories in minor engagements and had attracted Lord Gordon to the Royalist cause. Colonel Hurry's Covenanters had fallen back to the west from Elgin to entrap Montrose who, on 8 May, was camped at Auldearn with some 2,500 men. Hurry's attempt at a night march was detected and Montrose swiftly placed Macdonald on the right in full view at Boath Doocot, keeping the rest of his force concealed on a

The Battle of Auldearn, 9 May 1645
2 miles E of Nairn (16 miles E of Inverness) on A96. Follow National Trust for Scotland signs to Boath Doocot viewpoint.

reverse slope to the left and with no centre at all to speak of. Macdonald's 500 could not bear to wait for Hurry to attack and they hurled themselves off the hill at their 4,000 adversaries as they came on across the burn and bog. The Macdonalds were within an ace of being wiped out, but Montrose threw in Gordon's horse against Hurry's flank and followed with the infantry. The Covenanters crumbled; more than 2,000 of them perished.

Kinloss Abbey Burial Ground

3 miles NE of Forres by B9011. Commonwealth War Graves Commission.

The graves of men of No 19 Operational Training Unit which was at RAF Kinloss are here: 36 UK, 27 Canada, 6 New Zealand and 3 Australia. There are three other burials of World War II and one of a naval officer killed at the Battle of Jutland.

The Battle of Culloden Moor, 16 April 1746

5 miles E of Inverness by B9006. National Trust for Scotland Visitor Centre, open daily all year. Tel: (01463) 790607. Numerous landmarks and memorials also in the care of the Trust.

Prince Charles and Lord George Murray completed the withdrawal to Inverness on 21 February while William Augustus, Duke of Cumberland occupied Aberdeen on 27 February 1746. The Jacobites scattered to undertake various small actions during the next six weeks but were recalled in April when Charles moved to Culloden House; there were only some 5,000 of them. On 8 April Cumberland moved north with 9,000 professional soldiers including about 2,500 cavalry. By 14 April he was at Balblair, just south-west of Nairn. The next day the Jacobites were arrayed on the moor to the south of Culloden House, ready for battle. Nothing happened. It was Cumberland's birthday, and the English had the day off. Cold, wet and hungry, the Scots waited.

At Prince Charles's council of war that afternoon an audacious if not fool-hardy plan was adopted: a night march to attack the English. It started late, took too long and was called off in disarray before dawn. The exhausted Scots found themselves back at Culloden, and scattered to find food and rest. By 5.15am on 16 April the English were marching towards Inverness.

The Scottish line was formed, according to Stuart Reid, between the corner of the wall around Culloden House and the wall of the Culwhiniac enclosure to the south-east, ground chosen by one of Charles's advisers, Colonel John O'Sullivan. Lord George Murray with his Atholl Brigade was on the right, traditionally the position of the Macdonalds who reluctantly accepted the left. There was no coherent second line, but a few units were in reserve. Only some 3,800 men could be got together that morning. The Atholls faced an obstruction in the shape of a turf enclosure at Leanach and they pushed left and forward to stand clear of it, pulling the line out of shape. The English had been forming in three lines with their left, Barrell's 4th Foot straddling the road in front of the Well of the Dead, and this flank was reinforced when the movement of the Atholls was seen. The English front line was of some 3,000 men and the same number formed the second with James Wolfe's 8th Foot on the left. Down the slope to the River Nairn there were some 450 English horse with infantry support who were to break through the walls of the Culwhiniac enclosure and cross the burn to the south of Culchunaig farm to threaten the Jacobite rear during the battle.

At about one o'clock the Scots' artillery opened fire and the English replied in kind. The soft terrain ruled out the usual technique of sending shot skipping to the enemy, and the English aimed high to drop their cannonballs into the

Jacobite lines, but even this less effective fire was withstood for only ten minutes before the Highlanders on the right rushed forward. The English guns replied with canister. Murray's men smashed into Barrell's and Monro's men, who held bravely before being forced back, but by then Wolfe's and other units from the second line moved forward to contain and outflank the Scots. Nowhere else was the English line even dented, and musket and grapeshot whittled the Jacobites away. Unsupported and almost surrounded, the Highland right fell back. The collapse spread and the English swept forward. The rout began. The battle had lasted less than an hour.

The through-route of the Great Glen was secured at either end by castles and here a curtain-wall fortification was also established. It fell into decline after 1689, and most of the buildings date from the 17th century.

Urquhart Castle
17 miles SW of Inverness by A82. Historic Scotland. Tel: (10456) 450551. Open daily, Sundays afternoon only.

KINGUSSIE

Tourist information (summer): (01540) 661297.

The site of the medieval castle of the Comyns at Ruthven in Badenoch in the Spey valley had served as a garrison post in 1689 and was chosen as the site of one of the four barracks built in the aftermath of the 1715 uprising. Completed in 1724, it consists of two blocks facing each other across a square secured at either end with walls with musket-loops and a walkway above, enough to resist lightly armed troops but not artillery, and with corner turrets to enfilade attacks. The complement was 120 men. Stables for 30 dragoons were added in 1734. The barracks were taken by the Jacobites in 1746 and their forces regrouped here after the Battle of Culloden, only to disperse in despair when the order came to fend for themselves. The buildings, now roofless, stand much as they did then.

Ruthven Barracks
Historic Scotland.

In 1727 General Wade proposed a road from Loch Ness to Ruthven over the Corrieyairack Pass. It may be traced past Garvamore Barracks west of Laggan by car, but only on foot all the way to Glen Tarff and Fort Augustus.

The Military Road
Laggan, 11 miles W of Kingussie by A86, and minor road straight on up the Spey valley.

KIRKALDY

Tourist information: 19 Whytecauseway. Tel: (01592) 267775.

Built for James II between 1460 and 1463, this is, with Threave Castle, one of the earliest artillery forts in Scotland. Two huge round towers project forward of the front range into the ditch, with gunports arranged to enfilade the front. The guns had their own gunrooms, the earliest examples in Britain of real casemates. Of later date are the round-ended horizontal gun-loops above the entrance.

Ravenscraig Castle
Historic Scotland. On E outskirts of Kirkaldy, off Dysart Road. Open all year, Sundays pm only.

KIRKCUDBRIGHT

Tourist information (summer): Harbour Square. Tel: (01557) 330494.

The Stewartry Museum
St Mary Street. Tel: (01557) 331643. Open March to October Monday to Saturday.

This local history museum displays equipment of the Kirkcudbright Yeomanry Cavalry and the Ayrshire Yeomanry Cavalry as well as material relating to the American, John Paul Jones. In addition it has a collection of World War I recruiting posters. It is also open Sunday afternoons June to September; Saturday only November to February.

Threave Castle
Historic Scotland. 3 miles W of Castle Douglas (9 miles NE of Kirkcudbright by A711 and A75). Tel: (01831) 168512. Open April to September. Access by ferry and a long walk.

The massive tower-house of Archibald the Grim, third Earl of Douglas, built in about 1370, was strengthened some 80 years later with possibly the first artillery fortification in Scotland. The angle towers have gunports in the two lower storeys and may have had gun platforms above. The walls are slitted for bows or handguns.

LARGS

Tourist information: Promenade. Tel: (01475) 673765.

Vinkingar!
Barrfields, Greenock Road. Tel: (01475) 689777. Open daily all year.

The story of the Vikings in Scotland is told with the aid of modern multi-media technology from the first raids to their final defeat at the Battle of Largs.

OBAN

Tourist information: Boswell House, Argyll Square. Tel: (01631) 563122.

Dunstaffnage Castle
Near Dunbeg, 4 miles N of Oban by A85, on the shore of Loch Etive. Historic Scotland. Tel: (01631) 62465. Open daily April to September, Sunday afternoons only.

Loch Etive and Loch Linnhe command the south-western approaches to the Great Glen. This is one of a number of curtain-wall castles associated with the need for defence in the west against the Norsemen in the 13th century. It soon found a role in the control of the cross-country route to Inverness. Standing on a rocky outcrop on a promontory, it has walls 20 feet thick and rising 30 feet above the enclosure; twice that above the exterior. The entrance at one corner had a drawbridge and at the opposite, north-west, corner is the largest tower, the upper floor of which is entered from the battlements. The placing of the towers was influenced by the restrictions of the site. The slits for firing on attackers have been modified for muskets. A small chapel of the same period stands near by.

Carnasserie Castle
2 miles N of Kilmartin and 28 miles S of Oban on A816. Historic Scotland.

By the 16th century the tower-house had become less of a grim fort and more of a country house, with fine decoration as can be seen here. Open daily, Sunday afternoons only.

Dunadd Fort
1 mile W of Kilmichael Glassary, 4 miles S of Kilmartin on A816. Historic Scotland.

A well-preserved hill-fort which was the stronghold of Dalriada, the kingdom of the Scots, in post-Roman times. It stands on the site of an Iron Age fort.

ORKNEY

Tourist information: 6 Broad Street, Kirkwall. Tel: (01856) 872856.

The Bishop's Palace is a hall-house of the early 13th century with a drum tower at one corner added in the 1540s. There are arrow-loops on the lower floor.

The Bishop's Palace
Kirkwall. Historic Scotland.
Tel: (01856) 875461. Open
April to September.

The precise site of the battle is uncertain, but is probably to the south-west of Queenania and west of the north/south road. The circumstances are rather clearer. James III married Margaret, Princess of Denmark and thus, in 1468, the islands of Orkney passed to him against a pledge of dowry of 50,000 florins which was not redeemed. The earldom also became the property of the Crown by purchase from the Sinclairs two years later, but was leased back from James IV in 1489 and 1501 for £336 13s 4d. Henry Lord Sinclair fell at Flodden in 1513, but his widow, Margaret, maintained the lease.

The new Lord Sinclair evidently felt the lands should be his and, with the Earl of Caithness, invaded Orkney in 1529 – a purely private declaration of war. The governor of Kirkwall castle gathered the men of Orkney and, at Summersdale or Bigswell in Stenness – as the account goes – inflicted a heavy defeat on the interlopers. Caithness and 500 of his followers were slain, while Sinclair and all other survivors were made prisoner. Margaret's enjoyment of the land was relatively brief – a general act of revocation terminated the lease in 1540.

The Battle of Summersdale, 18 May 1529
Near Queenania, S of Finstown by road between the A965 and A964.

The broch is a structure unique to Scotland and was a safe haven for farm communities against lightly armed raiders. Here the tower is surrounded by Iron Age buildings.

Broch of Gurness
Aikerness, 14 miles NW of Kirkwall. Historic Scotland. Tel: (01831) 579478. Open April to September.

Probably one of the earliest stone castles in Scotland, this small tower was built around 1150 by the Norseman Kolbein Hruga (Kubbie being a Norse nickname for Kolbein). It has walls 5 feet thick, internal water-storage and is enclosed by a ditch.

Cubbie Row's Castle
On the island of Wyre. Historic Scotland.

This, together with the tower at Crookness, was built in 1814–15 to protect convoys assembling in Longhope Sound from American and French privateers. The design is similar to those on the English south coast with a 24-pounder on the roof. The nearby battery (in private hands) had eight 24-pounders on traversing carriages.

Hackness Martello Tower
SE end of Hoy. Historic Scotland.

An installation for two 6-inch guns to protect Scapa Flow in World Wars I and II.

Hoxa Head Battery
South Ronaldsay.

In World War II Italian prisoners of war were confined on this island overlooking Scapa Flow. One of them, Domenico Chiocchetti, organised the transformation of a Nissen hut into an ornately decorated chapel.

The Chapel, POW Camp 60
Lamb Holm Island

PERTH

Tourist information: 45 High Street. Tel: (01738) 638353.

The Black Watch Regimental Museum

Balhousie Castle. Tel: (01738) 621281. On the North Inch of Perth. Open May to September Monday to Saturday, October to April Monday to Friday. Admission free (donations welcome).

The original Independent Companies were raised in 1725, as the fortification of strongpoints stimulated by the 1715 uprising created the demand for troops. Their distinctive tartan gave them the name of the Black Watch and in 1740 they became a regiment. They saw their first overseas service in 1743, and thus the museum relates the history of the wars of Britain since then. They fought at Fontenoy, Ticonderoga, in the Peninsular War and at Waterloo, in the Crimea, the Boer War, two World Wars and in Korea.

Lochleven Castle

By boat from Kinross, 10 miles S of Perth. Historic Scotland. Open daily April to September, Sunday afternoons only. Entrance charge includes ferry trip.

The 14th-century tower-house was attacked in 1335 by John de Strivilin for Edward Baliol and thus can be dated with some certainty. It is very simple in design, with two barrel vaults forming the basement and first floor, with a connecting hatchway. The main entrance is on the second floor, into the hall, from which a stair goes down to the common hall below. While the basement could be entered from the outside for delivery of goods it was nonetheless secure as a result of these arrangements. Mary Queen of Scots was imprisoned here in 1567 and escaped the following year.

PITLOCHRY

Tourist information: 22 Atholl Road. Tel: (01796) 472215.

Blair Castle and Atholl Museum

Blair Atholl, 6 miles NW. Tel: (01796) 481207. Open daily April to October.

The 13th-century castle houses the museum of the Atholl Highlanders. Uniforms, guns and equipment of this regiment and of the Scottish Horse are to be seen.

The Battle of Killiekrankie, 27 July 1689

National Trust for Scotland Visitor Centre, 3 miles N of Pitlochry by B8079. Tel: (01796) 473233. Open April to October. Battlesite open all year.

John Graham of Claverhouse, Viscount Dundee, raised his standard in support of James II against William and Mary in April 1689. Glen Garry was a vital route for the Highland forces and Dundee, from the north, and government forces under General Hugh Mackay, from the south, both sought to secure it. Mackay had reached Urrard House by the afternoon of 27 July when Dundee's army was seen coming over the high ground above the road. Their forces were hastily drawn up above the River Garry, but for two hours little took place; Mackay could not launch an attack uphill and Dundee's men had the sun in their eyes. As dusk fell the Highlanders charged the over-extended government lines and swept them away, though 'Bonnie Dundee' died in the hour of victory. With the loss of their commander the Jacobites lost their coherence as a fighting force. On 21 August, under Colonel Alexander Cannon, they attacked government forces at Dunkeld, eight miles south of Pitlochry. For four hours the fighting around the church and the Earl of Atholl's house was ferocious, but in the end the Highlanders withdrew.

The exhibits include photographs, maps, uniforms and medals related to the regiment. It is open daily, Easter to September.

The Scottish Horse Museum
The Cross, Dunkeld. Tel: (01350) 724205.

While most bridges built as part of General Wade's road programme were of plain rubble masonry, the Tay Bridge, designed by William Adam and built in 1733, is a boisterous affair adorned with unnecessary columns.

Tay Bridge, Aberfeldy
On the B846 Tummel Bridge road, just N of Aberfeldy.

ST ANDREWS

Tourist information: 70 Market Street. Tel: (01334) 472021.

The 13th-century castle was strengthened by Cardinal Beaton in the 16th century with a massive circular blockhouse furnished with horizontal gunports. The siege works, a mine and counter-mine, of 1546 are the finest examples in Europe.

St Andrews Castle
Historic Scotland. In the town. Tel: (01334) 77196. Open all year, joint entry with cathedral.

On the surface apparently a peaceful farmhouse, Scotland's Secret Bunker extends 100 feet below ground. Here, during the Cold War, central government and military officials would have run the country, or what was left of it, in the event of a nuclear attack. There are, in addition to the operations rooms, two cinemas, a café and all the facilities for living and working in a radiation-proof environment. Open April to October.

Underground Nuclear Command Centre
Crown Buildings, near Kingsmuir and the junction of B9131 and B940. Tel: (01333) 310301.

Fear of invasion in World War II led to the construction of coastal defences. Polish soldiers were involved in building the line of anti-tank blocks and pillboxes still to be seen along the shore.

Tentsmuir Point
Nature reserve 4 miles NE of Leuchars (5 miles N of St Andrews by A91 and A919).

Most of the burials here are of Coastal Command men from RAF Leuchars. Some died on torpedo bombing strikes. There are 32 UK graves from World War II, 11 Canada, 10 Australia and 1 New Zealand. There are 5 UK and 1 Canadian grave from World War I.

Leuchars Cemetery
A mile from Leuchars (5 miles N of St Andrews by A91 and A919). Commonwealth War Graves Commission.

SHETLAND

Tourist information: Market Cross, Lerwick. Tel: (01595) 693434.

Built by Robert Mylne for Charles II in 1665–7, the fort was unfinished when the Dutch fleet approached, but luckily they had inflated ideas of its strength. It was Cromwellian in design, pentagonal with a zigzag wall facing Bressay Sound. The fort was left ungarrisoned in the Third Dutch War and burned when Lerwick was attacked in 1673.

Fort Charlotte
Lerwick. Historic Scotland. No charge.

   In the 1780s, in fear of American privateers such as the former Lowland Scot, John Paul Jones, a new fort was built on the same site. The general plan was the same but with a magazine and ammunition stores added. The barracks accommodated 270 men of the Sutherland Fencibles. It was abandoned after the Napoleonic Wars.

Mousa Broch

By boat from Sandwick (14 miles S of Lerwick). Historic Scotland.

The finest surviving broch stands here to a height of more than 40 feet. The nature and purpose of the broch is described in the entry for Glenelg Brochs in the Shiel Bridge section below.

SHIEL BRIDGE

The Battle of Glenshiel, 10 June 1719

About 5 miles SE of Shiel Bridge where the A87 crosses the River Shiel. A nearby cairn marks the old bridge. National Trust for Scotland information board.

The brief rising of 1719 was arranged by the Spanish Cardinal Alberoni. The plan was for a major landing in south-west Scotland by the Duke of Ormonde and a smaller strike further north at Loch Duich. Only the latter survived stormy weather to land at Eilean Donan Castle in April. Uncertainty and disputes undermined the Jacobites and they would have done well to withdraw, but hoping for reinforcement they took steps to block the pass at the narrowest point. They were joined by a few Highlanders, including Rob Roy. General Joseph Wightman led a small force of about 1,000 men from Inverness to oust them, bringing four Coehorn mortars. The 1,600 Highlanders were ranged up the hillside to the north of the road with 250 Spanish troops next to the river and Lord George Murray's men south of the river. The mortars played on the defences close to the river, doing no considerable damage except to morale, and the afternoon saw little action until 5pm when Wightman's right climbed round the Highlanders' left. Murray's men fell back and the Jacobites swiftly collapsed, fleeing into the hills. The Spaniards, with no such option, surrendered.

Bernera Barracks

8 miles W of Shiel Bridge via Glenelg.

The route towards Skye follows the old military road quite closely, and this way passed the Hanoverian troops seeking to secure the Highlands after the failure of the 1715 uprising. Bernera is one of four barracks built in the 1720s (see Ruthven) and it survives largely as it was in this beautiful place.

Glenelg Brochs

Glenelg. Historic Scotland. Open all year, no charge.

The broch is a structure found only in Scotland, and almost all of them in Caithness, Orkney, Shetland and the Western Isles. The massive stone towers – the two here still reach some 30 feet high – have galleries connected by stairways within their walls and appear to have been places of refuge for the inhabitants of the coastal farmlands, perhaps against slave-raiders of the 1st century when these regions were outwith Roman control.

STIRLING

Tourist information: Royal Stirling Visitor Centre, The Esplanade. Tel: (01786) 479901.

Stirling Castle

Historic Scotland. Tel: (01786) 447873. Open all year.

Situated on a rocky outcrop at the strategic heart of the country, the castle's impressive medieval buildings were augmented in the 1700s by Theodore Dury's outer defences. The gatehouse and the Elphinstone Tower now appear squat due to modification as gun platforms. The present defences are those remodelled by Talbot Edwards who completed Dury's work.

Regimental Museum of the Argyll and Sutherland Highlanders
The Castle. Tel: (01786) 475165. Open daily.
Raised in 1794, the regiment has been based at Stirling Castle for more than a

century. Its history includes service in the Crimea where the regiment formed the 'Thin Red Line', the Indian Mutiny, the Boer War and the two World Wars. More recently it has seen action in Korea, Suez, Aden and Malaya.

With the death of Alexander III of Scotland in 1286 and the failure of his plan to marry the heir, Margaret, with the future Edward II, Edward I imposed a puppet king on the Scots. The Scots eventually rose under the leadership of William Wallace and Andrew de Moray and, in Edward's absence in France, the Governor of Scotland, the Earl of Surrey, and the Treasurer, Hugh de Cressingham, moved to suppress them. The English, with 1,000 knights and 50,000 foot, reached Stirling to find the Scots, numbering some 10,000, at Abbey Craig, rising above the northern bank of the river over which a narrow bridge passed.

The Battle of Stirling Bridge, 11 September 1297
Causewayhead, on the N bank of the River Forth, and the Wallace Monument, Abbey Craig.

The exact location of the bridge is disputed. It may not have been far upstream from the 'Old Bridge', built about 1500, and a footbridge today. Cressingham rejected the use of the ford two miles further upstream at Kildean as being too far to go in the face of a puny adversary and took his men forward two abreast over the bridge. With less than half the English over, Wallace struck and, beyond the help of reinforcement, Cressingham and his men were destroyed. Surrey withdrew to Berwick and the newly knighted Sir William Wallace became Governor. Edward I was to be avenged at Falkirk in the following year.

Dr Ron Page carried out investigations in 1997, starting with a rowing boat and a 10-foot pole and going on to sonar, which revealed the existence of eight footings of what may well be the original bridge. If he is correct, the exact location of the battle may be fixed.

The final and decisive battle in the Scottish Wars for Independence was fought here. After Falkirk in 1298, Robert Bruce and John Comyn became guardians of the Kingdom of Scotland but Bruce slew Comyn in 1306 and was crowned King of Scotland at Scone. Edward I died the following year and his markedly less skilful son could not resist Bruce's steady progress until, in June 1313, Stirling Castle, the last defence of the Lowlands, was besieged. If no relief came it was to be surrendered after a year. Edward II left his effort to the eleventh hour, moving north with some 18,000 men, perhaps some 1,250 mounted.

The Battle of Bannockburn, 24 June 1314
National Trust for Scotland Bannockburn Heritage Centre, off M80/M9 at junction 9, 2 miles S of Stirling, Glasgow Road. Tel: (01786) 812664. Open daily all year.

Bruce, on the other hand, was well prepared. He had 6,000 men and some 500 mounted, and started to train them in April. The men were to form 'schiltrons', solid blocks of pikemen. He prepared to meet the English by occupying the ridge along which the A9 now runs south from Stirling. The approaching Edward detached 300 men to encircle the eastern flank while his main body came up to the Scots just south of the modern junction with the A872, close to the Heritage Centre. Sir Henry de Bohun saw Bruce in front of his troops, charged and was struck down by the nimble Scot. The thwarted English broke off their attack and camped near the river where the present A91 bridge stands.

On 24 June the adversaries faced each other across the Carse, the floodplain enclosed by Bannockburn on the south and the Forth on the north and east. The English knights failed to break the schiltrons and also shielded them from the fire of their own archers. As they wavered, some 3,000 Scottish followers rushed to join the action and the English broke. It was not the end of the war; Bruce was to take Berwick in 1318, and the recognition of his independence in the Treaty of Northampton came in 1328.

The Antonine Wall

See also GLASGOW for general information.

Rough Castle

Historic Scotland. From Bonnybridge (5 miles W of Falkirk by A803) follow signs 1 mile E by B816.

Here is the best-preserved length of rampart and ditch, together with the wall's most complete remains of a fort. A short length of the military road also survives.

The Battle of Sheriffmuir, 13 November 1715

E of Dunblane (5 miles N of Stirling), on minor road to Blackford via Pisgah. Macrae Monument where road kinks right and is joined by path from Dunblane.

The Earl of Mar lost his government post when George I came to the throne in 1714, so he switched allegiance to James, the 'Old Pretender', son of the deposed James II, raising his standard at Braemar on 6 September 1715. The Duke of Argyll moved the small government force of some 3,000 men to Stirling to prevent Mar's 7,000 moving into the south from Perth. Just as the Jacobite force at Preston was surrendering, Mar approached and Argyll moved to meet him near Dunblane. On the morning of 13 November they faced each other across the moorland, about a mile and a half apart, probably on either side of the site of the Macrae Monument, Argyll's men with their backs towards Dunblane. Their fronts overlapped, Argyll's right outflanking Mar's left, and Mar's right Argyll's left. The Scottish charge was held and repulsed by Argyll's right while his left was scattered and chased as far as Stirling. The battle front turned anti-clockwise and Mar's main body of troops was pushed back over the river at Kinbuck to the north-west. While neither side could claim a decisive victory on the field, the Jacobite cause received a fatal setback.

Doune Castle

Doune, 6 miles NW of Stirling. Tel: (01786) 841742.

A variation on the keep-gatehouse in which tower-house for the lord, kitchen-tower for domestics and a linking great hall form a single mass.

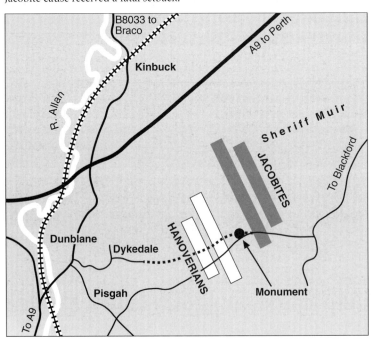

Edward I caught Wallace south of Falkirk and forced him to battle. The Scots formed up with archers before and between their schiltrons and cavalry to the rear on the south of Callendar Wood. Westquarter Burn was to their left, Glen Burn to their right and the marshy ground before them, so Edward's forces divided left and right. The rings of Scots spearmen, schiltrons, were left exposed by the retreat of the horsemen which allowed the English horse to scatter the Scots bowmen. The English archers did the schiltrons fearful damage before Edward's knights renewed their onslaught and won the day. The power of the longbow had had its first demonstration. Wallace reverted to guerrilla warfare after this defeat until he was betrayed, taken and brutally put to death in 1305.

After the failure in England, Prince Charles's forces besieged Stirling. Lt-General Henry Hawley brought 8,000 men from Edinburgh and Lord George Murray answered by moving a similar number to Falkirk Moor. Hawley was camped at Falkirk and had no idea that Murray was occupying the high ground; he was more interested in distracting himself at dinner with the author's ancestor, Lady Kilmarnock, who was doing her bit for the Jacobite cause. Murray anchored his left behind a ravine and formed two lines to the south towards Glen Burn, while Hawley belatedly hurried his troops into a line approximately through the site of the present hospital and, before they could settle, had his dragoons on the left charge. They were repulsed by a torrent of musketry and fell back through their comrades. Unable to reload because of the heavy rain, the Highlanders charged immediately, rolling the Hanoverians back. Only at the ravine, as good a protection for Hawley's men as for Murray's, did the line hold and the Scots found themselves enfiladed until Murray's reserves came up. In twenty minutes the English had been routed but the Scots were so scattered they could do no more than occupy Hawley's camp and enjoy his dinner.

The Battle of Falkirk, 22 July 1298

Near Glen Village, 2 miles S of Falkirk by B803 and B8028. Possible site between the canal and Callendar Wood, E of Glen Village.

The Battle of Falkirk, 17 January 1746

From Falkirk by B803, past junction with B8023, bear right opposite hospital and right to Bantaskin Park; monument and the ravine. Also, continue past hospital on B803, stop short of sharp left turn and look back from position of Jacobite right.

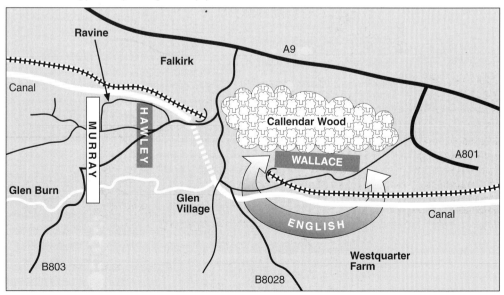

IRELAND

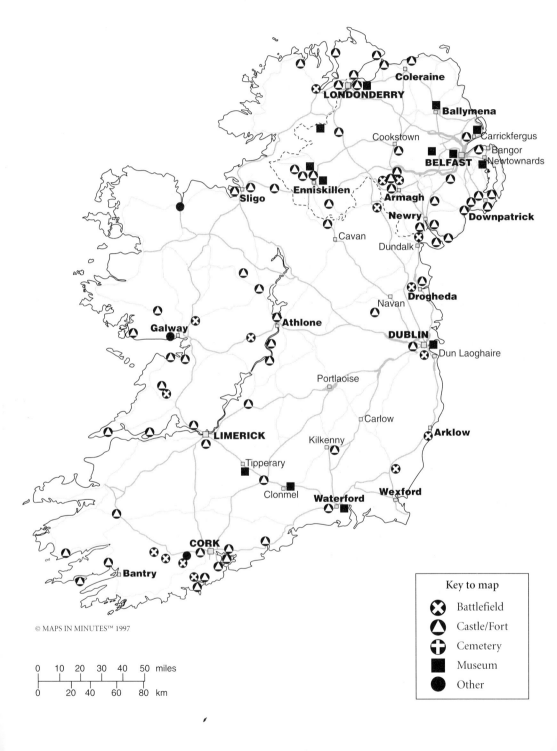

Coleraine

LONDONDERRY

Ballymena

Cookstown

Carrickfergus

Enniskillen

BELFAST

Bangor
Newtownards

Sligo

Armagh

Newry

Downpatrick

Cavan

Dundalk

Drogheda

Navan

Galway

Athlone

DUBLIN

Dun Laoghaire

Portlaoise

Carlow

LIMERICK

Kilkenny

Arklow

Tipperary

Wexford

Clonmel

Waterford

CORK

Bantry

© MAPS IN MINUTES™ 1997

| 0 | 10 | 20 | 30 | 40 | 50 | miles |

| 0 | 20 | 40 | 60 | 80 | km |

Key to map

- ⊗ Battlefield
- △ Castle/Fort
- ⊕ Cemetery
- ■ Museum
- ● Other

As G A Hayes-McCoy pointed out, plotting some 200 battle sites in Ireland reveals that no major action took place further than thirty miles from the sea and none at all more than fifty. Topography and politics rule.

The centre of the country is flat and wet. From the low coast round Dublin the land runs west marked by rivers and, before it was drained, bogs. To the north are the mountains of Ulster surrounding Lough Neagh and those of Donegal to the west. South of Dublin more mountains line the coast and the south-eastern shore is marked with the estuaries of the rivers Slaney, Barrow, Nore and Suir that drain the midlands to provide a welcome for invaders both in anchorage and in high roads to the interior. In the south-west the mountains prevail again and more secure anchorages are to be found. The west coast offers major access points at Limerick on the Shannon, at Galway and at Donegal Bay in the north, on a coast giving on to more mountains or at least country hard to traverse.

The Vikings were the first to make use of these landing places to establish towns at Dublin and on the friendly estuaries in the south and west, and the southern towns later served as entry gates to the Normans. From England the crossing from Cheshire to Dublin was a short voyage. Belfast Lough welcomed incomers from Scotland. While the estuaries and rivers offered an easy road, the Irish held the hills; south Armagh remains a haven for ambushers and irregulars to this day. In the centre only one clear line of defence exists, that of the Shannon. The Jacobites attempted to hold it against an advance from the east and the English fortified it in the Napoleonic Wars against invaders from the west.

The ease with which Ireland can be entered from Scotland, England and Wales works, of course, the other way round. In the 14th century Edward Bruce was able to threaten Edward II's England with a campaign in Ireland. The Tudor confrontations with Catholic France and Spain were coloured by the fear of invasion of, and then from, Ireland, as were later French wars, and in the wars of the 20th century lines of supply from North America were secure only if Ireland was at least neutral. The complicated consequences of internal strife and external interference are written on the face of the land.

ARKLOW

Tourist information: Tel: (0402) 32484 (mid-June to August)

**The Battle of Arklow,
9 June 1798**
At Arklow town.

The rise of the Irish Defenders, an anti-Protestant, millenarian pro-French Revolution movement, led to successive and increasing reprisals for their violent actions by the English and Protestant Irish. Insurrection was feared and even provoked by random and excessive use of force, beatings, burnings of houses and imprisonment of suspects. At the same time the war against the French was draining Ireland of regular soldiers and replacing them with ill-disciplined militia who contributed further to the miseries of the populace. That the English failed to foresee and provide for an uprising on the scale of 1798 is proof of their lack of understanding of the true situation. The revolt broke out at the end of May, soon to be suppressed in Meath and Kildare but County Wexford was a different matter. The North Cork Militia were defeated at Oulart, and Wexford and Enniscorthy were taken. The troops moving against the insurgents were worsted at Tubberneering. The government forces fled north through Gorey and Arklow to Wicklow. Extreme alarm gripped Dublin, but the rebels, without coherent leadership, dallied at Gorey while a makeshift force of about 1,000 men under Major-General Francis Needham was gathered and sent to Arklow on 6 June. Another 500 or so joined him on 8 June and the next morning.

The insurgents moved out of Gorey at 10am on 9 June, some 20,000 of them, marching through Inch and Coolgreany; the N11 follows a new route. They were armed with some muskets, pikes and various other weapons and had a couple of captured cannon. They reached Arklow around 4pm and split into two columns, one approaching the town from the west along the Coolgreany road, the other by Arklow Rock Road near the shore, now just a track, which ran towards the bridge over the Avoca River at the east of the main street. The first attack was from the west, Needham's outposts falling back to the barricades as the rebels came on. Encouraged by their apparent success, they charged the defences, to be met by musketry and grapeshot that cut them down in great numbers. The insurgents spread out to engage in a musketry duel at a distance while the other column attacked the eastern defences at the Fishery, setting a number of houses on fire and almost reaching the bridge. Needham's cavalry had been held on the northern bank of the river and now came storming forward but to small effect. However, the rebels failed to get into the main street itself and threw themselves fruitlessly against the musket fire and cannonade of the defenders. Here, as in previous engagements, the courage and determination of the rebels aroused the admiration of the English soldiers.

At about 8pm, with ammunition on both sides running low and the fire slackening, Fr Michael Murphy came up along the Coolgreany road and found men turning away. He rallied them to another charge and fell at their head. The musketeers had exhausted their ammunition and, ignorant of the fact that the defenders were in much the same state, started to withdraw. Others followed and as the insurgents drew back in the east the cavalry charged for a final time, but there was no general pursuit; they were all too tired. The thin defence of the road to Dublin had held, and the rebels trailed back to their camp on Vinegar Hill outside Enniscorthy.

Black Castle was built by Maurice Fitzgerald, a Norman incomer, in 1176 on a promontory immediately south of the harbour. In the late 19th century a battery was built to the south-west to mount four guns. The emplacements for two 6-inch breech-loaders of about 1900 survive. The battery was manned by the Wicklow Militia artillery. Two 9-inch RMLs of the 1860s are displayed on plinths overlooking the harbour.

Black Castle Battery
Wicklow, 16 miles N by N11 and R751.

ARMAGH

Tourist information: 40 English Street. Tel: (01861) 521800.

The regiment was raised in 1793 in response to the threat of the French in the preliminaries to the Napoleonic Wars. It saw service in Egypt, South America, the West Indies and Canada as well as Europe. The Crimean War and the Boer War, where they raised the siege of Ladysmith, were part of their experience. In World Wars I and II they distinguished themselves and went on to serve in Palestine, Korea and Aden. In 1968 they were amalgamated with the Inniskilling Fusiliers and the Ulster Rifles to form the Royal Irish Rangers.

The Royal Irish Fusiliers Museum
Sovereigns House, Mall East, Armagh. Tel: (01861) 522911. Open Monday to Friday (closed 12.30 to 1.30).

Navan, Eamhain Mhacha, was capital of the Kings of Ulster from 600BC to AD332. The hill-fort and the people associated with it are interpreted at the Centre with the aid of audio-visual and computer displays.

Navan Fort
Navan Centre. 2 miles W of Armagh by A28. Tel: (01861) 525550. Open daily, weekends afternoons only.

Hugh O'Neill, Earl of Tyrone, succeeded to his lordship in 1593. Rejecting English rule, as opposed to English suzerainty, he was declared a traitor in 1595. As defender of Ulster he had the wealth, the supplies, both from the Spanish and from English merchants happy to smuggle munitions to him, and the men, the well-disciplined Irish levies, the bonnachts. He worsted the English at Clontibret in 1595 and kept them on the hop to the extent of provoking the building of Blackwater Fort, just north of the modern crossing of the B128 from Armagh to Benburb. It was a poor thing, uncomfortable for the troops and badly designed for defence. When, in 1598, O'Neill threatened it, many were for withdrawal.

The Battle of the Yellow Ford, 1598
6 miles N of Armagh by A29 and B128.

However, Sir Henry Bagenal, the victim of Clontibret, was hot to move to the relief. On 14 August he marched his men from Armagh north on the east bank of the River Callan, the less obvious route, over open ground. O'Neill kept up a continuous harassment from the woods and bogs on the flanks and the advancing army became strung out as it veered westwards towards the Blackwater. Three little hills divide the Callan from the Blackwater, and between the two closest to Bagenal's objective O'Neill had a formidable trench dug across a cornfield, anchored at both ends by bogs. Sir Richard Percy took the vanguard beyond this obstacle, to the delight of the English in the fort, but the rearguard were still east of the Callan and Bagenal was rushing back and forth trying to regain control of his forces. The Irish fell on the vanguard and Bagenal was

Plan of the Battles of the
Yellow Ford and Benburb

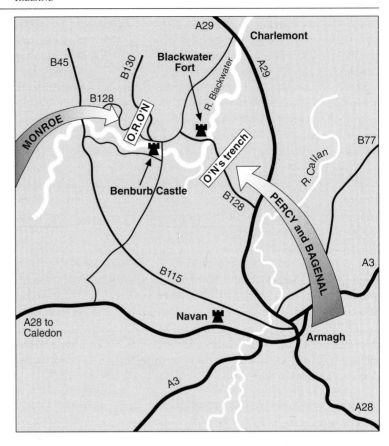

killed as he moved to support it. Percy, dazed, was among the very few to survive. The decision was taken to withdraw to Armagh, but some troops persisted in the advance and were cut to pieces. The gunpowder wagon blew up. A heroic charge allowed the foremost troops to rejoin their fellows in the rush for Armagh, there to set up what defensive positions they could, thence to retreat to Dublin leaving O'Neill master of Ulster.

The Battle of Benburb, 5 June 1646

Derrycreevy, W of Benburb, 7 miles NW of Armagh by A29 and B128.

With the outbreak of the rising in 1641 and the formation of the Confederation of Kilkenny, Owen Roe O'Neill, an experienced soldier who had been in the service of the Spanish in the Low Countries, returned to Ireland to train and organise the Catholic forces. In 1645 the arrival of John Baptist Rinuccini, the papal nuncio, with arms and money gave the Confederation fresh impetus. The planters' forces were under the command of the Scotsman Robert Monroe, who had served with the Dutch against the Spanish and with Gustavus Adolphus. In early June 1646 the Protestant armies planned to convene at Gladlough, west of Armagh, to attack southwards and O'Neill moved north from the Hill of Gallanagh, south of Cavan, to frustrate them. Taking his information from a prisoner, Monroe hastened to Armagh to attack O'Neill only to find his enemy already at Benburb on the high ground north of the river, near the old castle, dominating the crossing of the Blackwater. Monroe marched round by Caledon while O'Neill took up position on the hill of Drumflugh and sent a force forward over the River Oona to harry the fatigued Protestants; they had already marched 14 miles and they were marching into a trap.

The rising ground at Derrycreevy revealed the Irish beyond a small stream, drawn up in two lines. Monroe's men were on a narrower front with the Blackwater on the right and a bog to the left, from where he tried to turn the Irish left to drive them away from the river and into the arms of his allies advancing from Colerane – he failed. The Colerane force had already been scattered by Brien Roe O'Neill who now hastened to support his kinsman. The Irish moved to the attack. There was no swift victory; it took an hour of dour fighting to turn Monroe's left and force his men back to the river, but in the end they were broken. The tight-packed Protestants suffered fearful casualties both on the field and in the pursuit. O'Neill took the baggage, the artillery and a famous victory, but no long-term advantage.

Hugh O'Neill's triumph at the Yellow Ford was followed by defeat with his Spanish allies at Kinsale in 1601 at the hands of Charles Blount, Lord Mountjoy. To secure this part of troublesome Ulster, Mountjoy built a strong house and a fortified bawn at Charlemont. The house was a domestic dwelling of the period; three storeys high with large windows. The enclosure, however, was a serious military earthwork, square with bastions at each angle. The house was burned down in 1920, but the earthworks remain.

Ulysses Simpson Grant, the Union general of the American Civil War and 18th President of the USA, was descended from John Simpson who was born here in 1738. Audio-visual displays are used in the telling of the story of the plantation, and the connection with the USA. On Sundays it opens in the afternoon.

This hill-fort, from which there are magnificent views, was the headquarters of the O'Hanlans, Chief Justices of Ireland, who carried out the coronations of the O'Neills. The fort is unusual in having a bank but no ditch for defence. Hugh O'Neill was crowned here in 1593 and the stone inauguration chair was destroyed by Lord Mountjoy in 1602.

Hugh O'Neill first fought Sir Henry Bagenal in May 1595. The resistance to the English by the King of Ulster left Newry, Bagenal's home town, in the front line at the northern end of the Pale and Monaghan threatened to the west. Sir Henry marched with some 1,750 men to the relief of Monaghan with supplies and fresh troops, but was dogged by O'Neill as he went. The roads were poor but the country alongside impassable for an army on the move. By 26 May, after a number of skirmishes with O'Neill's men, they arrived in Monaghan and set out the next day by a more southerly route, roughly the modern N2. The journey proved no easier as the road still gave O'Neill numerous opportunities to harry and ambush the column.

Benburb Castle

Ruins above the River Blackwater in the grounds of Servite Priory, to be seen from Benburb Valley Park.

The house within the bawn, the area surrounded by the defensive wall, is private. The castle was built in 1611. In the Heritage Centre, Milltown Road, there is a model of the Battle of Benburb.

Charlemont Fort

Charlemont, 8 miles N of Armagh by A29 on banks of the River Blackwater.

Grant Ancestral Home

Dergina, Ballygawley. Off A4 13 miles W of Dungannon. Tel: (016625) 57133. Open daily April to September.

Tullaghoge Fort

Tullyhogue, 8 miles N of Dungannon off B162 Cookstown to Stewartstown road. Open site.

The Battle of Clontibret, 1595

Clontibret, 13 miles SW of Armagh, 22 miles by road by A31/N12 via Monaghan and SE by N2.

At Clontibret, which they reached about midday, Bagenal had to turn north for Newry. Here O'Neill fought him in earnest and, to the surprise and admiration of the English, showed the courage and steadiness of the Ulstermen. The issue was in the balance when a Palesman, Seagrave, burst throught the Irish lines to grapple with O'Neill himself, hurling him to the ground before losing his arm to the son of O'Cahan and his life to O'Neill. The English got on the move once more, making for Ballymoyer (near Newtownhamilton) and fighting as they went. By dusk they had got only as far as Ballymacowen where they halted for the night in battle formation, their powder almost gone and the officers' pewter being melted for shot. Fortunately the Irish were equally exhausted and, when reinforcements arrived from Newry next morning, they drew off to block the Moyry pass, leaving Bagenal cut off from Dublin. The English had to be resupplied and their wounded evacuated by sea and, when O'Neill hastened to the support of Donegal, they found refuge in Drogheda.

ATHLONE

Athlone Castle

Market Square. Tel: (0902) 92912. Open daily April to October.

The castle was built in the 13th century by John de Grey to control the strategic crossing of the River Shannon south of Logh Ree. It was a keep and curtain-wall structure, much modified early in the 19th century to create gun platforms against a possible Napoleonic invasion. In June 1691 Athlone was in the front line of the Jacobite enclave west of the Shannon. The Williamite army under Lt-General Ginkel moved from Mullingar, taking the forward position at Ballymore, and made to cross the river at Athlone. The Jacobites broke the bridge and Ginkel's men managed to put planks across, only to see them thrown down by the heroic Sergeant Custume who died in the act. The Jacobite General, St Ruth, was dilatory in reinforcing the position, and Major-Generals Hugh Mackay and Tettau succeeded in crossing and entering the town on 30 June. The castle surrendered the following day. During the Napoleonic Wars the walls and towers were modified to create 11 artillery positions as part of the Shannon Defence Line. Seven batteries were built to the west of the town in 1803–4, of which one survives.

The Battle of Aughrim, 12 July 1691

Aughrim, 20 miles SW of Athlone by N6. Aughrim Experience, tel: (0905) 73939. Open April to September.

After the fall of Athlone the Jacobite general St Ruth faced a difficult situation. He could retire on either Galway or Limerick, attempt to disrupt Lt-General Ginkel's supply lines or offer battle. The survivors of Athlone had fallen back to join the rest of the army at Ballinasloe and on 7 July Ginkel moved towards them. St Ruth took up position at Aughrim, on a ridge that ran south-east from the village with a stream and boggy ground before him, the ruined castle anchoring his left and more bog beyond it. On his right Tristaun Stream ran forward from the ridge to join the River Ballinure. A narrow causeway now beneath the N6 and a gravel ridge that now carries the Laurencetown road were the only crossing places. It was a wonderful defensive position for St Ruth's 20,000 men, but equally unsuitable for counter-attack.

On the morning of 12 July Ginkel left Ballinasloe with 25,000 men; Huguenots, Danes, Dutch, English and Ulster troops. The Danes made contact with the Irish right early in the afternoon and pushed slowly forward. Ginkel hesitated, but events were developing their own momentum and at about five in the afternoon St Ruth moved part of his cavalry, and later some infantry, to his right where Ginkel's men were pressing him amongst the hedges and ditches by the stream.

Near the castle the causeway was too narrow to allow the Williamites to advance in force and four English battalions struggled forward through the bog to battle their way forward hedge by hedge, until they could do no more against the tactical fighting retreat of the Irish. Meanwhile Mackay was moving against the castle and its associated positions as yet more of Ginkel's troops crossed the bog only to be driven back. Indeed, Jacobite hearts were lifted as Gordon O'Neill's regiment took a Williamite battery in their pursuit of the worsted attackers.

Mackay, together with the Marquis de Ruvigny, thrust the cavalry forward past the castle as Major-General Talmash brought the rest of the infantry across the bog to his left. For some reason the Irish cavalry near the village of Aughrim failed to react and as St Ruth moved north to resist the advance a cannonball took off his head; a plaque marks the possible location. Panic swept through the Irish troops. The Williamite cavalry were rampaging down their lines from the supposedly stronger flank, the left, while their own cavalry fled. Their right, too, started to fold and as darkness fell the Irish either ran or died. Some 4,000 Irishmen fell at Aughrim, together with about 2,000 of their foes.

The Jacobite cause in Ireland was lost. Between October 1691 and January 1692 some 19,000 Irish soldiers sailed for France with their families to serve, first, in James II's private army and then in the French Army. They were known as 'The Wild Geese'.

Ballintober Castle

Ballintober, 14 miles NW by N61, 60 and R367.

The ruins of a castle built by the O'Connors in the early 14th century, with a large courtyard defended by polygonal corner towers and a gatehouse. It was inhabited until the 19th century.

Roscommon Castle

Roscommon, 20 miles NE by N61, N of the town.

The ruins of a Norman castle built in 1269 by Robert de Ufford. It remained a stronghold for almost 400 years, being captured by the Confederates under Preston in 1645, but surrendered by him to Cromwell's forces in 1652 and then destroyed. Its position was additionally secured by marshy land which has now been drained.

Shannonbridge

On the Shannon, 10 miles S of Athlone.

The fear of French invasion in the Napoleonic Wars led to the building of strongpoints to form the Shannon Defence Line from the mouth of the estuary to Athlone. Work started in 1804. At Shannonbridge, where an enemy landing at Galway could be expected to arrive within 48 hours, there is an important river crossing with a bridge built in 1757. In July 1803 Lt-Colonel Benjamin Fisher, the commanding engineer for Ireland, was asked to design a *tête-de-pont*, a defence work on the vulnerable side of the bridge. The result is unique in Britain and Ireland and an outstanding example of military architecture of the time.

Four hundred yards west of the bridge the glacis commences, sloping up to a ditch 20 feet wide, on the other side of which is the west wall of the redoubt. In the ditch is a caponier, a bomb-proof shelter across the ditch with loop-holes for enfilading fire, and two galleries also cover the ditch. Above these is the gun platform for four 24-pounders on traversing platforms, to give cover from the north-west to the south-west. Behind is the courtyard from which a sunken road stretches back to the bridge with curtain walls on either side. At the river bank are two flanking defence works, a battery to the north and a barracks to the south, on the roof of which were three more guns on traversing platforms. On the river bank itself were half bastions. On the east bank there were more batteries, one of which survives.

Banagher

On the Shannon, 17 miles S of Athlone.

As the next major crossing south of Shannonbridge, Banagher also received fortifications in the early 19th century. The medieval tower on the east bank, known as Cromwell's Castle, was modified to provide a magazine and to mount a gun on top. On the west bank an oval Martello tower to carry one 24-pounder was built. Fort Eliza was constructed to the south-east of the bridge. It was a small five-sided battery for four guns with a salient at the rear with a gatehouse at the apex. The magazine was in the centre of the fort.

Harryville Motte

Above the Braid River in Ballymena.

All that remains of the Norman castle is the earthern motte.

There was a ford over the river four miles to the south which also needed protection. Keelogue Battery was built for this purpose. It is a D-shaped battery similar to those on the Shannon estuary, mounting seven guns and with a blockhouse at the rear with two guns on the roof. Meelick Martello Tower was built to carry three guns on its roof and a stone central pier supports the load.

BALLYMENA

Tourist information: Council Offices, 80 Galgorm Road. Tel: (01266) 44111.

Museum of the Royal Irish Regiment

St Patricks Barracks, Desmesne Avenue, Ballymena. Tel: (01266) 661355. Open Wednesday and Saturday afternoons.

The heir to all the infantry regiments of Northern Ireland, the Royal Irish Regiment came into existence in July 1992. Using touch screens and multi-media presentations the story of the soldiers of the Province is told from 1689 to the present day.

BANTRY

Tourist information: The Square. Tel: (027) 50229 (June to September)

Bantry Bay

Bantry stands at the head of the bay which extends some 20 miles to the SW.

During the winter of 1796–7 a French fleet carrying 15,000 troops under General Hoche, with Humbert as second-in-command, sailed from Brest. Wolfe Tone was with them. Fog led to the fleet being split up, but some ships, with over 6,000 men, came to anchor in Bantry Bay. A storm blew up before they could come ashore and the ships cut their cables in order to escape. The area was, at that time, entirely undefended and had a landing been achieved the consequences would have been serious. One of the abandoned anchors has been recovered and stands by the road south of the town.

Garinish Island Tower

Glengariff, 9 miles NW by N71.

Now a noted garden, Garinish Island was fortified to protect Glengariff Harbour in 1804. One of the earliest of the Irish Martello towers, with a vertical exterior face, stands here together with a battery.

Bere Island was a Royal Navy base until 1938. On the island are Ardagh and Coolaghlin Martello towers. They were built during the first phase of coastal fortification in the Napoleonic Wars in 1804. West of the town, at Dunboy Castle, are the remains of a star fort of the 17th century. Traces of the earthworks can be found around the castle.

Bere Island and Berehaven

Castletownbere, 27 miles W of Bantry by N71 via Glengariff and R572.

A restored drystone fort some 2,000 years old. The walls are up to 18 feet high and 13 feet thick with steps within to give access to the parapets. A bank and ditch form the outer defences. A similar fort, Cahergall, is near Cahersiveen, another 25 miles onwards on N70. Within its enclosure are a beehive hut and a rectangular house in drystone.

Staigue Fort

Castlecove, on N side of Kenmare River, 25 miles W of Kenmare by N 70 (25 miles N of Bantry).

Built on the shore of Lough Leane in the 15th century, a rectangular keep is surrounded by a bawn fortified with circular towers. The castle has been restored using medieval techniques of construction and furnished in the style of the period. It was the last stronghold in Munster to resist Cromwell and it was taken by a waterborne attack.

Ross Castle

Killarney, 19 miles N of Kenmare by N71. Tel: (064) 35851. Open daily.

BELFAST

Tourist information: St Anne's Court, 59 North Street. Tel: (01232) 231221.

World War II had an immense impact on Northern Ireland and Belfast itself suffered fearful casualties from air raids. Some 150,000 men and women from Northern Ireland and from the Republic served in the British Forces and more than 300,000 American and other Allied troops were stationed here. The story of the war is told in this exhibition and the comradeship amongst nations is commemorated in the Hall of Friendship. A memorial to the landing of the American troops stands in front of Belfast City Hall.

Northern Ireland in the Second World War

War Memorial Building, 9–13 Waring Street, Belfast. Tel: (01232) 320392. Open Monday to Friday. Admission free.

In 1793 Major William Fitch was granted a warrant to raise a regiment in Dublin – the 83rd Regiment of Foot. Major-General Cornelius Cuyler's Shropshire Volunteers were posted to Ireland in 1794 as the 86th Foot and these two regiments became, in 1881, the Royal Irish Rifles. In the Napoleonic Wars the 86th took part in the capture of Réunion, then called Bourbon, and the name was awarded as a battle honour. The regiment saw service in the Boer War and contributed 21 battalions in World War I. In 1921, in consequence of the partition of Ireland, the name of the regiment changed again, and it was under the new name that they served in the Far East and on the North-West Frontier before World War II took them to Europe, in part as glider-borne troops. In 1968 they were amalgamated with others to form the Royal Irish Rangers. The museum contains over 4,000 artefacts.

The Royal Ulster Rifles Regimental Museum

5 Waring Street, Belfast. Tel: (01232) 232086. Open Monday to Friday all year, preferably by telephone appointment.

Fernhill House

Glencairn Park. Tel: (01232) 715599. Open daily.

A museum devoted to the history of Greater Shankill includes sections on World War I, the Home Rule Crisis and Orangeism.

Langford Lodge Wartime Centre

Station 597, Gortnagallon Road, Crumlin. 12 miles W. Tel: (01849) 423896.

This was the US 8th Army Air Force base in World War II. Medals, maps, photographs and films form the displays. It is open weekend afternoons from April to October.

Carrickfergus Castle and Town Walls

Carrickfergus, 9 miles NE by M2 and A2. Historic Monument, DOENI. Tel: (01960) 351273. Open daily, Sunday afternoons only.

John de Courcy, a Norman knight, started work on this medieval stronghold in 1180. It was taken by Edward Bruce in 1315 and after recapture remained an English stronghold for 300 years. Artillery was provided for in the 1560s and the town itself was strengthened with earthen bastions. During the plantations of the early 17th century the walls were rebuilt in stone; the north-east angle bastion survives. Infantry barracks were built in 1715, the gatehouse modified to form gun towers and a battery was constructed to guard the north-eastern flank. In the late 19th century the east battery was developed to command the shipping route on Belfast Lough. The castle is arranged for informative visits.

In 1778 the American warship *Ranger* under John Paul Jones was challenged by HMS *Drake* sailing out of Carrickfergus. Jones captured the Royal Navy vessel.

Andrew Jackson Centre and US Ranger Centre

Boneybefore Carrickfergus, 2 miles E of Carrickfergus by A2. Tel: (01960) 366455. Open daily.

The 1st Battalion US Rangers was raised in Carrickfergus in 1942. The Rangers distinguished themselves in action on D-Day at the Pointe du Hoc in Normandy. Andrew Jackson, seventh President of the USA and victor of the Battle of New Orleans, was born here and the centre tells of his life and career and of the Ulster-Scots emigration to America. Open afternoons only at weekends.

Grey Point Fort

South shore of Belfast Lough.

With Kilroot Battery on the northern side, the battery's two 6-inch breech-loading guns commanded the waterway. The battery was first manned by the Antrim Royal Garrison Artillery in 1907. Gunhouses were added in World War II and searchlight emplacements built on the foreshore in 1936 and 1940.

The Somme Heritage Centre

233 Bangor Road, Newtownards. 9 miles E of Belfast by A20 and A21. Tel: (01247) 823202.

On 1 July 1916, the first day of the Battle of the Somme, the 36th (Ulster) Division achieved the only substantial advance on the northern half of the front at Thiepval, taking the Schwaben Redoubt and reaching the German second line. Their heroism is celebrated here in great detail with reconstructed trenches, audio-visual presentations and a wealth of historical information.

Hillsborough Fort

Hillsborough, 10 miles SW of Belfast by M1 and A1. Tel: (01846) 683285. Open daily except Mondays, Sunday afternoons only.

Begun in 1630 to command the route to and from Belfast and finished in 1650 by Colonel Arthur Hill, Hillsborough was declared a royal fort by Charles II. It is square, with a bastion at each corner. In 1770 the gatehouse on the north-west was converted to a place of entertainment and a new gateway was made on the north-east with a fanciful gazebo.

Dromore Mound

4 miles SW of Hillsborough.

A fine Norman motte and bailey castle overlooks a bend in the Lagan.

COLERANE

Tourist information: Railway Road. Tel: (01265) 447723.

Magilligan Tower
Magilligan Point. 12 miles W of Colerane by A2 and B202. Key to tower at pub in summer and at Magilligan Field Centre, Seacoast Road on A2 in winter.

In 1794 Sir David Dundas commanded a British naval squadron at Cape Mortella, Corsica, where a tower-mounted gun caused him considerable difficulty. He advocated the use of similar structures for the discomfiture of naval forces attacking the British Isles and the ten years from 1803 saw 'Martello' towers built both in England and Ireland. This example, built in 1812, worked with its fellow on the other side of Lough Foyle at Greencastle to protect the approaches to the magnificent anchorage and the port of Londonderry from American privateers. The entrance is on the first floor and the gun platform mounted two 24-pounders on the same central pivot.

Dunluce Castle
6 miles NE of Colerane, E of Portrush by A2. Open Monday to Saturday and Sunday afternoons, closed Monday October to March.

The original castle occupied the rocky outcrop separated from the mainland by a deep gorge. The oldest parts date from the 14th century. In the 16th century it was captured from the MacQuillans by the Scottish MacDonnells, the Lords of the Isles. The wreck of the Spanish Armada treasure ship *Girona* off the Giant's Causeway gave Sorley Boy MacDonnell the loot to finance the extension to the mainland with the construction of the courtyard and storage buildings, funnelling in towards the gatehouse which shows the Scottish influence with its corbelled turrets. The great hall was added in the 17th century by the Earls of Antrim.

Limavady Airfield
Limavady, 14 miles SW of Colerane by A2.
Relics of World War II are the old operations block and the dome trainer.

CORK

Tourist information: Tourist House, Grand Parade. Tel: (021) 273 251.
With its magnificent, sheltered anchorage and access to the rich farmlands of the valley of the Lee, Cork attracted the Danes and then the Normans. Cromwell took the town in 1649 and it was besieged again in 1690 after which most of its ancient fortifications were destroyed. The harbour was used by the Royal Navy during the American War of Independence and the Napoleonic Wars. A survey of defences was made by Lt-Colonel Charles Vallencey in 1777–8 and considerable construction followed.

Cork was a centre of republican action in both the War of Independence and in the Civil War that followed. On 11 December 1920 the Black and Tans set fire to buildings in the city, the greatest destruction being between Cook Street and Merchants' Quay along the south-eastern side of St Patrick Street.

Elizabeth Fort
Off Barrack Street, south of the city.

First constructed in 1601–2 at the behest of Lord Mountjoy in case of another Spanish invasion and rebuilt in 1603, it was entirely remodelled in 1625–6 and played an important role in the siege of 1690. It became a prison in 1835 and was burned down by the Anti-Treaty forces in 1922. The outer walls and bastions remain.

Barryscourt Castle

Off R624 to Great Island. Open daily March to October.

Built on land acquired by Norman incomers in the 12th century, the keep dates from 1420 and stands within a bawn which is formed in part of the remains of the great hall of the 13th century. The castle was attacked by Sir Walter Raleigh in 1580 after which the south-west and north-east towers were added.

Belvelly Tower

Great Island, 6 miles E of Cork by N25 and R624.

One of five towers built to protect Cork Harbour 1813-15. This one commands the bridge to Great Island and, like its fellows, has straight sides.

Cove Fort

Cobh (Cove), Great Island, southern shore.

The fort has three levels of gun emplacements overlooking the water. On the landward side part of the wall for defence by musket survives. The fort was built in 1743 replacing temporary batteries and was added to over the years, and rebuilt in 1804. The lower battery carried six 24-pounders, the middle battery thirteen and a single gun was on the upper level.

Cobh Heritage Centre

Cobh railway station. Tel: (021) 811 929. Open daily March to October.

Among other topics, the story of the development of Cork Harbour as a naval base is told, including events of the Boer War and World War I. The sinking of the *Lusitania* off Old Head of Kinsale by torpedo in 1915, a profound influence in bringing America into the war, is recounted. A monument to the victims stands in Casement Square.

Spike Island

South of Great Island.

During the American War of Independence a fort was built by Charles Vallencey at the southern end of the island on cliffs some 50 feet high, to be replaced by Fort Westmorland which covered most of the island. The armament consisted of 26 24-pounders, 3 13-inch mortars, 10 6-pounders and 5 small swivel guns. By 1809 it was half finished and it was still being added to and modified up to the 1860s. Between 1847 and 1883 it was used as a prison.

Youghal Town Walls

Youghal, 28 miles E by N25.

The town was a Danish stronghold in the 9th century and became a Norman one 300 years later. The walls were built in the 13th century and extended in the 17th, surviving as the most complete in Ireland with 13 towers still standing. In the 19th century a tower was refortified near the churchyard. Sir Walter Raleigh was mayor in the 16th century, during which time he introduced the potato into Ireland.

Royal Gunpowder Mills

Ballincollig, 4 miles W by N22. Tel: (021) 874 430. Open daily April to September.

The gunpowder mills were founded in 1794 by a Cork banker, Charles Leslie. They were bought by the British Board of Ordnance in 1805 to supply the war effort against Napoleon and closed at the end of that war in 1815. They reopened in 1833 and remained in production until 1903. An audio-visual presentation describes the history of gunpowder and of this mill, of which there is also a guided tour.

The Siege and Battle of Kinsale, 1601

S of Cork, 15 miles by N71 and R607.

Hugh O'Neill had fought a successful defensive war in Ulster since 1595 to avoid complete submission to England's vision of centralised control. Elizabeth I could not tolerate this, threatened as she was by the enmity of Catholic Spain and the possibility of an alliance with the Catholics in Ireland. Nor could O'Neill see a chance of lasting success without Spanish money, arms and men. Finally, in

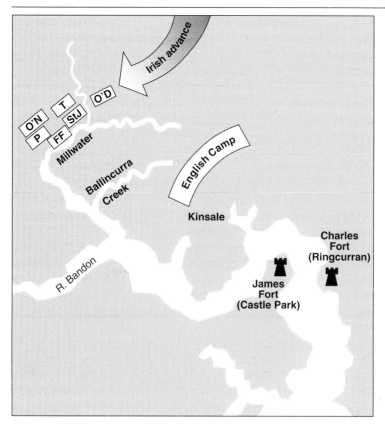

spring 1601, the Spanish mounted an invasion and landed at Kinsale on 21 September with 3,500 men. General Mountjoy moved swiftly, gathering his troops from all over Ireland, to contain them. By 14 October he had nearly 7,000 men in Cork. O'Neill at once raided southwards; by November, 22 villages had been burned in Meath alone. Mountjoy was not to be distracted by the damage done in the Pale, and pressure was instead exerted by reinforcing the English presence in Derry and Carrickfergus. Red Hugh O'Donnell, who had his cousin Neill bottled up in Donegal Abbey, also faced the dilemma of joining with the Spaniards or keeping his position in the north secure. In November both O'Neill and O'Donnell moved south for Kinsale. Mountjoy sent a force north via Cashel to meet O'Donnell, but they could not keep up with the swift pace set by the westward-moving northerners and turned back to Kinsale. The two Ulster armies met to the west of Bandon, just over ten miles from their objective and, in the first week of December, moved down the river valley to relieve the besieged forces of Don Juan del Aguila.

The English had Kinsale in a firm grip, having taken Ringcurran (where Charles Fort now stands) and Castle Park (the site of James's Fort), but although they had 7,500 men against Aguila's 3,000, they could not take the town. When O'Neill moved via Inshannon to Coolcarron with 6,500 men the English were cut off from supply from Cork and sickness and lack of forage for the horses sapped Mountjoy's strength. O'Neill was tempted to sit it out and let them rot,

Ringaskiddy Martello Tower

West of Cork Harbour.

Standing above Cork Harbour to the west, this drum-shaped tower was still in the building in 1813–15. It is unusual in having a surrounding ditch.

but the encouragement of the fiery O'Donnell and perhaps his own wish to achieve a decisive outcome led him to mount an attack in the early morning of 24 December.

The move was not a surprise to Mountjoy. For three days past his 'squadron volant' under Sir Henry Power had been held in readiness. The Irish advance was bungled. As they came south and then swung west to assemble by the little stream of Millwater, they became spread out, O'Donnell's rearward troops lagging behind as the English first saw O'Neill's men. As the Irish moved hestitantly forward as far as Ballincurra Creek, Mountjoy took some 2,000 men, Ffolliot's and St John's Regiments and Power's squadron volant, forward. The Irish fell back over Millwater, attempting to get in good order for battle as they did so, forming three large blocks with the addition of O'Donnell's men. The rest of the English horse were called forward from the reserve and the Irish horse turned tail, disrupting their footsoldiers as they did so. The English cavalry fell upon the Irish right and broke it and as Ffolliot's foot came up Richard Tyrrell, in command of the Irish centre, tried to move right in support. St John's Regiment charged to take Tyrrell in the flank and the centre also fell back and broke up. Seeing two-thirds of their number in flight, O'Donnell's troops dispersed. Mountjoy's speed in action had his troops back in camp by noon. The Spaniards surrendered Kinsale nine days later. Mountjoy was to have the satisfaction of accepting the Irish leaders' submission to the English Crown in 1603.

Charles Fort

Kinsale, on the E of the estuary. Tel: (021) 772 263. Open mid-April to mid-October daily except closed Mondays mid-April to mid-June.

Charles II's Dutch Wars gave rise to fears of an attack on Ireland and in 1678 work began to replace the earthworks at Ringcurran. William Robinson was in charge, assisted by Captain James Archer who actually carried out the project overseen by the Earl of Orrery. A two-tiered battery faces seawards, and behind it a bastioned defence work fatally overlooked by high ground inland. It had been intended to build a pentagonal fort to the rear, but this was never done. In 1685 Thomas Phillips carried out an inspection of Irish forts and found this well built as far as it went, but in need of strengthening to landward. No action was taken. In 1690, during the Williamite Wars, John Churchill, later the Duke of Marlborough, attacked the fort and succeeded in breaching the curtain wall next to the central bastion, at which point the defenders surrendered. Charles Fort is, notwithstanding, the finest example of 17th-century fortification in Ireland.

James Fort

Kinsale, on the W of the estuary by R600 and minor road S.

The pentagonal bastioned earthwork is the last work of Paul Ive, who died here, and was built between 1602 and 1604. The bastions are straight flanked and the ramparts revetted in stone. A building within, a square, demi-bastioned affair with two towers, was not completed until 1611. There is a blockhouse at water level some way to the north-west which is probably of slightly earlier date. The fort was taken by John Churchill in 1690 shortly before his success at Charles Fort.

The wild country west of Cork was well-suited to the guerrilla warfare waged against the British in the War of Independence from 1919 to 1921. It was also a stronghold of the Republicans who resisted the treaty that supposedly ended that war, and it was here that Michael Collins, attempting to suppress Republican opposition, met his death.

The Ambush at Kilmichael, 28 November 1920
S of Kilmichael, 25 miles W of Cork by N22, R584 and S on R587.
In the autumn of 1920 the activities of the RIC Auxiliaries against the civilian population made it imperative for the IRA to take action. Commandant General Tom Barry recounts that he was aware that his enemy made regular use of the road south from Kilmichael and that, in addition, the road kinked east for 150 yards before resuming its soutward line some one and a half miles south of the village. Here he set his ambush. The Command Post was at the eastern end of the west to east stretch, with three riflemen behind a low stone wall, and a section of 10 men were on the reverse slope of a rock immediately to the north. On the northern side of the road at the western end another 10 men were in position, seven able to fire south and the rest ready to act if the second of the two lorries expected failed to come round the corner. Another six men were south of the road and a like number in reserve north of the road lest additional lorries arrived. An overnight march brought them to these positions by 9am on that Sunday morning.

Cold, wet and with little to eat or drink, they waited. It was not until 4.05pm that the sentries gave warning of the Auxiliaries' approach from the north. Coming towards the concealed Command Post, the driver was puzzled by the appearance of a man in an IRA tunic. As he slowed a Mills bomb was thrown, a whistle blew and the riflemen opened fire. A savage fight left 11 Auxiliaries dead. The second lorry did turn the corner before halting and the men in it managed to take cover and return fire. As Barry and his companions moved to take them in the rear they heard shouts of surrender, only to see the IRA men shot at again as they rose to take their prisoners. In the ensuing battle no prisoners were taken – the Auxiliaries were wiped out. Three of Barry's men lost their lives.

The Battle of Crossbarry, 19 March 1921
Crossbarry, 8 miles SW of Cork by N71 and R589.
The British forces were operating in units of some 300 men early in 1921 and Tom Barry's Brigade Flying Column consequently consolidated all available men and weapons in a single group. On 19 March it became apparent that the British were mobilising at least four units to surround and destroy Barry's force. The operation was not, however, closely coordinated and Barry was able to set up an ambush at Crossbarry to deal with the first thrust which he knew was coming from the west.

The old road from Brandon to Cork passes through the little town and two roads from north to south cross it some 30 yards apart. Barry placed his men to the west of these crossroads, deployed to defend all sectors except the east, which was lightly guarded. Instructions were given that all sections should hold their positions unless expressly ordered otherwise, to guard against attack by other columns. The plan worked perfectly. One by one the British units came in, first from the west and, each after a convenient interval, from other points of the compass. Each was repelled with serious casualties until, the attacks ceasing, Barry was able to withdraw to the west in good order, only three of his men having been killed. The impact on the civilian population is not recorded.

The Skirmish at Beal na Bláth, 22 August 1922
Bealnablath, 9 miles W of Cork by N72 and R585.

The motive for Michael Collins's journey to Cork in August 1922 was ostensibly to inspect the South-Western Command in an area of strong Republican resistance, but there is also evidence that he planned to meet key figures in the Republican movement to seek resolution of their differences. The route selected itself exposed him to danger, taking his party in the early morning through the remote valley of Beal na Bláth on the way to Bandon. There they stopped to ask the way, speaking to Dinny Long, a member of Cork No. 2 Brigade of the Republican IRA. When the convoy had passed on its way, plans were made to ambush Collins on the return journey.

At 8pm the ambush party gave up, some of them making for the pub and five others clearing up the barricade and mine they had readied for the operation. As they did so they heard the sound of approaching vehicles and moved into position. When fired upon, Collins threw himself into the battle instead of attempting to evade his enemies. The exchange of fire lasted for perhaps half an hour before the attackers were forced to withdraw, but by then Collins was severely wounded on the back of the neck and he died shortly after. Countless conflicting versions of the incident have circulated over the years, but the likelihood is that a ricochet was the cause of the wound.

DOWNPATRICK

Tourist information: 74 Market Street. Tel: (01396) 612233.
The Mound of Down is a man-made pre-Norman motte on which the Normans later built a castle.

Clough Castle
Clough, 6 miles SW of Downpatrick by A25.

The Norman motte and bailey castle was of the most elementary type, with a mound on which a wooden palisade was erected. In the 13th century a stone tower was built on the motte.

Dundrum Castle
Dundrum, 2 miles S of Clough. Open April to September Tuesday to Saturday and Sunday afternoons.

This superb Norman castle was built by John de Courcey in about 1177 and surrounded by a ditch cut into the rock. The circular keep, added in the 13th century, was modified 200 years later by the building of a bridge from the original first-floor entrance to the curtain wall and the Lower Ward was built at much the same time.

Jordan's Castle
Ardglass, 7 miles S of Downpatrick by B1. Open May to August Tuesday to Saturday and Sunday afternoons.

Ardglass was, in the 15th century, the busiest port in Ulster, and the town was therefore geared to defence. Jordan's Castle is a tower-house of that period that had to withstand a three-year siege until relieved by Lord Mountjoy in June 1601. It takes its name from the owner of that time, Simon Jordan.

The tower-house, built in the 16th century, overlooks the harbour at the strategically important site of the mouth of Strangford Lough. The oldest surviving tower-house in the county is three miles to the south at Kilclief and another, Audley's Castle, stands two miles to the west.

Strangford Castle
Strangford, 8 miles E of Downpatrick by A25.

DROGHEDA

Tourist information: Tel: (041) 37070, June to August.
The town was founded by Norsemen in the 10th century and became a Norman stronghold in the 13th century when the town walls were built. Of these a portion survives at St Laurence Gate in Laurence Street and Butter Gate on Millmount south of the River Boyne. Millmount itself became the motte of the Norman castle. Drogheda was besieged by Sir Felim O'Neill in 1641 and the Catholic Convention defenders were relieved by Lord Ormond who was to surrender the town to the Parliamentarians six years later, and to regain it in 1649. Cromwell retook it later that year with fearful slaughter – some 2,000 people, men, women and children, were massacred.

The fort was built in 1808 to carry two 9-pounders on traversing platforms. The circular tower served as the magazine and living quarters for the garrison. Steps led down from Millmount to the barracks which, in 1815, had 340 men in residence.

Richmond Fort
Millmount.

In March 1689 James II came to Dublin from France to take up his position as king of a separate Irish realm. The army, officially disbanded by William of Orange, had been kept in existence by the Earl of Tyrconnell, who had been Lord Deputy before James's dethronement in England. There were three regiments of horse, one of dragoons and five infantry, including the Irish Guards. The northern Protestants resisted successfully at Derry and Enniskillen and in August their cause was strengthened by the arrival of the Duke of Schomberg with 2,000 men. That winter Ulster was in Williamite hands and Schomberg was at Lisburn, his force reduced by sickness to 7,000.

The Battle of the Boyne, 12 July (1 July Old Style) 1690
King William's Glen, 4 miles W of Drogheda by N51. Donore, W by minor road. Duleek, SW by R152.

    In 1690 James got support from the French with the arrival of the Count de Lauzun with 7,000 men in exchange for 5,387 Irishmen, the first of the Wild Geese, who were to become the Irish Brigade in the French Army. The Williamites welcomed a Danish contingent of 1,000 horse and 6,000 foot as well as English and Dutch regiments. When William himself arrived in June he also had French Huguenots in his service. On 3 July he moved south from Loughbrickland, six miles north of Newry, to Dundalk with 36,000 men. The Jacobite outposts fell back to the Boyne to join the main army on the ridge at Donore; some 25,000 men, of whom 1,500 were in Drogheda. William reached the Boyne on 11 July and camped at Tullyallen, four miles west of Drogheda, on the north bank. In front of him was the gully now known as King William's Glen, and offering cover, running down to the river at the hamlet, now gone, of Oldbridge. The river was tidal up to this point and the fords downstream only periodically useable. There were fords upstream at Rosnaree below Slane.

    At 5am on the morning of 12 July 10,000 Williamites moved upstream to

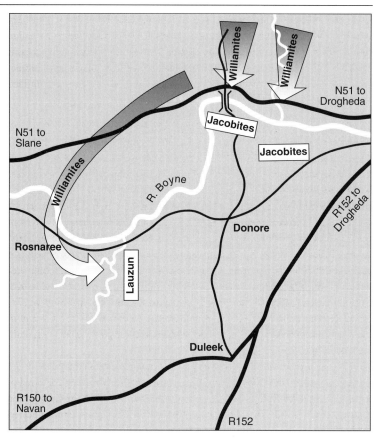

The Battle of the Boyne

cross at Rosnaree and other fords where they were resisted by Sir Neill O'Neill's dragoons for a short while. Once over they found all of Lauzun's troops and two cavalry regiments coming up to face them and this flank soon became static, with the opposing forces facing each other across a boggy rivulet, the Jacobites on the rising ground and Donore behind them. At about 10am William's Dutch Guards, the Huguenots and some English started across the river at Oldbridge, opposed by about 6,000 Jacobites. They were attacked by the cavalry and suffered fearfully, but held on. As the tide fell the fords downstream became, just, passable and 12,000 Danish and other Williamites got over, soon to be joined at noon by the cavalry coming over even lower down at Drybridge, neck deep. The pressure was too great for James's depleted centre and right to resist and while his left remained facing those who had crossed early in the morning the Jacobites were rolled back through Donore. The cavalry fought heroically; of 200 Jacobite Life Guards only 16 left the field unscathed. The whole Jacobite force fell back to come together at Dunleek and make for Dublin (whence James left for France) eventually to adopt a final line of defence on the Shannon from Limerick to Athlone and there to be defeated at Aughrim.

The ruins of Trim Castle stand on the south bank of the River Boyne. The keep is early 13th century and the walls were built some 25 years later. A wooden fighting platform was mounted on them and the holes for the supporting beams can be seen best in the riverside wall. A barbican and two drawbridges protected the Dublin Gate. In the mid-17th century the keep was lowered and infilled to become an artillery platform.

Trim Castle
Trim, 18 miles SW by N51 and R161.

DUBLIN

Tourist information: 14 Upper O'Connell Street. Tel: (01) 284 4768.

The River Liffey and the settlement that the Vikings called Dubh Linn give access to the midlands of Ireland and were key locations for incomers. The Norsemen's influence was checked by the High King of Ireland, Brian Ború, when he overthrew, at the cost of his own life, the forces of Sitric of Dublin, Sigurd from the Orkneys, Brodar from the Isle of Man and Maelmora, King of Leinster at the Battle of Clontarf on 23 April 1014. The fighting took place somewhere north of the point at which the River Tolka enters the bay. A century and a half later Leinster was to be the instrument of further incomers. Dermot MacCurrogh, King of Leinster, formed an alliance with Henry II of England to regain his lands. The Normans took Waterford and Wexford from the Norsemen and in 1170 Dermot and Richard FitzGilbert, known as Strongbow, ejected Haskulf, the Norse king, from Dublin.

The Norsemen returned in May 1171. The Normans fought them on the east of the town around the present Dame Street and were getting the worst of the affair when their leader, Miles de Cogan, sent his brother Richard out by the west gate and around by the south to take Haskulf in the rear. The archers cleared the way for the Norman heavy horse to slaughter the attackers. At much the same time another force under Rory O'Connor, the High King, blockaded the town with an encampment at Castleknock to the west. By September starvation threatened the town and Strongbow, de Cogan and Raymond le Gros led a surprise attack on the Irish camp with complete success. The Battles of Dublin left this vital gateway to Ireland in Norman hands.

King John gave instructions for the building of the castle in 1204, south of Dublin as it then stood. The medieval castle occupied the area now known as the Upper Yard, but much of it was destroyed by fire in 1684. There have been considerable changes since as the castle served as a centre of British power.

Dublin Castle
Open Monday to Friday 10am to 12.15pm and 2pm to 5pm, weekends and holidays 2pm to 5pm.

On 13 April 1922 men of the Dublin No 1 Brigade occupied the Four Courts and other buildings in the city. The Four Courts became the Republican military headquarters and demands were sent to the Secretary of the Dáil for the actions of the Cabinet in support of the treaty with the British that was intended to end the War of Independence to be repudiated. They warned that this was a last chance of saving the country from civil war.

By June the complicated events that left the status of the treaty unresolved had persuaded the British to lay plans to intervene and take the Four Courts. Fortunately they were not put into operation. On 27 June the Dublin City Guard

The Four Courts, April to June 1922
Ormond Quay.

Magazine Fort
Phoenix Park

Built 1736–8, this is a fort with four demi-bastions. A ravelin, a detached outwork, was added in the early 19th century. A 20th-century modification is the concrete pillbox for machine-guns built above the older loop-holes.

and the 2nd Eastern Division, on the orders of Michael Collins of the Provisional Government, threw a cordon around the buildings. At 3.30am the next morning an ultimatum was given that the Republicans should evacuate and, that being ignored, the attack started at 4.15. The attack made use of two 18-pounders lent by the British, but experienced gunners were lacking and ammunition ran short. The British supplied shrapnel, which was all they had, but it burst harmlessly against the walls and was used more to make a noise than to do damage. Continuous rifle fire was exchanged over a period of three days. Winston Churchill even offered Collins the use of British aircraft, painted in Irish colours, to bomb the Republicans out and end the impasse. On 30 June two mines laid by the defenders exploded, destroying the Public Records Office and documents recording hundreds of years of history, and fire swept through the complex. Resistance here ceased, but the Civil War had, in effect, begun.

The National Museum (Military Collection)
Collins Barracks, Benburb Street. Tel: (01) 677 7444. Open daily except Mondays.

Exhibits include Dublin 1000, which portrays the Viking settlement, and Road to Independence which gives an account of the rising of Easter 1916. The General Post Office in O'Connell Street still bears the scars of that event and the north end of Parnell Square is now a Garden of Remembrance of the rising.

Kilmainham Gaol Museum
Inchincore Road. Tel: (01) 453 5984.

The 'New Gaol' was built in 1792 and many of the Irish who fought for independence were imprisoned here. The museum traces the history of the risings from 1796.

Martello Towers
Joyce's Tower, Sandycove, Dún Laoghaire, 8 miles SE of Dublin. Tel: (01) 280 9265. James Joyce Museum open daily April to October, Sunday afternoons only.

The French landing in 1798 and the guerrilla action of Michael Dwyer in Wicklow reinforced fears of Napoleonic invasion and sea defences were few and feeble. A massive programme of construction was put in hand in 1804 and Dublin Bay was protected by 14 gun towers to the south and 12 to the north. The tower at Sandycove was occupied later by James Joyce and is now a museum of the writer's life and work. As such it is open to the public.

The Battle of Rathmines, 2 August 1649
Southern Dublin, between the Grand Canal and the River Dodder, astride the N11 Morehampton–Stillorgan Road.

The Marquis of Ormond held Dublin for Charles I while the Civil War gripped England, but support for this cause in Ireland was confused. The Catholic Confederation was anti-Parliamentarian, but also anti-English, and split between the rival influences of Owen Roe O'Neill and Preston of Leinster. Parliament was supported by the Presbyterian Scots-Irish. When Charles was defeated, Ormond, preferring English to Irish rebels, handed Dublin to the Parliamentary commander Colonel Michael Jones in June 1647. With Dublin were yielded up Drogheda, Dundalk, Naas and Trim, and Preston set about besieging the latter. Jones met forces from Drogheda at Skreen on 4 August and moved on Trim, from which Preston decamped to the shelter of Portlester but was drawn forth by Jones's attack on a Catholic castle. He then made a feeble thrust towards Dublin, but was caught by Jones at Dungan's Hill near Lynch's Knock (now Summerhill) and comprehensively beaten. At Knocknanoss in Cork Alasdair MacDonald and Sir Felim O'Neill were also defeated, leaving the Confederation shattered.

Ormond was back in Ireland in September 1648 to organise support for the Royal cause and continued in this after Charles I's execution in January. The victor of Knocknanoss, Murrough O'Brien, Earl of Inchiquin, had changed sides to join him and Preston was also with him. Owen Roe O'Neill persisted in his aversion to a Protestant king and was absent when Ormond, now in command of 11,000 men, moved tentatively on Dublin in June. He was joined by Inchiquin as soon as the latter had accepted the surrender of Drogheda and the other towns previously given up and they blockaded Dublin. An attempt to take the city was delayed and on 26 July Colonel Jones was reinforced by the first part of Cromwell's army. Ormond was camped at Rathmines with a view over open country to the city walls; they stood back from where the Grand Canal is today and Trinity College was outside them. Ormond decided to harry Jones by taking Baggotrath Castle, which stood about where Baggot Street Bridge crosses the canal, and making a trench to the Liffey where a fort would mount six guns.

After midnight on 2 August Major-General Purcell was sent to carry out the plan. By morning all he had managed was to cover the two miles to his objective; work on the defences had scarce begun. Jones was on the move (from the site of Merrion Square to the canal) so Ormond reinforced his advance party, stood the rest of the army to arms and went to bed. Jones attacked Baggotrath with all his 1,200 horse and a great part of his foot, killing or putting to flight all Ormond's troops in the front line, and wheeled to his right to advance towards Ranelagh. Ormond, aroused, hastened to organise his main force but Jones's men advanced, field by field while more of his men came up the Dodder across the present Clonskeagh Road and swung north over Milltown Road to attack Ormond's centre from the rear. Caught between two forces, the centre broke and the left collapsed soon after. In two hours Jones had, by unhesitating aggression, overthrown a much larger force and secured Dublin for Parliament. Oliver Cromwell and 12,000 troops landed on 15 August to suppress resistance throughout Ireland.

ENNISKILLEN

Tourist information: Wellington Road. Tel: (01365) 323110.

The original castle, a tower-house, built by Hugh Maguire in the 15th century, stood on an island. The Watergate, a tower with twin turrets, was added in the 17th century. Fears of French invasion at the end of the 18th century led to additional fortification, including barrack blocks of 1796 and 1825.

Enniskillen Castle
Tel: (01365) 325000. Open Tuesday to Friday and Monday afternoons all year, Saturday and Sunday afternoons in summer.

The Royal Inniskilling Fusiliers Regimental Museum
The Keep. Tel: (01365) 323142.
Formed from the 27th and the 108th Regiments of Foot, the history of the regiment goes back to the 17th century. It saw service in the Peninsular War and distinguished itself at Waterloo. The Boer War is of particular interest in this museum, and World Wars I and II receive thorough coverage, including the bugle that sounded the attack of the Ulster Division on the first day of the Battle of the Somme, 1916.

Enniskillen Forts

Forthill Park and a hilltop on the west of the town.

The revolution that brought William III and Mary II to the British throne in 1688 is styled the 'Bloodless' in England; a very biased view. In Ireland it was far from bloodless as the country became the arena for conflict between the Catholic and Protestant kings of England. The Williamite war lasted three years. Gustavus Hamilton, Governor of Enniskillen, raised defensive earthworks in 1689 on what was then known as Camomile Hill, now Forthill. The square, bastioned structure enjoyed protected access, a covered way, from East Bridge. A column, a monument to General the Hon. Sir G Lowry Cole, was erected in the middle of the fort in the 1850s and a cannon captured from the Russians in the Crimean War stands near by. A redoubt commanding the west side of the town was a structure of the Napoleonic Wars.

Monea Castle

5 miles NW of Enniskillen by B81.

Continued fear of Spanish support for Counter-Reformation resistance to British rule led James I of England and VI of Scotland to initiate a plantation of English and Scottish Protestant colonists. The incomers were obliged to construct defensible buildings and the ruined Monea Castle is an excellent example. It was completed by 1618 for Malcolm Hamilton. The Scottish influence is evident in the tower-house style and corbelled turrets. The main building is at one corner of a bawn or courtyard with two small towers covering its walls.

Tully Castle

10 miles NW of Enniskillen by A46. Open April to September daily except Mondays.

A plantation castle built for Sir John Hume in 1613. It is a rectangular tower-house along one side of a square bawn with square flanking towers at the angles. It was burned down in 1641.

Belturbet Fort

Belturbet. 20 miles S of Enniskillen by A509.

The Church of Ireland graveyard is fortified! In 1666 the townspeople built their own fortification and part of the earthwork bastions and ramparts still survive.

Castle Archdale Country Park

10 miles NW of Enniskillen by B82. Tel: (013656) 21588. Centre open June to September daily except Mondays.

The park is devoted to various outdoor activities, but there is an exhibition on the Battle of the Atlantic, the long, hard fight against the U-boats of World War II. Sunderland and Catalina flying boats operated from here. Near the north-east entrance are the ruins of the old castle where the gateway to the bawn survives.

Castle Balfour

Main Street, Linaskea. 12 miles SE of Enniskillen by A4 and A34. Free access.

A Scottish planter, Sir James Balfour, built the castle in 1618 and it remained in continuous occupation until the early 19th century.

GALWAY

Tourist information: Victoria Place, Eyre Square. Tel: (091) 63081.

In 1906 the Corrib Rowing Club bought two RMLs from the Admiralty and these were mounted, complete with their traversing platforms, outside the club.

The tower-house and bawn were built in 1520 and restored in 1924 and 1954. The original method of construction using wickerwork has left traces on the vault of the ground floor. The top floor is a modern sitting room.

The French incursions of the 1790s led to fortification of numerous sites around the coast of Ireland. At Aughinish Island and Finvarra Point two towers cam-shaped in plan were built to carry three guns each in about 1811.

The weakness of the English Crown in the 15th century, in continual dispute during the Wars of the Roses, coupled with the inclination of the Anglo-Normans to behave as independently as the Gaelic Lords, led to a reducing influence and the shrinkage of the territory controlled from London to the Pale, an enclave based on Dublin and reaching north to include Dundalk and inland scarce 50 miles. The Anglo-Irish magnates settled disputes amongst themselves, drawing on mercenary forces first seen at the time of Edward Bruce and known as *gall óglach* or gallowglass. They were families of fighters, brought from Scotland, MacDonalds, MacSwineys, MacDowells among them, who first fought for the Ulster lords O'Neill and O'Donnell, but as time went on entered the service of rulers further south such as the O'Briens of Thomond. They were hard professionals, mail-shirted and wielding long staves crowned with axe-heads.

When Henry VII came to power he found he could not dispense with the support of Gerald FitzGerald, Earl of Kildare and Deputy of Ireland. And when

Dunguaire Castle

Kinvarra, 16 miles S by N6, N18 and N67. Tel: (091) 37108. Open daily May to September.

Martello Towers

S side of Galway Bay, near Burren, 24 miles by N6, N18 and N67.

The Battle of Knockdoe, 19 August 1504

8 miles NE of Galway by N17 and N63, just W of the River Clare and N of N63.

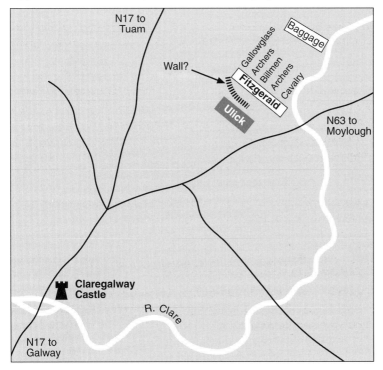

Ulick Burke or de Burgh, head of another Anglo-Norman house fell into dispute with the O'Kellys, destroying their castles, FitzGerald found himself both obliged to restore the King's peace and to help his kinsmen against their enemies. The alliances proliferated, so that eventually FitzGerald was at the head of a force that included such Ulstermen as O'Neill and the chief men of the Pale, as well as diverse other Anglo-Irish of the north and east, while Ulick headed the people of the south and west, Anglo-Irish and Gaelic. They met at Knockdoe, the hill of axes.

FitzGerald's army, including gallowglass, camped near Knockdoe on the evening of 18 August and took position on the hill next morning, facing west. A small wall lay to his front and right, so he positioned all his cavalry on his left, then his archers, then his billmen with their scythe-like weapons, then more archers and finally his gallowglass. Facing him Ulick had his infantry, with many gallowglass, on his right and the cavalry on the left, facing the wall. Ulick's gallowglass hurled themselves into the attack with three great shouts. The earl's archers replied with deadly effect before the two armies locked together in hand-to-hand combat. No records of manoeuvre exist; it seems to have been a long, static slogging. Ulick's horse moved round the Earl's right to despoil the baggage, but did little else, except to have one of their number die by being battered by the first gun reported on an Irish field. Eventually Ulick's men started to give ground and as dusk fell they were scattering, pursued, resisting, dying or fleeing. FitzGerald entered Galway the next day.

Rossaveal Martello Tower
Cashla Bay, 20 miles W of Galway by R336.
A one-gun oval coastal defence tower built in about 1811.

Aughnanure Castle
Near Oughterard, 15 miles NW of Galway by N59. Tel: (091) 82214. Open daily mid-June to mid-September.

The tower-house and bawn were built close to the river for defensive advantage, but the river itself has been the cause of its collapse. The tower is six storeys high and is looped for firearms. Two stages of building, an inner ward and an outer ward, can be seen.

LIMERICK

Tourist information: Arthur's Quay. Tel: (061) 317 522.
Limerick commands the entrance to the River Shannon and is thus of signal strategic importance. In 922 the Danes settled here but the incomers were ejected by Brian Ború nearly a century later. The Normans captured the town in 1194. It was besieged and taken by General Ireton in 1651 and long resisted as a Jacobite stronghold in 1690–91.

King John's Castle
Nicholas Street, on E bank of the Shannon. Tel: (061) 411 201. Open daily mid-April to October and weekends all year.

The Norman castle was built between 1200 and 1216 and represents an interesting transition from the idea of the keep as the heart of the castle. Here the defences depend on the mutual support of the gatehouse and the mural towers, linked by the curtain wall. Strong in defence because of the enfilading fire archers could bring to bear, it was also versatile as a base for counter-attack from its sallyports. The advent of artillery led to the building of an angle bastion to replace a tower on the south-east corner in 1611 and the other towers and curtain-wall walkways were lowered to take cannon. Used as a barracks in the late 18th century, the east wall and part of the bastion were demolished to make way for the parade ground. There is an audio-visual show and copies of medieval siege engines.

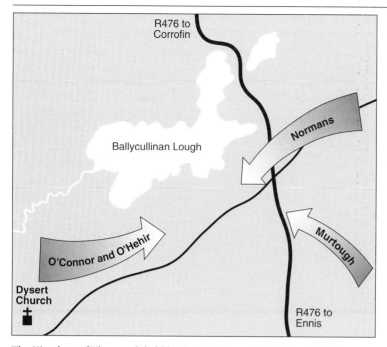

The Kingdom of Thomond, held by the O'Briens with Ennis as their base, was purportedly bestowed on Thomas de Clare by Edward I in the late 13th century and the de Clares thereafter allied themselves with one or other faction of the disputatious O'Brien family. In May 1315 Edward Bruce landed in Antrim and for three years harried the Anglo-Normans mercilessly, laying waste their lands and slighting their castles. The mayhem gave the Irish new opportunities to assert themselves. New generations were in conflict in Thomond. In 1317 Murtough O'Brien defeated Donough O'Brien and the de Clares at Corcomroe Abbey and continued to irritate by raiding Richard de Clare's cattle. Richard moved against him, entering the lands of Conor O'Dea and spreading his forces wide to plunder and destroy. He came upon the O'Deas driving cattle near Lough Ballycullinan and, approaching from the east, pushed them back across the stream that flows from the lough and across the modern Ennis to Corrofin road. Today a minor road runs south of the lough, marking the approximate edge of woodland at that time, and as the Normans pursued the Irish new enemies erupted from the wood both in front of them and behind them.

Richard was killed, but his men fought on, overcoming the attack to their rear and forcing O'Dea into the wood and surrounding him. Now the O'Connors and the O'Hehirs joined the fray and the Normans were pressing hard to overcome them when, from the south-east, Murtough arrived. Caught between two bands of Irish, the Normans fought doggedly on until almost all were killed. The de Clare stronghold of Bunratty Castle was set afire by Richard's widow as she fled to Limerick, and the power of the de Clares was broken. Thomond north of the Shannon remained a Gaelic kingdom until the 16th century when the O'Briens sided with the power of Elizabeth I against the O'Neills and O'Donnells.

The Battle of Dysert O'Dea, 10 May 1318

Dysert O'Dea, 29 miles NW of Limerick by N18 via Ennis, N85 and R476. Archaeology Centre, tel: (065) 37722, open May to September.

Lemenagh Castle

N of Dysert O'Dea, 6 miles by R476.

An O'Brien tower-house modified by its Irish owners during the plantations of the early 17th century to take on characteristics of an English-style residence.

Nenagh Castle

Nenagh, 25 miles NE by N7. Heritage Centre, tel: (0167) 32633.

The Anglo-Normans settled here in the 12th century and the castle, opposite the Heritage Centre, dates from about 1200. A circular tower survives.

IRA Exhibition

Canon Hayes Sports Complex, Tipperary, 26 miles SE by N24.

The exhibition records the activities of the 3rd Tipperary Brigade of the IRA in the War of Independence. It is open daily until 10pm in summer and 7pm in winter.

Bunratty Castle

Bunratty, 9 miles W by N18. Castle and Folk Park, tel: (0161) 361511. Open daily.

The castle was built anew in 1460, long after its destruction by the de Clares after the fight at Dysert O'Dea. The tower-house was restored in the 1950s and houses a collection of furniture from the 14th to the 17th century. The Folk Park portrays rural life in the late 19th century.

Kilkerin Point Battery

SE of Labasheeda, 25 miles W of Limerick by N18 via Clarecastle and R473 and minor road, on N shore of Shannon.

After the French invasion in 1798, attention was given to the coastal defences of Ireland and work was done in two phases, 1804–6 and 1811–14. The Shannon offered substantial facilities for an invader and was fortified as far north as Athlone. The shore batteries on the estuary were D-shaped and designed for six 24-pounder guns firing over a parapet, with a blockhouse at the gorge, on the roof of which two howitzers were mounted. This is reputed to be the best preserved of them. It faces Tarbert Island where there was a flat bastion-shaped battery, now replaced by a power station.

Doonaha and Kilcredaun Point Batteries

S of Kilkee, 58 miles W of Limerick by N18, N68 and N67.

The most westerly of the Shannon north-shore batteries, these are similar in layout and armament to Kilkerin, though Kilcredaun is rather smaller. There was another battery on Scattery Island to the east and at Corran Point on Carrig Island near the southern shore.

LONDONDERRY

Tourist information: 8 Bishop Street. Tel: (01504) 267284.

The Walls of Derry

Guided tours in July and August, starting from Tourist Information office.

When Sir Henry Sidney, Elizabeth I's viceroy, moved against Shane O'Neill in 1566 in order to restore Calvagh O'Donnell to power in Donegal, he went by sea to Lough Foyle and left Edward Randolph in garrison at Derry. O'Neill attacked the town and although Randolph was killed, the garrison held. It was not enemy action that overthrew it. The following spring, their gunpowder blew up and the English were obliged to retreat. The old defensive earthworks were eventually overrun in 1608 and in 1613 the City of London became responsible for the town. It was then that the stone-faced ramparts with nine bastions were constructed to the design of Captain Edward Doddington. When, in 1689, James II came to Ireland he found many men of the regiments officially disbanded by William of Orange ready to serve him under the command of the Earl of Tyrconnell. The Protestants took refuge in Derry and held out for 105 days until relieved by sea on 1 August. The walls are an outstanding example of 17th-century town fortification.

Amongst other displays relating to the history of the city are sections on the siege and on World War II. It is open daily in July and August.

The Tower Museum
*Union Hall Place. Tel:
(01504) 372411. Open
Tuesdays to Saturdays.*

This linear earthwork with a single bastion was constructed to enclose a peninsula where Lough Foyle narrows. It is the work of the Dutch engineer Jose Everaert and was built in 1600 by an English seaborne force. It was still in service in 1666 when it was one of the establishments listed as having a master gunner.

Culmore Fort
Off A2 on W of Lough.

A massive, circular stone hill-fort, reconstructed in 1870, and thus to be viewed with caution. Here was the seat of the O'Neills from the 5th to the 12th century until it was destroyed in retaliation by the King of Munster.

The Grianan of Aileach
*S of Speenoge, 5 miles W by
A2 and N13.*

In May 1567 Shane O'Neill made his bid to gain overall control of Ulster. His late brother Matthew had been preferred by the English and his son, Hugh, was now in England for his safety. Shane had gathered himself a mercenary force of gallowglasses, hereditary fighters originally from Scotland, further 'new Scots' and native Irish mercenaries known as bonnachts. He had already, on 2 May 1565, dealt a heavy blow to the power of the Antrim Scots at the Battle of Glenshesk near Ballycastle, though one of the leading MacDonalds, Alexander, was left alive. By 1567 his power was at its height and his men included peasants and other persons of lowly estate, the classes formerly excluded from bearing arms.

The Battle of Farsetmore, 8 May 1567
*On the Rathmelton road,
about 1 mile NE of
Letterkenny, 24 miles W of
Londonderry by A2 and
N13.*

Sir Henry Sidney's expedition to Derry in 1566 had succeeded in strengthening the O'Donnells of Donegal to Shane's disadvantage, though the English had been obliged to abandon Derry. In the spring of 1567 Hugh O'Donnell raided Tyrone; Shane had to react. He crossed the River Swilly in force to menace Hugh who held a small fort at Ardingary just east of Letterkenny. Hugh's small body of men could not prevent him, but managed to hold him up near Aghanunshin Hill while taking refuge in the boggy land to the north. Shane made camp, intending to use it as a base to scour the countryside, while Hugh awaited reinforcements. The gallowglass of Clan MacSwiney rallied to him and Hugh attacked. The details of the fight are not known, but the battle was long and hard. The O'Neills were eventually forced back to the ford, but now the tide had risen and the formerly easy crossing had become a death-trap. A sandbank there is still called the Marcaghs' (horsemen's) bed, for here they drowned.

St Columb's Cathedral
The mortar shell by which the message demanding surrender during the siege of 1689 was fired into the town is to be seen in the porch.

Shane's power was broken as also, it seems, was his sense. He went to Alexander MacDonald at Cushendun on the Antrim coast and there, together with the fifty horsemen who accompanied him, he was killed.

The ruins of a 14th-century Gaelic stone castle overlook the valley route. It was built by Henry Aimbreidh O'Neill who died in 1392.

Harry Avery's Castle
*25 miles S of Londonderry
via Strabane by A5 to
Newtownstewart and W by
B84.*

Castlederg Visitor Centre

26 Lower Strabane Road. 10 miles W of Newtownstewart.

Amongst other items of local interest is a model of the Alamo Fort, Texas, where Davy Crockett's last stand took place. His family originally came from this area. It is open March to October, Tuesday to Saturday and Sunday afternoons.

Doe Castle

NE of Creeslough, 17 miles N of Letterkenny by N56. Tel: (0174) 381124. Open daily 9am to 8pm.

The basic keep and bawn are protected by the sea and a rock-cut ditch. The round towers and Great Hall are later additions. In the 18th century the castle was turned into a residence by General George Vaughan Harte who had served in India and who installed a number of cannons taken at the Siege of Seringapatam. In the 16th century the castle was a stronghold of the gallowglass family McSweeney.

Dunree Fort

Dunree Head, 18 miles NW of Londonderry by A2 and R238 via Buncrana and minor road NW. Tel: (077) 61817. Open June to September daily, Sunday afternoons only.

In the late 18th century, for the first time in 200 years, Ireland became an exposed western flank for foreign invasion. There were five attempted expeditions by the French between 1793 and 1798. Dunree was given an earthen fort at that time and in the early 19th century it was upgraded as part of a wide programme of fortification of the coast. Knockalla Fort is on the opposite shore and was built at the same time. Buncrana became a British naval base; as recently as 1914 the entire British Grand Fleet was in Lough Swilly. The fort is now a military museum setting out the complete story and exhibiting the original guns.

Greencastle

N of Greencastle, 19 miles NE of Londonderry by A2, R238 via Moville and R241.

The ruins of the castle built by Richard de Burgo in 1305 overlook the entrance to Lough Foyle. It was taken by Edward Bruce in 1316 and was held by the O'Donnells in the 14th century. In 1812 a Martello tower was erected near by, a twin to the tower on Magilligan Point across the water.

NEWRY

Tourist information: Town Hall. Tel: (01693) 68877.

Newry commands an important route running north and south to Carlingford Lough and to Dublin. The early Christian hill-forts of Lisnagade and Lisnavaragh some nine miles north are evidence that this has been so from early times.

Narrow Water Castle

Warrenpoint, 7 miles S of Newry by A2. Open July and August Tuesday to Sunday, Sunday afternoons only.

A tower-house and bawn built at the outflow of the Newry River into Carlingford Lough by the English in about 1560. The entrance to the three-storey tower has a murder-hole, a loop-hole through which attackers could be fired on from within.

Greencastle

S of the A2 Kilkeel road, 12 miles SE of Newry. Tel: (01232) 235000. Open April to September Tuesday to Sunday and November to March weekends, Sunday afternoons only.

An Anglo-Norman keep within a rectangular enclosure with D-shaped corner towers surrounded by a moat hewn from the rock, commanding the entrance to Carlingford Lough and the route west of the Mountains of Mourne into Ulster. It was besieged by Edward Bruce in 1316 and was later an Elizabethan stronghold.

Hugh O'Neill controlled Ulster after the Battle of the Yellow Ford and was left alone when the Earl of Essex came as viceroy the following year. Essex was replaced by Lord Mountjoy in 1600, and the new commander immediately attempted to increase the pressure on Ulster by reinforcing Derry and, by way of the narrow Moyry Pass, the Gap of the North through which the road runs from Dundalk to Newry and where the modern railway goes, the other English toe-hold, Newry itself. On 20 September Mountjoy marched his 3,000 foot and 300 horse north from Dundalk to Faughart, where Edward Bruce had been defeated and slain in 1318, just short of the pass which O'Neill's men held. After sitting out the rain for four days, the English forlorn hope, the advance guard, moved tentatively into the pass along a road about 800 yards to the west of the modern road until they encountered barricades just south of the present site of the castle. They retired having taken a few casualties and stalemate ensued until 2 October. The next foray penetrated further into the pass, about a mile, but it was then clear there were yet more obstacles to overcome, not counting the swollen streams of Three Mile and Four Mile Water; the English withdrew again in a fighting retreat. A last effort was made on 5 October with an advance along the heights to the west, but this, too, was turned back and the attempt to take the pass abandoned. The English went to Newry by way of Carlingford Lough, but O'Neill himself withdrew to the west immediately thereafter, leaving the pass at last in English hands. Moyry Castle was built in 1601 to secure the pass.

The Battle of Moyry Pass, 1600

W of the A1/N1, 8 miles S of Newry.

Carlingford Lough Blockhouse

The lough's defences include a blockhouse on a small island. It may date from the mid-16th century or perhaps a little later, from Lord Mountjoy's time, about 1601.

Sharing the command of the entrance to Carlingford Lough with Greencastle and known as King John's Castle, it was built by Hugh de Lacey early in the 13th century and visited by King John in 1210. The eastern buildings were added in 1261.

Carlingford Castle

Carlingford, 12 miles SE of Newry by R173.

SLIGO

Tourist information: Temple Street. Tel: (071) 61201.

In the mid-17th century this small, square, bastioned earthwork was constructed. It formed an important part of the town defences in the Williamite Wars.

Green Fort

Outside Sligo town.

A Plantation castle, built by Captain Robert Parke in 1609 close to an earlier tower-house of which traces remain. It fell into disuse soon after 1652, having been attacked and captured in 1647, and thus is an unspoiled example of its genre. It has been carefully preserved and partially restored. There is an audio-visual presentation of the castle's history.

Parke's Castle

Lough Gill, 6 miles E by R286. Tel: (0171) 641149. Open June to September 9.30am to 6.30pm, April, May and October 10am to 5pm.

A fort of post-Cromwellian date, possibly early 18th century. It is a square masonry structure with corner bastions and now serves as a churchyard to the Church of Ireland church which stands within.

Manorhamilton Fort

Manorhamilton, 16 miles E of Sligo, on E of town.

Ballina

SE of Sligo, 37 miles by N4 and N59.

In late August 1798 General Humbert and some 1,000 French troops landed at Kilcummin on the western shore of Killala Bay and quickly took Ballina. A monument to him is in the town. He then moved south, gathering Irish supporters as he went, towards Castlebar, 26 miles to the south. General Lake, with a mixed force of English, Scots and Irish militia, offered battle but his force was scattered by the bayonet charge of the French veterans. The engagement became known as the Castlebar Races. Humbert drew off to the north-east, shadowed by Colonel Craufurd, as English forces gathered at Enniskillen and at Portuma and patrolled the coast to prevent reinforcement. Finally, Lord Cornwallis arrived at Tuam to take command. Humbert moved towards Sligo and then south-east, but the United Irishmen he had hoped would join him had already been defeated in Wexford and Meath. With no prospect of success the French laid down their arms on 8 September at Ballinamuck, County Leitrim, on honourable terms. Those Irishmen who had joined them were hanged as traitors.

Ballinafad Castle

Ballinafad, 17 miles S of Sligo by N4.

The ruins of the castle have the appearance of a medieval stronghold with four round corner towers. It was actually built in 1590 to command the pass in the Curlew Mountains. The last Irish success in the war against Elizabeth I was fought near here, the Battle of the Curlews, in which Hugh Roe O'Donnell overcame Sir Conyers Clifford in 1599.

WATERFORD

Tourist information: 41 The Quay. Tel: (051) 75788.

The Danes settled here in 853 and were defeated by Richard FitzGilbert and Raymond le Gros when they came to the assistance of Dermot MacMurrogh in 1170. The Normans extended the town's fortifications and substantial parts survive, notably at the Watch Tower, where Danish work is to be seen, and Reginald's Bar with its sallyports, near Reginald's Tower.

Reginald's Tower Museum

Tel: (051) 73501. Open daily April to October.

A stone fortress built by the Vikings in 1003 overlooks the Suir River. The museum relates the history of Waterford and has some items of military interest. It is closed on Sundays.

Kilkenny Castle

Kilkenny, 29 miles N by N10. Tel: (056) 21450. Open daily April to September, Tuesday to Sunday October to March.

Kilkenny was a centre of Anglo-Norman influence and grew to prosperity and importance in the Middle Ages. The pattern of the old town can be detected today. The castle was bulit in 1192-1207 and became the residence of the Butler family, Earls and Dukes of Ormond. It was substantially alterted in the 19th century.

Duncannon Fort

Duncannon, 7 miles E of Waterford via Passage East and ferry.

A protection for Waterford harbour was first built here by the Normans in the 12th century. It was modified for artillery in 1587-90 against possible attack by the Spanish Armada, and a sea battery for 25 guns was added in the 18th century, which was further modified during the Napoleonic Wars. It had the disadvantage of being overlooked by high ground to landward and was criticised for this fault, as was Fort Charles. Two Martello towers were built to correct this in 1814; both survive.

The County Museum displays items of relevance to the history of the county, and includes the World War I experience of the Royal Irish Regiment and the War of Independence and the Civil War. It is closed Sundays and Mondays.

Tipperary SR County Museum
Parnell Street, Clonmel, 28 miles W of Waterford by N24. Tel: (052) 25399.

The 13th-century castle was extensively extended in the 15th century. The keep is the original gatehouse, and the structure now has three wards. The north-west tower is 13th century with 15th-century windows, an indication of the shift from military to residential use. The great hall was modified in the 19th century. The site is said to be that of a building used in the 10th century by Brian Ború.

Caher Castle
Caher, 38 miles W by N24. Tel: (052) 41011. Open April to October 10am to 6pm, November to March 10am to 1pm and 2pm to 4.30pm.

WEXFORD

Tourist information: Crescent Quay. Tel: (053) 23111.
The Viking town was one of the first to fall in the Norman invasion of 1169 when Robert FitzStephen and his companions allied themselves to Dermot MacMurrogh in his fight against Rory O'Connor. The Normans fortified the town and the West Gate, built by Sir Stephen Devereux about 1200, and part of the walls survive. Wexford was the centre of the uprising of the United Irishmen in 1798. After the defeat of the insurgents at Vinegar Hill survivors slew about 70 Protestant prisoners on Wexford Bridge. The town fell to Sir John Moore on the afternoon of 21 June.

After their defeat at Arklow on 9 June, the insurgents withdrew to their camp on Vinegar Hill. They had few arms and supplies and their position was, although they appeared to be unaware of it, extremely vulnerable. English reinforcements were arriving in Ireland and by 20 June General Lake was able to put 20,000 men in the field. Lake approached along the eastern bank of the River Slaney with four columns. Battle was joined when only three had come up, but the artillery was there and did terrible damage. General Needham's column was late so the attempt to surround the hill failed and many of the rebels escaped. Those who did not, including wives and children of the insurgents, were killed. The rape, slaughter and plunder that followed the collapse of the uprising infuriated the new lord lieutenant of Ireland, Lord Cornwallis.

The Battle of Vinegar Hill, 21 June 1798
Enniscorthy, 12 miles N of Wexford by N11. Between the Wexford and Ferns minor roads, just E of the town.

FURTHER READING

This list is a select one, being limited to those books known to, and in most cases used by, the author. The list is in two parts: those titles of broad application and those that apply only to the geographical section of the work under which they are shown here. The references are to the most recent edition known and those books that are, in the personal opinion of the author, likely to prove the most useful to people new to the subject or to tourists are marked with an asterisk. The list finishes with web sites based on the information kindly given by Dr Martin H Evans.

Britain and Ireland

Baker, Anthony, *A Battlefield Atlas of the English Civil War*, London, Ian Allan, 1986.

Bennett, Martyn, *The English Civil War*, Swindon, W H Smith, 1992.

Black, Jeremy, *Culloden and the '45*, Stroud, Alan Sutton, 1990.

Boorman, Derek, *At the Going Down of the Sun: British First World War Memorials*, York, Dunnington Hall.

Boorman, Derek, *For Your Tomorrow: British Second World War Memorials*, York, Dunnington Hall, 1995.

Burne, Alfred H, *The Battlefields of England*, London, Greenhill Books, 1996.

Castles: A History and Guide, Poole, New Orchard Editions, 1985.

Daniell, Christopher, *A Traveller's History of England*, Moreton-in-Marsh, Windrush Press, 1993.

Dodds, Glen Lyndon, *Battles in Britain 1066–1746*, London, Arms and Armour Press, 1996.

The English Heritage Visitor's Handbook, London, English Heritage, annually.

Fairbairn, Neil, and Michael Cyprien, *A Traveller's Guide to the Battlefields of Britain*, London, Evans Brothers, 1983.

Freeman, Roger, *Airfields of the Eighth Then and Now*, London, After the Battle.

Freeman, Roger, *UK Airfields of the Ninth Then and Now*, London, After the Battle.

Fry, Plantagenet Somerset, *Castles of Britain and Ireland*, Newton Abbot, David & Charles, 1996.

Guest, Ken, and Denise May, *British Battles*, London, HarperCollins, 1996.

Haigh, Philip A, *The Military Campaigns of the Wars of the Roses*, Stroud, Alan Sutton, 1995.

Kinross, John, *Discovering Battlefields of England & Scotland*, Shire Publications, 1998.

*Kinross, John, *Walking and Exploring the Battlefields of Britain*, Newton Abbot, David & Charles, 1993.

Militaria Directory and Sourcebook, London, Windrow & Green, annually.

National Trust Handbook, London, The National Trust, annually.

*Platt, Colin, *The Castle in Medieval England & Wales*, London, Chancellor Press, 1995.

Ramsey, Winston (Ed), *The Battle of Britain Then and Now*, London, After the Battle.

Register of Historic Battlefields, London, English Heritage, 1995.

Reid, Stuart, *1745: A Military History of the Last Jacobite Rising*, Staplehurst, Spellmount Publishing, 1996.

Roman Britain: Historical Map and Guide, Southampton, Ordnance Survey, 1991.

*Saunders, Andrew, *Fortress Britain: Artillery Fortification in the British Isles and Ireland*, Liphook, Beaufort Publishing, 1989.

Seymour, William, *Battles in Britain*, London, Sidgwick and Jackson, 1979.

*Smurthwaite, David, *The Complete Guide to Battlefields in Britain*, London, Michael Joseph, 1993.

Their Name Liveth, Vol IV, Parts I & II, Imperial War Graves Commission/HMSO, 1958 and 1959.

20th Century Defences in Britain: An Introductory Guide, York, Council for British Archaeology, 1995.

Watson-Smyth, Marianne (Ed), *Deserted Bastions: Historic Naval & Military Architecture*, London, SAVE Britain's Heritage, 1993.

Wills, H, *Pillboxes: A Study of UK Defences*, London, Leo Cooper, 1985.

Wilson, R J A, *A Guide to Roman Remains in Britain*, London, Constable, 1988.

Wise, Terence, and Shirley Wise, *A Guide to Military Museums*, Knighton, Imperial Press, 8th Ed. 1994.

Young, Peter, and John Adair, *Hastings to Colloden: Battles of Britain*, Stroud, Sutton Publishing, 1996.

London

Tames, Richard, *A Traveller's History of London*, Moreton-in-Marsh, Windrush Press 2nd Ed. 1997.

Southern England

Burridge, David, *Twentieth Century Defence of Britain: Kent*, London, Brassey's, 1997.

Longstaff-Tyrrell, Peter, *Twentieth Century Defence of Britain: Sussex*, London, Brassey's, 1998.

*Saunders, Andrew, *Channel Defences*, London, B T Batsford/English Heritage, 1997.

Scarth, Richard, *Mirrors by the Sea*, Hythe Civic Society, 1995.

Wright, Peter Poyntz, *Hastings*, Moreton-in-Marsh, Windrush Press, 1966.

The West Country

*Saunders, Andrew, *Channel Defences*, London, B T Batsford/English Heritage, 1997.

Wales and the Marches

Griffith, Paddy (Ed), *The Battle of Blore Heath, 1459*, Nuneaton, 1995.

Hammond, Peter W, *The Battles of Barnet and Tewkesbury*, Stroud, Sutton Publishing.

Hodges, Geoffrey, *Ludford Bridge and Mortimer's Cross*, Logaston Press, 1989.

Hodges, Geoffrey, *Owain Glyn Dwr and the War of Independence in the Welsh Borders*, Logaston Press, 1995.

Central Southern England

Earle, James C, *Twentieth Century Defence of Britain: Berkshire*, London, Brassey's, 1998.

Foard, Glenn, *Naseby: The Decisive Campaign*, Whitstable, Pryor Publications, 1995.

Young, Peter, *Edgehill 1642: The Campaign and the Battle*, Moreton-in-Marsh, Windrush Press, 1995.

East Anglia

Gilman, Paul, and Fred Nash, *Fortress Essex*, Chelmsford, Essex County Council, 1995.

North Midlands

Osborne, Mike, *Twentieth Century Defence of Britain: Lincolnshire*, London, Brassey's, 1997.

The North

Boardman, Andrew, *The Battle of Towton*, Stroud, Sutton Publishing, 1994.

Twentieth Century Defence of Britain: Yorkshire, London, Brassey's, 1998.

The Borders

Fraser, George M, *The Steel Bonnets*, London, HarperCollins.

Johnson, Stephen, *Hadrian's Wall*, London, B T Batsford/English Heritage, 1989.

Twentieth Century Defence of Britain: Northumberland and Tyne & Wear, London, Brassey's, 1998.

Wesencraft, C F, *The Battle of Otterburn*, Doncaster, Athena Books (Publications), 1988.

Scotland

Burke, John, *A Traveller's History of Scotland*, London, John Murray, 1990.

*Cruden, Stewart, *The Scottish Castle*, Edinburgh, Spur Books, 3rd Ed. 1981.

Fisher, Andrew, *A Traveller's History of Scotland*, Moreton-in-Marsh, Windrush Press.

Historic Scotland: The Sites to See, Edinburgh, Historic Scotland, annually.

*Marren, Peter, *Grampian Battlefields: The Historic Battles of North East Scotland from AD84 to 1745*, Aberdeen, Aberdeen University Press, 1990.

*Reid, Stuart, *Like Hungry Wolves: Culloden Moor, 16 April 1746*, London, Windrow & Green, 1994.

Sadler, John, *Scottish Battles*, Edinburgh, Canongate, 1996.

Tabaham, Chris, and Doreen Grove, *Fortress Scotland and the Jacobites*, London, B T Batsford/Historic Scotland, 1996.

Ireland

Barry, Tom, *Guerrilla Days in Ireland*, Dublin, Anvil Books, 1989.

Bartlett, Thomas, and Keith Jeffery, *A Military History of Ireland*, Cambridge, CUP, 1996.

Foster, R F (Ed), *The Oxford Illustrated History of Ireland*, Oxford, OUP, 1989.

The GIs in Northern Ireland, After the Battle Issue No 34, London, 1981.

*Hayes-McCoy, G A, *Irish Battles: A Military History of Ireland*, Belfast, Appletree Press, 1989.

Hopkinson, Michael, *Green against Green: The Irish Civil War*, Dublin, Gill and Macmillan, 1988.

*Kerrigan, Paul M, *Castles and Fortifications in Ireland 1485–1945*, Cork, The Collins Press, 1995.

Kinross, John, *The Battle of the Boyne and Aughrim*, Moreton-in-Marsh, Windrush Press, 1997.

McAuliffe, Mary, *The Tower House and Warfare in Ireland in the 14th and 15th Centuries*, Irish Sword, Vol XVIII.

Neville, Peter, *A Traveller's History of Ireland*, Moreton-in-Marsh, Windrush Press 1992.

Townshend, Charles, *The British Campaign in Ireland 1919–1921*, Oxford, OUP, 1975.

Web Sites

The most comprehensive list of British museums of military interest is:

htpp://chide.museum.org.uk/

Other sites that may have useful information are:

http://www.cfcsc.dnd.ca/links/milhist/
http://www.compulink.co.uk/~flagship/
   Welcome.html
http://www.cs.ucl.ac.uk/local/museums/
http://www.cypass.com/greenwich2000/sea.htm
http://hants.gov.uk/museums/index.html
http://www.itl.net/vc/europe/London/Tourism/
http://www.museums.co.uk/alpha.htm
http://pc-78-120.udac.se:8001/WWW/Nautica/
   Museums/mm.html

ORGANISATIONS

There are many groups that offer members opportunities for study, the exchange of information or the chance to support an objective such as the preservation of the military heritage. The list that follows is certainly incomplete – groups with a restricted, local purpose being omitted intentionally, and others out of ignorance. Some public bodies are also included as sources of information. Re-enactment societies are very numerous and those interested will do best to consult the relevant section in *Windrow & Green's Militaria Directory and Sourcebook*.

Airfield Research Group. Research into airfields, both military and civil, in the UK and associated features. Publishes a journal, *Airfield Review*, three issues a year. Contact: John Nichols, 220 Woodland Avenue, Hutton, Brentwood, Essex CM13 1DA.

The Arms and Armour Society. The study, preservation and conservation of arms and armour from the earliest times to the present. Publishes a newsletter and journal. Contact: Field House, Upper Dicker, Hailsham, East Sussex.

The Battlefields Trust. The preservation of battlefield sites, particularly in the UK and Ireland, but with strong contacts elsewhere. Has been instrumental in influencing planning decisions. Publishes a newsletter and organises an annual conference and other meetings and expeditions. Contact: Michael Rayner, Meadow Cottage, 33 High Green, Brooke, Norwich, Norfolk NR15 1HR.

The Chariots Trust. Preservation of submarine history, particularly Human Torpedos. Contact: 6 Aycliffe Close, Bromley, Kent BR1 2LX.

The Cold War Research Study Group. Presentation of an objective view of Britain's national defence plans 1945–95. Contact: Malcolm Tadd, 65 Trindles Road, South Nutfield, Redhill, Surrey.

Commonwealth Forces History Trust. Provides history of units of the forces of the Commonwealth from 1066 to 1945; 7,494 regiments, corps and units covered. Contact: 37 Davis Road, Acton, London W3 7SE.

Commonwealth War Graves Commission. In addition to maintaining the graves of service people of the Commonwealth, the Enquiries Section assists members of the public to locate specific graves. Numerous publications including cemetery and memorial registers. The Commission cares for 23,194 burial grounds throughout the world in which 1,694,999 war dead are commemorated by name, and a further 208,707 are unidentified. Contact: 2 Marlow Road, Maidenhead, Berks SL6 7DX. Tel: (01628) 34221. Fax: (01628) 771208.

Crimean War Research Society. Research into every aspect of the Crimean War. Publishes a journal, *The War Correspondent*. Contact: David Cliff, 4 Castle Estate, Ripponden, Sowerby Bridge, West Yorkshire HX6 4JY.

The Defence of Britain. The compilation of a database of British 20th-century defence sites with a view to conservation and the stimulation of public interest in military heritage. Publishes a journal, *Defence Lines*, and a series of guides, *Twentieth Century Defence of Britain* (Brassey's). Contact: Imperial War Museum, Duxford, Cambridge CB2 4QR.

Fortress Study Group. Research and recording of artillery fortifications worldwide. Publishes a journal, *Fort*, and a newsletter, *Casemate*. Contact: Bernard Lowry (Secretary), The Severals, Bentleys Road, Market Drayton, Shropshire TF9 1LL.

Historical Radar Archive. Study of UK radar network. Contact: Ian Brown, 3 Kingsmuir Crescent, Peebles, Scotland EH45 9AB.

Indian Military Historical Society. The military history of the Indian subcontinent. Publishes a journal. Contact: Lt Cdr Maitland Thornton, 37 Wolsey Close, Southall, Middlesex UB2 4NQ.

Kent Defence Research Group. Originally formed to promote interest in Kent's defences, the membership and spread of interests is now much wider. Publishes a journal, *Ravelin*. Contact: David Burridge, 59 Markland Road, Dover, Kent CT17 9LY.

Mercia Military Society. Military history discussion group. Contact: Paddy Griffith, 24 Callendar Close, St Nicholas Park, Nuneaton CV11 6LU.

Mid-Wales Military Society. Contact: D E Davies, 10 Colwyn Terrace, Hundred House, Llandidrod Wells, Powys LD1 5RY.

Military Historical Society. British military history, all periods. Publishes quarterly bulletin. Contact: John Gaylor, 30 Edgeborough Way, Bromley, Kent BR1 2UA.

Military History Society of Ireland. Irish military history. Contact: Dr Pat McCarthy, University College Dublin, Newman House, 86 St Stephen's Green, Dublin 2.

Palmerston Forts Society. Study and recording of Victorian fortifications. Contact: D Moore, 17 Northcroft Road, Gosport, Hants PO12 3DR.

The Pillbox Study Group. Study and recording of pillboxes, local defence sites and volunteer and civilian activity in World War II. Publishes a journal, *Loopholes*. Contact: John Hellis, 3 Chelwood Drive, Taunton, Somerset TA1 4JA.

Scottish Military Historical Society. The study of Scottish military history. Publishes a journal. Contact: Tom Moles, 4 Hillside Cottages, Glenboig, Lanarkshire ML5 2QY.

Society for Army Historical Research. Study of the British Army. Contact: Dr Peter Boyden, National Army Museum, Royal Hospital Road, London SW3 4HT.

The 1940 Association. Study of British history 1939–45. Contact: Michael Conway, 43 The Drive, Ilford, Essex.

National Monuments Records. Aerial and ground photographs, drawings and modern and historic maps. England: NMR Customer Services, National Monuments Record Centre, Kemble Drive, Swindon SN2 2GZ. Scotland: NMR, RCAHMS, John Sinclair House, 16 Bernard Terrace, Edinburgh EH8 9NX. Wales: NMR, RCAHMW,

Plascrug, Aberystwyth, Dyfed SY23 1NJ.

The Naval Dockyards Society. All aspects of naval dockyards, hospitals, ordnance wharves and victualling yards. Meetings at National Maritime Museum. Contact: Philip MacDougall, 44 Lindley Avenue, Southsea, Hants PO4 3LJ.

Public Record Offices. England: Ruskin Avenue, Kew, Surrey TW9 4DU. Scotland: Scottish Record Office, HM General Register House, Edinburgh EH1 3YY and National Register of Archives (Scotland), West Register House, Charlotte Square, Edinburgh EH2 4DF.

UK Fortifications Club. Research and recording of UK military sites of all periods. Publishes a journal, *Aldis*. Contact: Peter Cobb, 4 Mablethorpe Road, Portsmouth PO6 3LJ.

Ulster Military Historical Society. The Royal Dublin Fusiliers and Irish Defence Forces, including period prior to 1922. Contact: Jonathan Maguire, 32 Clonmacate Road, Birches, Portadown, Co Armagh.

Victorian Military Society. International military history of the period 1837–1915. Contact: 62 The Links, St Leonards-on-Sea, East Sussex TN38 0UW.

The Western Front Association. Study of the period 1914–18 to perpetuate the memory of victims of the Great War. Contact: David Harrison, 16 Conway Road, West Wimbledon, London SW20 8PA.

TOURS

While the chief activity of specialist tour companies is arranging visits to overseas battlegrounds such as the Western Front, a number take an interest in history closer to home.

Holt's Battlefield Tours, 15 Market Street, Sandwich, Kent CT13 9DA. Tel: (01304) 612248. Fax: (01304) 614930.

Mercat Tours International, 47 Willowbrae Avenue, Edinburgh EH8 7HL. Tel: (0131) 661 4541. Fax: (0131) 661 4541. Web: http://www.mercat-tours.co.uk

Midas Historic Tours, The Old Dairy, The Green, Godstone, Surrey RH9 8DY. Tel: (01883) 744955. Fax: (01883) 744967.

Society of Friends of the National Army Museum, c/o National Army Museum, Royal Hospital Road, London SW3 4HT. Tel: (0171) 730 0717.